The Low Countries

Cover:
The Battle of Flanders – A silhouette.
At eventide on the Flanders Front

TLC

2014 # The Low Countries

ARTS AND SOCIETY IN FLANDERS AND THE NETHERLANDS

22

**Published by
the Flemish-Netherlands
Association
Ons Erfdeel vzw**

Contents

'I died in hell - (They called it Passchendaele)'
The Great War 1914-1918

Chronicle

Film and Theatre

History

Language

Literature

Music

Politics

Next page:
Menin Gate Memorial to the Missing, Ieper
(detail: poppies fall down through the opening in the barrel vault of the Hall of the Missing).The Monument contains names on stone panels of 54,896 Commonwealth soldiers who died in the Ypres Salient but whose bodies have never been identified or found. The poem of Ivor Gurney has been added by our designer. © In Flanders Fields Museum, Ieper

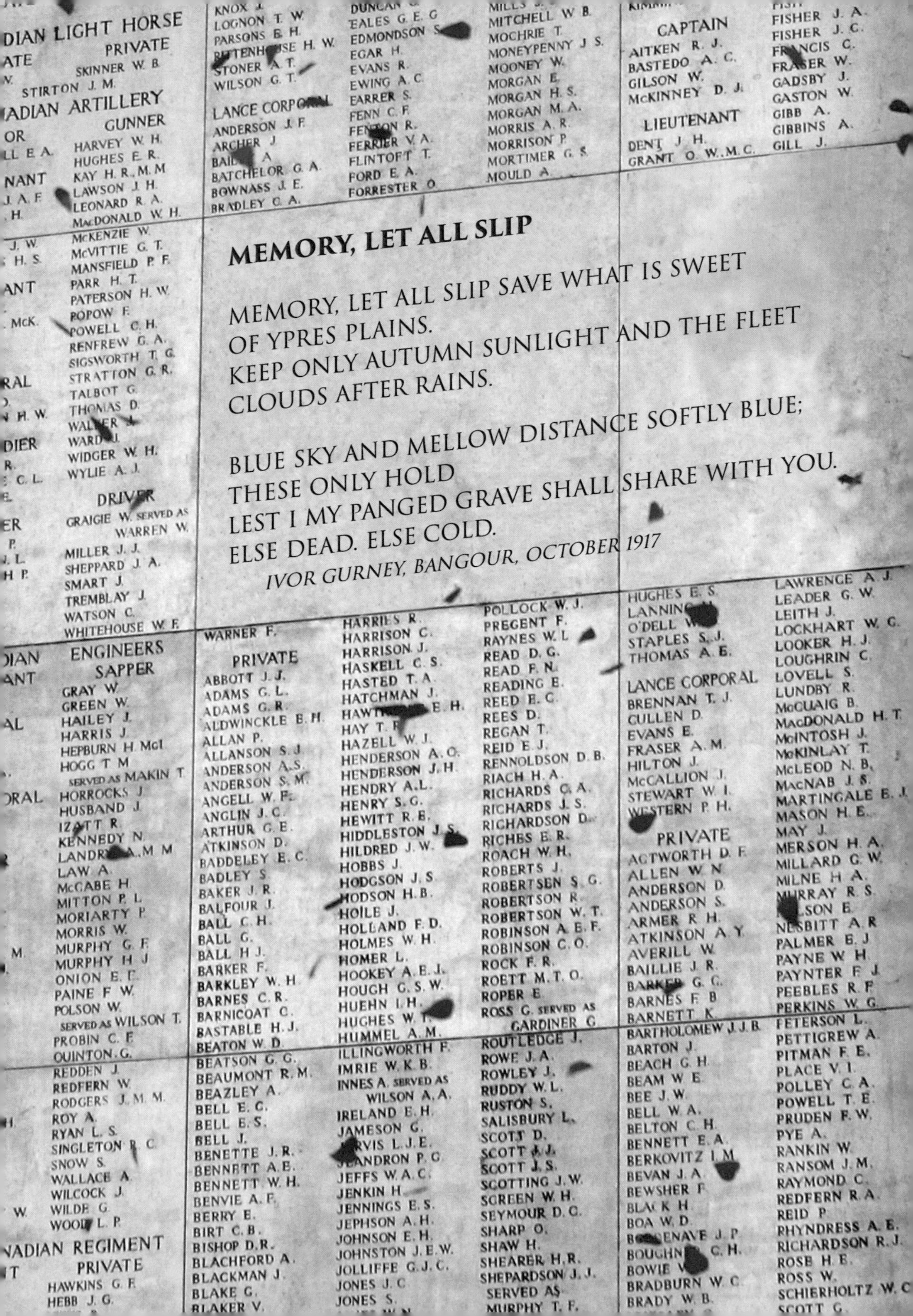

MEMORY, LET ALL SLIP

MEMORY, LET ALL SLIP SAVE WHAT IS SWEET
OF YPRES PLAINS.
KEEP ONLY AUTUMN SUNLIGHT AND THE FLEET
CLOUDS AFTER RAINS.

BLUE SKY AND MELLOW DISTANCE SOFTLY BLUE;
THESE ONLY HOLD
LEST I MY PANGED GRAVE SHALL SHARE WITH YOU.
ELSE DEAD. ELSE COLD.

IVOR GURNEY, BANGOUR, OCTOBER 1917

'On Being Asked For a War Poem'

I think it better that in times like these
A poet's mouth be silent, for in truth
We have no gift to set a statesman right;
He has had enough of meddling who can please
A young girl in the indolence of her youth,
Or an old man upon a winter's night.
W.B. Yeats (1915)

Yeats' refusal to write about the war and Gurney's melancholic attempt to retain only an impossible idyll of that war leave me perplexed. As it slips away into the annals of history, how does one write about the Great War? There are no veterans left and the last eye witnesses, children during the fighting, are dying out. That means this war will soon acquire a different place in the imagination and therefore a different place in history. Meanwhile, the commemorations over the next four years will be deafening, especially in Flanders, Belgium, France, Great Britain and the British Commonwealth. Less so in the countries of the vanquished, Germany and Austria.

According to the British historian Eric Hobsbawn, the twentieth century began in 1914 with the First World War and ended in 1991 with the fall of the Soviet Union. In his opinion the Second World War was a direct consequence of the First, which brought the end of the German, Austro-Hungarian, Ottoman and Russian empires. The Cold War was, in its turn, a consequence of the Second World War, and the fall of the Soviet Union a consequence of the end of the Cold War.

When the heir to the Austrian throne and his wife were shot dead in Sarajevo on 28 June 1914, a deadly machine was set in motion that catapulted the European superpowers into a war that no one seemed to have wanted, but that was nonetheless greeted with euphoria in all their capitals. That euphoria saw the war as an act of hygiene for the world, as Marinetti had written in his futuristic manifesto in 1909. By the end of 1914, however, the war had got bogged down in the mud of trench warfare. It was to last four long years and turned into a hitherto unseen *Materialschlacht*, in which, to quote Ernst Jünger, for the first time places rather than people became the targets. From Nieuwpoort at the North Sea to Switzerland, and from north-eastern Italy to Gallipoli in Turkey. For the Belgians the Yser became an iconic battlefield, for the British Ypres and the Somme, for the Canadians Vimy, for the French Verdun, for the Italians Caporetto, and for the Australians, New Zealanders and Turks Gallipoli. The Battle of Tannenberg was a debacle for the Russians. And for the Germans Langemark became the stuff of myth: there, in 1914, inexperienced German students advanced towards the machine guns of the professional British army.

How should we commemorate it all? Siegfried Sassoon thought the new Menin Gate in Ypres, which was officially opened in 1927, a scandal:

(...)
Here was the world's worst wound. And here with pride
'Their name liveth for ever', the Gateway claims.
Was ever an immolation so belied
As these intolerably nameless names?
Well might the Dead who struggled in the slime
Rise and deride this sepulchre of crime.
(On Passing the New Menin Gate)

Today we look with awe at the close to 55,000 names on this monument – names of soldiers whose bodies were never recovered. Perhaps the list is a war poem.

The Flanders Poppy as *Lieu de Mémoire*

John McCrae (1872-1918)

The scent of blood stains the Remembrance Poppy. In the black-magic fields of Flanders and the Somme, corn poppies are nourished by the memory of 'the missing'. It is as if the souls of those who died here between 1914 and 1918 have been transformed into a million blood-red flowers, whose enduring image reaches out to the farthest limits of our imagination. The Flanders Poppy is a volatile flower – a barometer of conscience and conflict, whose story reaches back into the distant past. How and why did such a humble flower become a universal symbol of remembrance and commemoration – a *lieu de mémoire*?

The story of the Flanders Poppy is strange and compelling. It is tragic and uplifting, deadly and comforting, intimately personal yet international in spirit. The poppy is an ancient symbol, yet also a modern icon of war and sacrifice. It collides with the First and Second World Wars, millions of war-dead, pacifism, and remembrance. Ironically, it is also embroiled in the international 'war on terror' through the billion-dollar trade in narcotic trafficking of the opium poppy and its derivatives.

The poppy's story is as old as civilization. Following its ancient origins, we glimpse a primordial world of sorcery, where Nature and humanity were joined imperceptibly by spirituality and ritual. Classical Greek myth tells that poppies flowered along the banks of the River Lethe which flowed to Hades, and from which the dead had to drink so as to forget their former existence in the world of the living. The association of the poppy with the anguish and suffering of war also appeared in the works of Homer. At a banquet in Sparta, Helen eased the Trojan War grief of her guests by spiking their wine with honey and opium.

The scarlet corn poppy (*Papaver rhoeas*) and purple-white opium poppy (*Papaver somniferum*) reveal their intimacy through a long relationship with war, not least because the 'long sleep' of death was so easily associated with opium narcosis, and also because of the corn poppy's ominous ubiquity on the freshly churned fields of war.

During the First World War, personal experiences juxtaposed images of the crimson poppy and scenes of carnage on the battlefields. Corn poppies were imagined as the spirits of the dead rising from the blood-drenched earth – 'thrusting from the lips of craters, undaunted by the desolation, heedless of human fury and stupidity' as the fighter pilot Cecil Lewis observed (1). Captain Rowland Fielding described soldiers wildly rushing across a No Man's Land ablaze with scarlet poppies, accompanied by a storm of rifle and machine-gun fire (2).

Messianic conversion in New York

It was the Canadian soldier-surgeon John McCrae who crystallised these feelings in his 1915 poem *'In Flanders Fields'*. Crouching at the entrance to his dugout, just outside of Ypres in Belgian Flanders, McCrae gazed on the small battlefield cemetery where he had just buried a close friend. From his grief he conjured his poem, immortalising the poppy in his opening stanza, 'In Flanders fields the poppies blow / Between the crosses, row on row'.

The poem became the touchstone of emotion for the war generation, striking a chord with soldiers and public alike. The corn poppy became the 'Flanders Poppy', an emblem for the souls of the dead, and a crimson palliative for those who had lost loved ones. Its ambiguous relationship with the opium poppy manifested itself in morphine, a powerful painkiller which made the physical agonies of war more bearable, and which was a derivative of opium.

In Flanders Fields established the corn poppy as the symbolic flower of the Great War, but did not guarantee its postwar emergence as an international symbol of commemoration for the English-speaking world. This final transformation took place in New York in the days leading up to the Armistice of November 11, 1918. It was here that an unassuming middle-aged schoolteacher named Moina Michael had nothing less than a messianic spiritual conversion.

Moina read McCrae's poem and imagined the voices of the dead clamouring for her to convert the scarlet flower into a sacred emblem of their sacrifice. She never married, and regarded the poppy as her 'spirit child', pledging her soul, she said, to 'that crimson cup flower of Flanders, the red Poppy which caught the sacrificial blood of ten million men dying for the Peace of the World' (3). In 1921, the poppy was adopted as the official remembrance flower of the United States. The 'Buddy Poppy', as it was soon re-christened, remains the national flower of war commemoration to this day, though most Americans wouldn't recognise it.

But this was a story of two women, for Moina's obsession was matched by Anna Guérin, an elegant French widow who championed the manufacturing of silken red poppies in the devastated areas of France, and sold them across the world to raise money for veterans and orphans of the Great War. Rivalry between the two women was unspoken but keen. Anna's early financial advantage was undermined when American veterans decided that their own disabled comrades should make poppies in the USA. Fashioned by crippled hands and missing limbs, the Buddy Poppy tugged at the nation's hearts every Veterans Day.

Anna Guérin sealed the poppy's international success by travelling to Canada, and her representatives to Australia and New Zealand, all of which adopted the commemorative flower. She visited London too, where she convinced the British Legion to embrace the poppy. This victory was short lived, as the Legion

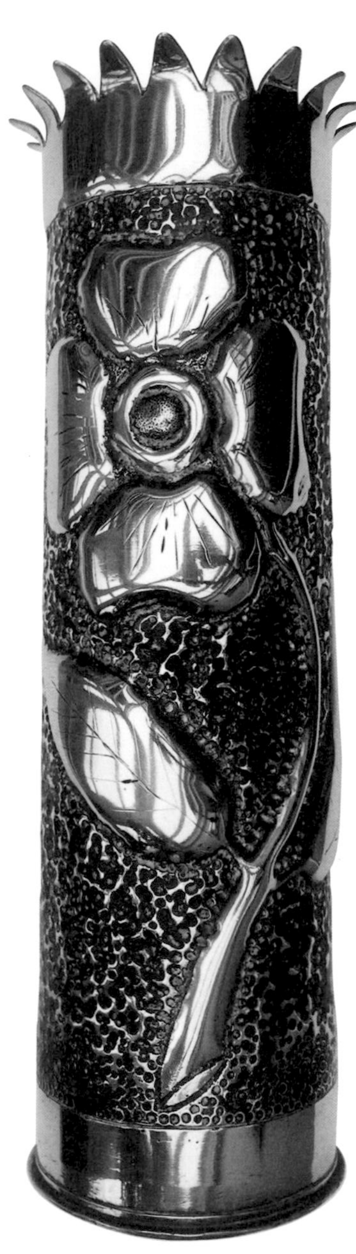

Trench art poppy shell
© J Brazier

soon began making its own artificial flowers for their Poppy Day Appeal, where the red cloth poppy on its wire attachment recalled for many a generation of youth sacrificed on the barbed wire of the Western Front.

In Britain, from 1921, buying a Remembrance Poppy directly supported the war-wounded who were employed in the British Legion's newly established Poppy Factory. The beginnings were modest, with just five disabled servicemen in a small room above a shop off the Old Kent Road in south-east London. As poppy wearing gathered momentum, the operation soon moved to Richmond in Surrey, and then, in 1933, it moved again to a purpose-built factory nearby where it remains to this day. The symbolism of this arrangement is as poignant and appropriate today as it was at the time. Men shattered by war created poppies to commemorate their fallen comrades, and to raise money to support the bereaved and themselves. The Flanders Poppy had become an evocative *lieu de mémoire*.

The inspirational spirit of giving associated with the poppy made a deep impression, and endured for decades. Some forty years later, in 1967, the First World War veteran Alexander Anthony, who had fought on the Somme and at Ypres, clung resolutely to the poppy.

> *'I'm a believer, you see. And to me that poppy means everything. ... I have been connected with these poppies for the last 50 years. ... When you know where your donation goes and the amount of money spent on destitute ex-servicemen who have given their all for their country, and you see these badly disabled servicemen making the poppies, then the light in their eyes when you bring them part of this donation is all the justification needed.'(4)*

Championed by Moina Michael – the 'Poppy Princess' – and Anna Guérin – the 'Poppy Lady', the Remembrance Poppy spread across the world, taking root in the hearts and consciences of men, women, and children in Canada, Australia, New Zealand, South Africa and beyond. During the inter-war years of 1919-1939, crimson cloth poppies for the living and counterpart wreaths on headstones and memorials became a new tradition. They bloomed for the dead and missing as thousands of pilgrims journeyed to the scenes of sacrifice, and countless more paid their annual respects from London to Sydney, New York to Vancouver. Battlefield pilgrims sought a rendezvous of the spirit which they had been denied in life when fathers, brothers, husbands and lovers did not return.

These pilgrims fell silent only to ponder or weep, to buy souvenirs, to fix their memories to a place, and a sky, and imagine their loved ones who had once passed this way. They set down their poppies, and returned home with strangely-shaped objects reverently placed on mantelpieces and in hallways: embroidered silk handkerchiefs, decorated brass artillery-shell cases, carved wooden boxes, and even fragments of earth.

By far the most popular of these battlefield mementos were the empty shell cases decorated with art nouveau floral designs – including the poppy. They served as 'flower vases', harking back to the prewar fashion for pastoral imagery, and an ageless fascination with flowers shared by the soldiers themselves. The power of these trench art ornaments to disturb later generations was part of the hidden world of the postwar years.

Early Remembrance Poppy
© J Brazier

A White Poppy rival

It was in this volatile and unpredictable landscape of memory that the Flanders Poppy flourished, renewing itself each year, and bringing hope and financial help to families decimated by the war. Wearing the poppy was an act of faith and solidarity with the dead and the living, and seemed to promise that such terrible sufferings would never be repeated – just as Moina Michael had intended. Battlefield pilgrimages were splashed with flowers, and the sight of crimson fields brought many to tears. Commemorating the war was becoming an industry, and the Flanders Poppy its peerless emblem.

Bizarre sights were seen in Britain. A poppy-decked elephant paraded the streets of Leeds in 1924, and in the same year a poppy-covered goat hauled a miniature replica of Wimbledon's war memorial around south London streets (5). The poppy fields of the Somme and Belgian Flanders were shrunk to more manageable size in the grounds adjacent to London's Westminster Abbey. A single wooden cross brought from the battlefield grave of an unknown British soldier stood alone for several years until 1928 when passers-by began planting their own poppies alongside. The Field of Remembrance was born, and still flourishes today in the days leading up to November 11.

Public enthusiasm for the Flanders Poppy gripped the English-speaking world. Poppy selling was mainly women's work, and would remain so until the Second World War. In 1930s' Britain, poppies were sold by 100,000 women of the British Legion's Women's Section, helped by 250,000 female volunteers (6). In the United States, volunteers for the soldiers' association known as the 'Veterans of Foreign Wars' were often pretty young women, who stood in front of giant 'stars and stripes' flags surrounded by poppy wreaths and patriotic posters, handing out poppies to the public for a donation. As the Second World War approached, Hollywood joined in, and female movie stars such as Ginger Rogers and Jane Wyman were chosen as Buddy Poppy Girls. Although too young to be a Poppy Girl, Judy Garland did her bit. In 1939, the film *The Wizard of Oz* saw her falling asleep in a field of magical poppies, overcome by their drowsy vapours.

The Remembrance Poppy was not accepted by everyone. In 1933, the Women's Co-operative Guild invented the White Poppy as an emblem of peace, to commemorate all war victims and express the hope for an end to all conflict. When the British Legion refused to manufacture what is regarded as a morally dubious rival, the newly-formed Peace Pledge Union began making them (and still does today).

Many First World War veterans were enraged by the White Poppy, regarding it as undermining their wartime sacrifices, and as too close to the white feather of cowardice and the white flag of surrender. Women lost their jobs for wearing it, and on Armistice Days white poppy wreaths were removed by red poppy wearers and trampled underfoot. Some saw both sides of the argument, and wore red and white poppies together.

Powerful and enduring symbol

9/11 is a date burned into the psyche of the West. The darker symbolism of the poppy stormed back into public consciousness in an apocalyptic vision of Islamic terrorism when the World Trade Centre came crashing down just a few blocks from where Moina Michael experienced her decidedly Christian revelation eighty years before. The U.S. response – the 'war on terror' – rejuvenated the connections between poppies, war, and violent death. As coalition troops flooded into Afghanistan, the nightmare of 1914-18 returned, and soon American, British, and Canadian soldiers were dying again amidst fields of poppies.

The invasion breathed new life into opium, and eradicating its poppy quickly became a key objective in winning the conflict. British soldiers last smelled opium winds in the summer of 1880, when a British army was all but annihilated by Afghan tribesmen at the Battle of Maiwand on the banks of the Helmand River. Now the British were back. The corn poppy remains a symbol of commemoration and war, but its opium-bearing cousin has become a reason for conflict. The two poppy varieties are locked together through conflict as closely today as they were in Homer's account of the Trojan War.

The conflicts in Iraq and Afghanistan rejuvenated the Remembrance Poppy's image and significance in Britain. Passengers at London's Heathrow airport were astonished in 2008 when confronted by a huge Poppy Man, towering five metres tall, and covered in 8,000 scarlet poppies. Poppy Man was a giant version of a smaller life-size figure invented for the Royal British Legion in 2007 (7). Poppy Man is hollow inside, yet his void is filled with the identity of loved ones by all who have been bereaved by war. More than this, he captures the transience of life, linking the war-maimed and disabled who make the Remembrance Poppy to thousands of poppy sellers who fill the streets in the weeks before November 11. He is unbearably poignant – a spiritual mannequin, covered in red.

The Legion launched its 2008 Poppy Day Appeal by taking him to southern Iraq, where he posed alongside British soldiers, calm and surreal amongst the chaos of war. He stood alongside troops in Basra at a service of dedication at a memorial wall commemorating fallen British soldiers in Iraq, and toured their barracks (8). Poppy Man taps into the core of the Remembrance Poppy – honouring the past, but resolutely contemporary, forever relevant to the young men who die and are wounded so far from home, and who leave wives, sweethearts and children behind.

The poppy is a powerful and ancient symbol, embodying ideas of war, death, eternal rest, and, ironically, of remembrance and forgetfulness. Its ability to change its meanings, and become relevant to new realities, shows how deeply rooted it is in human consciousness. Our imaginations play with the poppy's emblematic qualities, moving back and forth between the two varieties and forging the composite that is the Flanders Remembrance Poppy.

Every year, around 80 million people across the world buy a Poppy, participating in its message of remembering and honouring the war dead. Unknowingly, they acknowledge a deep-rooted and formative connection from the distant past, when the opium poppy was a sacred flower that floated the soul to an afterlife of never-ending sleep. Separate, but forever intertwined, the corn and opium poppies have generated more wealth, misery, hope and death than any flower in human history, and together have created the Remembrance Poppy, surely one of the most powerful and enduring symbols of our humanity. ■

NOTES

(1) Cecil Lewis, quoted in P. Fussell [1975] (2000), *The Great War and Modern Memory*, p 254. New York: Oxford University Press.
(2) Rowland Feilding. (1929), *War Letters to a Wife*, p 21, 23. London: The Medici Society.
(3) Moina Michael. (1941), *The Miracle Flower: The Story of the Flanders Fields Memorial Poppy*, p 79. Philadelphia: Dorrance and Company.
(4) Anthony Alexander, quoted in V. Newall. (1976), Armistice Day: Folk Tradition in an English Festival of Remembrance. *Folklore* 87 (2), pp 226-9.
(5) B. Harding. (2001), *Keeping Faith: The History of the Royal British Legion*, p 127. Barnsley: Leo Cooper.
(6) A. Gregory. (1994), *The Silence of Memory: Armistice Day 1919-1946*, p 111. Oxford: Berg.
(7) A. Hildebrandt. (2008), Poppy Man tours war zone to launch Remembrance Day appeal. *CBC News*, 23 October. http://www.cbc.ca/world/story/2008/10/23/poppy-campaign.html. Accessed on 24 October 2008.
(8) BBC. (2008). Poppy Appeal Launched from Basra. news.bbc.co.uk/2/hi/uk_news/7685840.stm. Accessed on 23 October 2009.

Nicholas J. Saunders' book, *The Poppy. A Cultural History from Ancient Egypt to Flanders Fields to Afghanistan*, was published by One World Publication, London, 2013.

Commemoration in Stone and in Silence

The Menin Gate and the Last Post Ceremony as *Lieu de Mémoire*

Who will remember, passing through this Gate,
The unheroic Dead who fed the guns?
Who shall absolve the foulness of their fate, -
Those doomed, conscripted, unvictorious ones?

Siegfried Sassoon used these words – and much stronger ones – to express his anger on the day after the unveiling of the Menin Gate Memorial (Menenpoort) in Ypres in 1927. This most uncompromising of the war poets hated the Menin Gate. He called it a 'sepulchre of crime' that the 'Dead who struggled in the slime' might indeed 'rise and deride'. Sassoon's criticism was undoubtedly prompted by the design of the Menin Gate. In 1919, architect Reginald Blomfield had already conceived of a triumphal arch to serve as a symbol of the 'enduring power and indomitable tenacity of the British Empire'. The first designs show a classical arch adorned with a lion keeping watch towards the east. Blomfield inspected several sites at Ypres, but from the outset he favoured the present site. This preference was based on a number of practical considerations, but also had to do with symbolism: it was the only point of entry in the east rampart, and thousands of British troops had marched past it on their way to confront the enemy. Blomfield's initial design was commissioned by the Battle Exploit Memorials Committee, which at the time was working hard to preserve the ruins of the Cloth Hall (*Lakenhallen*) and St. Martin's Church, as well as working on a new great British war memorial.

Memorial to the Missing

Initially, the intention was certainly not to build a funerary monument. The original plans were for a memorial to military actions (read: victories) by the armies of the British Empire, not for a memorial to the dead. This changed at the beginning of 1921, when the Imperial War Graves Commission decided to honour the missing – who have no known grave – by recording their names on specially designed architectural memorials. Because it would have been absurd and financially irresponsible to have two British war monuments in Ypres – one to

Construction of the Menin Gate Memorial, spring 1927 © In Flanders Fields Museum, Ieper

commemorate military action and the other to honour the missing – the two schemes were integrated. The Menin Gate project was transferred to the War Graves Commission. This proceeded relatively smoothly, since Blomfield was already one of the Commission's principal architects.

The Menin Gate that was unveiled on 24 July 1927 was indeed a 'double' monument – in form as well as meaning: its exterior is a triumphal arch, and the interior and sides are a funerary monument. On the east side, a watchful lion sits atop the memorial and on the side facing the centre of the town there is a cenotaph, as if to remind Ypres that all these men had sacrificed their lives for the town and its residents. Whereas a triumphal arch was the time-honoured way to commemorate military action, the concept of a monument for the missing was progressive as well as new. Never before had a memorial been erected for those who were missing on the battlefields and, in the case of the First World War, the British example would not be followed by the other belligerents. A Memorial to the Missing not only answered the needs of the families affected, who wished for a place to mourn, but is also evidence of the way in which the war was fought. The majority of the fallen were killed by artillery fire. If they had not already been literally blown to bits, it was very likely that their known grave would have been lost anyway in the later battles of this static trench war. A memorial to the missing was also the logical consequence of an earlier decision taken by the War Graves Commission to commemorate all those who had lost their lives in the service of Britain equally. This was a distinctly progressive stance, particularly for the class society that was the British Empire. It had everything to do with the composition of the British forces in the First World War; most of the rank and file were volunteers and, from 1917 on, conscripts. In short, the aim was to commemorate ordinary citizens in military service.

Now that I have explained what the Menin Gate is, it is important to emphasise what it is *not*. It is not a victory memorial, although it has the appearance of a triumphal arch. Neither is it a peace memorial, although many consider the thousands of names recorded there to be a powerful plea for peace. The Menin Gate is officially, exclusively, a place of remembrance for 55,000 subjects of the British Empire who died at Ypres and do not have a known grave. It therefore does not commemorate the losses suffered by other Allied powers – let alone the Germans – or the fallen at any other front. The names on the Menin Gate therefore do not include those who are buried in one of the 150 cemeteries at Ypres. It is important to remember that many more British soldiers went missing than are listed at the Menin Gate. A further 35,000 names are inscribed on a long wall at the Tyne Cot Cemetery in Passchendaele, and the Memorial to the Missing at Ploegsteert ('Plugstreet') records the names of those who lost their lives south of the River Douve. All other meanings attributed to the Menin Gate are interpretations, elicited by aspects such as its architectural form, the seemingly endless list of names and/or the events that take place there.

There were also writers who were more favourably disposed towards the Menin Gate. In 1928, Stefan Zweig described it in words very different to those used by Siegfried Sassoon a year earlier:

The broad vaulted gateway, Roman in the simplicity of its mass, towers on high, a mausoleum rather than a triumphal arch. On its front facing the enemy there lies on the summit a marble lion [in fact stone], *his paw heavily planted as if on his prey which he does not mean to let go: on the reverse side facing the town stands a sarcophagus, gloomy and stern. For this monument is to the dead, the six and fifty thousand English dead at Ypres whose graves could not be found, who lie somewhere crumbled together in a common grave, mutilated beyond recognition by shells, or disintegrating in the water, to all those who, unlike the others, have not their bright white polished stone in the cemeteries round about the town, the individual mark of their last resting-place. To all of these, the six and fifty thousand, this arch has been raised as a common tombstone and all these six and fifty thousand names are engraved in letters of gold – so many, so interminably many, that as on the columns of the Alhambra the writing becomes decorative. It is a memorial, then, offered not to victory, but to the dead – the victims – without any distinction, to the fallen Australians, English, Hindus and Mohammedans who are immortalized to the same degree, and in the same characters, in the same stone, by virtue of the same death. Here there is no image of the King, no mention of victories, no genuflections to generals of genius, no prattle about Archdukes and Princes: only the laconic, noble inscriptions – Pro Rege, Pro Patria.*

In its really Roman simplicity this monument to the six and fifty thousand is more impressive than any triumphal arch or monument to victory that I have ever seen, and its impressiveness is still further increased by the sight of the heaps of wreaths constantly being laid there by widows, children and friends. For a whole nation makes its pilgrimage every year to this common tomb of its unburied and unreturning soldiers.

Last Post Ceremony on Armistice Day,
11 November 1936
© In Flanders Fields Museum, Ieper

It seems to me that the impression that the Menin Gate made on Zweig is the prevailing impression among visitors today. This partly explains why the Menin Gate, despite all its imperial pomp, has only very rarely been the target of political manifestations. However, whereas in Zweig's day the 'heaps of wreaths' were still laid by 'widows, children and friends', this is now done by a much wider range of people: relatives, school groups, associations, and so forth. The fact that the Menin Gate is still used for funerary commemoration is one reason we can refer to it as a *living* memorial. Another reason is that names are still added when it is found that someone should be commemorated there and that, in theory at least, names are removed when it turns out that someone is commemorated elsewhere, either with a known grave or on another Memorial to the Missing.

Call to Attention

However, the main reason we can refer to the Menin Gate as a living memorial is the Last Post Ceremony, which, in June 2011, was officially recognised by decree of the Flemish government as part of the country's 'intangible cultural heritage'. The ceremony was held for the first time on 2 July 1928. After an interval during the first winter, the daily ceremony was reinstated on 1 May 1929. It has continued uninterrupted ever since, except during the German Occupation in the Second World War. It is impossible to overstate the uniqueness of this continuing daily remembrance, which will take place for the 30,000th time on 9 July 2015.

Although a British melody is used – the actual 'Last Post' – and the English name, the ceremony has an entirely local character. The content of the ceremony is determined by the Last Post Association (called the Last Post Committee until 1999). Anyone can become a member of this association, but the members of the Board of Administrators are residents of Ypres and the surrounding area, and are co-opted. This principle has caused some to describe it as elitist. The ceremony itself is performed by a number of Masters of Ceremony, eight

Adolf Hitler in Ypres, 1 June 1940, with the Battle of Dunkirk still raging buglers and, more recently, a bagpiper. The buglers were traditionally recruited from the local fire brigade and, although they take part at the request of the Last Post Association and some of them are no longer members of the voluntary fire brigade, they still wear its uniform.

Shortly before 8 o'clock each evening, the police stop the traffic on both sides of the Menin Gate. This is not only symbolic but also necessary: the memorial is situated on one of the busiest routes into the town centre and the roar of traffic echoes under the arch all day long. However, every day there is a brief period of silence, and the Gate regains the aspect of a quiet place of contemplation and remembrance. At precisely 8 o'clock, buglers on the east side of the memorial sound a Call to Attention. After a short announcement or address, the Last Post is played. The Exhortation is then recited by a member of the public or a member of the Last Post Association. The Exhortation is a verse from Laurence Binyon's poem 'For the Fallen', written in September 1914:

They shall grow not old, as we that are left grow old:
Age shall not weary them, nor the years condemn.
At the going down of the sun and in the morning
We will remember them.

Those present repeat the last sentence. The Exhortation is followed by a minute's silence – which many feel to be the most moving part of the ceremony – and the laying of wreaths. The ceremony ends with the sounding of the Reveille. The Last Post Ceremony rarely lasts more than five to ten minutes. If a piper is present, a lament is played as the wreaths are laid. If foreign dignitaries are visiting, their national anthem may be played at the end of the ceremony, but the structure of the ceremony has remained unchanged for decades. This does not mean that the Ypres Last Post Ceremony has not evolved. In the past, a day-to-day ceremony was often limited to stopping the traffic and the sounding of the Last Post by two buglers. The fire-brigade uniforms were worn only at weekends or on special occasions. During the week, the buglers wore 'civvies',

Last Post Ceremony in grand style

Sikhs during Armistice Day Ceremony, 11 November 2009 © Tijl Capoen

later with an overcoat and beret for a more official and uniform appearance. This has not been the case since around the beginning of this century. The increase in the number of buglers (who still wear uniform), the employment of a permanent piper, and the integration of the Exhortation and minute's silence in the weekday ceremonies too, have changed the character of the Last Post. Despite being firmly anchored in the local culture and daily life of Ypres, the ceremony now seems more formal and more British. Due to the considerable increase in the number of onlookers, particularly since the 1990s, the Last Post Association continually struggles to make it clear that the ceremony is more than a tourist attraction. Today, the public have to be expressly asked not to applaud during or after the ceremony, and the hundreds of flashing cameras, smartphones and iPads do not exactly make for a serene atmosphere.

The Last Post Ceremony as a 'blank slate'

But there is more. The strength of the Last Post Ceremony has always been that it is a 'blank slate', as it were, by this I mean that everyone can attribute his or her own meaning to it. Aside from being a homage to the fallen, it can be an inspiration for military personnel to persevere in their duties, while for pacifists it is a plea for peace. For some, the Last Post Ceremony is a reminder of the purpose of the war, while for others it is a reminder of its futility. In the past, the organisers of the Last Post have had to steer a careful course to preserve its intended neutrality. In a brochure published in the second half of the 1970s, the Last Post Committee wrote that the former enemy would be honoured too, and the hope was expressed that 'by remembering the suffering that war has caused, the desire for peace will be strengthened in men of goodwill everywhere, so that the nations of the world may live side by side in mutual understanding and harmony'. On 17 May 1985, while visiting the Menin Gate, Pope John Paul II prayed for world peace. The occasion is commemorated on a paving tile on the north staircase. However, since that time it has been

ANZAC Day,
25 April 2003

Army Cadets during Last Post Ceremony,
3 August 2012 © www.greatwar.be

Calling Home Ceremony of Canadian First Nations during Last Post Ceremony, 1 November 2005 © Tijl Capoen

noticed that the Last Post Ceremony has undergone a degree of 'militarisation'; I am referring primarily to the increased active participation of armed military detachments in the Last Post Ceremony. Some members of the public object when military personnel with rifle and bayonet are given a place of honour at a Last Post Ceremony, just as others would disapprove if the ceremony were used as a platform for political statements. Given the current level of interest, among military personnel from all over the British Commonwealth and others, it is certainly not always easy for the Last Post Association to maintain the neutrality of the ceremony in this respect. In order to preserve its uniqueness and universal significance in perpetuity, it is essential that the character of the ceremony as a 'blank slate' is strictly observed, and that all participants – including military personnel – are required to observe rules in order to safeguard the perception of strict neutrality.

Despite the different possible interpretations, such as those inspired by the architectural bombast, the Menin Gate should be thought of exclusively as a place of commemoration, and the Last Post Ceremony must remain a collective act of remembrance for people of all persuasions. It is only as symbols of remembrance that are open to interpretation that they can – and will – retain their powers of unification and connection until the next Great War Centenary. ■

Translated by Yvette Mead

FURTHER READING

D. Dendooven, *Menin Gate & Last Post. Ypres as Holy Ground,* Koksijde, De Klaproos Editions, 2001, 160 p.

www.lastpost.be

www.cwgc.org

On Passing the new Menin Gate

Siegfried Sassoon

Who will remember, passing through this Gate,
The unheroic Dead who fed the guns?
Who shall absolve the foulness of their fate,—
Those doomed, conscripted, unvictorious ones?

Crudely renewed, the Salient holds its own.
Paid are its dim defenders by this pomp;
Paid, with a pile of peace-complacent stone,
The armies who endured that sullen swamp.

Here was the world's worst wound. And here with pride
'Their name liveth for ever,' the Gateway claims.
Was ever an immolation so belied
As these intolerably nameless names?
Well might the Dead who struggled in the slime
Rise and deride this sepulchre of crime.

Begun Brussels, 25 July 1927;
finished Campden Hill Square, January 1928

They Went with Songs to Battle

Songs as *Lieux de Mémoire* of the Great War

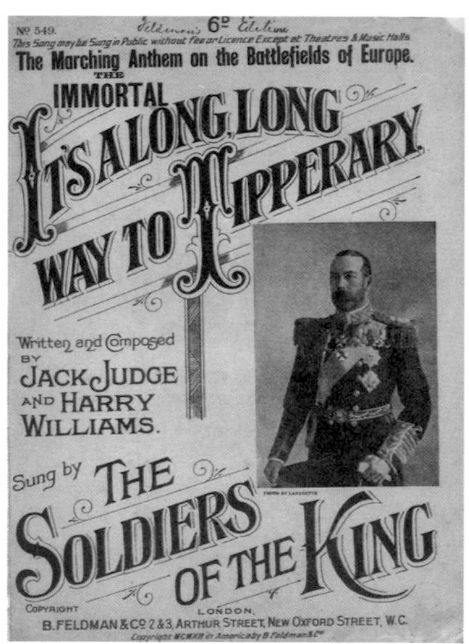

'It's a Long Way to Tipperary' – Sheet music cover B. Feldman & Co., England (Copyright 1912). The wartime cover highlights the song's use for marching

It was called 'the Ragtime war'. Soldiers sang as they marched; gramophones 'passed the time along' in every British Officers' Mess and the deepest German bunkers; composers provided songs that were sentimental, satirical, topical or bellicose for the Home Front and the theatre of war; Concert parties, with old favourites and hits from the latest shows, urged the men behind the lines to join in 'altogether now'; and the troops themselves created their own mordant musical commentaries on the conflict. The First World War exists with and in its own soundtrack. Each time 'Tipperary' or 'Pack up your Troubles', 'There's a Long, Long Trail' or 'Blighty' play, there's an intertextuality that immediately calls up blotched and flickering film of Tommies waving to the camera as they march through Flanders' fields - just as the jauntiest of the songs are now almost inseparable from a sense of desolation at our foreknowledge of what awaited those same Tommies at the Front. And their own words, stating the truth unvarnished 'Oh my, I don't want to die, I want to go home', equal the greatest of the Great War poets. Uniquely, the First World War is evoked by song.

How did song become the pre-eminent *lieu de mémoire* of this war? The songs that are its signifiers are disparate – some composed before 1914 with no military content, others so full of longing for home that they seem designed to foster nostalgia rather than battle. Even the wartime creations lack significant jingoism; the soldiers their texts describe are more humorous than heroic. These paradoxes are clearly present in the most famous of all the lieu de mémoire songs, 'It's a long way to Tipperary'. Despite its later status as 'the immortal ... marching anthem on the battlefields of Europe', initially 'Tipperary' had no bellicose associations – it was composed more than two years before the war and was reportedly written only to win a bet. On 30th January 1912, Jack Judge (1872-1938), a prolific songwriter and singer, was appearing at The Grand Theatre in Stalybridge, in the north west of England. A large, genial man who enjoyed a drink, Jack made a practice of offering a challenge to the company in pubs he visited during his theatre tours. He would bet five shillings (about a quarter of a skilled man's weekly wage at the time) that he could write a song overnight and sing it on stage the next day. That evening he took a bet and the following night sang 'It's a long way to Tipperary' to great applause. And though evidence of an earlier piece of his called 'It's a long way to Connemara' suggests the Stalybridge work was not such an impromptu composition as first appears, this performance at The Grand fixed the song's text and – as Jack could not write music – it was arranged with these lyrics by his friend Harry Williams, who became co-author as a result. Jack advertised the song and caught the attention of Bert Feldman (1875-1945), a major London music publisher. By September 1912 Feldman had the music in print (adding an extra 'long' to the chorus) and by 1913 it was featuring in the repertoire of the music hall star, Florrie Forde (1875-1940). Florrie and Jack sang 'Tipperary' around the halls and the sheet music sold well, but it was not until a reporter for the mass-circulation newspaper, *The Daily Mail*, wrote that the Connaught Rangers sang the song as they disembarked with the British Expeditionary Forces at Boulogne in August 1914 that it took off to become an international hit, indelibly associated with the Great War.

'There's a Long, Long Trail' – Sheet music cover West & Co., England (1913)

Pre-eminently of - but not about - the war, 'Tipperary' exemplifies the discontinuities that mark several of the popular songs which became its *lieux de mémoire*. For soldiers pounding along the narrow roads of rural France and West Flanders with full military pack, the 'long, long way' of its chorus made a particularly apt accompaniment. But the lyrics of 'Tipperary's' verses consist of elements from an existing comedic format, the 'Irish Mother's Letter to her Son', re-cast in the form of a love letter:

Paddy wrote a letter to his Irish Molly-o
Saying if you don't receive it, write and let me know
If I make mistakes in spelling, Molly dear, said he
Remember it's the pen that's bad, don't lay the blame on me.

'There's a Long, Long, Trail' – Postcard with drawing illustrating first verse and use in the war. Inter Art Co. 'Artistique Song' Series, England [ND]

Like their own endlessly repeated rationalisation 'We're here because, we're here because, we're here...', perhaps the troops only marched to the insistent, foot-raising beat of 'Tipperary's' chorus rather than the irregularly-timed old jokes of its verses. And given that the infantry were frequently expected to cover twenty kilometres per day to get to or from the line, despite a promising title, it seems unlikely that another early favourite, 'There's a Long, Long Trail' was often sung en route. Written by American students Stoddard King (1889–1933) and Alonzo Eliott (1891–1964) for a concert at Yale University in 1913, the gently swaying rhythm of its tune and the moonlit dreamscape of nightingales and reunited lovers in its text offer a refuge from reality rather than encouragement to stride out in step to face the enemy.

'It is a peculiarity of British humour to be derogatory to its own dignity,' wrote Royal Flying Corps Lieutenant Frederick Nettleingham (1893-1976), characterising the wartime songs soldiers made up for themselves. And satire was also the response to conflict of many of the songs composed in Britain during the war. Successful music hall writers like Robert Weston (1878-1936) and Bert Lee (1880-1946) echoed the troops' own irreverence with songs about the Home Front like 'Do You Want Us to Lose the War?' or 'Lloyd George's Beer' that were an antidote to jingoistic posturing. A marked absence of heroics also characterised 'Take Me Back to Dear Old Blighty', one of the wartime *lieu de mémoire* songs dealing directly with soldiering. Written 'in four hours' by Arthur J. Mills (1872-1919), Bennett Scott (1875-1930) and Fred Godfrey (1880-1953) after they saw a poster for a show called 'Blighty' outside the Oxford Music Hall in London in 1916, the song's verses portray a genial, amateur army. Featuring an airsick pilot, infantrymen taking tea and a soldier attempting to shave under enemy shelling, its tone is established in its opening verse by 'Jack Dunn', 'doing his bit' in the mud by day but spending his evenings listening to his gramophone. All the characters are depicted at war in France and each is named, but none is identified by military rank or role in combat. Even more significantly, 'Blighty's' extremely catchy chorus consists of a heartfelt plea to return to 'anywhere' in England and the comfort of sweethearts and home. Composed at precisely the time when the requirement to 'be offensive' was the subject of repeated orders from Douglas Haig, the Commander of the British Expeditionary Force, 'Blighty' highlights the gap between official zeal for 'an active Front' and the aspiration of individuals attempting to survive.

'Pack up Your Troubles in Your Old Kit Bag and Smile, Smile, Smile' – Sheet music cover Chappell & Co. (1915). The cover highlights the song's use for marching

Although they now act identically to evoke the Great War, the songs that are its *lieux de mémoire* were created under varying circumstances. Favourites from the music hall, written only months apart, reflect changing attitudes as the war became prolonged and the volunteers of 1914 had to be replaced – from January 1916 – by an army of conscripts. Unsurprisingly then, 'Private Perks' of 'Pack up Your Troubles in Your Old Kit Bag', an enthusiastic warrior with a disturbingly fixed grin created in 1915, contrasts markedly with the civilians in uniform of 'Blighty' in 1916; just as the insouciant 'Smile, smile, smile' of 'Pack up Your Troubles' chorus transformed into a damning title for Wilfred Owen's (1893-1918) poem of the 'sunk-eyed wounded' in September 1918.

Like other English *lieu de mémoire* songs, 'Pack up Your Troubles' was composed by professional songwriters and performers – the brothers Felix Powell (1878-1942) and George Asaf [Powell] (1880-1951). To catch the excited patriotism of the outbreak of war, the pair had written a form of the song but then discarded it as 'piffle'. In 1915, however, a revised version won a competition for morale-boosting pieces organised by the international publishers, Francis, Day and Hunter. Their sheet music proclaimed:

> 'What is best described as a PHILOSOPHY SONG is now being sung and whistled by the troops as they march along. We believe that it will become overwhelmingly popular.'

According to family sources, however, the success of the song became problematic for its writers. None of the composers of these English lieu de mémoire songs had personal experience of war at the time of their publication, but as ever greater numbers of men were needed to replace battle casualties, all were called up. Subsequently, both Powell brothers found their role as musical recruiters disturbing, and Felix - who served on the Western Front - suffered 'a kind of nervous breakdown' as a result.

Oh my I don't want to die

But troops did not need to rely on professional composers for songs to accompany marching or rest. Reportedly, famous *lieux de mémoire* like 'Tipperary' enjoyed only temporary favour - what was actually sung by soldiers were their own words set to the famous chorus:

'Take Me Back to Dear Old Blighty' – Postcard with posed photograph illustrating first verse – and gramophone. Bamforth's 'Song' Series, England [ND]

That's the wrong way to tickle Marie
That's the wrong way to kiss
Don't you know that over here, lad
They like it better like this
Hooray pour la France!
Farewell Angleterre!
We didn't know the way to tickle Marie
But now we've learnt how.

As well as music hall favourites, to a generation where church-going had been the norm, hymns provided a common fund of music for their own songs. 'What a friend we have in Jesus', 'The Church's One Foundation' and 'Holy, Holy, Holy!' lent their tunes and even parodied texts to 'When this Ruddy War is Over', 'We Are the Ragtime Army' and 'Grousing, Grousing, Grousing'. The latter was sometimes 'sternly suppressed by company commanders ... as being detrimental to good discipline' noted Lieutenant Nettleingham, who included all of these in his collections of *Tommy's Tunes*, published when he was on active service in 1917.

Concert parties formed by soldiers also created their own music. In Ypres with 1st Canadian Contingent, Lieutenant Gitz Rice (1891-1947) played the piano and wrote songs for military troupes like Princess Patricia's Canadian Comedy Company. The verses of Rice's 'self-satire', 'I Want to go Home' (1915) complained about Flanders' rain and mud giving him measles, 'flu and 'rheumatism in my hair', so that -

Tomorrow when the officer asks 'What would you like to do?'
I'm going to stand right up and say, 'If it's all the same to you –
CHORUS: *I want to go home, I want to go home*
The "Whizzbangs" and Shrapnel around me do roar
I don't want this old war any more
Take me far o'er the sea
Where the "Alleman" cannot get me
Oh my I don't want do die [sic]
I want to go 'ome.

The music hall patter of Rice's verses faded, but his jokey waltz-time chorus – an update of a song current in the Boer War - was poignantly taken up by British troops. Arriving in Ypres at night near enemy guns, William Cushing of the 9th Norfolk Regiment remembered:

'... someone started to sing *sotto voce* that haunting, nostalgic cry, taken up by all: "Oh my, I don't want to die, I want to go home." I can still hear that murmured wish and longing.... I wonder how many had their wish.'

It was even sung in the trenches, 'when strafe was at its hottest,' wrote the composer and poet Ivor Gurney (1890-1937) in June 1916 - 'a very popular song about here; but not military ... Nor a brave song, but brave men sing it.

I want to go home. I want to go home
The whizzbangs and shrapnel they whistle and roar.
I don't want to go in the trenches no more.
Take me over the sea
Where the Alleman can't catch me
Oh my! I don't want to die.
I want to go home.

Singing in the trenches was very important, remembered Corporal George Coppard (1898-1984), author of *With Machine Gun to Cambrai*. But asked if *lieux de mémoire* like 'Tipperary' were as popular with the troops as was believed, he replied 'Not so much as those which suggest something spicy.' From the merely racy to the downright obscene, the appeal of 'spicy' songs is well attested by contemporary sources. In fact, one 'famous heirloom of the British Army' provided the tune for over sixty songs of different subject, length and lewdness. A major key version of the tune for 'Johnny I Hardly Knew You', it already had military associations when it was fitted to 'Three German Officers Crossed the Rhine' - a parody of Johann Uhland's sentimental poem 'Der Wirtin Töchterlein' (1813) which replaced Uhland's three students sorrowing over a Rhenish innkeeper's dead daughter with three hyperactive Prussians and the obliging 'daughter fair' of a French innkeeper. A narrative song with 'about forty verses', its content meant that Tommy's Tunes could only offer 'a well-purged and diminutive' form. Other uses of the tune include the picaresque 'Mademoiselle from Armentières', which has the virtue of a verse commemorating the role of laundry maids behind the lines; 'Farmer Have You Any Good Wine?', in which an English 'soldier of the line' replaces the Three German Officers; and 'The Sergeant Major's Having a Time', other ranks' perennial complaint about the venality of their NCOs. 'Unprintable for general consumption', almost all the troops' 'spicy' songs form *milieux de mémoire* of the First War – a shared evocation of involvement that was only fully available to those who had experienced it directly for themselves.

From August 1914 and reports of the Connaught Rangers arriving in France, songs began their development into *milieux de mémoire* of the War. This was reinforced across contemporary culture. Sheet music publishers advertised the success of their wares as accompaniments to marching. Postcards depicting verses from popular songs were produced in sets and exchanged between home and the Front. Folklore grew up around songs – 'Roses of Picardy' (1916) was believed to portray the factual romance of its writer, a young lieutenant and a French widow. Although he was 68 and working as a lawyer in the south west of England during the war, its composer, Fred Weatherley (1848-1929), was happy to foster this battlefield mystique. Most resonantly, however, songs echoed through the poetry of the War – as clearly in Laurence Binyon's (1869-1943) poem 'For the Fallen' in 1914, proclaiming troops 'went with songs to battle' as in Siegfried Sassoon's (1886-1967) 'Song Books of the War' (1918), where 'a snatch of soldier-song' holds the risk of re-kindling young men's enthusiasm for fighting.

This process continued and diversified after the Armistice. Wartime concert parties took their songs and sketches on tour to a wider public into the 1930s. Composers revived their hits – an appearance by Fred Godfrey, co-writer of 'Take Me Back to Dear Old Blighty' at Exeter Hippodrome in November 1930 producing 'scenes of remarkable enthusiasm' as audiences 'revelled in the popular war-time chorus, the singing of which, however, was tinged with a feeling of sadness.... the atmosphere engendered by the appearance on the stage on Armistice Night of the man who wrote a ditty that will always be associated with memories of the war.' And different media began to assert the identity of songs and war. English feature films about the war frequently took their titles and inspiration from *lieu de mémoire* songs, including 'It's a Long Way to Tipperary' (1914), 'Mademoiselle from Armentières' (1926) and its follow-up 'Mademoiselle Parley Voo' (1928), 'Blighty' (1927) and 'Roses of Picardy' (1927). Later, even more complex intersections were created when the radio programme, 'The Long, Long Trail' (1961 and 1962), which used contemporary songs to provide a narration about the war, became first the musical drama 'Oh! What a Lovely War' (1963) and then a film (1969). Listeners today say that the songs offer them a brief, near-direct experience of the soldiers' war; the concerts and recordings planned for its centenary can only renew and intensify this unique fusion of the 'war to end all wars' and its music.

Acknowledgements: With many thanks to the staff of the Kenniscentrum, In Flanders Fields Museum, Ieper, Cyril Pearce and Jim Boyes for their generous, expert assistance. ■

John Stuart (left) as 'Johnny' in behind the lines concert party scene. Publicity photograph from the English feature film *Mademoiselle from Armentières*. Directed by Maurice Elvey (1926). Elvey directed a number of films with *lieu de mémoire* song titles – mainly after the war

In Flanders Fields

The Landscape of War as *Lieu de Mémoire*

We are sitting with a beer and some Turkish snacks at the only outdoor café on the bay. Young Turkish mothers are playing with their children down by the water in front of us. About thirty metres out to sea, a fisherman is gutting his catch on some flat rocks that show just above the water surface. A few rocks along, three seagulls wait impatiently for him to finish, so they can scavenge for entrails. It is the height of summer, the sea is smooth, with just the occasional ripple breaking almost silently on the narrow sandy beach, which turns into rocks after just a few metres. On the side of the bay with the café and the village and its medieval ruin, the land is a flat stretch of grass and stones. The opposite side of the bay is a sheer cliff face. A British burial ground nestles at the point where the flat land meets the cliff: V Beach Cemetery. The village is Seddülbahir, the Sud-el-Bar of the Irish folk songs, and the beach is V Beach, the deadliest of the Gallipoli landing beaches of 25 April, 1915. Turkish Fort No. 1 stands on top of the cliff with a memorial beside it that dates back to the 1960s and a statue with an Atatürk slogan from 1992. At the highest point is the Cape Helles Memorial to the Missing, erected in 1926. This site makes it easy to see how just a handful of Turkish defenders were able to offer such resistance to a landing force. Here, on V Beach, that landing force consisted of a converted collier, the SS *River Clyde*, and a number of smaller vessels. The collier's hull had openings cut into it to allow two battalions to emerge and go ashore. The strip of flat rocks is what remains of the landing stage that was constructed alongside the beached cargo ship. The first Munster Fusiliers who climbed out of the cargo hold were met with rapid fire from the Turkish forces, and so the rest wisely stayed put until darkness fell. Their fellow soldiers from the Dublin Fusiliers, in their launches, fared even worse. Their names fill V Beach Cemetery and the Cape Helles Memorial. After the landing, both units combined could muster barely one battalion, which they called the Dubsters.

Almost one hundred years later, this scene can still clearly be read in the landscape: the bay, the beach, the cliff and the monuments fix the crucial elements of the story, at least from the British perspective, or the Irish-British perspective, which was the same thing at the time. Almost nine months later, when the British and the ANZACs left Gallipoli, they had achieved nothing, at the expense of nearly 50,000 lives: a humiliating defeat.

Beach Cemetery at Anzac Cove, Gallipoli, the beach where the ANZAC troops (Australian and New Zealand Corps) landed on 25th April 1915

When the Ottoman Empire finally lost the war, the Imperial War Graves Commission returned to construct the cemeteries and monuments. The area where the Australians and New Zealanders had landed was effectively ceded by the new Turkish government under the Treaty of Lausanne, and became known as ANZAC. All of the roads on ANZAC were originally constructed by the War Graves Commission. Thirty-seven cemeteries and five memorials to the missing proved that dead men can still be used to demonstrate their leaders' cause. Many years after the British Empire's memorials, Turkish monuments were also installed. Gallipoli is, of course, also part of the epic tale of Mustafa Kemal, later known as Atatürk, the father of the modern Turkish nation. In 1992, a large part of the peninsula became a national park, and a third wave of monuments advanced across the former battlefield to mark the Turkish victory, with a religious significance that has been increasingly obvious since the rise of Erdogan.

Anthropological landscape

I know of no WWI landscape that is more extensive, better preserved and more clearly legible than Gallipoli, this final point of the Southern Front through Europe. However, it differs in very few respects from the region known as Flanders Fields, the most northerly section of the Western Front. The Westhoek, or the front zone within it from the beach at Nieuwpoort to the French border at Armentières, is certainly one of the less well-preserved battlefields. After the war, when it was suggested that the rubble of the city of Ypres should be preserved as a British monument, and later, when the idea was put forward that restricted areas should be created, based on the example of the French *zones rouges,* the returning population rejected these proposals. Stubbornly, they set to work on the soil, which had been poisoned with gas and weighed down with tons of ammunition and the debris of war, and made it fertile once again. Ypres, Diksmuide, Nieuwpoort and their hinterland were rebuilt, even without the aid of German reparations; only rarely could any traces of the new, post-war era be seen in this reconstruction. If the Belgians had their way, it would look as if there had never been a war there. Generations of local politicians combated the economic consequences of the war with plans and construction projects, refusing to be thrown off course by the remnants of war. The war had put the region far behind the rest of the country, so the only true victory over the war was progress. Motorways, industrial estates and new residential districts were constructed without the layer of war being permitted to impinge – until the late 1980s.

And yet the Westhoek is just as recognizable as a layered landscape of war as Gallipoli. All of the elements of such a landscape are still present: not only the remnants of the war, the features of the landscape where the fighting took place, the cemeteries and monuments marking memories that are almost a century old, but also countless narrative threads that extend into the present day. The anchoring of this last layer within the first three is the most important requirement for a fully-fledged landscape of war.

The features of the Flemish landscape that determined the location of those wartime positions are less dramatic and unambiguous than in Gallipoli, but they are just as visible. In the Westhoek, these key features are the polders and drainage systems of the Yser Plain, the bare land in one direction and the low ranges of hills to the east and south of Ypres, where the remains of forests, country estates, rows of trees to break the wind, and a multiplicity of hedges and small fields filled the landscape with backdrops for war. A century later, these two basic landscapes remain essentially unchanged. The water to the north and the slopes to the south resulted in two fundamentally different forms of defence and warfare. Their continued presence allows us to read the landscape and see how the war was fought in this place. However, recent developments in the agricultural industry, with its huge fields, massive fertilizer plants, greenhouses and deforestation, threaten the historical footprint of the old small-scale agricultural landscape where the war descended in 1914. Fortunately, there is an ecological countermovement urging farmers to plant new hedges and trees, while forests and nature are increasingly important for recreational purposes, particularly in the southern part of the Ypres Salient. If the literally linear dimension of the front lines could be highlighted more effectively in this region, we would literally still be able to read the war in the landscape,

Chunuk Bair, the highest point of the battlefield at Gallipoli, where the New Zealand National Monument and the statue of Mustafa Kemal Ataturk, founding father of the modern Turkish Nation, both demand our attention

Oblique photo of Kanaaldijk (Canal dike) close to Essex Farm (where John McCrae wrote the poem *In Flanders Fields*) and its surroundings. Note the cemeteries at Essex Farm, Bard Cottage and Marengo Farm, where Alexis Helmer was probably buried. Both the Marengo Farm cemetery and his grave have disappeared

as in Gallipoli. Some farmers, however, persist in seeing any such attempts as an attack on their freedom, sometimes wilfully destroying what has been part of their own heritage for decades or even centuries. Flemish law is ill-equipped to deal with such destruction, and lags behind the facts. This is because the landscape is still generally viewed as a utilitarian matter, particularly in agricultural areas, and rarely seen as part of a cultural-historical heritage that is of equal value to our patrimony of urban architecture.

Graves and monuments have naturally appeared in the immediate surroundings of the relatively narrow front zone too, stops on the many evacuation routes for the casualties of war, sometimes parallel, sometimes perpendicular to the front lines. More than just the historical trail of the medical services, these graves and monuments bear meaning for the post-war generations: how the grief of a generation that had sacrificed its husbands and sons was allayed by the honour and glory of the nation; and the subsequent generations, which either rejected this honour or reclaimed it for coming generations and for future wars. Following the 1918 armistice, commemoration of the war soon became an element of group identity and nation-building, in all the countries and for all the groups that had taken part in the conflict. However, commemoration is equally the private domain of every person. Etymologically speaking, the English *commemoration* and the French *commémoration* both involve remembering something together, a social act. The Dutch *herinnering* and the German *Erinnerung*, however, refer to our inner selves, an intimate process of internalization. In that sense, every landscape of war is also an anthropological landscape, a place where our relationship to the war as a phenomenon, both as individuals and as a society of people, is manifested over and over again.

If ye break faith with us

The landscape of war plays an important part in this relationship. Flanders Fields are a point of anchorage for our thoughts and actions about the war, for

In Flanders Fields

Hugo Claus

De grond is hier het vetst.
Zelfs na al die jaren zonder mest
zou je hier een dodenprei kunnen kweken
die alle markten tart.

De Engelse veteranen worden schaars.
Elk jaar wijzen zij aan hun schaarse vrienden:
Hill Sixty, Hill Sixty One, Poelkapelle.

In Flanders Fields rijden de maaldorsers
steeds dichtere kringen rond de kronkelgangen
van verharde zandzakken,
de darmen van de dood.

De boter van de streek
smaakt naar klaprozen.

In Flanders Fields

Here the soil is most rank.
Even after all these years without dung
you could raise a prize death leek here.

The English veterans are getting scarce.
Every year they point to their yet scarcer friends:
Hill Sixty, Hill Sixty-One, Poelkapelle.

In Flanders Fields the threshers
draw ever smaller circles round the twisting trenches of hardened sandbags, the entrails of death.

The local butter
tastes of poppies.

Translated by John Irons

A Pat of Butter

after Hugo Claus

The doddery English veterans are getting
Fewer, and point out to fewer doddery pals
Hill Sixty, Hill Sixty-one, Poelkapelle.

My dad's ghost rummages for his medals
And joins them for tea after the march-past.
The butter tastes of poppies in these parts.

Michael Longley

our rituals and our attitudes to war. They are the inspiration, the point of departure or the destination of all those narrative threads. The fields of Flanders are, in short, a *lieu de mémoire*, as is the poem "In Flanders Fields".

Canadian military doctor John McCrae wrote his famous poem on the night of 2 May, 1915[1]:

In Flanders Fields

In Flanders fields the poppies blow
Between the crosses, row on row,
That mark our place; and in the sky
The larks, still bravely singing, fly
Scarce heard amid the guns below.

We are the Dead. Short days ago
We lived, felt dawn, saw sunset glow,
Loved, and were loved, and now we lie
In Flanders fields.

Take up our quarrel with the foe:
To you from failing hands we throw
The torch; be yours to hold it high.
If ye break faith with us who die
We shall not sleep, though poppies grow
In Flanders fields

Ypres in the winter of 1917

Kanaaldijk (Canal dike) close to Essex Farm Cemetery in 2003

McCrae was prompted to write this poem by the death of his friend and fellow soldier Alexis Helmer. Tradition has it that Helmer was buried in a meadow near a dressing station that the British had named Essex Farm, alongside a high canal bank just to the north of Ypres. McCrae conducted the graveside burial service, and then returned to the medical station, where he set about writing this poem.

The first two strophes are elegiac, words to console the poet. Starting with his experience of trench warfare, and what he saw and heard around him – the poppies, the larks, the guns – McCrae turned his focus on death: "the crosses, row on row..." Like anybody who has to bid farewell to a loved one, he realized that death strikes us with despair, though we might ignore it in the midst of life, as it represents the destruction of that life, of our aspirations and our loves. All that remains is a grave, somewhere, nowhere, or here, in a field in Flanders.

However, this particularly private place, the hole beside which McCrae had read those last prayers, and into which he had seen his friend descend, was to become a public place, only a few hours after the funeral, in the third strophe of his poem "In Flanders Fields": the soldier's tomb, on the field of honour. Hold high the torch of our righteousness, so that these horrific deaths might serve a purpose, and these "failing hands" might yet prevail in "our quarrel with the foe": a heroic death for a sacred common cause, against enemies who must be sent to their deaths.

In those 15 lines, a personal relationship (you and I, we, the dead) becomes a very public fact (we, ye, the living); this shift is about immortality, victory over death, and keeping "faith with us who die".

Landscape as heritage

Throughout the commemoration of the First World War, the process within these fifteen lines has been repeated over and over again. The public space of Belgium, and the Westhoek in particular, is packed with similar exchanges between private and public commemoration – and therefore with meaning, identity and purpose. It is a peculiar process. The hole into which Helmer was lowered has been filled, and the field where – once again, as tradition has it – he was buried has since been known as Essex Farm Cemetery. High on the canal bank a monument is elevated, as is, given the lack of a marked grave, The Menin Gate Memorial to the Missing, where Lieutenant Alexis Helmer's name is engraved on panel 10 - for all eternity.

I emphasize "as tradition has it", as recent analysis of aerial photographs of the canal bank during the period when John McCrae was based at the medical station reveals that it is unlikely that any burials had taken place there at that time. There is, however, a site a few hundred metres to the north along the same canal bank that had been used for burials, but no burial ground exists in that location now. The Imperial War Graves Commission transferred the graves to another British burial ground, Bard Cottage Cemetery. Even there, however, there is no evidence of any Canadian presence during that phase of the war. So even the first grave has been lost.

But no *lieu de mémoire* is concerned about such details. The story of the doctor-soldier-friend-poet is so strong, the tradition so persistent and the interaction between private and public so successful that the detailed photographic analysis only adds mystery to the story. The more likely location of Alexis Helmer's

Right
The historic centre of Ypres is rebuilt, 1923. Reconstruction of the cathedral has started. At the Menin Gate the foundations of the first Memorial to the Missing in the world are laid

grave has long been built over, and is now the site of a matrass and duvet factory. Grant them eternal rest, indeed.

Clearly, however, we cannot allow ourselves to build over everything and to leave it all to tradition. On the contrary. The very fact that the war can still be read in the landscape even today has anchored these events within the culture of the front zone. It is estimated that Essex Farm Cemetery and Dressing Station receives over a hundred thousand visitors a year. The story is embedded in the landscape of war, the circumstances of the poem are tangible, and so remain accessible; those fifteen lines have a place where we can continue to visit them.

Visitor numbers are expected to increase over the next few years. We need to seize the opportunity of the centenary commemorations to culturally embed the legacy of the First World War. There are literally hundreds of texts, thousands of stories, both large and small, with a similar origin and destination. It is our responsibility both to draw attention to these stories and to preserve them. We can do so by approaching the landscape of war as a *lieu de mémoire*. It may be more effective from a political point of view to use the term "heritage". Just as history and the teaching of history were an important catalyst of nation-building in the 19th century, so heritage, the modern mix of history, culture and participation, is an important instrument within the much broader and more positive process of identity formation – from the local to the global, from the individual to the universal. With this in mind, the Westhoek is potentially one of the most international and fascinating war landscapes in the world. It is more complex than many other sites; our task is to ensure that this heritage is not lost. ■

Translated by Laura Watkinson

(1) "In Flanders Fields" was first published in *Punch* on 8 December, 1915, but it is generally accepted that McCrae started his poem at the dressing station at Essex Farm, shortly after Alexis Helmer's funeral.

Violence and Legitimacy

Occupied Belgium, 1914-1918

[SOPHIE DE SCHAEPDRIJVER]

When, at eight in the morning of 4 August 1914, the largest invasion army ever mobilized crossed the German-Belgian border, Belgium entered a war unlike that of the other belligerents on the Western Front. By November 1914, Belgian society had fallen apart into different segments: the government in exile, the army on the Yser, the small uninvaded corner behind the British and Belgian sectors of what was now the Western Front, the royal family on the westernmost Belgian coast, the refugees abroad – and, the largest segment of all, the occupied country. Belgium, at that point the most densely populated country in the world, was largely overrun: of its 2,636 communes, 2,598 were occupied. More than eight out of ten adult Belgians lived the war under military occupation. This made for an experience both marginal and central to the war. Germany, Britain and France (even if France was itself partially occupied) waged war through a division of labour between front and home front, their armies supported by domestic society. By contrast, the majority of Belgians, trapped inside the occupied country, neither fought at the front, nor produced munitions for the Yser army. Occupied Belgium stood at a remove from the raging war, since it was neither a front nor a home front. Yet at the same time occupied Belgium stood at the heart of the war on two essential counts. Firstly, the German capture of Belgium prevented the war from ending. The invasion was a massive breach of international law, since Belgium was a neutral state. Conceding permanent domination to the German Empire would allow military aggression to shape international law. Most of Entente opinion refused such a departure from the rule of law and considered a European postwar order without the restoration of Belgian independence unthinkable. (In neutral countries, many thought likewise.) By contrast, German opinion saw a redrawn map of Europe that reflected the actual balance of power as a better guarantee for future peace than international law. The wartime Wilhelmine elites wished for a satellite Belgium that would constitute an advance bulwark for the German Empire and a permanent obstacle to attempts to encircle Germany. It is important to note that, on both sides, this was not an unemotional disquisition on the international system: the hecatomb of the war's first months, with the bodies of young German, British, French and Belgian men strewn across Belgian soil, lent the issue a passionate intensity. Secondly, the occupied population was situated at the

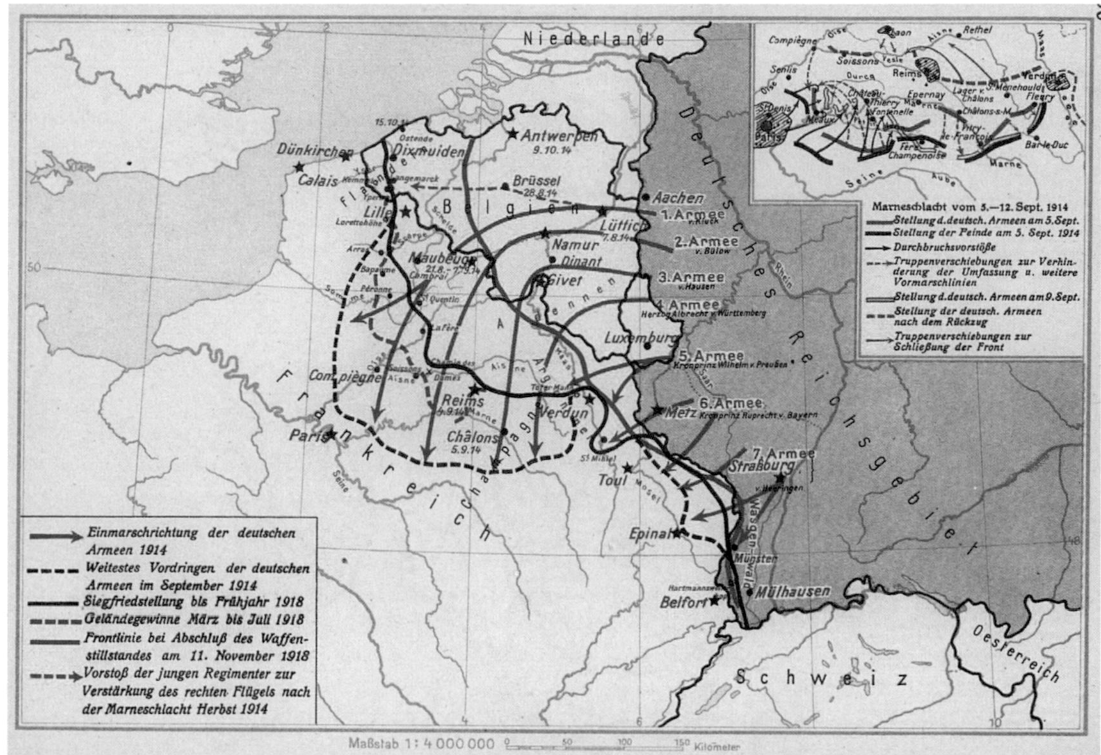

Map of conquest, The Western Front 1914-1918 (from Harms, Neuer Deutscher Geschichts- und Kulturatlas, 1934)

heart of the war. The two major visions of the conflict – the quest to roll back an order of things created by military aggression versus the notion that invading armies, because of their superiority, were justified in establishing facts on the ground – confronted each other in the occupied country in myriad ways that cut deep into civilian society. The question before Belgian public culture during the occupation years was that of the legitimacy of an authority built on violence.

Invasion and violence

The capture of Belgium, as it happened, started with an outburst of extreme violence beyond the boundaries of accepted warfare. The German armies, as they advanced through Belgium, avenged setbacks on civilians. From Liège to Diksmuide, invading troops destroyed houses, used locals as living shields, and massacred thousands of people on flimsy accusations of sniping. Some 5,500 men, women and children were killed in this way from August – when the bulk of the violence happened, with explosions of vengeful paranoia in places like Leuven, Aarschot, Dinant, and Tamines, left as smoking ruins with mass graves – to October, when the advance to Western Flanders occasioned a last series

An improvised Triumphal Arch: Bridge over the Dyle in Werchter, August 1914. (Undated, unwritten postcard, collectie Haachtse Geschied- en Oudheidkundige Kring (HAGOK), with thanks to Bart Minnen)

of smaller-scale bursts of ferocity along the route. Much ritual enacting of conquest accompanied the violence: local dignitaries – burgomasters, priests – were singled out for humiliation; survivors testified that people herded together were made to sing praise to the German Empire; an improvised triumphal arch put up on a bridge in the badly battered Brabant village of Werchter bore the inscription 'To The Victorious Warriors'.

These massacres would deeply affect the fifty months of the occupation. Not because they were a harbinger of things to come. After October 1914 and up until the Armistice, fewer than a hundred Belgian civilians died in similar outbursts of violence. But the massacres, and especially the silence imposed around them, disqualified the occupying regime from being accepted by the occupied population beyond the wary, ad-hoc modus vivendi needed to survive.

Occupation and permanence

The war's most outspoken statement against military conquest was made in Belgium at the start of 1915. 'Occupied provinces are not conquered provinces. Belgium is no more a German province than Galicia is a Russian one.' This pointed reference to the unacceptability of all military occupations, including those by Entente states, was made by Cardinal Mercier in his pastoral letter for the New Year, entitled 'Patriotism and Endurance'. Mercier used his position as head of the Catholic Church in Belgium to break through the enforced silence surrounding the massacres and to state that a regime established on violence could expect no acceptance. He did not call to revolt; the occupied should refrain from endangering their fellow citizens. But they should also steadfastly deny the occupying regime all legitimacy. The 'Power which has invaded your land and temporarily occupies the major part of it,' stated Mercier, 'is not a legitimate authority'.

The highest German authorities in Belgium reacted with affront. Belgium's Governor-General, the elderly East Elbian General Moritz von Bissing, called the letter's references to the violence of the invasion an insult to the honour of an imperial army that had acted in self-defence. His second-in-command declared the occupying authorities 'offended in their feelings'. These reactions are remarkable, because although Mercier had essentially called the new rulers usurpers, he *had* urged calm. A military occupation regime could scarcely ask for more. Yet von Bissing, in function since December 1914, did want more. His logic was no longer that of the offensive, but that of occupation. With the military outcome suspended, the German conquest of Belgium appeared to be an accomplishment in itself. Legitimacy was the key to rendering this conquest permanent; and that was precisely what Mercier's letter denied the occupying powers.

That same quest for legitimacy limited recourse to violence. Von Bissing certainly reacted with a heavy hand. He ordered the letter confiscated all over the diocese. This extended the confrontation over legitimacy to the parish level. Priests were made to relinquish the text under protest; underground copies instantly

'Patriotism and Endurance' as a devotional object (Miniature manufactured at Maredret Cloister, Namur, Pierpont Morgan Library, New York City)

Moritz Ferdinand Freiherr von Bissing, Governor-General of Belgium, December 1914-April 1917

multiplied; and, in the majority of parishes, the text was read from pulpits anyway - at least in Mechelen, Belgium's largest diocese, with 2.4 million inhabitants and 2,000 priests, and the country's largest cities, Brussels and Antwerp.

Elsewhere in Belgium the letter barely circulated, because all five Belgian bishops had declined to co-sign it out of caution. Ghent and Bruges were not in the German Government-General under von Bissing, but in the so-called *Etappengebiet* closer to the front, which was under direct, harsh military rule. In heavily garrisoned Tournai, on the border between *Etappe* and Government-General, the bishop had been taken hostage in September 1914 and, still shaken, died in early 1915. As to the dioceses of Namur and Liège, they had both been terribly maltreated during the invasion. The Bishop of Liège, Rutten, stressed how vulnerable the civilians were: those deported in August 1914 were still in German camps, hostages in all but name. Rutten had a point. In the diocese of Mechelen, too, memories of civilian helplessness cut short gestures of defiance. In several parishes of the Deanery of Aarschot, still reeling from the massacre, priests read the letter in part, then desisted under duress. But in Antwerp and Brussels, the letter was read in full before packed churches. In the big cities, the German military authorities showed a marked reluctance to threaten force, which is revealing. And, ultimately, even in villages, where the occupiers asserted their might more brutally, no priests were physically harmed, which was a far cry from the violence of the invasion. In January 1915, the time of extreme violence against civilians was over. What this means is that Mercier's assertion of non-acceptance was made at a time when the occupying power had made acceptance a priority.

Flamenpolitik

One way in which the occupying regime sought to rest its authority on acceptance was by seeking legitimacy among specific groups. In this context a cultural policy evolved that sought to accommodate the agenda of the Flemish Movement. This policy – eventually known as *Flamenpolitik*, Flemish policy – was more of a makeshift program than a strategic blueprint. But its symbolic value seemed beyond dispute: before international public opinion, *Flamenpolitik* redefined the invasion as an act of liberation. In occupied Belgium it was hoped that latching on to the Flemish Movement, and through it the Flemings, would help the regime acquire the legitimacy it needed to control civilian life.

Yet the prewar leaders of that very Flemish Movement refused these advances: in their view, too, violence precluded legitimacy. 'A river of blood runs between the German policies and the Belgians,' wrote one of the Flemish tenors, the Socialist Camille Huysmans, from his Dutch exile. In the occupied country, Flemish leaders called 'a policy based on race and language' incompatible with civic sense in 'these tragic circumstances'. They would continue to withhold acceptance all through the occupation in a steady barrage of manifestoes; some wound up in prisons in Germany as a result.

Yet *Flamenpolitik* did win recruits. The first were members of *Jong-Vlaanderen* (Young Flanders), a small radical Flemish-nationalist student group constituted in Ghent in October 1914. The success of *Flamenpolitik* in this corner is unsurprising. Under the occupation, young men of the privileged classes found themselves in an awkward spot. Because of the invasion, most Belgian men were not at the front. At the end of the war, only 20% of Belgian men of military age would have been mobilized, as against 54% in Britain, 86% in Germany, and 89% in France. In the occupied country, networks smuggled young men across the Dutch border so they could join the Yser army; an estimated 30,000 men left in this manner. Some did so of their own accord; others under pressure from their environment, which was especially intense in the middle class out of a sense of *noblesse oblige*. In these circumstances, a way out for some young men of the university-bound classes was to reject the idea of a common destiny altogether and present the occupation as a moment of liberation that only the boldest dared to seize; it was a choice that, as one of them quite candidly wrote at the end of the war, 'made us, comfortable bourgeois non-combatants, feel a brush with greatness'.

A 'home front'

Meanwhile, civilian forces had started to regroup. The invasion had left hundreds of thousands of people homeless and millions facing hardship. The government in exile was in no position to help. Yet local authorities had remained in

Occupation zones:
Government-General and Etappe

place. The mass flight of 1914 did not indicate the collapse of an entire system, as would happen in 1940; holders of public office considered themselves duty-bound to stay. In addition, an ad-hoc organization called the National Committee (*Comité National*), secured international aid through the US-led *Commission for Relief in Belgium*, a neutral organization that centralized funds, purchased and shipped food, and guaranteed it from German confiscation. The wartime feeding of Belgium was the largest food-aid effort in history up until then. In Belgium, the National Committee sold the imported food and granted aid; it was, in fact, a kind of proto-welfare state with 125,000 agents that effected some real benefits in national health (infant mortality actually declined relative to prewar years) and ensured a – relative – check on dearth and profiteering that maintained a minimal level of public confidence. Its very existence was a statement: it enacted, in a practical manner, the autonomy of civilian society vis-à-vis military power. The occupying powers knew full well that the National Committee detracted from their authority. It was part of what one might call Belgium's 'home front', not in the sense of a society streamlined to support an army, but in the more immediate sense of a 'home' that was a 'front', with daily life an ongoing theatre of confrontation, largely unarmed though never without risk.

One of the unique features of occupied Belgium was the explosion of the clandestine press, replicated nowhere else in occupied Europe during the First World War. Almost eighty periodicals emerged, not counting the proliferation of ephemera – open letters, satirical songs, brochures, cartoons. All protested the imposition of censorship and denied the occupying regime legitimacy. The longest-lived periodical, *La Libre Belgique* (Free Belgium), skewered German mendacity over various points from the violation of Belgian neutrality to the confiscation of mattresses. Most periodicals were in French, although there was a clandestine press in Dutch too, ranging from the colloquial *De Vrije Stem* (The Free Voice) in Antwerp to the more high-brow *De Vlaamsche Leeuw* (The Flemish Lion) in Brussels. The clandestine press thrived especially in 1915, the year when the extreme violence of the invasion receded while the exhaustion wrought by attritional warfare had not yet kicked in; the year, therefore, in which the standoff over legitimacy – the occupying regime's quest for it, the occupied population's withholding of it – was at its most intense. Not coincidentally, the national holiday of July 21 was widely celebrated that year in spite of the German ban – another confrontation over legitimacy that stopped short of violence, though offenders faced prison sentences as well as heavy fines that accelerated the already deepening material hardship.

By then, eight people had been shot at Liège for spying on the German armies, among them the mother of a little boy. After the war, a German war correspondent would write that 'nowhere, at any time, have people spied more fanatically and with more of a spirit of sacrifice than in Belgium'. Occupied Belgium was in a unique position as a hostile hinterland of the German army on the Western front, open to the neutral Netherlands. The Belgian, French and, especially, British military intelligence services sought out Belgians who had left, both men and women, and enticed them to return to the occupied country, collect information on military matters and smuggle their reports into the Netherlands.

German bulwark

In response, a German engineer corps closed off most of the Dutch-Belgian border with a lethal electric fence between May and August 1915. This astonishing venture, the first of its kind in the history of military occupation, was part of the German endeavour to turn the conquered country into a bulwark. From early 1915, the Germans concentrated on turning the Western front into an 'inactive' theatre to free up troops for the East. That required defensive buildup. By the autumn of 1915, the defensive belt on the front had thickened to three miles. The coastline bristled with batteries; a special army department closely supervised the railways, instructing troops to shoot anyone who approached embankments or bridges. The secret police had reached full strength and were able to dismantle one Entente spy network after another. By mid-1916, as the battle raged at Verdun, none of the Entente armies had a serious intelligence operation left.

'La grosse poire', undated cartoon, City Archives Brussels, Fonds Keym

The terrible battles of 1916 changed the outlook among the occupied. The phrase 'after the war' came up more. With the end of the war receding from sight, more and more people dismissed it as a parenthesis that interrupted their actual lives, and turned towards personal matters – family, social life, career, political interests, survival, or even just respite. This made for a sense of relative normalcy not unrewarding to the occupation authorities. Meanwhile, the pool of recruits for *Flamenpolitik* expanded beyond the extremist confines of *Jong-Vlaanderen*, as the Flemish militant rank and file welcomed German linguistic considerations and the German-controlled press inflated and sometimes forged francophone anti-Flemish slurs. Flemish refugees in the Netherlands, with contributions from Dutch-German circles, fashioned a separate identity for those who accepted German support. Choosing true nationhood over imposed state earned them the title of *activists*. By contrast, the majority of Flemish militants who persisted in refusing German support were dismissed as *passivists*. The question of loyalty rose urgently over the German-sponsored 'Flemishization' of the University of Ghent. 'Ghent' was the trump card of *Flamenpolitik* because it fulfilled a long-held wish of the Flemish Movement and discredited the Belgian state, which the occupying government hoped would consolidate its authority. The German official in charge, the mathematician Walther Von Dyck, praised the university as 'a mighty fortress, a trusty shield and weapon for us Germans'. (The paraphrase of the Luther hymn *Ein' Feste Burg ist unser Gott* gave his statement the required solemn impact.) In other words, the new Flemish university was considered part of the advanced defence works of the German Empire in that it established the occupying regime's legitimacy.

The Ludendorffian turn

Or so it was hoped. But the university's solemn opening in the autumn of 1916 coincided with the first wave of deportation of forced labourers from Ghent. These deportations heralded a return of terror that quite undercut what hopes of acceptance the occupation regime might have had. In Germany, the third Supreme Command under Paul von Hindenburg and, especially, Erich Ludendorff ushered in a harsh policy of winning the war at all costs; the result, for occupied Belgium, was a turn towards extreme exploitation. From October 1916, workers were deported in cattle-cars to German camps or to front-line labour. Of the 120,000 men taken, 2,500 died during deportation, a large number shortly thereafter, and many remained invalids. Brutal and messy, the deportations were more an expression of Supreme Command hubris than the implementation of a considered policy. They were halted in February 1917 for the Government-General, but continued until war's end in the *Etappe*.

To see Flemings subjected to forced labour was a considerable embarrassment to the recruits of *Flamenpolitik*. Most refrained from openly identifying as such, which indicated the extent of their awareness of ostracism. Still, surreptitiously, exasperation over the long war and mistrust of the government in exile continued to generate some degree of adherence to activism, all the more so as the occupying government's scission of the country created a great many administrative jobs for the recruits of *Flamenpolitik*, as well as positions in the newly created Walloon administration. Yet the new arrangements acquired little legitimacy, especially against the backdrop of ever-deepening exploitation as entire segments of Belgium's industrial infrastructure were hauled off to Germany.

Remobilization

The German spring offensive of 1918 seemed, to some, the ultimate blow: 'many people', as a municipal official in the city of Aalst recalled after the war, 'had become pessimists; they saw no other outcome than the victory of brutal force, the disappearance of our Belgium as an independent state'. The choice of terms is revealing: though permanent, such a conquest would lack legitimacy because it was a triumph of military aggression. It was around this basic refusal that the 'home front' remobilized. Though the clandestine press had reached a very low pitch, there was a revival, modest in quantitative terms but important qualitatively. From 1917, the high-profile *De Vlaamsche Wachter* (The Flemish Guardian) skewered *Flamenpolitik* and its champions. In mid-April 1918, *Le Flambeau* (The Torch) was launched in Brussels to combat anxieties over the German spring offensive. The much-persecuted *Libre Belgique* observed the German opposition closely and applauded its position on the war. A certain degree of sympathy with

Germans' plight reflected hopes of an eventual resumption of dialogue. However, the German retreat occasioned a renewal of violence: retreating troops engaged in looting, destruction and sometimes killing, and left explosives lying about near and in residences that would make for a long litany of deaths and mutilations – especially of children – until long after the Armistice.

Aftermath

When, on 22 November 1918, King Albert solemnly rode past the cheering crowds in flag-festooned Brussels, he was not presiding a classic victory parade so much as a reunion between the different segments of Belgium-at-war that had been separated for fifty months; a reunion that brought its share of tensions. Insistent exaltation of civilian valour, outbursts of brutality against those who had 'behaved badly' during the occupation, persistent material misery and disillusionment over the peace settlement made for a brittle mood. The return to a level-headed discussion of the language issue seemed postponed indefinitely. To some extent, the inevitable disillusionments of the postwar – inevitable because no postwar order could possibly satisfy the exasperated hopes of wartime – generated the very kind of discredit of the notion of common destiny that the occupation government had in vain tried to foster. Yet the very failure of the occupation government to gain a foothold – a failure now openly acknowledged by some in Germany – remained a source of genuine pride for the Belgian citizenry on both sides of the linguistic frontier, because it had demonstrated the unacceptability of an authority based on violence: many held on to this as a heartening thought amidst the pity of war. ■

Bulwark: 'Advance Base near Ypres' (from: Walther Stein, *Um Vaterland und Freiheit. Wirklichkeitsaufnahmen aus dem grossen Krieg nebst einer Einführung* (Hermann Montanus Verlagsbuchhandlung, Siegen/Leipzig, 1915, Volume 2, p.43))

Belgian Refugees in Britain

1914-1919

[CHRISTOPHE DECLERCQ]

When Germany invaded Belgium on 4 August 1914 and stories about atrocities by the German troops quickly spread, many Belgians fled their homes. Eventually, one out of five Belgians, some 1.5 million, sought refuge abroad. Initially more than a million went to the Netherlands, but by the end of the war barely 100,000 Belgian refugees were still in exile there. (1) About 325,000 refugees went to France, most of whom stayed there throughout the war, in part because the Belgian government in exile was located at Le Havre. Roughly a quarter of a million Belgians crossed the Channel during the war years. (2) Other destinations were Switzerland, Spain, Cuba, the United States, Canada, Australia and New Zealand. Only a few academic studies have uncovered anything about this little-known mass migration. (3) However, with the Centenary of the First World War approaching, the topic is receiving increasing attention.

From barbarism to safe haven

In the atmosphere of anti-German sentiment that followed the invasion of Belgium, most stories about German atrocities went to print uncorroborated in the British newspapers of the time. The alleged witness reports about German brutality sent shivers down the entire British society. On 16 September, Vera Brittain noted in her diary that 'the terrible stories of atrocities by Germans ... in Belgium' continued to come. (4) The atrocity stories were officialised in 1915 by the Committee on Alleged German Outrages in a report that is also known as the Bryce Report. This report concluded that during the invasion of Belgium, German forces had been guilty of widespread sadistic outrages. (5)

The first Belgians reached the southern ports of England in late August 1914. Initially in small numbers and mostly at their own expense, they moved inland and settled, usually in and around London. Jules Persyn, a Flemish literary critic of the time, and his family of eight headed for Ostend towards the end of August. Persyn had taken the family of Alfons Van de Perre, a Belgian MP, with him. On 30 August, they left for Folkestone at 11am and arrived in London at 7pm. (6) In the space of just a few weeks, the numbers of Belgians arriving

October 1914: Belgians sought refuge wherever they could. They would arrive some place and soon move on somewhere else. Here the SS La Pallice arrives at La Rochelle (author's collection)

in England increased dramatically. On 15 October, the day Ostend fell, an estimated 26,000 Belgians arrived in Folkestone alone. The ports of the southeast acted as a transition area: from there most Belgians were sent to dispersal centres in London, such as Alexandra Palace and Earls Court, and were allocated to a local community anywhere in Britain that had volunteered to host them.

As no official registration system was in place until early December 1914, no exact figures exist. Numbers range from 211,000 to 265,000. One of the official reports of the time mentioned the number as 225,572. However, this did not include Belgian soldiers who convalesced in Britain. Also, because the spelling of Belgian names was often difficult for British administrators, many entries were in fact duplicates. Arguably the most detailed overview of the Belgians in Britain was produced by T.T.S. de Jastrzebski, a Belgian statistician. In January 1916, he published a paper for the British Royal Statistical Society (7), in which he stated that 91,000 of the Belgians were under 25 years old. 40% of the refugees had come from the province of Antwerp. A total of 67.2% spoke Dutch, 18.3% spoke French. The remaining 19% of refugees had come from the province of Brabant (Brussels and 'martyr cities' such as Louvain, Aarschot, etc.), assessing language use for that area was difficult to gauge.

Location, allocation and relocation

During the war, more than 2,500 local Belgian refugee committees were formed. The central organisation was an effort shared by the newly established War Refugees Committee and the existing Local Government Board. The Belgians did not rely on British charity alone, official bodies such as the Belgian Legation in London and the Comité Officiel Belge worked alongside the British organisations. Equally pivotal to the well-being of the significant Belgian community in Britain were the charity events organised jointly by the Belgians and British.

One such occasion was the Emile Verhaeren celebration, held on 3 March 1917 and organised by the British Royal Society of Literature. Distinguished British

Postcard of Belgian refugees 'Driven from a Belgian village'. Notice that the group concerns an entire family, including the men and boys (author's collection)

men of letters such as Robert Bridges, Edmund Gosse and Thomas Hardy sat alongside Belgian authors such as Maurice Maeterlinck, Henri Davignon and Emile Cammaerts. In the many cultural circles, especially those in London, the Flemish/Dutch – Walloon/French differentiation seemed much less of an issue than among the working class and peasants who had taken refuge in Britain. Using English as a relay language, possible friction was already negated beforehand by offering official information in three languages. Belgians also enjoyed a true exile press, in which *L'Indépendance Belge* served the francophone refugees and *De Stem Uit België* those refugees who spoke Flemish/Dutch.

Because of the reception and accommodation by the British, Belgian refugees in Britain were able to continue their lives pretty much as they would have done at home, which contrasted starkly with the refugees in the Netherlands, most of whom lived in camps. In addition, as the Belgian men were not conscripted for most of the duration of their exile, theirs was not a story of absent fathers or grandfathers either. However, the Belgian 'able-bodied men', those who could enlist and join the forces at the front, did pose a problem.

A British shell crisis leads to a Belgian solution

With the war going on longer than anticipated, the initial wave of empathy for Gallant Little Belgium and the refugees waned. Friction arose within the host society. The different habits and customs of the Belgians caused many arguments. Women did not wear hats in public and alcohol consumption happened out in the open. However, that was nothing compared to the 'barbaric' habit of eating horse meat. This met with a wall of disapproval from the British. In Birtley, a Belgian labour colony just south of Gateshead, the Belgians of Elisabethville had at their disposal running water and electricity, whereas the local population did not. In the spring of 1915, pressure on local housing provision in Fulham even triggered a true anti-Belgian riot by local people.

One of the dormitories in Alexandra Palace, London, The Times History of the War, 1915, vol. IV, p.471

With nearly half of the entire group of Belgians in Britain under 25, the issue arose of able young men. Anywhere Belgians settled in Britain, the local people sent their men to the front, whereas Belgian families arrived and most of their able men remained on British soil. References to sentiments of discontent increased in number in the British press. Official organisations and cultural patrons continued to organise charity events, but across Britain many local communities became increasingly disgruntled.

Strangely enough, it was a British military crisis at the French front that saved the day for the Belgian exiles in Britain. In May 1915, a substantial lack of explosives was reported in *The Times*. This eventually led to the downfall of the Asquith Cabinet and the installation of a coalition government with the Liberal Lloyd George as Minister of Munitions. The solution to the problem of able Belgians was found in their employment in the war industry. The presence of existing factories such as Vickers or emerging munitions factories such as Armstrong-Whitworth in Birtley created labour opportunities for tens of thousands of Belgians. In fact, able men were brought from the Netherlands even. Large local Belgian communities, of several thousand refugees each, emerged in places like Dartford, Richmond, Letchworth, Barrow-in-Furness and Birtley, Gateshead.

Education in exile

Another major issue that needed a well-structured solution was the education of the Belgian refugee children. With the sustained support of the Catholic clergy and financial backing by local authorities, the Belgians were able to develop a system of education in exile. There were various reasons for establishing Belgian schools for the refugee children and not having them join local British schools. Not only were differences in learning programmes between British and Belgian schools substantial, the language issue convoluted any possible incorporation of Belgian school education into the British one. Moreover, the

Catholic Church viewed proper Belgian education as a means of keeping their pupils away from the influence of the Anglican Church.

In August 1916, elementary education for Belgian refugee children was in place in 70 schools, in which 4,500 pupils were taught. The network of schools increased in size and one year later 7,000 pupils were being taught in 111 schools. (8) The 'Gesticht van het Heilig Hart', Tulse Hill, London, was a secondary school for Belgian boys, mirroring the bilingual situation in Belgium: 48 boys were taught in Dutch and 97 in French. St Mary's in Glasgow had 361 boys and girls attending by mid-1918, over 60% of whom came from the Antwerp-Mechelen-Lier area. Despite the reservations of the Catholic clergy, most Belgian refugee children were successfully incorporated into the British education system. The number of Belgian refugee children admitted to elementary British schools came to approximately 30,000.

André Cluysenaar, La Grande Bretagne Accueille Les Réfugiés Belges, plate from A Book of Belgium's Gratitude, London, John Lane, 1916, p.ii

The school year 1918-1919 did not end with the Armistice. In fact, the majority of Belgian children continued their education in exile well after 11 November 1918. With the return of most Belgian refugees organised for early spring 1919, most schools remained open until as late as Easter 1919. The Belgian schools that kept classes running into 1919 were no longer funded by the British and subsequently received subsidies from the Belgian government, which had returned to Brussels.

Belgian refugees and British institutions of higher education also added to the history of education in exile. Early in September 1914, William Osler, the renowned Canadian scholar at Christ Church, Oxford, had initiated the effort to have Belgian professors come to Oxford with their families. Among them was the well-known historian Leon Van der Essen. One of the Belgian students in Oxford was the author Jozef Muls. In Cambridge, an association of Belgian professors was formed. The group offered many lectures to both British and Belgian students. Other universities also helped Belgian refugee students and usually waived fees, as they did at Birkbeck College, London, for example.

In the minds of the literati

The role and position of literature during the First World War has been the scope of numerous publications. With regard to the Belgian refugees, however, the difference could not be bigger. There has been no real output on the theme of Belgian exiles so far. And yet a whole pedigree of cross-cultural influences can be traced.

Emile Cammaerts, a Belgian who had come to Britain in the years before the war and who had married the Shakespearean actress Tita Brand, published several volumes of poetry, always translated by his wife, in *The Manchester Guardian* and *The Observer*. Not only did Cammaerts befriend G.K. Chesterton, one of Cammaerts' other relations, Edward Elgar, set one of Cammaerts' poems, *Carillon*, to music.

Before Virginia and Leonard Woolf moved to Hogarth House in Richmond, Virginia rented rooms overlooking the Green in Richmond from a Mrs Le Grys. In her diaries Woolf wrote about the dietary habits and noises produced by refugees visiting the house. In his letters to Forrest Reid, E.M. Forster expressed his amazement on how much Jules Quilley, the Belgian refugee he had taken into his house, could eat. Maria Nys, another refugee, became a housemaid at Garsington Manor first and a marginal figure of the Bloomsbury group next. Immediately after the war she married Aldous Huxley. Lalla Vandervelde, the wife of the Belgian politician Emile Vandervelde, befriended W.B. Yeats, H.G. Wells and G.B. Shaw.

The names of authors and artists involved was virtually endless, not least because Charles Masterman, a close friend of Winston Churchill, had called for dozens of writers to contribute to the war effort by publishing pamphlets and

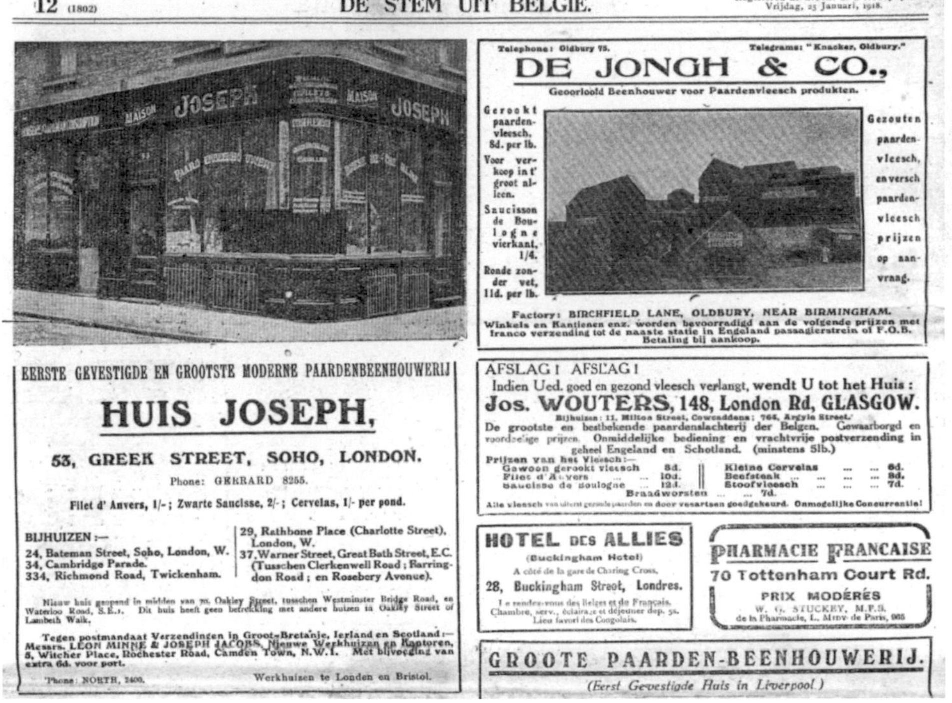

12 (1802) DE STEM UIT BELGIE. Registered at G.P.O. as a Newspaper. Vrijdag, 25 Januari, 1918.

Telephone: Oldbury 75. Telegrams: "Knacker, Oldbury."

DE JONGH & CO.,

Geoorloold Beenhouwer voor Paardenvleesch produkten.

Gerookt paardenvleesch, 8d. per lb. Voor verkoop in t' groot alleen. Saucisson de Boulogne vierkant, 1/4. Ronde zonder vet, 11d. per lb.

Gezouten paardenvleesch, en versch paardenvleesch prijzen op aanvraag.

Factory: BIRCHFIELD LANE, OLDBURY, NEAR BIRMINGHAM.
Winkels en Kantienen enz. worden bevoorradigd aan de volgende prijzen met franco verzending tot de naaste statie in Engeland passagierstrein of F.O.B. Betaling bij aankoop.

EERSTE GEVESTIGDE EN GROOTSTE MODERNE PAARDENBEENHOUWERIJ

HUIS JOSEPH,

53, GREEK STREET, SOHO, LONDON.

Phone: GERRARD 8255.

Filet d' Anvers, 1/-; Zwarte Saucisse, 2/-; Cervelas, 1/- per pond.

BIJHUIZEN :—
24, Bateman Street, Soho, London, W.
34, Cambridge Parade.
334, Richmond Road, Twickenham.
29, Rathbone Place (Charlotte Street), London, W.
37, Warner Street, Great Bath Street, E.C. (Tusschen Clerkenwell Road; Farringdon Road; en Rosebery Avenue).

Nieuw huis geopend in midden van 70, Oakley Street, tusschen Westminster Bridge Road, en Waterloo Road, S.E.1. Dit huis heeft geen betrekking met andere huizen in Oakley Street of Lambeth Walk.

Tegen postmandaat Verzendingen in Groot-Bretanje, Ierland en Scotland:— Messrs. LEON MINNE & JOSEPH JACOBS, Nieuwe Werkhuizen en Kantoren, 5, Witcher Place, Rochester Road, Camden Town, N.W.1. Met bijvoeging van extra 6d. voor port.

'Phone: NORTH, 2400. Werkhuizen te Londen en Bristol.

AFSLAG! AFSLAG!
Indien Ued. goed en gezond vleesch verlangt, wendt U tot het Huis:
Jos. WOUTERS, 148, London Rd, GLASGOW.
Bijhuizen: 11, Milton Street, Cowcaddens; 764, Argyle Street.
De grootste en bestbekende paardenslachterij der Belgen. Gewaarborgd en voordeelige prijzen. Onmiddelijke bediening en vrachtvrije postverzending in geheel Engeland en Schotland. (minstens 5lb.)
Prijzen van het Vleesch:—
Gewoon gerookt vleesch 8d.
Filet d'Anvers ... ... 10d.
Saucisse de Boulogne ... 12d.
Kleine Cervelas ... ... 6d.
Beefsteak ... ... 8d.
Stoofvleesch ... ... 7d.
Braadworsten ... ... 7d.
Alle vleesch van uiterst gezonde paarden en door veeartsen goedgekeurd. Onmogelijke Concurrentie!

HOTEL DES ALLIES
(Buckingham Hotel)
A côté de la gare de Charing Cross.
28, Buckingham Street, Londres.
Le rendez-vous des Belges et de Français.
Chambre, serv., éclairage et déjeuner dep. 5s.
Lieu favori des Congolais.

PHARMACIE FRANCAISE
70 Tottenham Court Rd.
PRIX MODÉRÉS
W. G. STUCKEY, M.P.S.
de la Pharmacie, L., Mrov de Paris, 965

GROOTE PAARDEN-BEENHOUWERIJ.
(Eerst Gevestigde Huis in Liverpool)

Advertisements on page 12 of De Stem Uit België, Friday 25 January 1918: The horse meat trade clearly set the Belgian butchers in exile apart from the British butchers (author's collection)

including a pro-war tone in their publications. This War Propaganda Bureau is also known as Wellington House. Several of the Masterman authors contributed to the many gift books such as *King Albert's Book, Queen Mary's Gift Book and The Book of Belgium's Gratitude*. The proceeds of each of these publications went at least partly and often entirely to the distress relief of Belgian refugees in Britain.

One author who did not contribute was W.B. Yeats. After he was asked by Henry James to contribute to a gift book compiled by Edith Wharton, he first

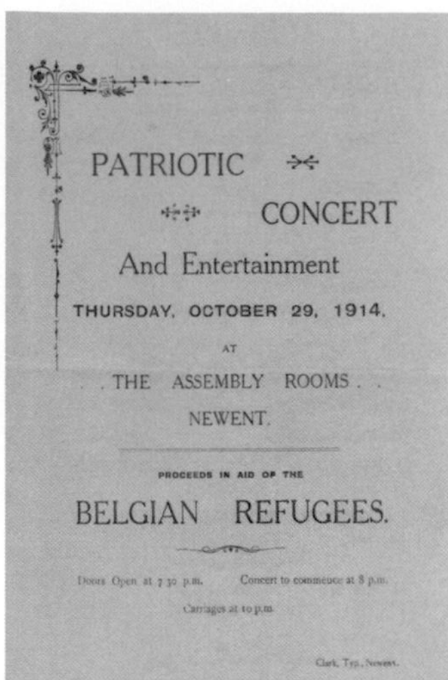

PATRIOTIC CONCERT

And Entertainment

THURSDAY, OCTOBER 29, 1914.

AT

THE ASSEMBLY ROOMS

NEWENT.

PROCEEDS IN AID OF THE

BELGIAN REFUGEES.

Doors Open at 7.30 p.m. Concert to commence at 8 p.m.

Carriages at 10 p.m.

Clark, Typ., Newent.

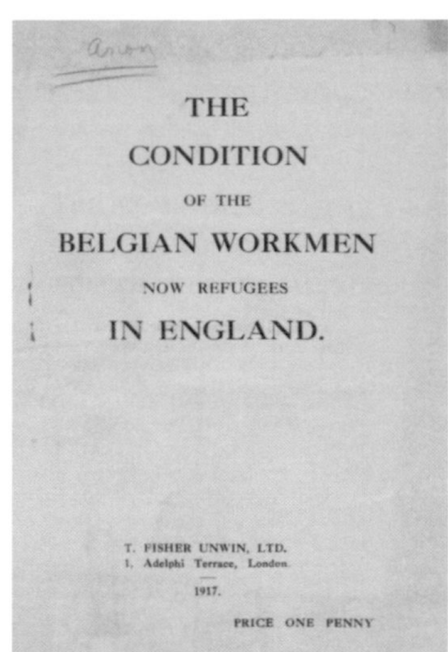

Anon

THE

CONDITION

OF THE

BELGIAN WORKMEN

NOW REFUGEES

IN ENGLAND.

T. FISHER UNWIN, LTD.
1, Adelphi Terrace, London.

1917.

PRICE ONE PENNY

Cover page of a booklet produced for a charity event in Newent, Wales, proceeds were in aid of the Belgian refugees (author's collection)

Throughout the war, the refugees formed part of a propaganda battle between Britain and Germany. This leaflet, The Condition of the Belgian Workmen now Refugees in England, was one of the many publications, providing proof that Belgians were treated well in Britain (author's collection)

declined with the cynical 'On being asked to write a war poem' and wrote 'Easter 1916' next. (10) On 23 March 1916, *The Times Literary Supplement* published a posthumous essay by Henry James, virtually the last thing he wrote, on the subject of Belgian refugees. James regularly visited convalescent Belgian soldiers at Crosby Hall, adjacent to his Chelsea residence.

Strangely enough, the most renowned literary merit and legacy of the Belgian refugees is a fictitious character by Agatha Christie. She had finalised her character of Inspector Poirot after becoming acquainted with Belgian refugees and treating wounded Belgian soldiers in Torquay Town Hall.

Upon return

Even though the war dragged on for more than four years and despite strained resources, most Belgians had a source of income as a result of their work in the British war industry. When the war ended in November 1918, however, the Belgians were not immediately sent back. The British government was more concerned with bringing their own armed forces back first. In addition, the winter of 1918/1919 was a harsh one and Spanish influenza was a major issue too. The organised return of Belgians would last well into March 1919. The first to return were Belgians from the factories in Birtley. They were deemed skilled enough to help rebuild Belgium's destroyed infrastructure. Upon return, 'British Belgians' were often looked at with contempt, as if they had been traitors, leaving their fellow countrymen alone under German occupation. And yet, other than those Belgians who had been forced to work in Germany, it can be argued that those who went to Britain worked hardest during the war. The fact that they might not have suffered the most can be seen at the start of the Second World War, when the government no longer went into exile in Le Havre but headed straight for London. (11)

Pupils of the Belgian school in Letchworth, where a community of refugees resided around the Belgian Kryn and Lahy steel factory (Varlez 1917, author's collection (9))

The legacy of the Belgians in Britain during World War I is more than a pathway into World War II. Today many sites, memorials and gratitude plaques commemorate the Belgians in Britain. Lasting relations between host families and their guests continued for decades too. With over 5,000 Belgians staying in Britain officially, it can be argued that more unofficial Belgian ancestry can be traced as well. Anecdotal evidence of the 'long lost great-uncle in Glasgow', the illegitimate child from Cardiff that was adopted into a well-off family, all prove that there is still so much more to uncover. ■

Everyman's Special Belgian Relief Number, November 1914, London, Wyman&Sons
The issue included contributions from authors such as H.A.L. Fisher, Maurice Maeterlinck, G.B. Shaw, Hilaire Belloc and Emile Cammaerts

By THOMAS HARDY

SONNET ON THE BELGIAN EXPATRIATION

I dreamt that people from the Land of Chimes
Arrived one autumn morning with their bells,
To hoist them on the towers and citadels
Of my own country, that the musical rhymes

Rung by them into space at measured times
Amid the market's daily stir and stress,
And the night's empty starlit silentness,
Might solace souls of this and kindred climes.

Then I awoke : and lo, before me stood
The visioned ones, but pale and full of fear ;
From Bruges they came, and Antwerp, and Ostend,

No carillons in their train. Vicissitude
Had left these tinkling to the invaders' ear,
And ravaged street, and smouldering gable-end.

The chimes were mentioned in a poem by Thomas Hardy too, written especially for the publication of King Albert's Book, 1914, page 21 (author's collection).

NOTES

(1) For an analysis of the Belgians in the Netherlands during the First World War, see Evelyn de Roodt, *Oorlogsgasten. Vluchtelingen en krijgsgevangenen in Nederland tijdens de Eerste Wereldoorlog.* Zaltbommel, Europese Bibliotheek, 2000, 464p.

(2) For a comprehensive appreciation of the British politics behind the British distress relief for Belgians in Britain, see Peter Cahalan, *Belgian refugee relief in England during the Great War,* New York, Garland Publishing, 1982, 552 p. The PhD thesis that lay at the basis of this book can be found through McMaster University's Digital Commons, http://digitalcommons.mcmaster.ca/opendissertations/717/

(3) For a comparative history of Belgians in these three main destinations, see Michaël Amara, *Des Belges à l'épreuve de l'exil. Les réfugiés de la Première Guerre mondiale; France, Grande-Bretagne, Pays-bas* 1914-1918, Brussels: Editions de l'Université de Bruxelles, 2008, 422p.

(4) Vera Brittain. *Chronicle of Youth, Great War Diary* 1913-1917. London, PhoenixPress, 2002, p.103.

(5) For an elaborate analysis of the German atrocities, see John Horne and Alan Kramer, *German Atrocities* 1914*: A History of Denial,*Yale University Press, 2001, 608 p.

(6) Jan Persyn. *Jules Persyn* 1878-1933 *Een slachtoffer van arbeidsdrift en politieke onwil Tevens bescheiden gezinskroniek.* Antwerpen, Stichting Marie-Elisabeth Belpaire. 2001. pp. 28-29.

(7) T.T.S. de Jastrzebski, 'The Register of Belgian Refugees', in: *Journal of the Royal Statistical Society,* Vol. 79:2 (March 1916), pp.133-158, also available through JSTOR at www.jstor.org/stable/2340812.

(8) In comparison, there were only 71 primary schools for about 13,000 Belgian children in the Netherlands, where refugees shared the Dutch language, (1917/1918 figures).

(9) Armand Varlez. *Les Belges en Exil.* London/Brussels : Libraire Moderne. 1917. page H7.

(10) For an appreciation of the setting in which this poem was written, see Marjorie Perloff, 'Easter 1916', from Tim Kendall (ed.) *The Oxford Handbook of British and Irish War Poetry*, Oxford University Press, 2007. Chapter available from http://epc.buffalo.edu/authors/perloff/articles/Perloff_Yeats-Easter-1916.pdf

(11) Contrary to the history of Belgians in Britain during the First World War, the history of Belgians in Britain during the Second World War is much clearer, not least because there is comprehensive archive material. For an analysis of the latter, see Robert W. Allen, *Churchill's Guest: Britain and the Belgian refugees during World War II,* Wesport, Praeger Publishers, 2003, 212p.

An Extract from *Across the Channel*

By Annelies Beck

On the pretext of a summer holiday, Marie Claes travels to Glasgow with her parents in 1914. It soon becomes clear, though, that there is no question of returning. War has broken out and Belgian refugees are pouring in by the thousands. Initially the Glaswegians are full of sympathy at the arrival of 'their Belgians', but as the realisation dawns that the war will not be over quickly, the inevitable frictions surface. The Belgians in Glasgow try to create a place for themselves, but how far can you go as a guest? Cracks start to appear in the close-knit community. One person's misfortune is another person's opportunity. And the Scots have their own problems. Rents skyrocket and more and more people are evicted from their homes. The refugees are safe and sound while the men of Glasgow are fighting at the front. This novel gives readers a glimpse of a society in disarray, a world which, confronted with strangers, is confronted with itself.

Life is there to be lived. Perhaps that was it? Even after all those years she still couldn't explain it. In a community in exile, where everyone has at least one story of a broken heart, fear, sadness and loss, people seek each other out and live it up every so often with a big party. Shameless, innocent, without scruples. As if the group makes a silent pact: we grant one another a night's respite, a moment's freedom from waiting for the end of the war, from longing to be reunited with loved ones. It had been wonderful, the party: the ecstatic atmosphere and the feeling of being beautiful. But for her that evening would always be associated with what came next. As if it hadn't been permitted after all. Not without punishment. But in that case how should you live?

When it came to parties the Belgians had a reputation to maintain. Funnily enough they never had to defend or explain these events to the Scots, who were all too happy to join them drinking and dancing. Of course there was always the good cause that served to reconcile potential conscientious objectors with frivolities like parties. There was always a game or tombola, the takings going to our boys at the front, or to the home front. Conscience soothed, refill your glass. Anyone who still found it necessary to trot out arguments in justification of this or that explained it as a way of thanking the host city and the men and women who had been so welcoming.

It had been a close call according to some members of the organising committee. The riots in London had been big news in Glasgow too and stubborn rumours were doing the rounds about Belgians taking advantage of the situation. Do we have to come out with this just now, make ourselves so conspicuous? The discussion between those for and those against a party had been undecided, but those for had won out and the preparations had now been under way for weeks. It was a question of supplies, lights and location, bar staff and hands to fetch and carry, money, flags and representation, speeches or the absence thereof, cleaning and security. Her father sometimes came home dead tired after yet another consultation.

'Now we've had to decide all over again if every association should have their own placard or if we should just have one big banner for all the Belgians.' Her father gestured to her mother to sit down; he wanted to get something off his chest. 'Really, it's enough to drive you mad. Even in these circumstances some people just can't manage to leave politics at home.'

Her mother pushed a glass towards him. 'Did you come to an agreement?'

'Well, yes, long may it last.' Her father laughed. 'The only one who still manages to bring some character to those meetings is August.' Her mother looked happy. It turned out August had a talent for party committees. In Aalst he'd been a member of the maypole society, not just as a carpenter, but as one of the organisers. He could keep a group of people together and get them enthusiastic about a communal task – at least for a party. His aptitude had first surfaced in his own neighbourhood, but now he was invited along whenever a Belgian or Flemish association organised anything.

Marie had mixed feelings. Naturally she was looking forward to dancing and having a jolly evening. She had asked Edith along, and of course August would be there. He was coming, but he had omitted to mention that he would be bringing Mary – Marie had to hear that from Edith.

It was a beautiful evening. The dark blue of the sky seemed to light up and the little lamps around the dance floor added colour. The food was set out on long tables on the edge of the lawn. An improvised bar had been decorated with flags: Belgian and Flemish, but also Scottish and British. Someone had even found a poster of Glasgow's coat of arms. The baking and cooking went on all afternoon. Marie and her mother had contributed too, not just pancakes this time, but an apple pie and three dishes of stew. As seven o'clock approached they had gone home to get ready and pick up her father.

Her dress was a bit on the long side. Specially selected and bought for the occasion, a first real ball gown. The shop assistant had held another one up to her, exactly her size, but Marie wanted this one, completed with feminine detailing. She would work something out. Now she was fussing with an elastic band. Not very elegant and it took some effort to hide it in a fold so it looked as if it was meant to be that way. Really she was a little disappointed that her appearance wasn't quite complete. She hoped the elastic would at least hold.

'I hope you can enjoy yourself, this evening.' Marie stood at the mirror brushing her hair. She felt caught in the act when her mother came and stood behind her.

'I have something for you. For the belle of the ball.' She held one of her necklaces in front of Marie: a little silver pendant on a gossamer-thin chain. Marie looked and looked and had to bite her lip not to cry. What was that all about?

'Hair loose or in a plait?'

'Whichever you feel like. I'll put it up for you if you want.'

Marie couldn't get enough of the woman she saw in the mirror, as if with her pinned up hair and exposed throat two images were suddenly overlaid: herself and her mother in one. Her mother stood close to her, gazing as if she saw Marie for the first time.

'Just enjoy it.'

Compliments from Edith and her father who asked her for the first number on her dance card. Marie felt light and strong when she arrived at the party. The orchestra was warmed up and a couple of pairs were already venturing onto the dance floor.

'Let's have something to eat first. I want to try that stew of yours,' said Edith. 'Gives us a chance to take a good look at who's here.' Marie was happy to follow along. If she had said yes, she could have had a glass of beer or cider in her hand moments later, but she declined. 'Why didn't you bring anyone yourself?'

They stood leaning against a table, on one side of the dance floor, with a view of the bar opposite. To the left they saw the latecomers arriving. To the right people sat in groups eating and talking. Edith wiped some sauce from her mouth. 'I'm here with you, aren't I?'

'Yes, but strictly speaking I brought you. Do you have a fiancé?'

'No.'

'Isn't there anyone you like?'

'Well you're very forward! Why do you ask?'

Marie shuffled back and forth. 'Just wondering. Sorry.'

'I don't mind. There was someone, briefly, but not anymore.'

'What happened?'

Edith thought a moment. 'Let's just say we wanted different things.'

Marie tried to imagine what that might mean. Edith looked at her teasingly, as if daring her to keep asking. When Marie said nothing, she asked, 'What about you, Marie?'

'What?'

'Still unhappy about August?'

Something inside Marie broke open.

'I'm sorry.' Edith looked away, as if she regretted her question but couldn't take it back. 'I've seen how you look at him.'

It was a moment before Marie could hear the music again and understand what Edith was saying.

'I'm going to get another drink, would you like one?'

'Yes please.'

Marie watched Edith walk away, crossing the dance floor with confidence, in between the dancing couples, laughing cheerfully whenever she bumped into anyone. Everyone seemed to think it was funny. No one was offended by her. Apparently Edith knew her better than she knew herself, and that wasn't a pleasant feeling.

Edith was now on the other side. There was a queue for the buffet, but she didn't join the back. She stepped up to a man in the middle of the line, opening her arms. He saw her and wavered a moment as she embraced him. Everyone backed away from the passionate greeting. Marie had to move her head from side to side to see what was happening between the dancing couples. Was that the lover of 'not anymore'? He was a good-looking man, tall and dark, somewhat older than Edith, she thought, with a short beard. They didn't kiss, but they stood talking animatedly. He struck Marie as vaguely familiar. A glass of cider in each hand, Edith nodded to her, and the man turned in her direction. Marie half raised her hand. Did they want her to go over there? He didn't really seem to see her. Before she could decide Edith was back, walking slowly to minimise spillages.

'There you are! Already dying of thirst?'

'Thanks. Who was that?'

Edith took three big gulps of her cider.

'That was William. Just back from the front.'

'Your fiancé?'

'What? Mine? God, no! No, no. William was married to my eldest sister who died.'

'I didn't know you had another sister. Or that she died. Sorry.'

'Doesn't matter. Her name was Cathy. It was two years ago. William's still family, even if we see less of him now.' Edith leaned against the table and tapped her foot to the rhythm of the music. Marie tried not to stare at Edith; she hadn't seen her this way before. At the bar she saw William making jokes with other drinkers.

'Soldier?'

'No, he was at the front before, but...'

'Ah, here's the lady on my dance card!'

'Daddy!'

Edith set her glass on the table, took a step back and gestured towards the dance floor with a theatrical bow.

Marie had seen her father's disapproving look at her drink, but she didn't care. She laid her hand on his arm and let him lead her to the dance floor. This was her father at his best. Graceful, that was how Marie imagined herself on the dance floor, graceful in the arms of her father. He seemed to be enjoying himself too. During their second dance they crossed paths with Edith and William.

'I'm dancing the next one with your father,' Edith called out to her.

'Do you think she's already had too much to drink?' whispered her father in her ear.

'I think she just wants a good dance partner.' He laughed.

'Changez!' shouted her father when they crossed paths again and in three nimble steps he took over from William and waltzed away with Edith.

'Miss Claes, may I?' William had a deep, gravelly voice.

Marie nodded. She felt small, deserted by her gracefulness. 'Sorry. I'm not a very good dancer.'

'Nonsense. You're doing fine. Edith tells me you've learnt perfect English in no time.

'Not perfect.'

'Marie, isn't it?' He pronounced it right. She smiled.

'Yes.' She relaxed and decided to enjoy it, dancing with strangers. 'Edith said you'd been at the front, but not as a soldier.'

'No, as a journalist.'

'Where?'

'Near Neuve Chapelle. Among other places.'

It didn't ring any bells for Marie. 'Do you write about it in the newspaper then?'

'Yes, "War Notes".'

'In The Glasgow Evening News? That's you? Edith told me about you, I remember now.'

Her father and Edith came up to them again. Her father winked at her. He seemed tireless and she'd never seen Edith so elated. Marie nodded and then saw how Edith's face tightened and her eyes narrowed to slits. Marie followed her gaze, just as William manoeuvred her into a lock step and with light pressure on her shoulder blade steered her into a most elegant turn. And so she saw August and Mary sweep by, August with his arm around Mary's middle. Mary was stunningly beautiful, in a colourful gown, with a flower placed as if nonchalantly in her loose, dark hair. A bohemian with a style quite out of keeping with the setting, but with that polished dandy at her side she immediately gave the party that sparkle which had been missing until then. Drink, dance and that image. Marie took leave of William and went to rest on the side.

The musicians were finished with the waltz and she saw Edith part company from her father and approach August and Mary. August quickly withdrew his arm. Edith tried to take Mary aside, but she resisted. Mary tried to ignore her sister, but when that didn't work, she snapped a couple of words at Edith and made her way to the buffet, August in tow.

Other people were observing the couple too now. A pair of young men by the bar commented, laughing. William stood a little way from them drinking his beer. Marie's mother looked troubled, trying to catch sight of her father. Looking at Zech-Dupont, who had taken up position by the tombola table, Marie couldn't tell whether he was smiling or biting back a grimace.

Plate in hand the couple slowly made their way round the semicircle of the dance floor to Marie.

'Hello Marie.' August, cheerful as always. Or perhaps a little nervous after all? 'You look splendid, Marie. Your hair really suits you that way. More grown up.'

'Hello August. Mary.'

'Are you all on your own over here?' He held his plate out to her. 'Want a bite?'

'I've just overdone the dancing a bit. And it's nice to watch people.' She took another sip. 'Why was Edith so cross just then?'

'Oh, Edith. She always worries much too much.' Mary pulled a face as she said it.

'Worries? What about?'

August wanted to keep it friendly, but Mary was ahead of him.

'You know, Marie, things aren't always as simple as Edith likes to imagine. I couldn't care less what she does or doesn't do with her life, but she shouldn't tell me what to do with mine. Nor you for that matter.'

'Anyone for another drink?' asked August.

Mary must have thought she had made Marie uncomfortable with her violent reaction against Edith, as a little later, when they all had full glasses in their hands, she added, 'Don't let it bother you. Sisters quarrel sometimes. It'll be fine.'

Marie didn't really care. She thought. But when August came a bit later on to cut in with a tap on the shoulder and take over from her Scottish dance partner, she was surprised to find her legs momentarily shaky.

He complimented her on her necklace. Was it her birthday perhaps? Marie felt herself floating along. The dance could go on forever. Before he could step back and relinquish her, she said, 'Another one. It's not often I get to go to a dance.'

He laughed and grabbed her hand. The next dance was faster and Marie gladly let him set the pace and rhythm, one hand firmly on hers, the other on her lower back, steering her. Her feet naturally synchronised with his. Eyes closed she was almost in ecstasy. The belle of the ball after all.

When she opened her eyes again, she saw August look over her shoulder at something happening behind her. With every turn, or half-turn, he kept his eyes fixed on what was going on. Mary of course. She was standing further up, surrounded by three men and two women.

August turned her away from him. 'Sorry, Marie, just going to see if everything's ok,' and he left her standing on the dance floor. The ring around Mary opened for him and suddenly it was five against two. Marie pushed her way through the dancing couples to where her glass was, not far from what was beginning to look like a real stampede. She drank a couple of sips of her cider and moved a little closer.

'Aha, look, the Belgian, high and dry. Nice and easy, huh, a bit of partying with our girls?'

'And in the meantime her sweetheart's fighting at the front.'

August attempted to smooth things over. 'We're just friends, nothing more.'

'Yeah yeah, just friends and just in Glasgow, while we fight for your country.'

The orchestra switched to a slow waltz. One of the women turned to Mary. 'And you! Have you nothing better to do than run around making a spectacle of yourself? With your peculiar clothes and sweet talk.'

'A proper "new woman".' It was an older woman speaking now.

'Let your sister be an example to you. At least she knows what's important.'

Mary squared her shoulders and stuck her chin in the air, aloofness personified, but Marie saw her clasp her hands behind her back until the knuckles went white. The woman who had just spoken gave Mary a firm push. 'Whore!'

August pulled Mary behind him in one swift movement and raised his hands to the woman. 'Stop that. This is a party. We're not here by choice.'

'And talking down our hospitality too!' The man spat directly at August's face. The waltz grew louder and the tempo quickened. Suddenly other Belgians emerged behind August, including the young men who had been standing at the bar. 'Problems?'

With an emphatic flourish the orchestra concluded the waltz; the final note hung in the air, loud and shrill. The mood had turned. Marie emptied her glass in one gulp and went in search of Edith and her parents, even Zech-Dupont if need be. Someone had to do something. But she wasn't even half way across the dance floor, when the first chair flew through the air and someone yanked the Belgian flag from the bar. Marie stumbled over the hem of her dress; the elastic had given up.

The party ended in havoc, police and injuries – nothing serious, a few cuts and bruises, although the memory would remain with a number of Belgians and Scots. The party food had made the least damaging missiles, but a couple of chairs and tables hadn't survived the evening either. And Marie had missed the lot.

She had never been so sick. She barely made it beyond the dance floor in search of help, because when she fell over everything began to spin and whether she lay flat on the floor or bent forward, nothing helped. Until she suddenly bent double and threw up. After that she had collapsed where she stood and closed her eyes. When she opened them again, she was at home in bed and indescribably thirsty. On the bunk below hers, beside the stove, lay August, apparently dead to the world, one eye swollen shut and an ugly cut in his cheek.

Her mother sat at the table, her back to them.

'Mama, water.' Her mother was at her side immediately. She dabbed her lips and helped her up so she could drink.

'What a party.' Marie had no reply. 'Sleep a bit more. It'll get better, you'll see.' She sounded gentle, her mother, Marie thought as she slipped away again. ■

Translated by Anna Asbury

From *Across the Channel* (*Over het Kanaal*, De Geus, Breda, 2011)

The Belgian-Dutch Border During the First World War

A Second Belgian Front?

74

[ALEX VANNESTE]

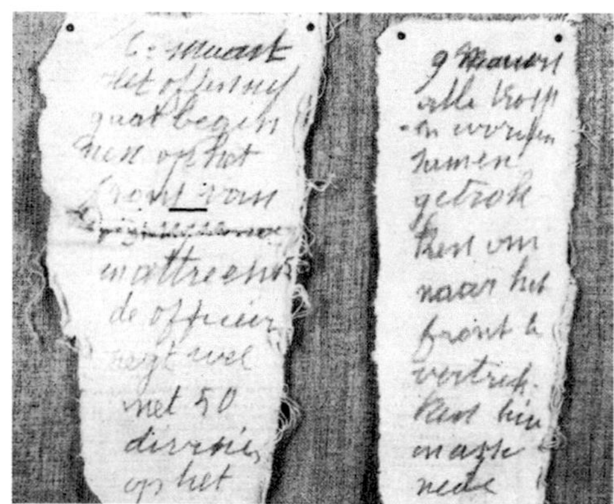

Of the war-related events in Belgium during World War One, the greatest attention is invariably, and rightly, given to the dramatic hostilities at the Western Front on both sides of the now legendary river Yzer and the heavily-hit area round the three frontline towns, Nieuwpoort, Diksmuide and Ypres (Ieper). One should however not lose sight of the fact that the civilian population of the whole country suffered greatly during the more than four years of German occupation and the havoc that the German advance at the beginning of the war and the withdrawal at the end of it created. Not so well-known are the forms of resistance at the Belgian-Dutch border, which, more than anywhere else in the country, were very intense and specific.

In contrast to the Second World War, Germany had several strategic and political reasons not to involve the Netherlands, a neutral country, in the war. This meant that the nearly 300 mile long Belgian-Dutch border was the only Belgian border with a country that was not at war. This would have far-reaching consequences for Belgium, the Allies and the Netherlands itself. For from what follows it will become apparent that the Germans were not able to seal off that border with regular manpower.

The clandestine paper *La Libre Belgique*, which is still published today, began to appear in February 1915 on an irregular but more or less weekly basis. Initially an edition of 1,000 copies was printed but a year later it had grown to 25,000 copies. This is the front page of issue no. 62, February 1916. The caricature of the German Emperor has as its subject the fruitless search by German counterespionage for the printer of the paper, its distributors and its readers. The text below it reads: 'For more than a year I've been looking for you, night and day, you disgusting little girl, and you keep getting away.' (Archive La Libre Belgique)

Left
Information, collected by spies, noted on pieces of linen that could easily be hidden or sown into clothes. The text on the left reads: 'The offensive will begin on the Péronne-Bapaume Front, and will be carried out - as the officer says - with 50 divisions upon the British Front, as rapidly as possible. There are also on the east Imperial troops - 15-20 divisions. He says that it will be on a broad front.'

NUMÉRO 62 DEUXIÈME ANNÉE FÉVRIER 1916

PRIX DU NUMÉRO — élastique, de zéro à l'infini (prière aux revendeurs de ne pas dépasser cette limite)

LA LIBRE BELGIQUE

Acceptons provisoirement les sacrifices qui nous sont imposés..... et attendons patiemment l'heure de la réparation. A. MAX.

J'ai foi dans nos destinées; un Pays qui se défend s'impose au respect de tous: ce pays ne périt pas! Dieu sera avec nous dans cette cause juste. ALBERT, Roi des Belges (4 août 1914).

FONDÉE LE 1er FÉVRIER 1915

Envers les personnes qui dominent par la force militaire notre pays, ayons les égards que commande l'intérêt général. Respectons les règlements qu'elles nous imposent aussi longtemps qu'ils ne portent atteinte ni à la liberté de nos consciences chrétiennes ni à notre *Dignité Patriotique*. Mgr MERCIER.

CHAGRIN D'AMOUR

Composition de G. Lafrosse   Portrait extrait du *Die Wochenschau*   Dessin de E. Papeur

Depuis un an déjà je te cherche nuit et jour,
Petite abhorrée, tu m'échappes toujours.

At the start of the hostilities, the Belgian army consisted of about 200,000 troops. After its retreat behind the Yzer, less than half of those remained. These heavy losses were of course due to the fighting during the German advance after the invasion on August 4, 1914. In addition, even before the fall of Antwerp, on October 9, 1914, more than 30,000 Belgian troops had fled to the Netherlands, where they were interned. This led to King Albert and the army command issuing an appeal, especially via Dutch newspapers, to all able-bodied Belgian men who hadn't been mobilized, to join the diminished Belgian army behind the Yzer. Around Christmas 1914 there followed a second, similar appeal, from Cardinal Mercier this time, in the form of a pastoral letter, *Lettre pastorale sur le Patriotisme et l'Endurance* (1914) that had to be read in all Belgian churches. The result of all of this was that of the more than 30,000 Belgian volunteers who would go to the front during the course of the war, a large part did so immediately after the two appeals. Recruiting agents in the occupied areas saw to it that volunteers were enlisted and they were then escorted to the Dutch border. There they were led across by experienced passeurs or border-crossing guides. In Flushing (Vlissingen) they were taken by boat to Folkestone

The Flight, a pastel by the Antwerp painter Eugeen Van Mieghem (1875-1930). (Private collection)

and from there to a harbour in northern France. After that they were assigned to fighting units behind the front line.

During the course of the first few months of the war, the allied intelligence services were able to join forces and put themselves under the coordinating command of a number of British agents, who were planning to establish themselves in the Netherlands (Flushing, Rotterdam). The British intelligence services were at that time much better organized than the Belgian or even the French. Espionage in the occupied territory was organized from the Netherlands. Around 7,000 agents were active in Belgium and northern France, spread over some three hundred local, regional and national services of varying sizes. Some only had a few agents, others several hundreds. They were used for air observation (around airports), territorial observation (the movement of troops), and in particular for railroad observation. Agents from all levels of society, young and old, men and women, carefully recorded which trains were coming from where and where they were going, with how many and what sort of troops, what kind of weaponry, at what time, etc. All this information was recorded in the most creative ways, sometimes in code and on all sorts of materials (pieces of paper, clothing, packaging, etc.), and relayed by couriers in an equally inventive way to the border, where message smugglers were able to get them to agents in the Netherlands. The central interallied intelligence services analysed and assessed the messages and sent the relevant information on to Folkestone or London, where military staff could use them to advantage.

In Belgium the regular post was in the hands of the occupier and strictly censored. This led, from the very beginning of the war, to the creation of clandestine organizations – like *Le Mot du Soldat* or *Familiegroet* – dedicated to collecting the letters of people with relatives fighting at the front – a father, brother, child, or other beloved one. Again through couriers, this secret post was transported to the border, brought to the Netherlands by letter smugglers and via Flushing to Folkestone, and then to northern France, behind the front line, where the letters were distributed to the soldiers at the front. The answers then travelled the opposite route.

Classic food smuggling along the Belgian-Dutch border was already flourishing before the war and assumed much greater proportions during it. The collapse of commerce, trade and the general economy had created a shortage of just about everything, especially of products that were quite readily available in the Netherlands (rice, coffee, oil, butter, flour, beans, etc.). This kind of smuggling was of course carried out by Belgians, but also by Germans stationed at the border and especially by the Dutch. Some did it out of pure necessity and earned little or nothing from it; while others, especially the Dutch, became rich smuggling, in spite of intense surveillance by Dutch soldiers along the Belgian-Dutch border, and great efforts by the Dutch authorities to thwart the traffic in contraband, not least, and with reason, to prevent a shortage of these products in the Netherlands.

A different form of contraband was the smuggling of Dutch newspapers. With the exception of the clandestine *La Libre Belgique*, which was founded during the war, and some small local papers, the Belgian press was also strictly censored. Belgians who wanted information about how things were going at the various fronts could only get it from newspapers smuggled in from the Netherlands and sometimes from Great Britain, which often reported extensively on these topics.

It is quite clear from all of this that the Belgian-Dutch border was a line that was often crossed by all kinds of people and for different reasons, and that it happened throughout the war. But there is more.

Flying Monday

One of the most universal results of the outbreak of war in a certain region or country is the sad fact that it nearly always occasions a substantial part of the population to flee. Either civilians are forced by the aggressor to run, driven away usually by military pressure; or the situation is so harrowing that they seriously fear for their personal and social safety; or the socio-economic situation becomes so wretched that civilians seek refuge somewhere else out of sheer misery, fear or panic. World history offers many examples of this, in every shape and form, and the First World War was certainly no exception to this rule. Germany never resorted to systematic expulsion or deportation of certain sections of the population during the Great War. The population took flight *itself*. This happened in several waves.

A first wave of refugees was created immediately after the German offensive, in the first week of August 1914. Heavy bombardments caused some 20,000 Belgians, primarily from Liège and the surrounding area, to flee to Limburg under pressure from the onrushing invaders. The majority hoped to reach the neutral Netherlands. The residents of hard-hit Visé, in particular, tried to escape from the chaos, as well as countless people living in the border villages of Voerland. A day after the invasion a quarter of the 650 residents of the municipality of Moelingen, for example, had already fled to the Netherlands. Many traveled in the direction of Brussels and France, but even more went via Limburg and the Kempen (Campine) to the Netherlands. From Flanders, too,

Antwerp refugees in Dutch Roosendaal reading messages, hoping to find relatives and friends who had also fled. For 8 months Roosendaal was host to about 25,000 Belgians. (From *The Illustrated War News*, October 21, 1914)

especially from the Antwerp Campine, refugees could already be seen traveling to the Netherlands. Towards the end of August the number of refugees from the Liège area was still increasing substantially, again especially in the direction of the Netherlands. In just the first few weeks of this world conflict, in August 1914, about 100,000 people fled to Dutch Limburg and North Brabant, and this number would only continue to grow.

When the Germans swept across Wallonia they drove - particularly as a result of the battles near Charleroi and Mons around August 20 - a new wave of refugees from Hainaut, Namur and Luxemburg in front of them, this time towards France; whole villages in the Sambre-Meuse valley were emptied. Meanwhile, the fear of German brutalities grew among the whole Belgian population, fuelled by numerous accounts in the press, which was still available. Yet a large part of the population, especially in the provinces of Namur and Luxemburg, were actually surprised by the rapid advance of the Germans, so many stayed where they were.

From the moment the Germans made moves to occupy northern Belgium, an exodus began from Flanders towards Antwerp and subsequently the Netherlands. The big flight from Flanders that began on August 24, 1914, became known as *Flying Monday*, or sometimes *Crazy Monday*. To get away from the dreaded bombardments, fleeing in the direction of Antwerp was the only option. Then from the port city many traveled on to Ghent. Most of these refugees ended up in West Flanders and France, and a number of them in the Netherlands.

The Dutch refugee centre Kloosterzande in the town of Hontenisse in Zeeuws-Vlaanderen, where Belgian refugees found temporary shelter in barracks and tents. The camp had room for about 4,000 people. Because it was impossible for private individuals or the local authorities in the Dutch border towns to house the enormous number of Belgian refugees, many of them were soon sent on to more northerly or easterly state refugee centres. (Collection C. Buijsrogge, Terneuzen)

When it became apparent that Antwerp was also threatened, refugees could still go in three directions: to Great Britain via Antwerp's port or by train from Central Station through East Flanders to one of the North Sea harbours; to France via East or West Flanders; or, finally, to the Netherlands via the Campine. The number of refugees increased sharply, especially in September. In that month 10,000 fled to Great Britain, 20,000 to East and West Flanders and 20,000 to the Campine and the Netherlands. When the Germans announced, on October 7, that Antwerp would be bombarded, it led to a massive exodus from the city and it surroundings. On October 7 alone 30,000 Belgians arrived in Roosendaal and soon afterwards there were no less than half a million Belgians staying in North Brabant. Many refugees also traveled to Ghent and towards the coast. In the extremely short space of just three or four days after the bombardments and the massive exodus, Antwerp had become a ghost town, an empty city.

The surprise attack on East and West Flanders finally led to a last wave of refugees, who were driven towards the coast, from where some of them went to Great Britain, to the Netherlands and to France. When the first battle of the Yzer became imminent (October 15, 1914) even more residents of the threatened area fled to France.

So after several months of war, residents from all the Belgian provinces could be found in the Netherlands, France and Great Britain. In the Netherlands, refugees from Antwerp, Brabant, Limburg and Liège were in the majority. In France there were mainly residents of Hainaut and West Flanders,

The massive arrival of Belgian refugees in Dutch Bergen op Zoom. (Collection F. Duinkerke, Bergen op Zoom)

while in Great-Britain there were chiefly people from Antwerp and Brabant. The largest number of refugees was to remain with our northern neighbours, others traveled on to Great Britain and from there sometimes even to France, and a small number even farther, to Canada, the United States, South America, South Africa, New Zealand and a few other countries.

Refugees weren't always registered very carefully in the host countries, which makes it hard to determine their exact number. Nevertheless there is a consensus that the Netherlands, with its 6 million inhabitants, took in 1 million refugees. France took in almost 350,000 and Great Britain about 250,000. Since France and Great Britain were combatants in the war, many refugees could be put to work there in the war industry and in agriculture. Most of the refugees therefore stayed there till the end of the war or even nearly a year later.

But in the Netherlands the situation was different. The Netherlands was a neutral country and wasn't really allowed to put refugees from a warring country to work. It had no choice but to restrict itself to humanitarian help. The many refugees were taken in by private individuals and local governments or were housed in one of the many so-called state refugee centres. Providing the refugees with food and drink, clothing and shelter was a gigantic challenge for the Dutch, and forced the authorities to dig very deep into their coffers. It seems to us – and to many others – that Belgium could have been a bit more forthcoming in offering its thanks to its northern neighbour after the war.

On top of that the Netherlands also had to look after more than 30,000 interned soldiers, and thousands of German deserters during the war.

Under pressure from the Germans most of the refugees returned to Belgium from the Netherlands at the end of 1914 and during the first months of 1915. Even so, throughout the war many more Belgians fled to the Netherlands, both agents from the intelligence services, who were being pursued by German counterespionage, and civilians. It is assumed that at least 100,000 Belgians stayed in the Netherlands during the course of the war.

Killing wire

It is evident that the occupier could not tolerate any form of exfiltration especially of Belgians to the Netherlands, be they civilian refugees, army volunteers, letter, message or common smugglers, or deserters. Until the spring of 1915 crossing the border was, given the circumstances, relatively easy. After all, the Germans could not deploy endless numbers of troops to seal off the border hermetically. That is why they decided, in the spring of 1915, to completely fence in Belgium with electric wire: a triple fence of which the middle one carried a deadly charge of 2,000 volts.

The electric wire fence, here at Wortel, near the village enclave of Baarle-Hertog, along the Belgian-Dutch border. One can clearly distinguish the central electric wires (2,000 volts) and the two fences that protected it on each side. This barrier was guarded night and day by armed border guards, who as a rule patrolled on the Belgian side. Contact with the central wires mostly resulted in instant death, which is why the fence was commonly called the *killing wire*. (Collection H. Janssen, Merkplas)

On top of this, the fence was guarded by armed patrols and border guards who had been given instructions to foil any attempts to cross the border with the use of firearms. Along the border a *Grenzgebiet* was established where the most rigid safety measures and controls prevailed and inside that zone there was a closely guarded *Grenzstreife* , 100 to 500 meters wide, an area that was strictly forbidden to all civilians and even to German troops, with the exception of border guards.

All of this did not however prevent the busy border traffic from continuing in both directions. Clever passeurs - mostly former smugglers - continued to guide volunteers across the border. Agents - spies - at the border continued to smuggle thousands of secret messages across it for the use of the allied intelligence services. Letter smugglers did not hesitate to tackle the fence to smuggle hundreds of thousands of letters to the Netherlands for soldiers at the front, and vice versa. Smuggling continued to flourish. Deserters took great risks in order to escape the horrors of war.

Tens of thousands of times people passed through the lethal fence, either alone or in small or larger groups led by *passeurs*. In spite of the 'killing wire', as it was commonly called, the resistance at the border remained extremely active. It will therefore not come as a surprise that the fence also claimed victims: nearly one thousand, who were electrocuted or shot by border guards. The majority of victims were Belgians, but British, French, Russian and German citizens died at the fence too.

It goes without saying that the number of victims of the electric fence falls far short of the number of victims among the troops fighting at the front: about 600,000 in Belgium alone, 550,000 of them in the mud of the Ypres Salient. Even so, the recruiters, couriers, intelligence agents, message and letter smugglers from the areas bordering the Netherlands deserve our gratitude and thanks for their unremitting contributions in the fight against the occupier – on *their* front. ■

Translated by Pleuke Boyce

One of the techniques for safe passage through the fence was by using a *passeur's* or folding frame. With some training and with the help of a border guide, one was able to get 'to the other side' that way. Nonetheless there were many fatalities, even with the use of this type of frame. (Frame belonging to the Historical Society Marcblas, Merksplas; photo by H. Jansen, at the reconstruction at Zondereigen)

Belgium's Finest Hour?

King Albert and Queen Elisabeth in Wartime

[LUC VANDEWEYER]

The second King of Belgium, Leopold II, was not popular either in Belgium or abroad. Furthermore, he had no son to succeed him. It was his nephew, Albert, born on 18 April 1875, who had to prepare for that role. The young man received a military education, which deeply influenced his beliefs and ideas. Then, on 2 October 1900, the Prince married Elisabeth of Bavaria, a lady of high nobility. In fact the Belgian royal family had been intermarrying with various European royal families for generations. Finally, in 1909, Albert became head of state of an unusual country with many limitations, of which he was very well aware.

A neutral state

Belgium was a young state. It had broken away from the Netherlands in 1830 after an armed uprising. In return for support fromthe European great powers for its independence, the country had to undertake to maintain an armed neutrality. It had to defend its borders against all invaders but could also rely on the military support of the great powers who had agreed to guarantee its independence. All the European great powers had set their signatures to this.

So, the country had to defend itself - but it was small. Obviously it would not be able to raise an army capable of resisting one of the great powers. The Belgian strategy was therefore directed at preserving the core elements of the state, including its army, within a large stronghold built around the seaport of Antwerp. Outside it, mobile troops were available to discourage any invasion by a foreign army and if necessary to obstruct it as much as possible. It was hoped that discouragement would be enough to protect at least the more populous regions to the north of the Sambre and Meuse valleys against foreign troops passing through.

There was, after all, a threat of war in Europe because of the sharp conflict of interests between the great powers. For Belgium, the antagonism between France and Germany was the most dangerous. The situation became more acute after 1900 and led to the formation of two hostile coalitions with Russia, France and Great Britain on one side and Germany, Austria-Hungary and the Ottoman Empire on the other. In particular, the fact that the British abandoned their 'splendid isolation' after 1904 and ultimately signed an agreement with France

Le Petit Journal

ADMINISTRATION

5 CENT. SUPPLÉMENT ILLUSTRÉ 5 CENT.

ABONNEMENTS

26me Année — Numéro 1.282

DIMANCHE 18 JUILLET 1915

LES SOUVERAINS BÉNIS

Le roi des Belges apportant dans ses bras un blessé à l'hôpital où la reine Élisabeth soigne les soldats

In this French weekly you can see King Albert carrying a wounded soldier into the hospital. Queen Elisabeth is watching

caused alarm bells to ring in Brussels. There was no great power left which, from a neutral standpoint, might dissuade the hostile coalitions from resorting to arms or, if this failed, could limit conflicts geographically with its powerful fleet.

Throughout his formative years as a young officer, Albert's mind was filled with the strategic problems facing his country. He was also particularly interested in all forms of technology. The army was just the place for him because there were many younger officers who were equally fascinated by the new possibilities which machines, motor vehicles, armour plating, artillery and such like could offer the armed forces of a small country with a large and efficient heavy industry. The budget, however, was limited. Only in the autumn of 1909 was national service made more or less universal. For the first time in many years it was possible to fundamentally strengthen the army. But it would need time.

The royal couple presented a totally different image from Leopold II and they soon became hugely popular. Their popularity grew even more after Albert became king. He made a point of wearing military uniform at official functions in order to emphasise the fact that constitutionally he was the supreme commander of the army.

Meanwhile there were rumblings in the Balkans and the sabre-rattling raised tensions throughout Europe. Germany drastically strengthened its army by the law of 3 July 1913. It was followed by France on 7 August, and Russia and Austria-Hungary also followed suit. The arms race led to an unprecedented

King Albert inspecting an aircraft on the beach of De Panne.© Archives Royal Palace Brussels

militarisation of Europe. Berlin had already made it known that it felt so threatened that - if it was necessary in order to defeat France - it would not respect the neutrality of Belgian territory. King Albert was informed of this personally and found it seriously worrying.

On 28 June 1914 the heir to the Austrian throne and his wife were assassinated in Sarajevo by a Serbian nationalist. The police investigation uncovered links to the Serbian capital of Belgrade. Vienna threatened war. Would this unleash a disastrous chain reaction? Albert feared that it would.

Belgium was obliged to defend the neutrality of its territory with force of arms. To avoid any misunderstandings on this score, the country announced on 29 July that its army had been put on an 'armed peace footing'. The barracks were filled with the four most recent militia intakes. The decision was intended to show that Brussels was serious.

The German invasion

King Albert had known for years that Berlin had plans ready for marching through Belgian territory. If this should happen, British and French forces would support Belgium. But could London and Paris deploy sufficient forces to prevent the Germans from overrunning the country? It seemed extremely unlikely. Belgium therefore banked on the stronghold of Antwerp. It was believed that it was strong enough to withstand a lengthy siege and that the political core of the state, including the royal family, would be secure within it. The country would then still count for something after the conflict.

On 2 August, Berlin sent Brussels an ultimatum. Germany demanded free passage for its troops through to France. The Belgian government, under Albert's leadership, refused. It had no choice. Immediately after that, the King announced that he was taking over the effective leadership of the army. He then left for the military headquarters which he had set up in the town hall of the city of Leuven. In fact, most of the mobile field units were concentrated well inside

Belgium, in east Brabant. The army leadership did not want to place too many of its troops close to the border where they ran the risk of being immediately annihilated by a surprise attack.

The King and his ministers were therefore geographically separated. But King and Ministers needed each other's signature for decisions to be lawful. Of course, the distance between Brussels and Leuven was not great and communications were good.

On 4 August, German armed forces invaded Belgium *en masse*. On 18 August, Albert was compelled to order his army to retreat rapidly to Antwerp where the government had already moved. From there, on two occasions, he would send massive numbers of troops to attack the relatively weak German north flank which proved to be vulnerable, compelling the German command to draw on troops from the main force. In that way the Belgian army helped to save the French and British forces. Meanwhile, with the Royal Navy under the command of Winston Churchill, London sent reinforcements to Antwerp in the form of Royal Marines.

This freedom of movement did not last long. At the end of September, the German High Command was determined to wipe out fortress Antwerp. The pressure on its forts was greatly increased. This gave rise to a problem which nobody had foreseen in the pre-war planning, namely the fall of Antwerp. Withdrawal or surrender were now the only alternatives left to King Albert.

Where could the King, the government and the field army go? The only way out was towards the sea and the only real chance of survival was to link up with the British and French armies. On 8 October the exodus began, but with the German army hot on their heels, the retreat turned towards the French border in the hope of finding some sorely-needed military support.

The Belgian government and the army command ended up in the little frontier town of Veurne. Watching them streaming in stood a disconcerted Jozef Gesquière. He noted on 14 October: "It is said that the King and Queen are in the area and intend to stay here, probably in De Panne." The rumours were right. On the following day, Gesquière heard that the headquarters had been installed in the town hall, where the large upper chamber was converted into an office for the royal supreme commander. That morning he saw the King himself step out of a car. "On his flushed face, one could see that he was worried", he noted. His arrival was almost furtive: "No cheering crowds. Hardly anybody noticed the King's arrival. Everything happened so secretly and so quickly."

The King's absolute power

From Veurne, the army command could direct the army, which had set itself up along the River Yser in order to hold back the advancing enemy. But what about the ministers? The Chief Minister, Charles de Broqueville, tried to remain in Veurne while the other ministers travelled on into France. But the King made it quite clear to him that there was little he could do and that it would be better if he too left for France. Their relationship had become fairly icy. There was now not only a physical but also a mental separation between King and government.

After the Battle of the Yser at the end of October 1914 the presence of the royal supreme commander at headquarters was less necessary. He now

Queen Elisabeth taking pictures. De Panne, 1915. © In Flanders Fields Museum, Ieper

resided virtually permanently at De Panne. At the westerly edge of De Panne there were four villas, set somewhat apart from the rest of the village. Queen Elisabeth, the three children and a small entourage of staff and military advisers also stayed there, relatively undisturbed, until 1917.

De Panne was suitable, the King decided. One reason was that new headquarters were set up in the border village of Houtem. It was also in Houtem that the King and his ministers held their meetings in the early phases of the war. Otherwise, the ministers concentrated their rather meagre administrative staff in a suburb of the French seaport of Le Havre. So the distances involved were considerable, which made the ministers uneasy. They realised that Belgium had to have unity of leadership but this could not be guaranteed so long as the King insisted on remaining on Belgian soil within range of the heavy German artillery. Supreme authority over Free Belgium was therefore geographically scattered even if in the eyes of citizens and soldiers this was not the case. After all, was not De Panne now the capital? The royal couple had become the pre-eminent symbol of the Belgian nation. Furthermore, their entourage did everything it could to build up this image among the troops and the public. The idea was further boosted by high-ranking visits to De Panne with the associated parades and ceremonies.

The King and Queen did not shut themselves away. Albert often went out, as did the Queen. And this was not limited to beach walks on horseback or on foot. They showed themselves everywhere behind the Belgian lines and even in the trenches on the front. Virtually every soldier got to see the royals at close quarters. Queen Elisabeth was often observed in the field hospitals. However, she did not do any actual nursing, although the propaganda suggested that she did. It goes without saying that this proximity did much to boost the morale of the troops.

His view of the war

In 1917 an 'inner cabinet' was created. This small group of ministers met in De Panne whenever the king wanted to exercise his 'presidency' of the government. The allies quickly realised that there was only one government. If they wanted to discuss strategic decisions and input from the Belgian army, they had to do so with the King. He was the real leader of the Belgian forces, the man who had the final word. However, the King could never be persuaded to take part in allied offensives or allow his troops to play a major role outside Belgian territory. He wanted to be absolutely certain that an offensive would be successful. Until well into the summer of 1918 events proved him right. All the allied offensives bled to death.

King Albert put his stamp on the diplomacy because he was utterly convinced that it was the only way for Belgium to survive the conflict and thereby maintain its independence, its social model and its monarchy. Furthermore, the country remained obliged by treaty to be 'neutral'. Belgium may have fought on the same side at the front, but in his eyes it was never one of the 'allies' like the French and the British. That was his guideline. He had strong doubts whether the civilian politicians properly appreciated the all-consuming nature of the war. This belief in fact led him in 1916 to put out feelers in Berlin to see whether a compromise peace might be possible. He was ignored.

The King followed a highly personal course and kept the civil authorities very much at arm's length. He was, however, happy to allow his ministers free rein to look after the numerous Belgian refugees in Le Havre.

As well as that, an impressive network of Belgian training camps, factories, hospitals and nursing homes was built up on French soil. The Belgian army was, after all, seriously handicapped because virtually the entire country was occupied by the Germans. It had therefore to be all the more creative in order to maintain itself in a war of attrition in which weaponry and tactics were evolving rapidly. At the same time, it had to try to retain as much autonomy as possible from the French and British forces.

The King regarded that autonomy as very important. He was horrified by the terrible loss of human life suffered by the armies of the great powers. He was appalled by the slaughter of a generation of young men on the battlefield. He wanted to spare his own soldiers and their families such suffering and in his eyes he could only do that if he was in complete control. He considered most politicians to be irresponsible, certainly if they were the mouthpiece of movements in Belgian society which he mistrusted: the Catholics and Socialists, for example, parties with an anti-militarist tradition. They were responsible for the weakness of his army, or so he believed. But he also mistrusted the party supporters in France.

Queen Elisabeth and Doctor Lepage visiting wounded soldiers at L'Océan, Vinkem. Photo © Archives Red Cross Flanders. Mechelen. Painting by Alfred Bastien

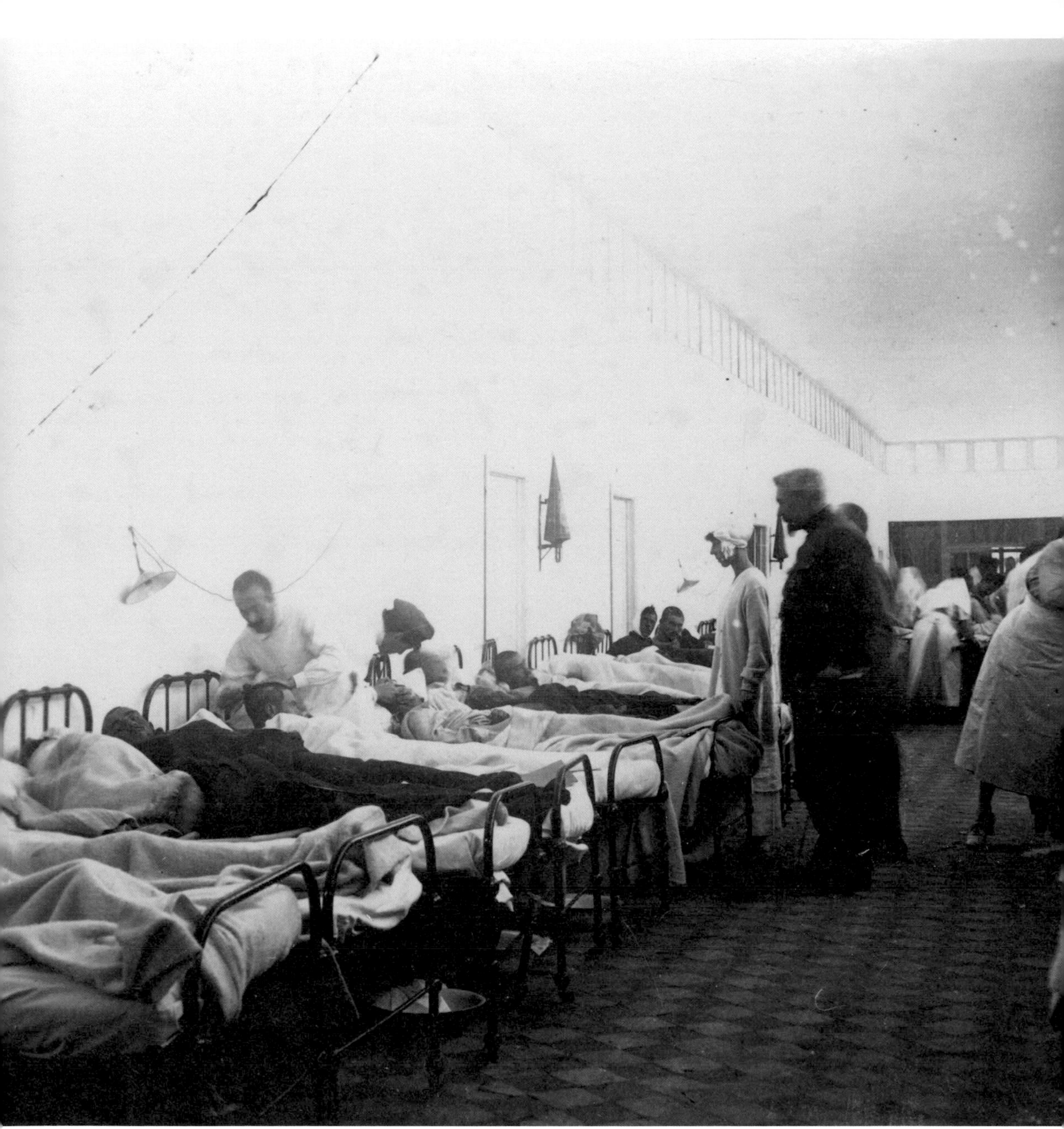

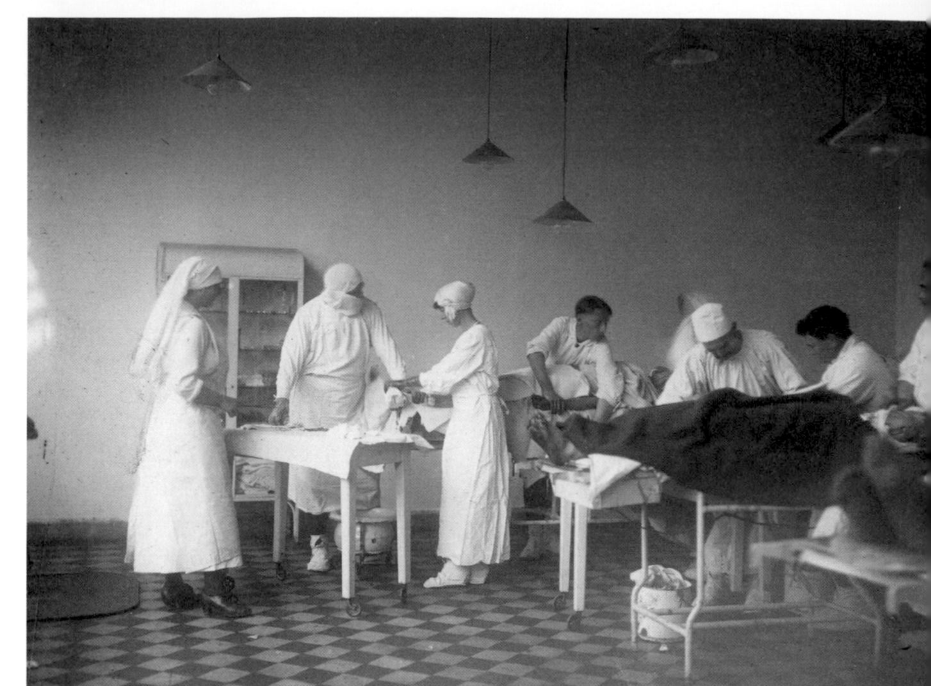

Queen Elisabeth assisting Doctor Lepage at L'Océan, De Panne. © Archives Red Cross Flanders. Mechelen

King Albert I and Maréchal Foch, De Panne © In Flanders Fields Museum, Ieper

Albert believed in a determinist concept of history which Charles Lagrange had taught at the Military School. He had developed the so-called laws of Nicolas Brück, a 19th century Belgian officer, in conjunction with a collection of Biblical arguments. Furthermore, changes in the Earth's magnetism and the chronology of the Old Testament also played an important role. These laws revealed that the French as a nation and civilisation had been in irreversible decline since 1870. The future lay with the Anglo-Saxons and would do so till the end of time, which would inevitably occur within a few hundred years. This partially explains Albert's actions as a military leader.

After the war

The King was rightly concerned about Belgium's future. After all, the conflict had lasted far longer than anyone could have foreseen in August 1914. The warring states held each other in a stranglehold and they had gradually dragged each other down towards the abyss. The first great power to fall into it was Russia, in 1917. Albert saw very clearly that the war of attrition threatened to destroy the social order in all the warring states. But he also believed that societies where order and discipline were deeply rooted had a better chance of survival.

It was only as the autumn of 1918 approached that Albert agreed to join the offensive. The German army was by then seriously weakened. In the King's eyes, only now was success truly certain. The country was indeed liberated. But what then? Albert succeeded in mediating an important step towards democratisation which gave every adult man one vote. Women, however, were still excluded. The country also experienced coalition governments for the first time. Nobody could claim a political majority any more. The great political groupings now had to learn to collaborate, though the process went in fits and starts.

The King found it rather difficult because democratisation also threatened his own power. Albert particularly wanted to maintain close supervision of the armed forces and foreign policy. He was nervous of growing too close to France. But on the other hand, the British were trying to free themselves from close ties with the European continent. International relations remained bitter. The experience of war would not be digested or assimilated for at least a generation. The war veterans of 1914-18 would form the grassroots of numerous authoritarian movements which would lead, two decades later, to the Second World War.

But by that time, King Albert was no more. His love of risky physical challenges had long made ministers and generals nervous. During the war, it had taken him into the frontline trenches and led him to fly in the rickety aircraft of the time. In the end, it would take him to his death on the slippery chalk rocks of the Meuse valley near Marche-les-Dames. On 17 February 1934 he breathed his last. Belgium's Knight-King was dead. ■

Translated by Chris Emery

The Great War That Largely Passed Us by in the Netherlands

[M.C. BRANDS]

'If we want to understand and ultimately to put behind us the cataclysmic record of European history in this century, we must revisit the war that set in motion these enduring centrifugal and centripetal forces, propelling us away from and towards a unified Europe'.

Jay Winter, *Sites of Memory, Sites of Mourning: The Great War in European Cultural History,* Cambridge 1995, p. 1

During a conference for the Institute for War, Holocaust and Genocide Studies (NIOD) in 1997, I gave a lecture on 'The Great War' that passed us by – a blank spot in the historic consciousness of the Netherlands.

My lecture focused on the question of how far we in the Netherlands were aware that the First World War had opened a chasm between the world before 1914 and the world afterwards, and where that chasm could be seen.

Did the World War perspective penetrate the Dutch consciousness, and if so, to what extent? In other words, did we begin to realise that this war had been a watershed event in the history of Europe – and even in the history of the world? This brought about, amongst other things, the end of stability in Europe, now this *Urkatastrophe* ('great seminal catastrophe')[1] had caused so many chain reactions in Europe.

It is the Second World War that is ingrained in the collective memory of the Dutch as a national trauma. There can be no misunderstanding: when people in the Netherlands talked – and talk – about 'the war', we mean the Second World War. That is *the* great caesura in our own national history.

This sets the Netherlands apart from neighbouring countries where 'the Great War' still means the First World War. This war, a watershed event for the whole of Europe, has not become – or hardly – part of our collective memory in the Netherlands. For the Dutch, what the Germans refer to as historische *Erfahrbarkeit*, or experience of history, does not extend back as far as 1914-1918; it goes back no further than the Second World War.

That is why November is not a month of remembrance in the Netherlands. In our country, the poppy has not become an especially symbolic flower. There are very few First World War monuments in the Netherlands, in contrast to other countries such as France, where the Great War resulted in a veritable monument industry.

Belgian soldiers in the Smitskerkje, Bergen op Zoom, October 1914

In his great work on the 20th century (1988), the French historian René Rémond wrote:

'La célébration du 11 Novembre éclipsera toujours celle du 8 mai 1945.... Ce n'est que vingt ans plus tard que l'affectation d'un numéro d'ordre, à l'instar des Anglo-Saxons - World War One, World War Two -, déclassera cette guerre unique, réduite à n'être plus désormais que la première d'une série désignée par des adjectifs numériques.'[2]

For the Netherlands, it was and is an inestimable privilege and advantage that the Great War passed us by. But this has its disadvantages too. By not experiencing this trauma first-hand, our country missed a crucial turning point in the modern history of our continent. The decline of the old Europe passed almost unnoticed. Consequently, after 1914, the Netherlands kept to its own chronology that continued until the next caesura: the Second World War. Our historical timeline diverged from that of all the countries that had experienced the *Urkatastrophe*.

Partly for this reason, the 'short' 20th century (1914-1989) was even shorter in the Netherlands, and many lines of development from the 'long' 19th century (1789-1914) continued uninterrupted. Consequently, our picture of the violent

Otto Dix, *Dance of Death Anno* 1917. (Der Krieg, 1924) © SABAM Belgium 2014

20th century has remained largely incomplete, compared to our neighbouring countries. We can even speak of an 'amputated', truncated perspective, as a result of which the Second World War has remained centre-stage. It resembles a Greek tragedy of which one sees only the second act.

And that is certainly the case in a country where historical awareness is poorly developed and historical questions in general do not play an important role in day-to-day, public life.

Knowledge of history from books is a poor substitute for first-hand experience. There can be no doubt about it: the First World War is 'beyond our national sphere of remembrance'. Events that people have not experienced for themselves are not internalised, or only to a limited extent, and do not become part of the national historical experience.

In that respect, it is a serious disadvantage, in terms of knowledge, to have underestimated the significance of WWI, or have even overlooked that great watershed event in the history of Europe – and even in the history of the world – for so long. As a result, we in the Netherlands were less aware than our neighbours of not only what was called a 'new Europe', but also of the *Selbstentmachtung* (self-disempowerment) of Europe. This also meant that the Dutch failed to perceive the Second World War as one of a series of disasters in what historians call the 'short twentieth century', and this did nothing to help the Dutch towards a more realistic understanding of the balance of power in Europe and of Europe's position in the world after 1914.

Some degree of understanding of the century's history and the structural problems that led to major conflicts in Europe is indispensable in order to make sense of the post-Cold War Europe in which we live today.

Umwertung aller Werte

There are many issues in history on which historians do not agree, and in many cases they are the subject of a never-ending discussion. However, it can be said that there is consensus among today's historians on the significance of the First World War. They nod in agreement at terms such as *Umwertung aller Werte* ('transvaluation of all values'), and agree that the First World War was the major catalyst for the many disasters later in the 20th century; the beginning of an era of tyrannies and dictatorship, a war that continued its natural progression into another war, and yet another – albeit a 'cold' one.

The First World War gave birth to a tradition of mega-violence. What other event prompted mobilisation on such a scale as WWI? It was a new dimension of horrors that Karl D. Bracher described as 'the paradigm for the great wars of the future'.

The 1914 war was therefore the first 'democratic' war in history. The war affected people at all levels of society in every country that was involved. It was a war not only of motorisation and mechanisation, but above all of large numbers: soldiers, resources, materials and deaths; a *Materialschlacht*, a 'war of resources'.

When the war finally ended, Europe found itself in a state of profound sorrow and confusion, but at the same time it eagerly anticipated and had great expectations of a better world. Modris Eksteins highlights the explosion of artistic creativity unleashed by and after this uprooting.

The war had abruptly undermined the idea of steady progress. Politics fell into the grasp of totalitarian ideological movements, political schools of thought in which everything became an issue. The 'old' had lost its significance; in the world that replaced it people were swept along by increasingly extreme opinions.

It was the birth of an age of extreme consequences and cumulative extremism (Hans Mommsen). Sensibilities were heightened, partly due to an extensive friend/enemy propaganda machine. At the same time, these years were characterised by a strong urge for a return to stability – an urge so strong that it only made things more unstable.

A new era of European instability had begun, in terms of the balance of power, national borders and social and political regimes.

A peace made for the dead

The war had dragged on endlessly in the mud. For years, the powers that be proved unable to bring it to an end.[3] Europe changed in all respects. The old empires had crumbled, and many new states were constructed at the end of the war, as if on a drawing board or with a Meccano set. 'It was the thought of the new Serbia, the new Greece, the new Bohemia, the new Poland which made our hearts sing hymns at heaven's gate', the British eye witness Harold Nicolson wrote about Versailles in his *Peacemaking*, 1919 (p.33).[4]

The Fabian, Beatrice Webb, saw everywhere 'new things around which all who are discontent with the old order foregather' (Beatrice Webb, quoted in Mayer, p.390).

What was still referred to in 1919 as the Spring of Nations, Masaryk's *The World Revolution*, a liberation from the 'prison of nations', was seen as the opposite ten years later. The history of Europe is a constant battle between stability and freedom. After 1919, stability was based on revolutionary principles (A. Sharp).[5]

Contemporaries, among them the Dutchman Ernst Heldring, spoke of a 'scandalous and impracticable peace treaty that will keep Europe in a state of unrest'. In Paris, on 2 March 1919, Heldring wrote in his diary: 'I have the impression that all the discussions of the diplomats and statesmen here will soon

Lloyd George, Georges Clemenceau, Woodrow Wilson. Versailles, 1919

be swept away by the great wave of revolution that is about to engulf the world. The French, in particular, are proving largely unaware of the serious times that are ahead of us'.

The Dutch historian H.Th. Colenbrander spoke in 1919 of 'a peace – made for the dead – that we, the living, must now submit to'. In the words of Paul Valéry during a lecture in Zürich in 1922: 'The storm has abated, yet we are still restless and do not feel at ease, as if the storm could break again at any moment'.

And that is what happened: the war continued after 1918, albeit in other ways. Revisionism became one of the highly destabilising factors after Versailles. At best, the perception was that Versailles had created at least as many problems as it had solved. At worst, Versailles was seen as dynamite that made stable relations impossible.

In the words of John M. Keynes in his book about Versailles that was as critical as it was famous: 'The Treaty includes no provisions for the economic rehabilitation of Europe - nothing to make the defeated Central Empires into good neighbours, nothing to stabilize the new States of Europe, nothing to reclaim Russia; nor does it promote in any way a compact of economic solidarity amongst the Allies themselves; no agreement was reached at Paris for restoring the disordered finances of France and Italy, or to adjust the systems of the Old World and the New' (I. Clark, *Globalization*, p.52).

Versailles lacked what was known as an 'oblivion' clause, that salutary peacemaking 'forgetting', the amnesty clause of earlier peace treaties that were oriented to reconciliation rather than to retribution and reparations. In the aftermath of war, a policy of letting bygones be bygones is a prerequisite for an effective peace treaty that restores stable relations. In his classic work, *The Twenty Years' Crisis: 1919–1939*, the British historian E. H. Carr speaks of 'the unprecedented vindictiveness' of the peace treaties of 1919 (p.61).

The League of Nations was a plaster that was too small for the large, deep wounds of war. Critics referred to the League as a pill to cure an earthquake, but their objections did nothing to quell the 'No More War' sentiment.

Not only did the European state system unravel in 1919, but also, as contemporaries were already pointing out, Europe's position in the world was seriously undermined by this self-disempowerment. According to A.J.P. Taylor, 'In January 1918 Europe ceased to be the centre of the world'. In 1924, the French historian René Grousset spoke of a 'réveil de l'Asie' – a reawakening of Asia. He argued that, following the Europeanization of Asia, Asia would revolt against Europe. The 'old continent' continued to rule its colonies but it was the beginning of the end, although few noticed.

In order not to give the impression that everything was new after the great *Umbruch* of 1914, it should be emphasised that, despite this 'earthquake', many lines of continuity in institutions, behavioural patterns, mentality etc. remained. As the German historian H.U. Wehler once remarked, the two World Wars worked as an accelerator as well as a brake.

Germany was an extreme example of the overlapping of continuity and discontinuity. German history in general is characterised by a continuity of fractures. Karl D. Bracher's crucial question: 'Wie tief ist der geschichtliche Bruch, wie stark die Kontinuität der Vorkriegswelt?'- 'How deep the historical fracture, how strong the continuity of the prewar world?' - would not be out of place in the library of many a historical institute.

Cognitive maps need to be revised

What consequences did the First World War have for the position of the Netherlands in the fabric of the European state system that had been so drastically rent asunder, and what were the consequences for Dutch colonialism?

Few Dutch contemporaries saw the consequences of the major changes in the years after 1919. [6] In his short memoirs of the post-World War Two period, Beyen (1897-1976), the Dutch Minister for Foreign Affairs and a great European, compared 1914 with the fall of Constantinople, the discovery of America and the French Revolution. In his view, 1914 had been a much clearer caesura, but he emphasised that 'back to normalcy' soon became the motto again after 1918. With regard to the Netherlands, he added that it was governed between 1918 and 1940 by what he referred to as two 'nineteenth-century' figures: Colijn and De Geer. 'They ended on the debris of their politics. But people did not see this until the next war' (p.117). Unlike most of its neighbours, the Netherlands did not lose its naiveté and innocence in the period 1914-18.

During and after the First World War, the Netherlands was accused, mainly by the British, of using its professed neutrality to camouflage a pro-German stance. Publications such as *The Economist* calculated how much profit the Netherlands had made from the war. In short, the world was not terribly impressed with us in 1919. It is even more surprising, then, that the government, aware of how vulner-

able the Netherlands was during those years, remained so obstinate regarding the German emperor's controversial escape into exile in the Netherlands.

Since 1945, the historiography of the First World War has remained largely incomplete; too little attention has been paid to this area of research. There is still a great deal of lost ground to make up in terms of our knowledge of WWI and the post-war period.

Our view of history urgently needs to be 'Europeanized', if only to bring it back into line with that of our neighbours after all these decades.

As mentioned above, there are still many questions relating to the Netherlands and the First World War that have not been researched. There is much that historical research can clarify, particularly with regard to the nature of Dutch neutrality.

Just as in 1919 we can now ask about the position of the Netherlands in today's Europe, after the great *Umbruch* of 1989/91, after the end of the division of Europe. Have our 'cognitive maps' of Europe been properly updated since 1989? Are we aware that we are now living in a completely different Europe?

The era of the Second World War – including its sequel in the Cold War – does not end until the revolutions of 1989/91. Not until then is the division of Europe – and therefore of Germany – come to an end, followed by the fall of the Soviet Union. It means the end of that exceptional period in which so many structural elements of European history were temporarily thrown out of action.

In the *International Herald Tribune* of 18 April 1997, the renowned American columnist Flora Lewis warned that 'History is not fatality, but European history has brought too many tragedies to risk slipping back into the old ways'.

There is not yet a clear answer to the question of how our continent must or can continue after the major crisis of 2008. At the very least, we should disentangle and analyse the lines of development that lead to the present.

Us too

There are historians who are almost unable to formulate a single sentence without using – either implicitly or explicitly – the terms 'construction', invention' or 'representation'. This school itself freely indulges in all manner of constructions and is consequently no longer hindered by constraining proportions of extent such as great or small. They frequently aim to give the impression that the Netherlands was involved – in one way or another – in the major episode in history known as the First World War. After all, this too is a matter of how you present it.

Although relatively little attention was paid in the Netherlands to the First World War before the 1990s, since then there has been a sort of 'appropriation' hype, with all its confusing reactions: an 'us too' sentiment, 'the war didn't pass the Netherlands by', 'we're part of it too, a lot of things happened here in 1914-18'. The revision of established views of history often leads to overemphasis.

But for goodness' sake let us not needlessly complicate things even further: in the years 1914-1918, the people of the Netherlands enjoyed a level of security, freedom and prosperity that was so painfully lacking in other countries – like Belgium, for example.

Let us not lose sight of the hard facts: the numbers of dead and wounded. Was a whole generation of men wiped out, as in Britain? 'More undead in the Netherlands', it was said in London at the time. How great was the destruction of buildings and infrastructure in the Netherlands? Yes, the army was mobilised. But there were few victims. There were civilian casualties, however, in the merchant navy and the Navy. But there were no battlefields, no trench warfare, no air raids (as on Leuven), no minorities issue, no morbid absurdism in the arts. The end of the kingdom, the beginning of the republic.

We cannot speak of a collective experience of immense violence and slaughter. There was no urgent demand for women to work. There were many war refugees, and there were border incidents, but this did not make the Netherlands into one of the countries that had truly suffered during the war.

Is this not a form of 'levelling', of putting problems of widely varying importance on a par? Matters of life and death on the one hand, and on the other the question of how people survived. [7]

'The war was not a deluge which swept all before it, but at best a winter storm which swelled the rivers of change'. ■

Translated by Yvette Mead

NOTES

1. A concise summary of the many major effects of WWI can be found in Wolfgang J. Mommsen's introduction *Europe on the Eve of the First World War:*
'The debate about the First World War and its origins goes on up to the present day with unabated vigour. This is in no way surprising if we consider the momentous changes effected by the First World War and its political, social, economic and cultural consequences. It destroyed a system of culture dominated by an elitist intelligentsia closely interrelated with the rising commercial and industrial classes and reflecting their self-confidence and high self-esteem, but also a comparatively sophisticated life style. It resulted in the breakdown of the European system of powers and the rise of new superpowers, the U.S., and, with some delay, the USSR. It led to a long period of instability and political crisis which paved the way for the rise to power of Fascism and National Socialism on the one hand, Soviet Communism on the other. It also marked the end of the European hegemony over the rest of the globe and initiated the process which eventually led to the collapse of the older European empires, even though decolonisation began in earnest only after the Second World War.' (In: J.J. Becker and S. Audoin (eds.), *Les sociétés européennes et la guerre de 1914 - 1918*. Nanterre 1990, p.23).

2. 'The celebration of 11 November will always eclipse that of 8 May 1945. Yet only twenty years later the attribution of a number, in the Anglo-Saxon fashion – World War One, World War Two - was to downgrade this unique war, to reduce it from then on to nothing more than the first of a series referred to by numerical adjectives.'

3. cf. D.C. Watt, *How War Came. The Immediate Origins of the Second World War.* 1989, (p.12): 'What was disastrous for Europe was not so much the outbreak of the First World War, but the inability or unwillingness of anyone in the seats of power and authority to bring the war to an early end'.

4. In the introduction to *Peacemaking*, 1919 (ed. 1943), Nicolson wrote these pessimistic words: 'We succeeded in balkanizing Europe, although we Europeanized the Balkans'.

5. cf. E.H. Carr, *Crisis*, pp.129 and 123: 'The impulse which it (WWI) gave to the pursuit of autarky was immediate and powerful'. 'The victors of 1918 "lost the peace" in Central Europe because they continued to pursue a principle of political and economic disintegration in an age which called for larger and larger units.' (p. 230).

Homecoming, Australia, 1919

Otto Dix,
Near Langemark
February 1918.
(Der Krieg, 1924)

6. Colenbrander's opening sentence in 1920 was as follows: 'One of the most remarkable phenomena in the recent history of the Netherlands is the indifference that recently arose here with regard to our position and role in international politics. Although newspaper readers in the Netherlands were in the habit of saying that they read detailed correspondences on what was happening in the world, they had become unaccustomed to asking – let alone answering – the question of how events abroad might influence the fate and interests of their own country. It was as if it went without saying that no-one would trouble the Netherlands.' (H.T. Colenbrander, *De internationale toestand van Nederland tijdens, vóór en na den wereld-oorlog.* In: H. Brugmans (ed.), *Nederland in den oorlogstijd.* Amsterdam 1920, p.103).
Regarding the strong German orientation of the Netherlands, Colenbrander remarked: 'The Dutch had a high regard for Germany....Beatific admiration for all that was German was all too common, and slavish imitation was a real danger'. (p.110)

7. The Netherlands did experience these aspects of the war: mobilisation, a foodstuffs act, food distribution, civilian casualties (e.g. at sea), minefields at sea, smuggling, an electric fence between the Netherlands and Belgium constructed by the Germans, border incidents, air raids on towns and villages in the province of Zeeland (Zierikzee and Sluis were particularly badly hit), large numbers of refugees. In the end 80,000 Belgians stayed in the Netherlands for the duration of the war. They were housed in refugee camps.

Paul Schulten and Martin Kraaijenstein (eds) *Leven naast de catastrofe. Nederland tijdens de Eerste Wereldoorlog. Hilversum 2001,* p.169: 'The greatest and most famous monument to the reception of refugees is undoubtedly the Belgian Monument near Amersfoort. It is a symbol of Belgium's gratitude to the Netherlands for taking in so many refugees. Political difficulties between the two countries after the war made an official ceremony impossible. It was not until 22 September 1938 that the Belgian King Leopold III unveiled the commemorative plaque'.

I am largely in agreement with the criticism expressed by my colleague Piet Blaas. He wrote: 'For a long time we have lacked a 'First World War' perspective. We were unaware – or not sufficiently aware – of the serious structural consequences of conflict on international relations… In his lecture, Brands makes a second claim that could be regarded as more or less following on from the first, namely that since 1945, the historiography of the First World War has remained largely incomplete; too little attention has been paid to this area of research'. I think this statement could be more nuanced'. Blaas is right about this, and also about the fact that I should have mentioned the Utrecht historian and commentator G.W. Kernkamp. In: M. Kraaijenstein and P. Schulten (eds.), *Wankel evenwicht. Neutraal Nederland en de eerste Wereldoorlog.* 2007, p.15 ff.

Three Questions That Do Not Go Away

The Netherlands and the Shoah

There are some cruelties that over time seem to acquire more significance rather than less. As more facts about them become known and as the perspective of memory widens into history, their true proportions become more and more apparent and so their commemoration gains ever more significance. One such historical enormity was inflicted on the Dutch population, namely the five years of terrorizing occupation by Nazi Germany and especially the systematic murder of approximately 104,000 Dutch Jews in the years 1940 to 1945. There seem to be three crucial questions with regard to that period of Dutch history, three questions that dominate the historical debate up to the present day, three painful questions that – despite countless studies, articles, autobiographies and interviews – simply do not go away. Before addressing these three questions, let me make some preliminary remarks.

In the year 2010 it was 65 years since the German occupation of the Netherlands ended. This prompted the Dutch government to set up a publicity campaign under the title 'The Second World War is Retiring'. The idea seems to have been that The War was now so long ago that its commemoration would cease to be meaningful for new generations and that the time had come to put it away in the Retirement Home of history, among the many other historical episodes in our nation's past, like the 80 Years War with Spain in the 17th century or the years 1810-1813, when the Netherlands was made a part of the French Empire. In another attempt to take the sting out of World War II memories, the Dutch government has in recent decades broadened the scope of the official yearly commemoration of wartime victims on 4th May to include Dutch citizens who died in subsequent wars and so-called international 'peace operations'.

In my view, these attempts to reorganise the collective Dutch memory of the war against Nazi Germany and the ugly years of occupation from 1940 to 1945 have had some alienating effects for individual groups of victims and their descendants. It is quite tragic for a family to lose a son or a grandson in a UN peace mission in Afghanistan, but it is a totally different tragedy from the tragedy of a man whose father was executed by the SS as a resistance fighter during World War II, or the tragedy of Dutch Jews who lost their parents or grandparents in the Shoah.

In an even more fundamental way, and from the very beginning of the Dutch post-war period, the Dutch government tried to appropriate the memory of the German occupation by establishing an official government agency in 1945 called the State Institute for War Documentation. The good thing about this official institute was its collection and preservation of many thousands of documents about the war period that would perhaps otherwise have been lost. The bad thing was that the State Institute was a state institute. The questionable role during the German occupation of so many state officials such as the police, the judicial authorities, railway functionaries etc. warranted a much more independent approach to the historiography of the wartime years in the Netherlands. As a consequence, many unpleasant truths or even downright scandalous episodes concerning the Dutch authorities in their dealings with the Nazis were not or not sufficiently covered by the 14-volume official Dutch national history of the war. Instead they were revealed over time by independent historians and publicists, whose work is still going on. In recent years, even since the so-called 'retirement' of the Second World War, new facts have come to light about the behaviour of civil servants, of state museums, of the Supreme Court, including the sometimes unjust or even inhuman attitude of the Dutch authorities towards victims of Nazi persecution after the war ended.

Out of all these books, studies and articles, and the many autobiographies and diaries that are still being published, three central questions emerge that continue to trigger fierce debate whenever an opinion is expressed about them. Together, these three questions seem to summarise the ethical dilemmas that underpin the story of the Nazi occupation of the Netherlands and of the genocide inflicted on Dutch Jewry.

The first question is: was it always possible for ordinary people, living in the midst of daily reality, to distinguish clearly between good and evil, to choose between resistance and collaboration? Over the years, as the heroic first-person narratives of former resistance men and women have died away, historians and journalists with more detachment have maintained that rather than a choice between black and white, living in the Netherlands under Nazi occupation was a question of nuances, that it was often impossible to distinguish between what and who was good, on the one hand, and what and who was bad, on the other. In the words of one of these recent historians, wartime reality was by definition a grey zone.

In my view, this line of reasoning is used more often than not to whitewash stories of collaboration, to quench a feeling of guilt or simply to blur the distinction

between perpetrators and bystanders on the one hand and victims on the other. In such a view of the years 1940-1945, all Dutch people become victims of history, the only difference being that some resisted more and others less, and that some survived and others did not. I must confess that I cannot accept this reductionist and opportunistic view of morality in wartime. There are undoubtedly many forms and nuances of morally reprehensible behaviour, but I think it is important to acknowledge and admire those who did act when it was necessary, who did protect other people at the risk or sometimes even at the cost of their own lives. There is nothing grey about that, and if the ugly history of Nazi occupation can produce anything by way of a moral lesson, it is that impossible dilemmas are the truest test of human morality and human courage. Those who did pass that test, for example those who helped the Anne Frank family, should be put on a metaphorical pedestal and not dragged down to the level of confusion, compromise and collaboration where so many others struggled.

The second uncomfortable question that does not seem to go away is the question: why did such a high percentage of Jews in the Netherlands perish in the Shoah, while in other European countries the percentage was much lower? In the Netherlands only 25 percent of the Jews survived Nazi persecution. In Belgium, for example, the figure was 62 percent, while in France, with its strong tradition of anti-Semitism, no less than 75 percent of the Jews survived. Even in Germany itself, a Jew had more chance of surviving the Nazi persecution than in the Netherlands. The reasons for these shameful statistics, especially for a country like the Netherlands that likes to pride itself on its longstanding tradition of tolerance and humanism, are quite complex, and they cannot be summarized in a few sentences. According to the most recent studies on the subject, the poor record of the Netherlands in protecting its Jewish population should be seen in the light of the characteristics of the civilian regime that the Nazis established in the occupied territory of the Netherlands and the all-powerful German police in our country, whose raids and deportation programmes met with little protest or resistance, and in many cases with indifference or even collaboration. But even if 10 or 100 more studies on the subject were to be undertaken, analysing still further the fate of the Jews in the Netherlands as compared to other European countries, ultimately there is only one conclusion to be drawn: in 1940-1945 the Netherlands failed its Jews; the Dutch people did not do enough to protect them. Everybody – including the Jewish population itself – should have done more to resist, to escape, to go into hiding. This conclusion is rarely drawn, for two reasons, firstly because it is too simplistic and secondly because it is useless, as history has already run its course and cannot be altered.

But if there is something like national pride, there should also be something like national shame, and I think it is proper and useful for a country to express and to maintain this shame as an integral part of its national heritage. On a personal note, I should add that my own grandfather resisted his persecution and that of his wife and three children as much as he could. After a failed attempt to flee the country in May 1940, he succeeded in 1943, with the help of forged legal documents, in getting out of the transit camp Westerbork, where the family was taken after being arrested by Dutch policemen. Thus the family was spared further deportation to the East and was able to hide and avoid further torment at the hands of the Nazis. The lawyer who assisted my grandparents and their children to survive the war in this way was honoured, on the initiative of my father, by Yad Vashem as a Righteous Among the Nations. His name was Ysbrand Nijgh. His courage and determination to save people were unfortunately all too rare. That, to my mind, is the final truth about the high percentage of Dutch Jews exterminated in the years of the Nazi occupation of the Netherlands.

The third question that persistently crops up, to the point that it will never fully go away, is the question: did people know about the fate that awaited Jews who were deported to the East? This is an important question, because if people were aware of what was happening or going to happen to the Jews, then their feelings of shared responsibility, even of guilt by association, and certainly their resulting shame should be greater in proportion to their knowledge. If, on the other hand, they knew nothing and could not have known, there is at least some possible justification for their not resisting harder, helping more and protecting more generously and more effectively. This issue is not just a Dutch question, and it is perhaps even more complex than the other two questions. So I cannot answer this third question by summarizing the literature on the subject, which is simply too vast to read even in a lifetime. Different historians come up with different interpretations, depending on their evaluation of documents, radio speeches, newspaper reports, diaries and autobiographies. Some authors say: at the time people did *not* know about the fate of the Jews, but in their heart of hearts, on the basis of persistent rumours, they feared the worst. Other authors say: of course many people *did* know; the reports and rumours were clear enough, but they did not want to accept the truth until it was too late. In my view, there is no real contradiction between these two interpretations.

This may sound strange to you, but it has to do with the semantics of two crucial words in the question 'Did people know about the fate of the Jews?' Firstly, what do we mean by 'people'? There are individuals, families, colleagues, friends, neighbours. All those people hear, read, tell others things. Under enemy occupation, without press freedom, without radios and under a perverted state regime, everyone is thrown back on a small circle that can be trusted. One of the pernicious consequences of an enemy occupation is precisely that no one is to be trusted until the contrary can be proved, and that the people in a general sense, or 'public opinion', ceases to exist. So it is impossible to say that 'people' knew or that 'people' did not know. Any such opinion is a construction in retrospect.

The second ambiguity in the question is the verb 'to know'. 'Did people *know* about the fate of the Jews?' What is 'to know'? Is it: 'to have strong indications'? Is it: 'to assume something'? Or is it: 'to be absolutely certain of something?' or 'to have no doubt about it?' Knowing comes in countless nuances of certainty, and in a time of war, a time of lies, disinformation and diabolical deceit, it is impossible to talk unambiguously about anything that is not before your very eyes. Even in our present time of peace it is difficult to act upon what you know.

For example, I know that our way of living, travelling and consuming gravely endangers the environment, that there is no solution to the problem of nuclear waste, that the world economic crisis will only get worse. But what does this knowledge mean for my daily conduct? I do my job and try to make a success of it. What do I tell my three children? I tell them to do their homework and to make sure they pass their exams. And I trust that sometime in the future, when grave problems present themselves, problems that may even threaten our very existence, we will together have the strength and resourcefulness to solve them. I hope for the best, and I prepare for the worst, but I do not tell my family each day that the end is nigh. So, as I said before, there is no real difference between '*not knowing* but fearing the worst', on the one hand, and '*knowing*, but not wishing to accept the truth', on the other.

I am aware that the three questions I have addressed may be too complex to tackle in a brief text. But I still wanted to talk about them, not only because in the Netherlands these historic issues keep coming back to trouble the conscience of historians and non-historians alike. In fact they are certain to obsess anyone who reflects on the history of the Nazi occupation of the Netherlands and the persecution of Dutch Jews. But I also wanted to talk about them because these three questions illustrate so vividly the need to safeguard well-informed public opinion, an open and democratic society, in which the government at all levels can be held accountable for its adherence to and enforcement of the rule of law and its respect for the constitutional rights of its citizens. It is in such a society that we can hope to find citizens who are able to distinguish between resistance and collaboration, between good and evil, citizens who have the curiosity, the commitment and – if necessary – the courage to live up to their moral responsibility. ■

This is a slightly edited version of a talk given under the auspices of the Instituto Holandés de Buenos Aires at the 2013 Feria Internacional del Libro in Buenos Aires. Maarten Asscher is a writer and bookseller living in Amsterdam. His latest book is Appels en peren. Lof van de vergelijking (Apples and Pears. In Praise of Comparing), published in 2013.

All photos from NIOD (Institute for War, Holocaust and Genocide Studies, www.niod.nl), Imagebase, Beeldbank WO2

Bodybuilders in Haarlem

Startling Aspects of Cornelis van Haarlem's Art

[ILJA VELDMAN]

Cornelis Cornelisz van Haarlem was born into a well-to-do Catholic family in 1562. He was four when the Iconoclasm took place and nineteen when Haarlem officially converted to the reformed faith. What was a budding painter full of ambition to do in a period when art was disappearing from the churches and commissions for religious art were dwindling? A generation earlier, painters had become famous for their monumental altarpieces. Cornelis' fellow townsman, Maarten van Heemskerck, who was his great example, had been able to demonstrate visibly to everyone in those altarpieces that - thanks to a year spent in Rome – he had mastered the style of Michelangelo, Raphael and the ancients.

Once commissions for the churches dried up, portraiture became an important part of a painter's repertoire. It was intelligent then of Cornelis' parents that they placed him in the charge of the portraitist Pieter Pietersz. As early as 1583 Cornelis obtained the honourable commission to paint a group portrait of the corporalship of the Haarlem Civic Guard's Hall (1583). His example was Dirck Barendsz' *Banquet of the Eighteen Guardsmen of Squad L* in Amsterdam (1566), but Cornelis' composition is a lot livelier. He and his teacher, Pieter Pietersz, can be recognised in the two men at the top left. The motif of the inclined flag would be adopted later by Frans Hals in his portraits of guardsmen. In 1599 Cornelis was commissioned to paint the officers of the civic guard as well (Frans Hals Museum, Haarlem).

Collaboration with Goltzius and van Mander

Although he would still paint portraits now and then, portraiture was not really where the young Cornelis' aspirations really lay. He had become friendly with Hendrick Goltzius, a talented engraver and draughtsman, who had settled in Haarlem in 1577. Along with Karel van Mander, an emigrant from the Southern Netherlands who had moved to Haarlem in 1583, they established a sort of brotherhood, which they called an 'academy' in the Italian fashion, with the intention of drawing 'from life' together. Their most important subject was the nude male body. They probably drew very few live models, as that was rather unusual at the time. Instead they copied casts of ancient sculptures and

Cornelis van Haarlem, *The corporalship of the Haarlem Civic Guard's Hall*, 1583, oil on panel, 135 x 233 cm, Frans Hals Museum, Haarlem

modern bronzes of very muscular male nudes like the ones Willem van Tetrode, a sculptor from Delft, used to produce. Drawings and prints also served them as models. After Van Heemskerck's death, Cornelis got hold of his Roman sketchbook, which contained many sketches of ancient sculptures. The three artists were much impressed by the work of Bartholomeus Spranger, too, the court painter of Emperor Rudolf II in Prague, who had worked in Rome for years. Goltzius made prints from some of his mythological drawings.

Cornelis had a predilection for extremely gruesome scenes, probably in an attempt to rouse respectable citizens with his knowledge of classical culture. His painting *The Dragon Devouring the Companions of Cadmus* (1588, National Gallery, London) shows a scene from Ovid's *Metamorphoses*. Cornelis based it, amongst other things, on Van Heemskerck's *Torso Belvedere* in the Vatican, which would reappear in many of his figures with muscular backs. With the bitten-off head in the foreground, the picture could rival the bloodiest scenes from a modern science fiction film. Goltzius made an engraving of the painting and dedicated the print, 'as the first fruit of their partnership', to their common friend Jacob Rauwaert, a print lover and art dealer.

In the background of all the anatomical violence of Cornelis' *War of the Titans* (ca. 1588, Copenhagen) a tangle of falling bodies can be seen. Cornelis developed the motif in his print series *Four Falling Figures* (1588). The figures, brought down

Left: Hendrick Goltzius after Cornelis van Haarlem, *Fall of Ixion,* 1588, engraving, Prentenkabinet Museum Boijmans Van Beuningen, Rotterdam

Right: Cornelis van Haarlem, *Fall of Ixion,* ca. 1588, oil on canvas, 192 x 152 cm, Museum Boijmans Van Beuningen, Rotterdam

by their pride or sinfulness, are Phaeton, Tantalus, Icarus and the less well known Ixion, who was thrown out of heaven because he had tried to seduce the wife of Jupiter. Paintings on that subject existed as well, but only the *Fall of Ixion* has been preserved (Museum Boijmans, Rotterdam). Cornelius did not reserve his muscular nudes only for mythological representations. A print like *Cain slaying Abel* shows that the Bible, too, offered opportunity enough for what seemed almost to be Cornelis' obsession: the depiction of human figures in hopeless situations, from which, despite their physical strength, they cannot escape.

Working for the Stadholder and the Prince's Court in Haarlem (1590-1593)

Goltzius himself left for Italy towards the end of 1590 to study ancient art. In the meantime Cornelis had made such an impression with his new style that the commissions were pouring in. His *Massacre of the Innocents in Bethlehem* (1590) is a monumental composition in which unbelievably muscular naked male bodies carry out their murderous work in complicated positions amidst women fighting back, pale lifeless babies and babies that are only just alive. Because the subject demanded so much action and drama it was popular in the print art from the school of Raphael. Cornelis endeavoured to surpass all his predecessors by producing a painting with strong colours in gigantic format. Such cruelty, inflicted on defenceless women and children, was an unusual theme and will have been perceived as a form of realism by the Dutch public. Nonetheless, we can point to an example from antiquity of faces drawn by anguish: the agonised faces of Laocoön and his sons, the famous statue from the Vatican in Rome. There is a provocative motif here of which Cornelis' was particularly fond: a naked man in the foreground, kneeling, with his behind towards the viewer. It is thanks only to the refined use of shadow that we

Cornelis van Haarlem, *Massacre of the Innocents*, 1591, oil on canvas, 268 x 257 cm, Frans Hals Museum, Haarlem. Photo by Tom Haartsen

do not look straight at the man's pendulous sexual organs. Where bodybuilders are shown from the front their private parts are covered by a flimsy scarf. As it is mentioned in the inventory of the Oranges in the 18th century the painting was probably made for Naaldwijk Palace, which the States General put at the disposal of Stadholder Maurits.

Cornelis must have enjoyed success with this work, because shortly afterwards the burgomasters of Haarlem gave him an honourable commission to produce paintings for the walls of the Prince's Court, the residence where Stadholder Maurits stayed when he was in Haarlem. Cornelis had to make a new centrepiece to go with the two side panels of Van Heemskerck's *Drapers' Altarpiece* (1546) - which had been transferred from Saint Bavo's to the Prince's Court - as the middle had been lost during the Iconoclasm. Once again Cornelis opted for a *Massacre of the Innocents* (1591, Frans Hals Museum). The second version shows the same gruesome details and anatomical tours de force. The question is why anyone would come up with the idea of presenting a picture like this to Stadholder Maurits and his court. Probably we should see the Biblical massacre of innocents as an allegory for massacred innocence and King Herod, who ordered it, as the prototype of a tyrant. The tyranny of Philip II was still fresh in people's memories. Haarlem had had to withstand a long siege and plundering by the Spaniards and it was the task of Stadholder Maurits to continue to safeguard the Republic from despotism. So the paintings could be seen as a (very present) visual exhortation.

A second painting – even larger than the *Massacre of the Innocents* – was destined for Maurits' bedroom. It depicts the *Marriage of Peleus and Thetis* (1592/93). In the foreground naked gods and goddesses feast on fruit and drink. Ceres and Bacchus, entwined in the middle ground, catch the attention immediately, the symbol of delicious food and drink. The extremely muscular figure seen from the back in the left foreground is Vulcan. On the left Pan embraces a pale nymph. In the bottom right-hand corner a muse, lying in a rather daring pose, is served wine by Ganymedes. The muse to the left of her adds to the merriment by playing on her lute. Inconspicuous in the far background – a typical Mannerist trick – the bridal couple, the real subject, sit at table feasting.

Cornelis van Haarlem, *Nun and Monk,* 1591, oil on canvas, 116 x 103 cm, Frans Hals Museum, Haarlem. Photo by Tom Haartsen

This subject was not only chosen for its eroticism. For those who knew their classics this marriage was the start of much misery. Eris, the goddess of discord, who is flying away in the top left of the picture, had thrown a golden apple into the assembled company with the inscription 'for the most beautiful'. Paris, Prince of Troy and the only jury member in the beauty contest that followed (depicted in the right background), chose neither Juno, who promised him wealth, nor Minerva, who would give him wisdom. He chose Venus - or sensual love. In return she gave him the most beautiful woman on earth. Unfortunately, however, the beautiful Helen was already married. Her husband started the Trojan War, with dramatic consequences for all concerned. The lesson an erudite person might draw from this was mainly the importance of making the right choices.

A third painting, which Cornelis created for the Prince's Court and that hung above one of the doors, was a life-size *The Fall of Man* (1592, Frans Hals Museum). Adam and Eve are portrayed in graceful postures: ideal male and female beauties according to the ancient canon. Cornelius borrowed the composition from the famous engraver Albrecht Dürer. Apart from the pleasure that the nudes will have given, the violation of the commandment not to eat from the tree of knowledge can be interpreted as a warning here as well.

The burgomasters of Haarlem also bought Cornelis' *Nun and Monk* (1591) for the Prince's Court. This satire of a monk, who, under the influence of drink, pinches a young nun's naked breast, is highly appropriate for the stadholder's surroundings too. After all, Maurits was the figurehead of the Protestant faith, which had exposed the wrongdoings of the Catholic Church. It is typical that an attempt was made by a Haarlem city archivist in the 19th century to interpret the scene as a 'wonder', whereby wine instead of milk spurted from the nun's breast. That would prove that she was not pregnant as wicked tongues had claimed.

A real eye-catcher in a more homely environment will have been Cornelis' *Bathsheba* (1594). There is not a trace of King David. It is the viewer himself who acts as a voyeur, with a good view of the super white, naked Bathsheba sitting at the edge of a pool of water. Her feet are being carefully washed by a pitch black, naked servant helped by a white colleague. A bright yellow garment cast off by her lies provocatively in the foreground.

Cornelis' later period

It is not always an advantage, as a painter, to become so old. Cornelis had to make sure he kept up with all the developments in the art world, which was evolving incredibly fast at the beginning of the 17th century, especially in Haarlem. His later work is sometimes treated with a degree of pity. It looks as if he used up

Cornelis van Haarlem, *Marriage of Peleus and Thetis*, 1592/93, oil on canvas, 246 x 419 cm, Frans Hals Museum, Haarlem. Photo by Tom Haartsen

all his energy with the visual violence of his early years. But he himself must have recognised that the success he had enjoyed earlier was over. Apart from (group) portraits there was hardly any work for large-format artists. The Court of Orange-Nassau was not interested in giving commissions during that period. And which ordinary citizen would want that sort of dramatic scene on the wall? With the growth of a middle class that was eager to buy, it was small, less expensive decorative paintings – known as cabinet paintings - that became fashionable. Cornelis bravely tried to adapt to the new fashions and to a certain extent he was successful. He produced a number of small paintings showing Bible stories that made attractive wall decorations for both Catholics and Protestants. Even his *Juda and Tamar* (1596), a rather spicy Bible story after all, was very decent. The style is reminiscent of van Mander, but Cornelis is better as far as composition and use of colour are concerned. Cornelis also tried the modern genre of half-figures, with a preference for mythological or allegorical characters. Especially witty and original are the rather melancholy looking *Neptune and Amphitrite* amidst rare shells (1616/17). The panel is considered to be a *portrait historié*, showing the Haarlem textile dealer Jan Govertsz van der Aar as Neptune.

At the end of his life Cornelis tried painting scenes from everyday life, a genre that was very popular in Haarlem at the time. But the heads of his smoking, drinking peasants are still reminiscent of his idealised gods from earlier years. Sometimes Cornelis did not know when to stop. One or two years before his death – he died in 1638 – he repeated the sexually explicit pose of the Muse in his *Marriage of Peleus and Thetis* in a panel with (naked!) children playing marbles (1636/7, private collection). But this time he used the pose for a completely naked, barely pubescent girl. Would that not have caused offence then? Gods and goddesses are forgiven a great deal, but in ordinary people – and certainly children – something like that quickly looks dubious.

Cornelis' reputation in later years

That Cornelis was one of the top Dutch painters during the years 1583-1599 is clear from the prestigious commissions he obtained. In social terms he was successful too. He had many pupils and belonged to various associations. In 1603 he married a wealthy widow, a burgomaster's daughter who died a few years later. The painter did not marry a second time, but he did have a relationship with his housekeeper, with whom he fathered a daughter who was to become the mother of the artist Cornelis Bega. Contemporaries considered Cornelis 'exceptionally diligent' and praised his use of colour in particular. But Constantijn

Cornelis van Haarlem, *Neptune and Amphitrite,* 1616/17, oil on panel, 72 x 94.5 cm, P. and N. de Boer Fondation

Cornelis van Haarlem, *Bathsheba,* 1594,
oil on canvas, 77.5 x 64 cm, Rijksmuseum, Amsterdam

Huygens comments venomously in his biography that the painter can thank fortune that he was not born thirty years later, because his work at the end of his life was 'past it'.

It cannot be denied that it was with the exaggerated musculature of his early period that Cornelis won his spurs. Other painters, too, such as Utrecht-born Abraham Bloemaert and Joachim Wittewael, painted comparably dramatic scenes with nudes for a few years while they were under his influence, but were quick to revert again afterwards. It was exactly this extraordinarily Mannerist style that would later evoke distaste. The tragedy of all the Dutch artists who tried to introduce the modern style of the famous Michelangelo and the ancients into the North is that it really did not seem to fit into the canon of Dutch art as people had clung to it for centuries: typical Dutch landscapes, still-lifes and genre scenes apparently taken from very ordinary, everyday life. Inventive and experimental painters like Van Heemskerck and Cornelis van Haarlem were the victims of that. They were shunned for a long time as 'too international', which is exactly what these painters had tried so hard to become.

Interest in the sixteenth century Dutch Mannerists was only revived in the 1960s. In 1999 the recently deceased Pieter van Thiel published his comprehensive monograph on Cornelis van Haarlem. But the first retrospective of the painter was staged only in 2012, in the Frans Hals Museum in Haarlem, of course. A retrospective like this is important, because much of Cornelis' work is privately owned and had therefore never been seen before. Paintings from every period of the artist's life and all the corners of the world were brought together. To complete the retrospective it would have been interesting and useful if a selection of the graphics designed by Cornelis had been on view as well, or a small bronze nude by Van Tetrode, for example. The real bodybuilder demonstrating his art in the educational film in the room before the *Massacre of the Innocents* was a nice idea, but visitors could have thought that up for themselves too. ■

Translated by Lindsay Edwards

Writing is Gilding

The Monumental Oeuvre of A.F.Th. van der Heijden

[ARNOLD HEUMAKERS]

When A.F.Th. van der Heijden (Geldrop, 1951) debuted under the pseudonym Patrizio Canaponi with a short story in the literary magazine *De Revisor* early in 1978, it was immediately clear that this heralded an extraordinary talent. At the time, however, no one could have suspected what a remarkable writer he would become. Not satisfied with separate novels or stories, he set his work in one great, all-encompassing cycle (*De tandeloze tijd*, 'The toothless time') and, when that proved insufficient, coolly started work on a new cycle (*Homo duplex*) before the first was complete. So van der Heijden, who relinquished his pseudonym after a collection of stories and a novella, is working on two cycles simultaneously. Several parts of each have been published, amounting to thousands of pages in total.

It can be difficult for readers to keep pace and remember which is which. Nevertheless this ambitious body of work also exhibits remarkable coherence, traces of which can already be found in *Een gondel in de Herengracht* ('A Gondola in the Herengracht', 1978) and *De draaideur* ('The Revolving Door', 1979), the two books van der Heijden published as Patrizio Canaponi.

Anyone who has read the published parts of *De tandeloze tijd* will recognise events and anecdotes in the baroque, mannered stories of young Attilio Sandrini, showing that van der Heijden was already drawing on the same autobiographical source. Equally present, both in the stories and in the novel, are the writer's Oedipal obsessions, formally placed centre stage in *Homo duplex*, as the main character Movo (abbreviation of 'Moeilijke Voeten', 'Difficult Feet') is seen as a contemporary reincarnation of Sophocles' Oedipus. There is also an aestheticizing drive, which immediately emerges in the quasi-Italian setting with its southern glory and splendour. However humble reality turns out to be, literature lays a layer of gold on top. Writing is gilding.

Forming an alliance

This is how Attilio's grandmother sets about telling of her late husband in *Een gondel in de Herengracht*: 'His widow took everything that was black about him and sang it into the purest gold.' She spoke of Attilio's grandfather only

A.F.Th. van der Heijden (1951) © Klaas Koppe

in the 'noblest of poetry'. Gold is also the central metaphor in the description of Attilio's discovery of auto-erotica, when he stands in the attic in a 'pillar of sunlight', 'a column of pure gold dust', which completely fits him like a 'long, straight, sparkling dress'. The suggestion is unmistakeable: this unification with sunlight, associated with a 'pyramid' that serves to allow Attilio 'to reach the heights', refers not only to the 'small, sweet sin' of masturbation but also to the artistry symbolically awakened within the main character, who brings forth the first product of his imagination in the 'pearl' with which a number of rats' tails are sealed into a 'rat king'.

Van der Heijden himself playfully emphasises the coherence of his oeuvre, by making Patrizio Canaponi a character in the third part of *De tandeloze tijd.* In the reality of the novel he is called Patrick Gossaert, a writer of brilliant style but lacking content, who forms an alliance with Albert Egberts, the main character of the cycle. Albert, who sees his life as a continuous 'experiment', has material for stories in abundance. The result, as suggested by a characteristic baroque mirroring effect, is *De tandeloze tijd*.

This too belongs to a literary game, but it fits well with the shift that has taken place in van der Heijden's work since he began to publish under his own name. Through Albert Egberts, in many respects the writer's alter-ego, he returns to Geldrop in Brabant, the place he really comes from: the departure from the Italian guise appears to be coupled with a generous dose of realism. *De tandeloze tijd* describes the career of Albert Egberts, the son who is the first in his working class family to go to university (studying philosophy in Nijmegen) but who then moves down in the world to become a junkie in Amsterdam. In the later parts we also catch a glimpse of him after he has dried out in prison and made something of a name for himself as a playwright.

In his first cycle van der Heijden paints a panoramic picture, peopled with many characters besides the central figure, drawing on the great drama in the Netherlands after the Second World War, the transition from a class-based society to mass democracy with all the associated conflict, from workers' emancipation to depillarisation (*ontzuiling*) and from secularisation to urbanisation. In fifty years the Netherlands transformed (before mass-immigration brought new drama) and van der Heijden sketches the universally recognisable traits of this change. In the Canaponi books everything centres on a strictly personal literary mythology, in *De tandeloze tijd* he places his mythologizing tendencies (still clearly evident) in a story that concerns not only himself but his entire generation.

Events proceed with a grandeur and largesse that could only be called baroque. Mannerism may have retreated into the background as realism takes its toll – as a writer van der Heijden has in no way conformed to Dutch thrift. In a country where verbal reticence ('not a word too many') is often seen as a valuable quality, van der Heijden defines himself by wealth and abundance. His eloquence is a cornucopia, his descriptions impress with their expressive power, his words awaken a suggestion of overflowing reality, continually gilding it, however humble, ignominious and even outrageous it may be. Van der Heijden has not forgotten the lesson of Attilio's grandmother.

Turning mud into gold

This emerges almost programmatically in *Asbestemming* ('Ash Destination', 1994), the 'requiem' in the margin of *De tandeloze tijd*, which van der Heijden dedicates to his father, who died at the age of 67. We recognise the father from *De tandeloze tijd* again, an alcoholic domestic tyrant, someone who frequents the pub and lands his moped in the ditch blind drunk on more than one occasion. The portrait his son paints of him is humiliating, albeit not on a literary level; there the bond between father and son is confirmed. 'I was constantly making poetry of even the shabbiest aspects of him, worship without end,' says Albert of his father in *Vallende ouders* ('Falling Parents'). The same is true of *Asbestemming*. The more shameful and scandalous the father's behaviour, the greater the triumph of the son when he succeeds in making it something beautiful, even 'holy', revealing the personal need behind this poetry.

In *Vallende ouders* Albert Egberts speaks to his friend Flix of 'reforging, melting down into something beautiful which at the same time – intensifying – buries the memory of the horror inside'. This theme returns repeatedly. Like a second Baudelaire, van der Heijden continues to transform mud into gold. This is part of his own history, but changed into the material of his novels it symbolises the entire reality. Van der Heijden's aestheticism rests on a rather pessimistic view of humanity and the world, in which only literature with its 'alchemistic' magic power can offer a counterweight.

Behold the inherent ambition of van der Heijden's writing, continually haunted by a longing to write a 'humanly impossible' book that is all-encompassing, one which makes all books superfluous, to chime in with Gerard Reve. Van der Heijden emulates earlier examples such as Mallarmé's dream of *Le Livre*, or Jean Genet's cycle *La Mort*, which he never accomplished. The cyclic form of his own oeuvre, in which the One Impossible Book is effectively cut into pieces, should be seen as a cunning final attempt at that Impossible Book, a series which eventually turns out to be endless.

Life in breadth

In *De tandeloze tijd* this ambition finds its counterpart in Albert Egbert's ideal of 'life in breadth'. In the prologue of *De slag om de Blauwbrug* ('The Battle at the Blauwbrug') this notion of life in breadth is placed in contrast to life in length, as he writes of '*breadth*, where everything happened faster, there was more movement, no earthly time was lost: where all events happened simultaneously, instead of following one another, robbing one another of time'. The ideal exhibits a striking resemblance to what Jung called 'synchronicity' and the modernists of the early twentieth century term 'simultaneity'; it amounts to an attempt to capture as much reality as possible in its entirety and is therefore a good match for what van der Heijden hoped to achieve with his Impossible Book.

Within the cycle of the novel Albert Egberts does not achieve his ideal, except in the glow of his heroin addiction, a caricature of his original intention. But as a writer van der Heijden comes close to his aim, continually increasing the scale and narrative density of his novels. In the fourth part of *De tandeloze tijd*, *Advocaat van de hanen* ('Punk Lawyer'), the 'binge drinker' and lawyer Ernst Quispel joins Albert Egberts as a second lead character whose murky history runs in parallel to Albert's. In the third part, published shortly afterwards and consisting of two substantial halves, *Hof van barmhartigheid* ('Court of Mercy') and *Onder het plaveisel het moeras* ('Under the Pavement the Swamp'), that account turns into an overloaded 'polyphony' of voices and stories, from which van der Heijden cunningly cut and pasted to make a separate novel, *Doodverf* ('Death Paint'). Even before that, alongside the cycle, *De sandwich*, *Weerborstels* ('Rebels'), and *Het leven uit een dag* ('Life in One Day') were published as 'satellite books', showing how difficult it is, if not impossible, to encapsulate everything in a single unit.

Stopping time

We should not, therefore, be surprised that around the turn of the millennium van der Heijden started a second cycle alongside *De tandeloze tijd*. It shows that his ambition has only grown with time; in his essay about the novel *Kruis en kraai* ('Cross and Crow', 2008) he himself speaks openly of 'megalomania', even if its ultimate goal comprises nothing other than a 'monumental failure'. How could it be otherwise, when both 'life in breadth' and the Impossible Book are attempts to stop time, to escape from its teeth, one of the meanings of the title of van der Heijden's first cycle? This is where we should look for the real motivation behind his writing.

Of the eight to nine parts originally announced for the new cycle *Homo duplex*, four have now been published: an enormous 0th part, *De Movo Tapes*, and the even more voluminous *Het schervengericht* ('The Ostracism') not even mentioned in the original plan, as well as *Drijfzand koloniseren* ('Colonising Quicksand') and *Mim*, which are considerably more restrained in volume. It remains uncertain how the cycle will look in the end. Perhaps part of the reason van der Heijden began this new cycle was to go beyond the autobiographical framework of *De tandeloze tijd*. In *Homo duplex* Brabant seems remote; the narrator appears as the Greek god of light Apollo, although he can no longer bear this name, having 'sold out' to NASA. His task is to entertain the gods of Olympus by causing as much tragedy and misery on earth as possible.

In *De Movo Tapes* this results in a real war between Amsterdam and Rotterdam football hooligans, in *Het schervengericht* the action moves to California, where we witness a confrontation in prison between the French-Polish director Roman Polanski and Charles Manson, the leader of the sect that murdered Polanski's pregnant wife. It is worth noting that this confrontation is also mentioned in *Advocaat van de hanen*, as the subject of a play Albert Egberts has decided to write, so the two cycles are not entirely separate.

Homo duplex only began to take shape with the newly published parts. So far we know that at a certain point there must be a 'World Strike', a 'war of All against One', which must bring an end to human futility and the pointlessness of existence. In some sense this is a counterpart to what we find in Harry Mulisch's novel *De ontdekking van de hemel* (*The Discovery of Heaven*): instead of heaven withdrawing its hands from humanity, humanity tries to elicit a sign of life from heaven. 'I aspire to raise the need so high that even if no God ever existed, at that moment one *comes into* existence...', says the main character Tibbolt Satink, who, transformed into Movo, must proclaim the World Strike.

Death of a son

It all sounds quite bizarre, even over the top. We might wonder whether van der Heijden will ever succeed in making a convincing tragedy of these curious facts, worthy of Sophocles, if that is his aim at least. For the time being fate has thrown a spanner in the works, as in 2010 on the night of Whitsun, van der Heijden and his wife Mirjam Rotenstreich's only son Tonio died in a traffic accident. In an attempt to express his grief van der Heijden wrote the only 'requiem' he had probably expected never to have to write, *Tonio*. The 'monumental failure' that had always been his aim now became a real failure. Literature can keep the memory of the dead alive, but cannot bring the dead back to life. Van der Heijden needs the many pages of *Tonio*, full of shame and guilt because he was unable to prevent his son's death, the flipside of his megalomania, to distance himself as long as possible from this realisation. At the same time it comes ever closer as he tries to reconstruct the hours before the fatal accident in as much detail as possible. In van der Heijden's view Tonio's death throws a black shadow over everything he has written, and inevitably on what he has yet to write.

Has the writing lost its shine?

Since the death of his son the author has been showered with prizes, including the P.C. Hooftprijs in 2013, the Netherlands' most important literary prize. A new book also appeared for that occasion, a relatively short novel by van der Heijden's standards, *De helleveeg* ('The Shrew'), part of *De tandeloze tijd*, surprisingly, rather than *Homo duplex*, a sign that the first cycle still cannot be seen as complete. In the bibliography at the back of *De helleveeg* van der Heijden mentions two titles 'in preparation': a new part of *Homo duplex* and a historical novel. If we are to believe his expression of thanks for the P.C. Hooftprijs, however, he has yet to return to business as usual. The veil of guilt and shame which has covered everything since the death of his son (a feeling he describes with the neologism 'beshaming'), also determines the flavour of his new work. This is already clear in *De helleveeg*.

The aestheticizing force which previously characterised van der Heijden's writing is absent from this novel about a woman who goes through life embittered and full of venom. The literature no longer gilds, but grotesquely exaggerates the horror. *De helleveeg* is about child abuse, abortion and hypocrisy, pulled together to form a pitiless attack on the world of Catholic Brabant from which the writer comes. Although the novel is certainly no less well written than his earlier work, the transformation to a higher aesthetic plan still eludes him. Pessimism must stand alone, without its glittering counterweight. The writing has lost its shine. The extent to which the same is true of the parts of *De tandeloze tijd* and *Homo duplex* still to come is something we can only await in fear and trembling – and suspense. ■

Translated by Anna Asbury

Extract from *Falling Parents*

By A.F.Th. van der Heijden

Sometimes, when after a period of careless living and casual fasting I felt myself losing weight, I imagined that I had the fragile and languid quality of Thjum himself.

I was wrong. I was too broad-shouldered. My sturdy frame got in my way. Nothing seemed more ridiculous than someone with my shoulders in the role of a sickly youth. Thjum's build might have been able to make me the poet for which I was sometimes taken. My ribcage was too big for poetry...

Oh yes, I wanted to penetrate the world passionately, to *partake* of it instead of just being part of it. But at the same time I wished to remain the little angel, the immaculate boy, mummy's darling, in whose chops no character at all must be carved...

I wanted to penetrate the world, but not to be affected or eroded by it. Time should preferably pass me by toothlessly. And if there were really no alternative, I should be sucked like an acid drop, so that painlessly and imperceptibly slowly I gradually became less and less... and finally at the age of eighty or ninety disintegrated in blissful ignorance...

From *Falling Parents*
(*Vallende ouders*, *De tandeloze tijd 1*, Amsterdam, Querido, 1983)

Extract from *Movo Tapes*

By A.F.Th. van der Heijden

On the corner of Exilstraat two men were rummaging in full rubbish bags. Not fly-by-nights, they were working too systematically for that with their full-length kitchen gloves. Rubbish that had been put out a day too soon. They were mainly interested in the paperwork. Sometimes they studied an envelope and took it to a doorway to check the house number and nameplate. I cast a glance into the very heart of Western civilisation. Rooting around in people's rubbish on Sunday morning in order to retrieve the address of the woman who has put out her far from rat-proof bag at the wrong time.

Civilisation is... having a Secret Garbage Service brave the throwaway needles of diabetic patients, a comb caked with cradle cap, dog vomit in a newspaper, the toothbrush with shoe polish on it, the two-month miscarriage in a Tupperware lunchbox and the apple peel curled round cat poo, in order to make the local residents aware of their civilised obligations.

Civilisation is... enclosing the address wrapper sent to one of the neighbours with the rubbish before putting the rubbish bag out in the street two days too early.

The Dutch nose-picking monopoly. The ability to convince yourself that you are the only one who sneakily throws away a ball of paper or a piece of chewing gum in the street. Others more or less keep to the rules, nobody sees me anyway, and on a world scale it doesn't matter, no more than peeing in the swimming pool matters or a ball of snot under the kitchen table. A waste peel and box logic that is also strictly adhered to with regard to environmental legislation. Dumping used heating oil, or laboratory poison in all the colours of the rainbow, is rather like masturbating in secret. No one sees it, and what you get rid of you're done with. It was all taught us tacitly. By our educators, who every so often thought they were invisible, and still didn't know where to keep their hands.

Traces? 'It could just as well have been someone else.' That is how the murderer dumps his body, like a hard lump of snot that you stick to the bottom of the chair with its own slime.

From *Movo Tapes*

(*De Movo Tapes*, *Homo Duplex 0*, Amsterdam, Querido, 2003)

Translated by Paul Vincent

The Lost Highway

Journey along the Kortrijksesteenweg

The plan was to drive from Ghent to Kortrijk on the old Kortrijksesteenweg. There was no reason to do it, none at all. It makes much more sense to take the E17 motorway, which will get you there in 26 minutes if there are no delays. But on the way you see nothing. You miss almost everything that is interesting. So, choosing the road less travelled, I programmed the satellite navigation to take me to Kortrijksesteenweg 1, Ghent, the start of the road.

0 km

A curved white neoclassical building stands on the corner. The ground floor is occupied by a restaurant named La Rotonde that had seating around a circular bar. It was too early for lunch, so I programmed a new destination into the satellite navigation and set off back down the road. 'Continue on the present route', said the pleasant female voice.

1 km

Ghent's Kortrijksesteenweg is a grand nineteenth-century boulevard lined with town houses in various eclectic styles. They keep their secrets well hidden behind solid walls, but occasionally a dusty bronze plaque will reveal something about the inner life of the street. The house at Kortrijksesteenweg 128 offers one of those rare insights. 'Miss Edith Cavell,' reads the plaque. 'The glorious victim of German barbarity was secretly harboured in this house in April 1915.'

Her profile is etched on the plaque. She looks like a strict, determined woman, a forerunner of Margaret Thatcher. 'The lady is not for turning', you could well imagine her saying to her German captors. As I walked back to the car, I wondered what secret mission had brought Edith Cavell to the Kortrijksesteenweg in April 1915. But it had to remain a mystery. The road was all that mattered for the moment.

After ducking under the railway line, the steenweg to Kortrijk skirts a residential quarter called the Miljoenenkwartier, the Millionaires' Quarter. It was developed as the site of the 1913 Ghent World Fair because of its location close to the new Sint-Pieters Station, and later became a fashionable residential district. I took a quick look at the quarter, hoping to find something like the mad delirium of Cogels-Osylei in Antwerp, but Ghent's millionaires seemed to prefer a dull historical architecture.

3.5 km

As it leaves the city, the Kortrijksesteenweg becomes straight and wide with two lanes of traffic in each direction. Marked on maps as the N43, this is a national highway, one of the straight four-lane roads built in the 1930s. But these routes became obsolete in the 1960s when the faster, safer motorways came along.

The old routes were abandoned, left to decay. They have become back roads with their own memories. They are the roads that the Canadian jeeps drove down in 1944 to liberate Ghent, the routes along which families went on holiday in the 1960s. They shaped history for a couple of decades and then lost almost all significance.

You could see them now as museums of travel with their streamlined Art Deco architecture and slender Atom age street lamps. Or you might view them as places where utopian dreams have gone sour.

So a journey down the N road is a lesson in history. You slip back five decades in the time it takes the satellite navigation voice to instruct you to take the second exit at the next roundabout.

6 km

Most of the houses along the steenweg look as if they were put up in the 1930s when this was a fashionable place to live. They were designed in a streamlined brick modernism that was popular at the time in Belgium. They are now a bit crumbing and neglected, because no one wants to live here anymore.

These days houses are surrounded by hypermarkets, car showrooms, furniture warehouses, the architecture of late twentieth-century consumerism. You can find everything you need on this road. But it might still leave you wanting something more.

7km

One of the houses looks a bit strange. You slow down to take a look. The walls are painted pink. A neon sign reads Tropical. Beside it, the word Parking in large red letters. The house next door has a heart-shaped sign with the invitation Kiss Me.

These are roadside brothels, drive-in sex clubs. The highway to Kortrijk is lined with them. There are apparently more than 35 along the 41-kilometre route linking Ghent and Kortrijk, or almost one brothel for every kilometre of road.

Many of these places have English names, like The Dolls and The Cotton Club. Others are French, like the aristocratic Madame Du Barry and L'Emeraude, or they have names that do not fit neatly into any recognisable language, like Gl'amour. But the bar owners seem to shy away from Dutch language names, as if these places are not truly part of the territory. They lie across a border, even if it is an invisible ethical one.

A handwritten sign had been placed on an empty bar stool in the window of the Tropical. Demande Serveuses, it says. But only in French. It seems that strict language rules do not apply when recruiting waitresses along the Kortrijk road.

7.2 km

I pulled off the road to take a photograph of the O'Bar. It was a strange isolated house with black walls, symmetrical windows and two giant pink flower-pots. It was the sort of house a child of six would draw, one window on either side of the door. But it had an underlying sense of menace. It seemed like a place where dreams could easily turn into nightmares.

It was still morning and the place was closed, but you could see into the front windows. Two steel-framed bar chairs with leopard-skin padded seats were placed in the window. A sign pointed to the back of the house where clients were offered 'discreet parking'.

I have talked to people from Ghent about this strange road that leads to temptation. No one finds it scandalous. Some even enjoy driving down the road at night just to look at the strange row houses lit up in purple and pink neon. 'I take all my visitors there,' one local told me.

The Flemish film-maker Felix Van Groeningen shot his debut film Steve + Sky along this strip. The film charts the tormented relationship between Steve, who is trying to go straight after coming out of jail, and Sky, a dancer in a night club on the Kortrijksesteenweg.

It is filmed mostly at night as Steve cruises the strip in search of motorbikes to steal. The action is framed by brash sex bars, brightly-lit petrol stations and gaudy Chinese restaurants. It makes the steenweg look sexy, the Las Vegas of the Low Countries.

Van Groeningen is not alone in his obsession. The photographer Thomas de Bruyn has taken strange eerie photographs of the brothels along the route and the Ghent folk singer Berlaen released his first song accompanied by a video filmed in one of the brothels.

Despite the glowing neon and the exotic names, the clubs look sad and tragic places. Many seem to have closed down for good, like Club Le Rose Garden's,

which once entertained clients in a strange isolated modernist house with two circular windows. It now lies empty and abandoned, the neon sign slowly disappearing under ivy. A fitting punishment, some might argue, for Le Rose Garden's errant apostrophe.

8 km

The presence of this sex strip seems all the more strange when you turn down one of the side roads. For you immediately find yourself driving along leafy rural roads lit by old wooden lampposts that look as if they might be relics of the eighteenth century. It is as if you have gone from 2014 to 1714 in the time it takes to change down a gear.

I drove for a while through this idyllic countryside, past old farmhouses with horses in the fields, huge villas with neatly clipped hedges and old country houses. The landscape looks as if it has hardly changed since Emiel Claus painted his cows. The only modern touch is the black BMW 4X4 in my rear mirror nudging me to drive faster.

10 km

At some point on the road through Sint-Martens-Latem, the name changes to Xavier de Cocklaan, commemorating a local artist who painted the flat countryside around Sint-Martens-Latem. It then becomes Emiel Clauslaan as the roadside sprawl of Sint-Martens-Latem comes to an end and open farmland stretches off to the low Flemish horizon. The next village is Astene where in 1883 the painter Emile Claus settled in a villa called Zonneschijn, or Sunshine.

After Astene the highway goes through another identity change that turns it into Dorpstraat. It then becomes Kapellestraat, then Gentsesteenweg, followed

by Kortrijkstraat and finally, just beyond the roundabout on the edge of Deinze, back to Kortrijksesteenweg.

The N43 is well-maintained for a Belgian N road. Even the bus shelters look immaculate. They are De Lijn's latest design with bright yellow stripes on the windows and blue benches. No one has smashed the glass so far. But then no one ever seems to wait for a bus in this part of Flanders.

19 km

A side road off the N43 leads to the village of Machelen-aan-de-Leie, where the painter Roger Raveel lived until his death in 2013. His works can be seen in a beautiful white museum designed by the Ghent architect Stéphane Beel in 1999. The Raveel Walk takes you from here down to a bend in the River Leie and along an old country path. It feels as if nothing has changed here in a hundred years, though if you stand still long enough you can hear traffic rumbling along the E17.

On the edge of the village, a French flag flaps lazily in the breeze. It marks a French military cemetery from the First World War with row after row of simple crosses. The 750 soldiers who lie buried in Machelen died in the final weeks of the war, in October and November 1918, many of them buried under Islamic headstones. No one now seems to remember these Muslim soldiers far from home who died to liberate Ghent.

20 km

Even if the occasional bus passes, the Kortrijksesteenweg was built for the car. It represents a utopian dream where you can live your entire life on the road. You even see shiny bread automats at the side of the road where you can stop to pick up a fresh loaf on the way home.

The car is rapidly losing its appeal in cities like Ghent and Kortrijk where pedestrian zones are becoming increasingly popular. But out on the Kortrijk highway it is still 1966. The road is the place to be, the car still as an object of desire. The route is lined with shiny glass car showrooms selling expensive brands like Porsche, BMW and Harley Davidson. The Ferrari showroom is the most spectacular on the strip with sleek yellow models displayed behind huge glass windows.

25 km

The people who live near the N47 maintain perfectly manicured front gardens although they never seem to use them. The gardens are decorated with sculptures that sometimes seem quite bizarre. They come from large garden centres like the one specialising in Italian Renaissance replicas on the outskirts of Sint-Martens-Latem where a fake Michelangelo's David costs 237 euros according to the label tied around his neck.

Another place outside Harelbeke has a vast garden that has a hint of Hieronymus Bosch's Garden of Earthly Delights. Here you can pull off the road to buy a life-size elephant, or a bust of a French philosopher, or a classical temple, or three children astride a tortoise. Anything you want, you can find it on the N43.

30 km

The road runs straight through the centre of Zulte, passing a modern roadside hotel with a large blue sign on the roof that reads HOTEL-CAFÉ while a smaller sign above the entrance says RALLYE. I went into the bar to see if I could find out more about the Rallye. Several old men were sitting at the counter, smoking and drinking Stellas. It was not yet 11.30, but they looked as if they had settled down for the day.

The Café Rallye stood here up until 1971 when the building was demolished to widen the road. But the road expansion never happened, so the hotel-café built in the 1970s sits on a quiet side road set back from the N43.

I picked up a copy of the local newspaper. The main news story involved a plan by Zulte council to carry out some road repairs. An incident in Kortrijk was treated like foreign news. A story from Antwerp might as well have happened on a different planet.

Flanders is like that. It sometimes seems as if everyone is driving on fast roads and at other times as if no one ever intends to move from their favourite stool at the bar.

42 km

Omleiding. Diversion. My heart always sinks when I see that sign. It means that I might as well give up trying to get to the destination, because there is never going to be another sign to direct me back to the route. But it is not always such a disaster to be diverted. Sometimes you come across some hidden feature that you would otherwise never find. That is how I came to step inside the most

extraordinary modern church I have ever seen in Belgium. It is dedicated to St Rita, the patron saint of the impossible, and looks from the outside like a giant lemon squeezer. The interior of this vast concrete structure is filled with an astonishing baroque light that streams through a round window in the roof.

39 km

Back on the road, I was nearing the end of the road trip when I glimpsed a statue of a caribou perched on a rock beside the road. I couldn't stop to look at it more closely because it was standing next to a busy junction. But I found out later that it was a relic of the First World War commemorating soldiers from Newfoundland who had died in Belgium. Otherwise I might have thought it came from the garden sculpture centre down the road.

41 km

I was almost there. The road was no longer called the Kortrijksesteenweg. It was now the Gentsesteenweg. 'You have arrived at your destination', the satellite navigation voice announced.

It did not look like a destination, so I drove on into Kortrijk and parked on a square next to the site of the Battle of the Golden Spurs. I walked through a little park and came eventually to a narrow passage leading into the Begijnhof.

This was more like it. The Begijnhof is a perfect little community with narrow cobbled lanes and old whitewashed brick houses. The last Beguine died a few years ago, but the place still has a religious stillness. It represents a different way of moving, not in a fast car, not in a straight line, but slowly, more thoughtfully. It felt like the end of a journey, a place to stop for a while. ■

All photos by Derek Blyth

Misanthropes, Boring Assholes and Amoral Winners

The Literary Work of Herman Koch

[JEROEN VULLINGS]

It is exceptional for a writer from a small language region to break through in the United States, but Dutch writer, TV producer and actor Herman Koch (1953) has done just that. Never before has a novel originally written in Dutch risen so high on the American bestseller list.

Looking back, in the comfortable tradition of the successful, there is only one success story: that of the continuous rise, without hitch or setback. Not so for Koch. In the course of his literary career he has had to work hard for this, picking himself up after many a fall to re-enter the fray. He debuted almost silently in 1985 with the collection of stories *De voorbijganger* (The Passerby), and achieved some success with his novel about angry adolescents, *Red ons, Maria Montanelli* (Save us, Maria Montanelli, 1989), but after that it was some time before the publication of *Het diner* (*The Dinner*) in 2009 brought Koch to a large readership. In the preceding decade he wrote four novels, and many stories, without arousing significant interest.

Koch could have commanded that success much earlier if he had picked the easy route. As co-creator and actor in the innovative, satirical TV programme *Jiskefet* (1990-2005) – in the tradition of *Monty Python* – he became a popular Dutch celebrity. Had he produced literary work resembling *Jiskefet*, the masses would have devoured his books.

But his literary work was not about vanity, and he refused to play the clown. His prose was reserved for the serious, anguished, solitary Herman Koch. *Red ons, Maria Montanelli* came across as a spontaneous, accessible, youthful work, but in his next (negligible) book *Eindelijk oorlog* (War at Last, 1996), Koch exhibited quite the opposite of naivety – rather a hyperconsciousness, as if the leaden prose could prevent the author being identified with the types he satirised so hilariously in *Jiskefet:* nasty men, sly sadists, sniggering practical jokers, suspiciously pernickety inspectors, inhumanly formal superintendents.

In the satirical novel *Eten met Emma* (Eating with Emma, 2000) too, that hyperconsciousness undermines the urgency of the narrative. Yes, his prose up to then had known many good scenes, the dialogues were well-timed, the style precise, but it didn't quite form a compositional and thematic whole. Too fickle to restrict himself to the novel form, I thought at the time.

Herman Koch (1953)
© Klaas Koppe

Finding a balance

I adjusted that view after the publication of the novel *Odessa Star* (2003). There Koch presents the misanthrope Fred, who, beyond his hatred for others (his invalid elderly neighbour from downstairs, his brother-in-law or his former French teacher) despises what he himself has become: a boring member of the middle class. He prefers the scenes of gangster films to life with wife and son in his terraced house, scenes which give his existence that special glow. He sees his chance when at the cinema he bumps into a friend from his youth, Max G., now a glamorously infamous criminal. Fred immediately imposes himself on Max.

Koch had rich material in his hands there, familiar to us from gangster films. Childhood friends, one from the underworld, the other from the straight world, pick up where they left off after years apart. Who turns out 'good' and who 'bad'? What better setting could you wish for? Add to that the fact that Max is modelled on Dutch mafia boss Klaas Bruinsma (1953-1991), nicknamed 'de Dominee' ('the Reverend'), who still appeals to the imagination.

But in this novel again Koch's hyperconsciousness rears its head. He could not simply write an entertaining page-turner. Perhaps he was bored by the lack of depth. That, at least, would explain his almost irrepressible tendency towards satire, repeatedly undermining the authenticity of his realistic story. *Odessa Star* is told from Fred's perspective; Max has been murdered in the meantime and Fred is looking back. It is the choice for Fred's perspective that causes trouble for *Odessa Star*: Fred is too Jiskefet. For pages we share in his hatred of elderly Belgians plundering hotel buffets, people with Down's syndrome who, in his opinion, should be put away, and English tourists with their preference for greasy junk food. In *Odessa Star* the Fred-&-Max intrigue shifts into the background, destroying the intended suspense.

Koch's big problem as a writer was now exposed: he needed to find a balance. His brand remained diffuse. His handicap was that he was too intelligent, thought too abstractly to tell a story straight, to write a 'light' novel. The big question was how to proceed.

Koch's salvation from this destructive hyperconsciousness is simple: he must limit himself, keep his subject small, not go off at a tangent. He did this in his novel *Denken aan Bruce Kennedy* (Thinking of Bruce Kennedy, 2009), limiting himself in his choice of subject, but at the same time immersing himself in the finest details of a woman's life. Miriam is the wife of sidetracked Dutch director Bernhard Wenger, who is the only one who believes religiously in his talent. That would make him at worst a sad case, were it not for the fact that he is cursed with virulent jealousy towards anyone more successful. Koch wisely leaves it ambiguous whether Miriam's plight is due to the difficult task of living with Bernhard, or to depression. The fact is that she has made a run for it, to spend a week recovering by herself in a hotel in southern Spain. There she meets 68-year-old star Bruce Kennedy, a contemporary of actors such as Clint Eastwood, a living alcoholic film legend. A love affair begins, the home front laments, but then Bruce dies. Miriam returns home after his death, leaving the message of this moving novel clear, as in a striking, old-fashioned parable about modern human life: against the background of personal disasters such as cancer and death, vague relational discontent does not amount to much. Koch was now a fully fledged writer, but still almost no one could see it.

Instinct wins over morals

That changed with *The Dinner*. The novel is deceptive from the outset: the first person narrator Paul appears as a rather stiff figure, referring very properly to 'my wife'. A stickler for details, moreover, who takes pleasure in explaining at length that his spouse's name is Marie Claire, but that because of the magazine of the same name she prefers Claire. The structure of the novel follows the stages of a dinner, from aperitif through to tip. The reader prepares for the worst: a whole evening in the company of a bore like that; in familiar Kochian idiom, an asshole – gives you the creeps.

But Paul Lohman turns out to be a fascinating, nasty piece of work, cursed with a good dose of malevolence and no stranger to violent fantasy. The tension lies in the fact that two married couples with little to say to one another must spend an entire evening in conversation. Wolfing their food down in silence is not an option. They need to talk, as we know from the start.

The other couple, Paul's brother Serge and his wife Babette, are a source of further tension. Babette enters in tears: a row. The fact that Paul cannot stand Serge, the opposition leader and a dead cert for new prime minister, is not conducive to the desired atmosphere of serenity at the table. Koch feeds us slowly, moving from one ominous announcement to another shameful situation, inside the increasingly claustrophobic universe of *The Dinner*.

It is as if the merest breath of wind might knock over the pieces on the chessboard: Serge's flirting with the clumsy waitress; the manager who repeatedly moves his fingers too close to the food as he introduces the dishes; an intrusive fellow diner who wishes to immortalise his daughter in a photo with Serge; lengthy incoming and outgoing telephone calls at the table during dinner.

Of course the story comes to us through Paul, and we are given more and more reason to doubt his reliability. The fantasy of punching the manager in the teeth, for instance, appears to come from a volcanic mind, which might erupt periodically. Paul apparently threatened a bicycle maker with a pump in the presence of his own eight-year-old son Michel; he beat up the headmaster who did not like Michel's project about taking the law into one's own hands; he apparently hit Serge over the head with a frying pan, and so on. It is difficult to distinguish fantasy from reality, but the increasingly frequent, nonchalant mentions that Paul has been suspended from his job as a history teacher and has not been taking his medication for some time have a disconcerting effect.

Together all these carefully arranged fragments make the tightly plotted novel *The Dinner* completely compelling; the reader is witness to a personal disaster on the point of completion. On another level, however, this tense relationship between the brothers might be seen to stand for the cleft between citizen and politician: an opposition leader without solutions versus the dissatisfied, assertive, even explosive electorate.

Koch limited himself in *Denken aan Bruce Kennedy*; here he achieves the same effect with a small group. We find ourselves inside Paul's sick head and through him in the heads of Serge, Babette and Claire as well, as he registers and interprets their verbal and non-verbal responses. We even see inside Michel, Paul and Claire's adolescent son, who along with his cousin (Serge and Babette's son) has an act of senseless violence on his conscience: the nocturnal molestation and immolation of a homeless woman, filmed by the boys, in the spirit of the age, with a mobile phone. An event no parent expects – certainly not if he's a prominent candidate at election time.

The plot proceeds through the courses, but the essence of *The Dinner* is the question: how far would you go as a parent to protect your child? A long way, says Koch's unpredictable, amoral novel. Instinct wins over morals.

How to get away with the crime

What does an alchemist do when, after decades of stirring the cauldron, he knows the secret of making gold? Keeps stirring, probably, to produce the highest carat and transform the associated softness into hardness. After the international bestseller *The Dinner* Koch did something along these lines. In *Summerhouse with Swimming Pool* (*Zomerhuis met zwembad*, 2011) he has refined his method. How? He skips the foreplay. In the first chapter, as he sketches the line of the story and presentation of the main character (misanthropic family doctor Marc Schlosser) there is mention of the suspected murder of a patient (famous actor Ralph Meier) and a case with the medical disciplinary board. A thriller, the reader realises.

The main character's early confession gives Koch the chance to exploit the tension to the full. His affiliation with the thriller genre dictates that he build suspense into every scene and close every chapter with a cliff-hanger. But the formidable tension in *Summerhouse with Swimming Pool* rests mainly in what we do not know. What is Doctor Marc capable of? What does depraved actor Ralph have on his conscience? Will Marc's affair with Ralph's wife Judith continue, will it be discovered, and if so, when? Will Marc's 13-year-old daughter's hormones play up? Is Ralph's 15-year-old son Alex a culprit too? Is Marc's wife Caroline up to no good either? What is the dark role played by Ralph's family friend, famous film director Stanley Forbes? Because there is so much we do not know, every scene is crucial and every word counts, as a clue, oracle or omen. Continually wrong-footing us and then turning out right after all, inserting fragments of truth everywhere, Koch's thriller is Hitchcock and situation comedy in one. That's the way to make a page-turner.

But for a book to be a page-turner the characters must also be interesting. Koch uses four methods to suck the reader into the life of his characters.

One: they rest on past success. Recycled success. Marc is a version of the father from *The Dinner* (2009), whose moral dilemma was: would you go so far for your child as to deny their crime, cover it up and become an accomplice yourself? In *Summerhouse with Swimming Pool* this dilemma is resumed and logically continued: would you go so far as to kill for your child?

Actor Ralph is the prototypical successful baby boomer characteristic of Koch's prose. Everything comes to him easily, and he gets away with everything. Americanised Dutchman Stanley is a resurrected Bruce Kennedy, the mythical film star from *Denken aan Bruce Kennedy*. Stanley's function in the story is to bring the reader into contact with a glamorous, glossy world he otherwise would not have access to. The story effect.

Two: the larger than life effect. The writer must offer readers familiarity – to some degree – but not the mess or incompleteness of their own existence. Peeking in on interesting neighbours is much more fun. You introduce readers into a world of power: the doctor has power over others, even over life and death. We see into his head, hearing our real chances of survival and his cynical thoughts about patients and their conditions. Such insights and grim prognoses are not what you hear in your average four-minute chat with your own doctor. Doctor Koch supplies them. Marc's friendship with Ralph takes him (and the reader) into the world of Dutch glamour. Ralph brings us into the homes of the artistic elite, even Stanley, who makes international series for the Dutch television channel, HBO. Stanley takes us to Hollywood. He is the man who can make and break everything, just as lawless and amoral as Marc – an echo of Koch's flirtation with super-villains in *Odessa Star*.

Three: the attraction of evil. None of the characters are really good. By far the most interesting is Marc, who, instead of conforming to prevailing moral standards, takes the law into his own hands, deliberately settling the score. His child is more important than the rule of law, his own interest or that of society. He does not care about democratic decisions and legal procedures; he trusts no one, least of all government authority. He may be a megalomaniac with a god complex, a common trait in doctors and teachers, but it is more than that. His type is always present in Koch's work, but the changing political times accentuate his profile. Doctor Marc appeals to the populist uprising and social unease of current times. Seen in this light he is the strong man who imposes order, outside the elite of the Randstad region, political regents and government. He could not care less about their standards, values and the contemporary culture of affected moral perfection, of solidarity and condescension.

Robust malevolence suits this type of character, propped up by Marc's biological and social Darwinian convictions. Malevolence towards the 'boring asshole', the nobody with his mortgage payments, with whom women become involved quite unromantically when their biological clocks start ticking, the kind of dimwit that nice girls and fading older women end up with. These ostensibly insignificant, resoundingly witty passages have a message, drawing the line between winners and losers. Koch's characters are winners, great winners with successful children. Even the victims in this book are elevated above the losers. The reader persists in the hope of unravelling the secret of the winner's success.

Four: age-old stereotypes work their magic. Such as the myth of the false innocence of young girls (who turn out smarter than originally assumed) and the myth of the needy, naïve woman. Women are weak, oblivious to what is happening, lacking in self-control, and useless in an emergency. *Summerhouse with Swimming Pool* is about the supremacy of the macho man: he is terrible, but he defends his wife and daughters like no other against the wolves at the door. A right-minded, refined, soft family man would not do that: he would run away and call the (corrupt) southern European police. Doctor Marc on the other hand commits murder to restore order. Koch's thriller teaches us not only how to restore your existence outside the law, but also how to get away with crime. All that time, due to Koch's choice of intimate narrative perspective, you empathise with a scoundrel who appeals to the most primitive in men. After all, he stands for the rightness of evolution. His life is no romanticised existence outside middle-class conventions. No, he is a middle-class outlaw, someone who could just as well be your neighbour. Ordinary, but with the power to move things his way.

All together it seems Koch has found the perfect mix. ■

Translated by Anna Asbury

FURTHER READING

De voorbijganger (The Passerby, stories, 1985)
Red ons, Maria Montanelli (Save Us, Maria Montanelli, novel, 1989)
Eindelijk oorlog (War at Last, novel, 1996)
Eten met Emma (Eating with Emma, novel, 2000)
Odessa Star (novel, 2003)
Denken aan Bruce Kennedy (Thinking of Bruce Kennedy, novel, 2005)

The Dinner, translated by Sam Garrett,
Atlantic Books, London, 2013;
Hogarth/Crown/Random House, New York, 2013
(*Het diner*, 2009)

Summerhouse with Swimming Pool,
translated by Sam Garrett, Hogarth/Crown/Random House, New York, 2014
(*Zomerhuis met zwembad*, 2011)

An Extract from *Summer House with Swimming Pool*

By Herman Koch

I am a doctor. My office hours are from eight-thirty in the morning to one in the afternoon. I take my time. Twenty minutes for each patient. Those twenty minutes are my unique selling point. Where else these days, people say, can you find a family doctor who gives you twenty minutes? – and they pass the information along. He doesn't take on too many patients, they say. He makes time for each individual case. I have a waiting list. When a patient dies or moves away, all I have to do is pick up the phone and I have five new ones to take their place.

Patients can't tell the difference between time and attention. They think I give them more attention than other doctors. But all I give them is more time. By the end of the first sixty seconds I've seen all I need to know. The remaining nineteen minutes I fill with attention. Or, I should say, with the illusion of attention. I ask all the usual questions. How is your son/daughter getting along? Are you sleeping better these days? Are you sure you're not getting too much/too little to eat? I hold the stethoscope to their chests, then to their backs. Take a deep breath, I say. Now breathe out nice and slow. I don't really listen. Or at least I try not to. On the inside, all human bodies sound the same. First of all, of course, there's the heartbeat. The heart is blind. The heart pumps. The heart is the engine room. The engine room only keeps the ship going, it doesn't keep it on course. And then there are the sounds of the intestines. Of the vital organs. An overburdened liver sounds different from a healthy one. An overburdened liver groans. It groans and begs. It begs for a day off. A day to deal with the worst of the garbage. The way things are now, it's always in a hurry, trying to catch up with itself. The overburdened liver is like the kitchen in a restaurant that's open around the clock. The dishes pile up. The dishwashers are working full tilt. But the dirty dishes and caked-on pans only pile up higher and higher. The overburdened liver hopes for that one day off that never comes. Every afternoon at four-thirty, five o'clock (sometimes earlier), the hope of that one day off is dashed again. If the liver's lucky, at first it's only beer. Beer passes most of the work along to the kidneys. But you always have those for whom beer alone isn't enough. They order something on the side: a shot of gin, vodka or whisky. Something they can knock back. The overburdened liver braces itself, then finally ruptures. First it grows rigid, like an overinflated tire. All it takes then is one little bump in the road for it to blow wide open.

I listen with my stethoscope. I press against the hard spot, just beneath the skin. Does this hurt? If I press any harder, it will burst open right there in my office. Can't have that. It makes an incredible mess. Blood gushes out in a huge wave. No general practitioner is keen to have someone die in his office. At home, that's a different story. In the privacy of their own homes, in the middle of the night, in their own beds. With a ruptured liver, they usually don't even make it to the phone. The ambulance would get there too late anyway.

My patients file into my practice at twenty-minute intervals. The office is on the ground floor. They come in on crutches and in wheelchairs. Some of them are too fat, others are short of breath. They are, in any case, no longer able to climb stairs. One flight of stairs would kill them for sure. Others only imagine it would: that their final hour would sound on the first step. Most of the patients are like that. Most of them have nothing wrong with them. They moan and groan, make noises that would make you think they found death staring them in the face every moment of the day, they sink into the chair across from my desk with a sigh – but there's nothing wrong with them. I let them reel off their complaints. It hurts here, and here, sometimes it spasms down to here... I do my best to act interested. Meanwhile, I doodle on a scrap of paper. I ask them to get up, to follow me to the examination room. Occasionally I'll ask someone to undress behind the screen, but most of the time I don't. All human bodies are horrible enough as it is, even with their clothes on. I don't want to see them, those parts where the sun never shines. Not the folds of fat in which it is always too warm and the bacteria have free rein, not the fungal growths and infections between the toes, beneath the nails, not the fingers that scratch here, the fingers that rub there until it starts to bleed... Here, doctor, here's where it itches really badly... No, I don't want to see. I pretend to look, but I'm thinking about something else. About a roller coaster in an amusement park, the car at the front has a green dragon's head mounted on it, the people throw their hands in the air and scream their lungs out. From the corner of my eye I see moist tufts of pubic hair, or red, infected bald spots where no hair will ever grow again, and I think about a plane exploding in the air, the passengers still belted to their seats as they begin a mile-long tumble into eternity: it's cold, the air is thin, far below the ocean awaits. It burns when I pee, doctor. Like there are needles coming out... A train explodes just before it enters the station, the space shuttle Columbia shatters into millions of little pieces, the second jet slams into the South Tower. It burns, here, doctor. Here...

You can get dressed now, I say. I've seen enough. I'll write you a prescription. ■

Translated by Sam Garrett

From *Summerhouse with Swimming Pool,* Hogarth/Crown/Random House, New York, 2014
(*Zomerhuis met zwembad,* Anthos, Amsterdam, 2011)

Thanksgiving Came Via Leiden

The Influence of Holland on the Pilgrim Fathers

[DIRK VANDENBERGHE]

It is well known that the American tradition of Thanksgiving originated with the Pilgrim Fathers. Less well-known, however, is that the inspiration for that feast came from the Dutch city of Leiden. Indeed, the Pilgrims' brief stay there was responsible for a number of Dutch influences on modern America.

Strolling through the narrow streets behind St Peter's Church in Leiden one might suddenly end up in the William Brewster alley. Similarly, in Plymouth, Massachusetts, when walking from the Pilgrim Memorial State Park to the First Parish of Plymouth, the easiest route is via Leyden Street. It is the town's oldest street where the early colonists once built their wooden houses.

These street names bear witness to an aspect of history which is increasingly being forgotten, namely that the English Pilgrims, who set sail in 1620 for the north-east coast of America in the Mayflower and established a colony there, made an important detour via the Dutch city of Leiden. Their stay lasted for scarcely twelve years, but it has exerted a strong influence on American culture right up to the present day, and not only in the feast of Thanksgiving. For, although the English Pilgrim Fathers did not leave many traces behind in Holland, they did take several Dutch customs and practices with them to the other side of the Atlantic.

Scrooby

Already by the end of the sixteenth century, English Calvinists, who were unhappy about what they regarded as the lax attitude of Queen Elizabeth and the Anglican Church towards Rome, were leaving for the Netherlands. In contrast to the Puritan reformers they were seen as separatists, who had broken completely with the Church of England. These separatists were led by the Reverend Robert Browne from Cambridge who, in fear of persecution for himself and his followers, known as Brownists, fled to Middelburg in 1578.

As pressure on the small religious community increased in England and those who distributed anti-Anglican pamphlets risked being murdered, growing numbers fled to the more tolerant Netherlands. A community from the village of Scrooby in the county of Nottinghamshire attempted unsuccessfully to escape to Amsterdam in 1607. They were betrayed by the ship's captain and imprisoned. A year later some of them did finally make their way to the continent, though not to Amsterdam but to the somewhat quieter Leiden, then Holland's second city. A couple of months later even their imprisoned members were allowed to leave for the Netherlands, since they had been so clever as to take the precaution of disposing of all their possessions, leaving nothing for the authorities but the expense of their imprisonment. One of their leaders, William Brewster, started a small clandestine printing business and contributed to the spread of forbidden books in England. The alley where his printing shop stood is now named after him.

Brewster and his followers were of humble origin. He himself had been a postmaster and his small congregation in England had met in the post office

Charles Lucy (1814-1873), *Departure of the Pilgrims from Delft Haven*, oil on canvas, England, 1847. Pilgrim Hall Museum, Plymouth MA (PHM) 0065, Gift of Gov. Alexander H. Rice, 1880

to pray. Most of them were clothworkers, so for them the choice of the cloth town of Leiden was a logical move, even though it was always their intention to return to England when possible.

Leiden was then a city of 40,000 inhabitants, a third of whom were immigrants, mostly from what is now francophone Belgium. Initially the English were accepted by the local community like the other religious refugees. For the majority of them, ordinary manual workers, life was extremely hard and because of their puritan customs they tended to live apart from the other townspeople.

However, the most important of their leaders, John Robinson, regularly took part in theological debates at Leiden University. During the early years in Leiden, Robinson and Brewster had time to develop their ideas about small

Gilbert Tucker Margeson (1852-1940), *Mayflower at Sea*, oil on canvas, Massachussets, before 1920. PHM 0038, Museum Purchase, 1920

democratically-governed religious communities. They believed in the moral purity of small groups who chose their own leaders and pastors, and they faithfully followed the precepts of the Old Testament even though this did estrange them from the world around them. Meanwhile, the English refugees were also making contact with like-minded French-speaking Calvinists, one of whom was Philip Delano who would sail on the Mayflower in 1620. This Frenchman was a distant ancestor of Franklin Delano Roosevelt, president of the USA from 1933 to 1945.

Mayflower

Life in Leiden became steadily more difficult for the English, added to which the previously so tolerant city regarded them increasingly as strange and eccentric. Furthermore, the original Pilgrims were becoming concerned that the younger generation were only too willing to adopt pernicious 'Dutch customs'. They saw their teenagers playing truant from Sunday Bible study in order to join their friends in the taverns, and choosing to follow dishonourable careers such as trading or the army. The older generation considered Leiden's youth to be a bad influence on their own offspring.

Initially they considered moving south to Zeeland, but it was Hollanders who made them aware of the possibility of emigrating to America. As well as enjoying complete freedom of faith, they would also be able to begin a completely new life. Nothing would deter them, not even the news that, on an earlier expedition from England, 150 of the 180 emigrants did not survive the dreadful voyage.

In September 1620, 35 Pilgrims left Delfshaven for Plymouth where they were joined by over 60 others from London and Southampton to board the Mayflower for America. Navigation errors and storms meant that they would never reach their original destination, although in London it was also whispered that the captain had been bribed not to put them ashore at the Hudson River, where New York would later be built. That area was already regarded as potentially fertile land for new colonies.

Finally, in the middle of December, they landed to the north of Cape Cod, an area to which they had no claim according to the agreement they had signed with the English company that had financed their voyage in exchange for future returns. They nevertheless disembarked and named the territory 'Plymouth Colony'. Their first winter has gone into the mythology of modern America. The hard frosts made it impossible to build houses or cultivate the land and more than 50 colonists died. At one point, no more than seven men were able to work in the inhuman conditions of the American winter. The reduced colony certainly worked hard in spite of many setbacks, both in cultivating the land and in their relations with the English company, with which they finally reached an agreement which legalised their position, although the company was far from happy with the Pilgrims' emphasis on religious freedom and their failure to keep up with their payments.

Edgar Parker (1840-1892), after Robert *W. Weir, Embarcation of the Pilgrims*, oil on canvas, Boston, MA, 1875. PHM 0031, Pilgrim Society Commission, 1875

The local Wampanoag Indians did not see the small settlement of whites as a threat, and it was only thanks to them that the colonists were able to survive the first winter. The Indians taught them how to cultivate local crops and showed them which waters were rich in fish. The survival of the first colonists led, over a period of years, to at least another 125 Pilgrims setting out from Leiden to America. Relations between the settlers and the local population remained good for decades and only deteriorated when the settlements became much larger and new settlers moved west in search of fresh uncultivated land. The great leader of the Pilgrims, John Robinson, died in Leiden in 1625 without ever visiting the colony. The Pilgrims who remained behind in Leiden became reconciled with the other church communities.

In the early autumn of 1621, to show their gratitude towards the Indians who had saved their lives the previous winter, the colonists presented a meal to them made of local ingredients. That event is regarded as the first Thanksgiving, which is still one of the most important festivals in modern America.

It was originally assumed that Thanksgiving went back to an English or even a heathen tradition, but later research has shown that the Pilgrims drew their inspiration for it from Leiden. After 1574, the lifting of the siege of Leiden during the Eighty Year's War was commemorated each year on 3 October and indeed is still commemorated now. In those days it was celebrated with a church service and a communal meal, elements which the Pilgrims took with them to America. Only the turkey was added, since there were so many of them living in the wild around the Plymouth Colony. Incidentally, the tradition, which became an annual celebration, was only named Thanksgiving in 1633 or 1634. It was moved, much later, to early November and became a national holiday after the Civil War, under President Abraham Lincoln. After World War 1, when Thanksgiving and the Armistice occurred in the same week, Thanksgiving was moved again, this time to the end of November. It was President Franklin Delano Roosevelt, a descendent of the Pilgrims, who decreed in 1941 that from then on Thanksgiving would be celebrated on the fourth Thursday of November.

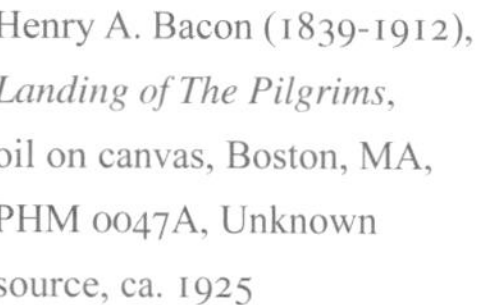

Henry A. Bacon (1839-1912), *Landing of The Pilgrims*, oil on canvas, Boston, MA, PHM 0047A, Unknown source, ca. 1925

Social contract

Thanksgiving may be the most tangible, but is certainly not the only thing which the Pilgrims introduced into America. On their way to America the colonists drew up a document which they called the Mayflower Compact. They decided on this when it became clear that they would not be disembarking where they had expected, and also on the assumption that they could make up their own laws and regulations. In contrast to the other settlements, the colonists wanted to withdraw from the rule of law as laid down by the English monarchy and the Church of England. Freedom of religion and the autonomy of the small community were central and the leaders of the community would be elected by a democratic majority. Although the original document has been lost, it is regarded as the first social contract in America and as such a forerunner of the American constitution.

The Pilgrims had picked up the idea of electing local representatives in Leiden, where the inhabitants of 77 separate districts elected their representatives. The emphasis on local roots ('ask your local congressman') and the election of officials such as judges and police commissioners continue to be a feature of the American political system.

In Leiden the Pilgrims were also introduced to the civil registration of marriage, a practice which was developed further by the colonists in America. It is one of the most visible aspects of the division between church and state and has been a characteristic of the United States of America since the beginning.

Standards for newcomers

In the decades following their arrival in the Massachusetts Bay Colony, the Pilgrims were reinforced by tens of thousands of Protestants, mainly from England and to a lesser extent from Scandinavia and Germany. The hard life in New England levelled out religious differences between the various Protestant groups, though everyone continued to follow their beliefs in complete freedom. The colony soon prospered; Boston became a well-functioning port where ships were being built by the 1630s, and in 1636 the first American university was founded at Harvard.

The Pilgrim Fathers' view of themselves as the chosen people and their conviction that the religious individual should live righteously and be wary of any interference from the government became firmly rooted in American society. The sceptical attitude of many Americans - not just conservatives - towards government and the elite dates back to that time. So the first colonists laid down standards for the many newcomers from Eastern and Central Europe as well as later Catholic Irish immigrants fleeing the ravages of the potato famine in the 1840s. Furthermore, religious freedom continued to attract immigrants for centuries, from the French Huguenots to the Amish with their German roots. Sometimes defence of communities' own congregations had pernicious consequences, such as the hanging of the early Quakers until they found a safe haven in the new state of Pennsylvania. Time softened the sharper edges, but because the followers of Calvin and the Old Testament were the most successful colonists, their Protestant ideals spread out from the north-east to the

Edward Percy Moran (1862-1935), *Signing of the Compact in the Cabin of the Mayflower*, oil on canvas, New York, 1899-1901. PHM 0048, Gift of J. Ackerman Coles in memory of James Cole, 1919

south-western United States. In this way, and helped by the North's victory over the southern states in the Civil War, hundreds of Protestant churches and congregations put their stamp on the United States.

Land of the free

The decision of the Pilgrims to undertake the perilous journey to what was then an inhospitable part of the world is still regarded as a tribute to personal freedom, even though that freedom had been dedicated to the service of God. The Pilgrims saw their crossing literally as a pilgrimage to the Promised Land that God had given to them and they continued to make a daily pilgrimage, to walk with God and converse with Him.

Initially, the idea of freedom blended well with the enlightened ideals of the Founding Fathers who eventually drew up the Constitution of the United States. The Christian charity of the Protestant colonists combined with the Founding Fathers' ideal of liberty were sources of inspiration for the abolitionists who fought to put an end to slavery.

At the same time, however, many of the divisions in modern-day American politics can be traced back to differences between the enlightened Founding Fathers and the religious Pilgrim Fathers. Take for instance the fierce disagreement on the theory of evolution. To enlightened America it is a valid, well-established theory, but for many American believers it is the work of the devil which undermines the very foundations of the Bible and therefore of America itself. For if America is no longer a part of the Divine Plan, as many Americans believe, what remains of America itself? The theory of evolution is not only diabolical, it is also terribly un-American.

Jenny Brownscombe (1850-1936), *The First Thanksgiving at Plymouth*, oil on canvas, Pennsylvania or New York, 1914. PHM 0046 Gift of Emilie S. Coles, 1919

Torchbooks

Although the first colonists initially regarded themselves as progressive, their influence is now felt mainly in the strictly religious and conservative corners of society. This is not a recent phenomenon and some Americans have long been aware of it. In the 1950s and 60s the US Information Agency distributed special books on American history, such as 'The Immigrant in American History' by the well-known historian Marcus Lee Hansen, published by Harper Torchbooks. These publications contained a concluding letter to the reader. 'Overseas there is the strong impression that we are a country of extreme conservatism and that we are unable to adapt to social change. Books about America may persuade readers abroad of the opposite', wrote the director of the American Information Service, followed by an appeal for money to support the 'Books USA' campaign.

It was a remarkable phenomenon. The descendants of colonists and pioneers used these books to convince the families who had stayed behind in the Old World that they were not nearly as conservative as Europeans might think. Just after the Second World War the puritan restraint which had prevailed in American society was slowly relaxing and being replaced by the luxury culture of television sets and full refrigerators. It was precisely then, in the 1960s, that the image was created of the USA as the country of unlimited possibilities. Nevertheless, the attitude of 'God bless America' and the toleration of thousands of small, often extremely conservative, religious communities still remain - as does European incomprehension of so much seemingly extremely naive religiosity. ■

Translated by Chris Emery

FURTHER READING

Wallace Notestein, *The English People on the Eve of Colonization,* Harper & Brothers, 1954.
Marcus Lee Hansen, *The Immigrant in American History*, Harper Torchbooks, 1964.
Marcus Lee Hansen, *The Atlantic Migration*, Harper Torchbooks, 1964.

Director of Characters

The Sculptures of Folkert de Jong

[DAVID STROBAND]

The artist Folkert De Jong (Egmond Aan Zee, 1972) has been bringing odd characters into the world for more than ten years now. Sometimes they appear in groups, sometimes alone. They are frozen in a pose and seek confrontation with us, the viewers. When the viewer encounters these carefully created characters, he is both seduced and frightened off, kept at a distance and at the same time invited to become more closely acquainted. Beauty and wonder – sometimes even bafflement – take turns.

De Jong speaks stirringly of his characters, whose roots often lie in (art) history. He tries, searchingly and contemplatively, to provide them with stories and meaning. In the course of defining his characters, De Jong unfolds a world where history seeps into our contemporary world and where our contemporary view colours history. His characters attempt, on the basis of both past and present, to shed light on how the world around us works and what our position in it is. They tell exploratory stories.

Attraction and repulsion

De Jong made his first sculptural piece – *The Iceman Cometh* – in 2001. What you see is a still from some gruesome story. Figures with various defects wander around in a chilling landscape, an island whose blueness has a wintry feel. It contains a procession of figures in ecstatic poses, led by a bent figure with big rabbit's ears, a pistol in his right hand and a penis standing proudly erect. He is followed by, among others, a soldier with a weapon in one hand and a Mickey Mouse doll in the other, and a figure that seems to be raising the stumps of his arms in jubilation. One of the more important sources of inspiration for this work is the paintings and drawings of the German Expressionists at the start of the twentieth century. De Jong was especially struck by the restrained emotional effect of a self-portrait drawn by Otto Dix, done in a trench during the First World War. Dix's satire and vivid colours make it simpler for the viewer to look at these horrors. De Jong's figures are also part of a satire: they show emotions that have been magnified as a consequence of their shortcomings. And moreover, they are brightly coloured.

The Iceman Cometh, 2001. Styrofoam and polyurethane foam. Photo by Jannes Linders. © Studio Folkert de Jong / André Simoens Gallery, Knokke

De Jong's sculptures have lifelike human dimensions and are made of chemical products such as Styrofoam and polyurethane foam. These materials are often used in building, and also in the Hollywood film industry, and are therefore very well suited to creating effects and illusions. De Jong uses them to give his sculptures an extraordinary layering. The material looks hard and industrial. De Jong cuts his robust shapes out of Styrofoam and assembles them quite roughly. It is precisely the combination of the forms cut from this building material and their clear and actually quite lively blue or pink colour which one moment repels and the next attracts.

The caverns of the artist's soul

As of 2001, Folkert de Jong's work reflects increasingly on his position as an artist in relation to society. It is through his characters that he defines his position in the consumer society of the West, which is so forcefully driven by the media. And how does he relate to (art) history? De Jong's materials look very temporary, but in fact they are strong and durable. Their seeming transience gives something very paradoxical to the often historical figures he makes with them.

In the 2003 work *Life's Illusions*, an ungainly figure with no arms sits drinking from a cup through a straw. His head appears to be completely covered in blood. Near him you see a green monster that looks like a Michelin man. Nearby a laughing woman in a flowery dress waves two axes around. Between the three of them burns a camp fire in blue, green and purple colours, and at an appropriate distance stands a horse mounted by a little man in an orange-coloured outfit with a variety hat atop his grinning face. This scene is surrounded by small walls that have been blown over and lots of building debris, all made from the same material as the frightful figures that seem close to madness. This work combines many of De Jong's fascinations: American comics, Bfilms, freaks, and the gruesome, dark and bizarre sides of man. He has also been influenced by artists from the West coast of America, such as Paul McCarthy and Mike Kelley. *Life's Illusions* shows a singular encounter between characters with twisted horror-like heads. They live in a world entirely their own, one that

De Jong likes to visit because he can examine the caverns of the human soul there. The bright colour accents that De Jong introduces into this scene using pigment put the potential madness of the characters into sharp focus.

Round 2006 Folkert de Jong meditated even more on his position as an artist. As a rule, artists aim to develop a new idiom, and thus distinguish themselves from their predecessors. But one is also undeniably part of a tradition – works by predecessors repeatedly enrich one's own vision. It was in this period that De Jong created *Gott mit uns*, a large installation featuring well-known sculptures by such typically twentieth-century sculptors as Hans Arp and Constantin Brancusi. These sculptures are threatened and mocked by a number of theatrical figures from military history who are near to madness. De Jong here emphasises the noncommittal nature that seems to characterise so many works of art, in this case abstract works. Arp and Brancusi did their non-figurative work in tranquillity and seclusion. During the Second World War they simply carried on. While battles were being fought outside, these artists were indoors creating universal beauty. In the first place De Jong was amazed that these artists did not seem to be interested in what was going on around them, but afterwards he concluded that they were able to reduce the turbulent events to an essential visual idiom that deliberately withdrew from the misery caused by mankind. Ultimately he admires the spiritual, contemplative position these artists adopted.

Life's Illusions, 2003. Detail.
Pigmented polyurethane foam and Styrofoam.
Photo by Jannes Linder.
© Studio Folkert de Jong

Restrained and concentrated

Round about 2006 De Jong's method and visual idiom evolved from those used in *The Iceman Cometh* (2001) and *Lost Illusions* (2003). This method involved less cutting and carving of Styrofoam, and more components of the works were made by casting. After some intensive research he developed a process for casting his materials (polyurethane) in moulds. In the course of casting (during which poisonous substances are released) De Jong adds pigments. This results in a more refined formal idiom related to painting and in subtler gestures in the characters. Such materials as jute and bubblewrap are also added to the casting process, leading to the creation of unusual structures in the work. You can see that De Jong makes the grotesque and ecstatic elements of his visual idiom merge into a more restrained and concentrated figurative idiom.

Round 2007 De Jong worked on *Les Saltimbanques* (acrobats, or circus performers). In this series, carnivalesque figures adopt still, inward-looking poses. They appear to have been inspired by the *commedia dell'arte*, but in fact derive from a series of works by Pablo Picasso. In his 1905 painting *Famille de Saltimbanques* and a series of drawings from the same period, Picasso shows performers at their most introspective. They clearly operate in a small niche in society and look only inwards, at themselves. In *Les Saltimbanques*, De Jong abandons the highly expressive features of his earlier work. No more exuberant gestures or frantic facial expressions, no more skulls or clashing of arms, only retiring and contemplative figures who pay no heed to the world or who view it from a great distance. Later works in this series – *Balancing Act 'Laura'* (2007) and *Circle of Trust (Mother and Son)* (2009) – can be seen more as 'traditional' sculptures. Here, too, it is apparent that De Jong hardly cuts his material at all anymore and assembles these forms less showily. He no longer translates his gestures and actions directly into the material, but models his forms in a more detached way by means of casting. A mother holding her little son in her arms, a girl performing a balancing act on an overturned oil drum: reflections on the human condition play a part in all these scenes. The costumes of these (circus) performers indicate that these characters accentuate human behaviour. They offer insights into the human psyche, but probably also say something about our species in present-day society, with its structures of economic and political power. The oil drum, for example, is an essential and recurring element in *Les Saltimbanques*.

Folkert de Jong has in the meantime developed into a consummate director of characters in all sorts of settings: 'I can spark off a process of associations and involve the public closely in the subject I am exploring. That fascinates me. We receive so much information. It is extremely difficult for an artist to add anything. I hope I can break open this chaos and create a moment of stillness.' [i]

For several years De Jong has been inspired by portraits of historical figures. They have included Benjamin Franklin, Jan Pieterszoon Coen, Abraham Lincoln and the crucified Jesus Christ. They make their appearance in the present time, take up a new position there and meet other historical characters. De Jong raises questions and makes room for reflection on our perception of history. How do we interpret it? And do we learn from it? De Jong is concerned by the condition of mankind down the ages. He does not make any moral or absolute statements, but his work contains enough metaphors that hold up a mirror to us.

Les Saltimbanques, The Joker and Human Pyramid, 2007. Pigmented polyurethane foam and Styrofoam. © James Cohan Gallery / Studio Folkert de Jong. Private collection

The immortals

This is apparent in his latest installation, *The Immortals* (2012), made at the Glasgow School of Art, which was an important and internationally renowned arts centre in the late nineteenth and early twentieth centuries. In a monumental room containing classical-looking plaster sculptures stands a big wooden scaffold; on top of it a female character looks out over the room. Diagonally behind her a man stands on a lower step, one foot on a yellow bucket covered with a sheet of Styrofoam, and like her he is looking out into the room. Both have the precise and refined modulation of the figures in *Les Saltimbanques*, are made using the same casting methods and are also distinguished by their lively range of colours. These two characters are Charles Rennie Mackintosh, the architect of the Glasgow School of Art, who was associated with the Arts and Crafts movement, and his wife Margaret MacDonald Mackintosh, who was also an artist. In another part of the room two men being embraced by a woman stand on a sheet of Styrofoam. They are again Mackintosh and his wife, while the second man has the features of William of Orange. Here, too, figures from different historical periods meet, which gives them a metaphorical import.

De Jong once explained in a conversation [ii] that during his study trip to the Glasgow School of Art he became fascinated by the man-woman relationships of the time. Margaret MacDonald Mackintosh remained in her husband's shadow artistically, but did work in the upper levels of the school, whereas the men populated the lower regions. Men traditionally represent power, and De Jong here examines a possible reversal: Mackintosh stands behind his wife on the scaffold and the woman enfolds the two men in her arms. De Jong is fascinated by apparent contrasts between good and evil, beautiful and ugly, man and woman. He thus appears to play the part of *The Storyteller*: a seated figure playing the guitar on a chair that closely resembles those designed by Mackintosh. This artist is at a suitable distance from the other scenes, adding lustre to what is going on, and probably also providing a commentary. Another woman, Margaret again, stands in a proud pose on a small wooden construction, her

Les Saltimbanques, Accordeon Player, 2007. Pigmented polyurethane foam and Styrofoam. © James Cohan Gallery / Studio Folkert de Jong. Private collection

eyes closed as if in ecstasy. She is wearing a summer hat made of underlayment, a plywood material that De Jong has used more frequently recently. Margaret's face is modelled on the famous late nineteenth-century death mask in *L'Inconnue de la Seine*. It was cast from the beautiful face of a dead woman, probably a suicide, who was pulled out of the Seine. Her mask was duplicated many times, adorned many a studio and was a major source of inspiration for artists. By means of this sort of reference, De Jong gives his characters many layers of meaning; this includes the title of this group of figures: *The Immortals*.

The court jester

A bronze figure by Folkert de Jong will soon be appearing on the Koningsplein, an oval open space in the stately and distinguished part of The Hague where the royal court resides. He uses this extremely traditional artist's material in his very own way. He adds a patina so that all manner of 'funky' colours appear on its surface. His fascination with graffiti on statues and monuments led him to add colourful patches and patterns to the tradition-laden bronze. In this way he refers to the fact that lots of people like to make their own visual contribution to statues and monuments. They are fascinated by their magnificence and durability and want to match themselves against it.

Left:
Les Saltimbanques, Balancing Act Laura, 2007. Pigmented polyurethane foam and Styrofoam. Photo by Aatjan Renders. © James Cohan Gallery / Studio Folkert de Jong. Private collection

Right:
Mother and Child , 2009. Pigmented polyurethane foam, Styrofoam and adapted Euro pallet. Photo by Aatjan Renders. © Studio Folkert de Jong. Rabobank Art Collection

The Immortals, 2012. Detail. Pigmented polyurethane foam, spray paint and wood. Photo by Glasgow School of Art Scotland. © Studio Folkert de Jong / André Simoens Gallery, Knokke

The character De Jong will install on the Koningsplein is a court jester, a figure that will appropriately provide gently ironic comment on institutions that have a sense of perpetuity. On this square, the bronze court jester acts as a landmark, it is the needle on the record-player: everything revolves around him at a set tempo and he makes this visible. ■

Translated by Gregory Ball

www.folkertdejong.org

NOTES

(i) Michaël Amy, 'Confronting the Grotesque; A Conversation with Folkert de Jong', in Sculpture, vol. 27, no. 5, pp. 24-33.

(ii) Noted down during a conversation with the artist on 7 November 2012.

The Highs and Lows of Hendrik Conscience

The case of the Flemish author Hendrik Conscience (1812-1883) is unique. Having set himself up as a professional writer at a time when Flanders had no publishing industry to speak of, he went on to produce a hundred novels and novellas to immense success. Translations into German, French, English and other languages made him a European celebrity almost overnight. No author writing in Dutch, past or present, has been translated on such a scale and with such intensity. A statue in his honour was erected during his lifetime. Upon his death he was awarded a state funeral with full military honours; tens of thousands lined the streets to pay their respects.

His fame did not last. Translations into foreign languages petered out within years of his passing. Very few if any of his works are currently in print. His masterpiece, *The Lion of Flanders* (*De Leeuw van Vlaenderen*, 1838), the iconic Flemish novel of the nineteenth century, remains unread today and is widely regarded as unreadable. What happened? What went wrong? What's left?

Hendrik Conscience grew up with two languages and never felt entirely at home in either. Born in Antwerp to a French father and an illiterate mother, he began by writing in French. However, in those heady romantic days he would not be bound to a single tongue. A short satirical play from 1836, 'Lucifer, or Satan Converted', which mercifully remained unprinted, had Lucifer reading an edict from God that consisted of 'words scrambled from eight languages':

Loïti faquïen tolanchä Consay
Oquïendo Quichen tatès Satanas,
figènoïïama Chimantès, Suntïen
Cum érodal; paguïa olam canchïa
Chèquëam Mocaïjoij: Coquinez
faxibol, Jehova, BungoCooij
Comboodoässi, outénobista!?

The initial sketches of his first novel, *In the Year of Wonder* (*In 't Wonderjaer*, 1837), were in French, but then he made a conscious decision to continue in Dutch. In a letter from October 1838 he described a scene from his new work,

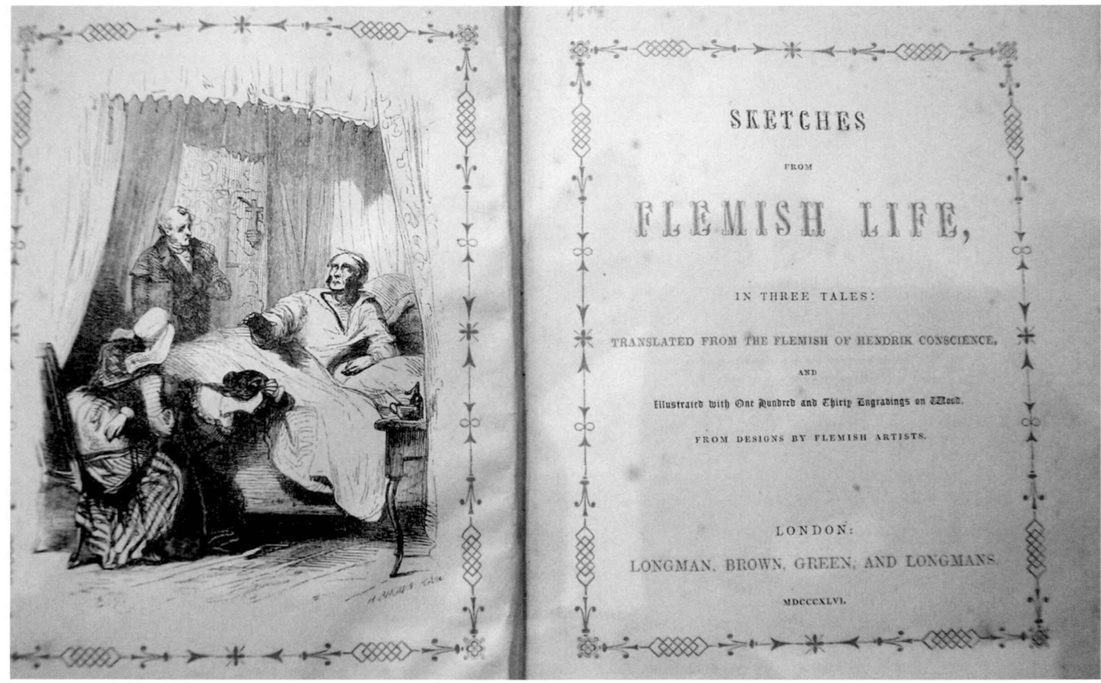

SKETCHES

FROM

FLEMISH LIFE,

IN THREE TALES:

TRANSLATED FROM THE FLEMISH OF HENDRIK CONSCIENCE,

AND

Illustrated with One Hundred and Thirty Engravings on Wood,

FROM DESIGNS BY FLEMISH ARTISTS.

LONDON:

LONGMAN, BROWN, GREEN, AND LONGMANS.

MDCCCXLVI.

The Lion of Flanders, still switching from one language to the other: "in the evening Breydel and his friend De Coninck are sitting in a tent, ils mangent des betteraves cuites sous la cendre et boivent du vin...". In later years he taught himself German and some English, and occasionally translated from German into Dutch.

He also engaged in translation of a very different kind, transforming himself from the defiant romantic of his youthful years into a pillar of Belgian society, and of its Catholic establishment in particular. Both *In the Year of Wonder* and *The Lion of Flanders* appeared in amended editions in 1843. In the case of the *Lion of Flanders* the revisions did not amount to much more than toning down the rough or excessively passionate language of individual characters. *In the Year of Wonder*, its title now shortened to *The Year of Wonder*, became a different book altogether, with a different ending. The freedom-loving Protestant rebels of the first edition were now portrayed as a lawless bunch of anti-Catholic fanatics. A friar who had a minor part before was made into a central character, so that the book as a whole clearly supported the preservation of the Catholic faith. The fiery authorial introductions championing the Flemish cause which adorned the first editions of both novels were quietly omitted.

Conscience's conversion to Catholic conformism was a feather in the cap of J.B. van Hemel, director of the main seminary in Flanders and a powerful man in this predominantly Catholic region. Among other things, he sat on the commission that decided on books to purchase for the nation's schools, hospitals

Hendrik Conscience ca. 1845. Letterenhuis, Antwerp

and prisons. In a suave letter full of veiled threats Van Hemel insisted on the necessary changes in return for bulk orders. His demands answered the political circumstances of the period. In the early 1840s, following ten years of unionist governments, the Catholic and liberal camps that together had achieved Belgium's independence in 1830 were drifting apart and consolidating into sharply antagonistic parties. Van Hemel was merely strengthening his own side.

For Conscience, the money mattered, too. He had to pay for his early books to be printed. His debut novel *In the Year of Wonder* had cost him the equivalent of a year's salary. Even though *The Lion of Flanders* proved a runaway success, it had been expensive to produce and made only a modest financial profit. As Conscience pointed out to his publisher many years later: if he wanted to live off his pen, he needed to sell books.

In meeting Van Hemel's ideological demands Conscience may have compromised his artistic integrity, but his talent for storytelling remained undiminished. Longer and shorter narratives rolled from the presses. He continued to write historical novels but branched out into edifying village and small-town tales. In 1846 he signed a fixed-term contract with a publisher, and similar contracts followed in subsequent years. Henceforth he would be paid by the page and could tailor his narratives to a desired length. He was now a professional writer.

Numerous translations

He was also well on his way to becoming an international celebrity, in numerous translations. The first few translations of Conscience's work appeared in Francophone Belgian newspapers and magazines, but they had little effect. The breakthrough came in Germany in 1845, when Melchior von Diepenbrock, the newly appointed Bishop of Breslau (today Wrocław), brought out a collection of three of Conscience's stories in German translation. He had come across them by accident. The little book sold 14,000 copies in two years and was in turn translated into English, Italian and Czech.

Things moved rapidly from then on, especially in Germany. The year 1846 was remarkable, as publishers rushed to issue their versions of Conscience's work. Aschendorff in Münster produced three novels – *The Year of Wonder, The Lion of Flanders* and Conscience's third novel, *Hugo van Craenhove* – and two collections of stories, one of these containing the same stories Von Diepenbrock had translated a year earlier, but now in a different version. In Stuttgart, Franckh published two novels, *The Year of Wonder* and *Hugo van Craenhove*, in their own translation. *The Year of Wonder* was brought out by another Stuttgart publisher, Hallberg, in a third German version. In Bonn, A. Marcus came with three titles: *Hugo van Craenhove* in yet another translation, another version of *The Lion of Flanders*, and a collection of stories which largely but not wholly overlapped with that issued by Aschendorff in Münster. A fourth version of *Hugo van Craenhove* saw the light in Leipzig with C.B. Lorck, and Overmann in Cologne produced a fifth translation, just when the publisher Pustet in Regensburg printed its own version (the fourth translation) of *The Year of Wonder*. The total for 1846 adds up to fourteen titles in translation, in more than twenty volumes printed for seven different publishers in six German cities.

When Conscience's novel *The Poor Gentleman* (*De arme edelman*) appeared in 1851, three publishers in Leipzig and one in Düsseldorf each presented their own versions to the public within a year. Two years later Aschendorff brought out a fifth version that was reprinted four times in its first ten years and continued to be reissued about once every decade until after the First World War. In the meantime Reclam, another Leipzig publisher, came with yet another version, the sixth, which was reprinted roughly every five years from 1877 till 1920. To close the series the Westphalian publisher Hamm produced a seventh translation in 1900. A bibliographical inventory of German renderings of Conscience's works runs to 449 entries in book form; the number of translations in periodicals is unknown. In 1942 the publisher Aschendorff calculated that their own translations of Conscience had, over the years, sold around 400,000 copies.

Some of these German translations appeared in series of world literature, but before long many began to slip from reading matter for adults to collections

Hendrik Conscience meets Hugo Claus in 1965
© Roland Minnaert

Hendrik Conscience ca. 1830. Painting by Xavier de Cock. Letterenhuis, Antwerpen

aimed at adolescents. The English translations show a similar pattern. Whereas Conscience's early work found a place in series like Constable's Miscellany of Foreign Literature or, for the shorter pieces, Half-Hours with Foreign Authors, many of the later translations appeared in The Amusing Library, Dunigan's Home Library, Duffy's Popular Library and other such lowbrow series. *Veva, or the War of the Peasants* (*De boerenkryg*, 1853), a novel set in the aftermath of the French Revolution and translated into English not from the original Dutch but after a French version, was cut up into episodes apparently designed to serve as 'railway literature', the new lightweight genre that catered for those travelling by train. The downward slide from high literature into popular reading is unmistakable.

It will not have troubled Conscience unduly. In January 1854 he signed a contract with the Paris publisher Michel Lévy stipulating that everything he had written so far and everything he was still to write would be translated into French. Lévy consequently published Conscience's collected work in French translation in sixty volumes, with another edition after the author's death in eleven volumes. For their part, Aschendorff in Münster brought out a German collected edition in seventy-five volumes. English translations were not quite so spectacular, but even here we encounter editions in up to ten and twelve volumes. Between 1854 and 1889 the story *Blind Rosa* was printed at least eight times in English translation, *Wooden Clara* ten times, *The Village Innkeeper* (*Baes Gansendonck*, 1850) eleven times, *The Conscript* (*De loteling*, 1850, also translated as *The Recruit*) twelve times, *The Poor Gentleman* fourteen times. Most of the English translations appeared without the name of a translator.

Plagiarised but not paid

The author assisted his translators when he could, carefully fashioning his self-image in his correspondence with them, enabling some of them to translate from the proofs instead of having to wait for the printed book, and authorising them to make changes in the texts to suit the taste of the intended audience. But there was much that remained beyond his control. The most searing episode involved none other than Alexandre Dumas, who plagiarised a French version of the novella *The Conscript* and expanded it into a three-decker novel. Dumas reckoned he had paid homage to Conscience by stealing from him ('je lui faisais bien de l'honneur en le volant...'). Two novels, one called *The Miser* and the other *The Village Innkeeper*, appeared in London in 1868 and 1871 respectively, both signed by one Hope Inslow (almost certainly a pseudonym) as the author, both plagiarised from Conscience.

In the nineteenth century the legal framework governing intellectual property was still under construction, and this explains the contrast between the proliferation of German translations and the exclusive contract with Michel Lévy's company in France. International copyright law did not yet exist, only bilateral treaties. In the absence of copyright agreements between Belgium and the German states, German publishers could publish whatever translations they pleased. As a result, we know the names of over forty German translators of Conscience, and many other translations appeared anonymously. Following the copyright agreement signed between Belgium and France in 1852 and the contract with Lévy in 1854, Conscience had just two translators into French, first Léon Wocquier and then, from 1860 onwards, Félix Coveliers. Every title issued by Lévy featured a dire warning to the effect that any infringement of intellectual property would lead to prosecution. The copyright agreement concluded between Britain and Belgium in 1855 protected English translations published in the British Isles but not those in the USA.

For all the personal satisfaction that Conscience may have derived from seeing his work blossom in such a stupendous number of foreign translations, they brought him little financial reward. Lévy paid only intermittently, and Conscience had to chase him and beg for his money constantly. The many hundreds of English, German and other translations afforded the author not a penny.

Talent for storytelling

Although Conscience, always hungry for recognition, relished his status as an international celebrity, that status proved short-lived. The popularity of his work brought him a large but not necessarily a very discerning readership. As book production steadily increased and literary fashions moved on towards the end of the nineteenth century, the downward slide in his standing as a writer proved fatal. As early as 1855 George Eliot had put the knife in. Both as a critic and as a novelist she championed realism in fiction and objected to sentimentalism, moralising and idealisation. Writing in the *Westminster Review* about the five volumes of Conscience's *Tales and Romances* brought out by the London publisher Lambert & Co., she showed herself aware of 'the high praise bestowed on these fictions in many quarters' and conceded that the books were 'in demand among a large class of persons.' But her own reading experience did not match her expectations. She confessed to being 'utterly disappointed,' finding the stories tendentious and lacking in both plausible characters and natural dialogue.

From our contemporary vantage point Eliot's criticism seems entirely justified. But we need to remember the angle from which Eliot was writing. Of course, the poetics she was promoting had the future. The novel was developing towards greater realism, a focus on psychologically complex characters, and aesthetic rather than didactic concerns. Subsequent modernist experiments would only radicalise these trends. They left Conscience looking outmoded and simplistic.

Nevertheless, it is worth asking what made Conscience appeal to such a large class of people, not just in his native Belgium but in other countries and languages as well, for half a century. The answer is likely to be found in his singular talent for storytelling. He was no linguistic virtuoso, his narratives are sentimental, his plots unreal and their moral judgements conservative to the point of being reactionary, but he knew how to draw the reader into a fictional world.

The brief evocations of nature which often introduce new scenes hold the reader's attention. Several stories employ frame narratives presenting a first-person narrator who directly addresses the reader so as to suggest both familiarity and distance. The changes of pace which punctuate the rhythm of the narratives make the reader aware of how expectations are built up and manipulated. The descriptions of mass scenes are epic in scale.

Interrogate these stories again

However, the sheer fluency with which these narratives unfold also invites us to read them against the grain, for the paths not chosen as much as for what is there. To take a single example: in *The Village Innkeeper* (*Baes Gansendonck*) the protagonist, a haughty man, causes his daughter irremediable heartbreak by thwarting the love affair between her and the local brewer's son because he prefers to see her married to a parvenu from the city. The story ends tragically: the girl pines away and dies, the boy goes mad. We may wonder why the girl never blames her father for destroying her life and why the boy, too, while still compos mentis, forgives him but seems intent on cutting the parvenu's throat. We may also wonder about the ending itself: surely the innkeeper could have been shown to find humility without the tragic denouement running its full course? What is it in the ideology sustaining the story that dictates such a brutal fate?

The contrast between Conscience's huge success for a good part of the nineteenth century and the oblivion that has befallen him in more recent decades is so stark it must raise questions about why and how he was read then and how he can and perhaps should be read now. No doubt he is to be read only selectively, as indeed most writers are. But we owe it to generations of international readers to interrogate these stories again, from every possible angle. ■

FURTHER READING

Arents, Prosper. *De Vlaamsche schrijvers in het Duitsch vertaald.* Brussel 1944.

Arents, Prosper. *De Vlaamse schrijvers in het Engels vertaald 1481-1949.* Gent 1950.

Hermans, Theo. '"Tusschen Europeaensche vermaerdheden." Het vertalen van Hendrik Conscience.' *Filter* 18, 2011 (3), 27-34.

Keersmaekers, August. *Hendrik Conscience. De muze en de mammon.* Gent 2009.

Simon, Irène. 'George Eliot and Hendrik Conscience', *Revue des langues vivantes* 26, 1960, 386-89.

Wellens, Oscar. 'De kritische receptie van Conscience in Engeland', *Handelingen Koninklijke Zuidnederlandse Maatschappij voor Taal- en Letterkunde en Geschiedenis* 36, 1982, 259-71.

An Extract from *Veva, or the War of the Peasants*

By Hendrik Conscience

The general made a sign to the company of Waldeghem, which immediately advanced and ascended the rampart, the whole army moving slowly after it. The troops, however, who were crowded against the inner fortifications, were in such haste to escape that they began to scale the outer ramparts in five or six different places, and grouped themselves in a mass on the approaches to the bridge.

Whether it was that the plan of the flight from the city had been betrayed, or that the French sentinels on the heights which commanded the Herenthals Gate could hear a certain noise caused by the confusion on the bridge, the report of a cannon was heard, pealing terrifically over the city and the surrounding country.

That ominous signal awakened the most terrible alarm in the hearts of the patriots. The companies who were in the rear of the column pushed on violently towards the bridge those who were before.

Immediately there arose a thrilling shriek of distress from the depths of that terrified crowd, and not a heart was there that did not throb with the most dreadful apprehensions.

No longer having any care for the general safety, each person rushed forward. A confused multitude scrambled over the rampart and poured like a torrent upon the bridge, the only means of egress from the devoted city. A hideous crash then mingled with the roar of the cannon and the rattle of the musketry. The bridge had yielded with the weight of the densely-packed mass of fugitives, and had fallen into the water, carrying with it its unhappy burthen.

This terrible accident, however, did not arrest the course of those who were behind. In the deep darkness of the night, and urged on by a mortal fear, they continued to throng forward, precipitating themselves from the ramparts and falling headlong into the moat. The cries and shrieks of their mangled and drowning brethren, far from stopping, only increased the frenzied impatience of the others to quit the city. The moat was soon completely filled with the corpses of the unfortunate villagers: it became a scene too horrible for language to describe.

Meanwhile the French companies who had advanced nearest to the bridge drew up quickly in order of battle before the great floodgate, and commenced firing in the direction from which the cries and shrieks proceeded.

While the patriots were stifled or crushed by hundreds in the moat, the enemy's shot, like a murderous hail, poured upon those who were fortunate enough to reach the other side of the water.

At the end of about half an hour the fearful tumult had ceased; all had relapsed into dreary silence. But the shadows of night were spread over five hundred dead!

From *Veva, or the War of the Peasants* (De Boerenkryg, 1853). Anonymous translation. London: Burns and Oates, s.d.

The Decline of the Belgian Car Industry

The car industry in Belgium has been going downhill for years, but the pace of decline has quickened markedly in recent years. In 2006, the Volkswagen Vorst plant was subsumed into Audi Brussels, a move which cost 3,000 of the 5,000 jobs. Four years later, in 2010, the Opel plant in Antwerp closed, axing 2,600 jobs in the process. And in 2012, Ford decided that its factory in Genk also had to close, with 4,000 job losses. Ten thousand direct jobs in the car industry were thus lost within the space of a few years. And all this after Renault, without any prior warning, abruptly closed its plant in Vilvoorde in 1997, putting more than 3,000 employees out of work. There is now only one car assembly plant left in Belgium: Volvo in Ghent. And the Volvo management, too, has hinted that the future of this plant cannot be guaranteed, however good its productivity figures may be. What is going on here? Or, to put it in automotive terms: why is the engine stuttering? Time to lift the bonnet and have a look.

Let us first take a step back in time - because there was a time when Belgium even had its own car makes which were famed and desired far beyond the Belgian borders. The best-known was probably Minerva in Antwerp, along with Excelsior in Zaventem and Imperia in Nessonvaux. The Minerva company was founded in 1897 and initially made bicycles, then motorcycles, and from 1904 onwards cars, too. Minerva became synonymous with beautifully crafted, luxurious, fast and even customised cars. The cars were easily identified by the distinctive mascot in the form of the head of the Roman goddess Minerva adorning the radiator cap. The cars were sold to members of the royal houses of Belgium, Romania, Thailand and India, as well as to members of the nobility and film stars. The legendary carmaker Henry Ford is also said to have driven one.

The golden age for Minerva was the 1920s: in 1927 the company employed more than 6,500 workers. During that period, the company was keen to expand further and went in search of new investors. However, those ambitious plans were thwarted by the stock market crash in New York on 24 October 1929. The economic crisis in the 1930s made its presence felt and demand for luxury vehicles slumped. In 1934, the recession forced Minerva to throw in the towel. Twelve hundred workers lost their jobs overnight. Today, Minervas are still highly sought-after vintage cars, and there is also a model gracing the MAS (Museum aan de Stroom) in Antwerp.

Around the time that Minerva was in its heyday, foreign carmakers came to Belgium in droves to set up business. This was the result of a requirement by Belgian law, which stipulated that any foreign carmaker which sold more than 250 vehicles in Belgium had to have a vehicle assembly plant in the country. First came the Americans, starting with the Ford Motor Company in 1922, which opened a factory in Antwerp. Two years later, Ford was followed by GM, which wanted to build Chevrolets in Antwerp; after the Second World War, this would become the Opel factory.

After the Americans came the French, with Citroën opening a plant in Vorst in 1926, followed a year later by Renault with a factory in Vilvoorde, and in 1938 Peugeot also crossed over the border. The Belgian company D'Ieteren had by this time already been assembling American Studebakers for four years, and from 1954 onwards built Volkswagens as well. In fact, the company is today still the Belgian importer of VWs, along with sister brands such as Audi, Porsche and Skoda. And then there was Mercedes-Benz, which began assembling cars in Mechelen.

This was just the first wave, as the 'golden sixties' and rising prosperity brought even more car manufacturers to Belgium. Ford laid the first stone for a new factory in Genk in 1962. In 1964 Morris, MG and Land Rover (all British Leyland brands) began building cars in Seneffe, in Wallonia, and a few years later Volvo opened an assembly plant in the port of Ghent. Later arrivals were Simca in Nivelles, Daihatsu in Aartselaar and Saab in Mechelen. It would be only a slight exaggeration to say that at a certain point it seemed as if Belgium was just one large car factory. In fact it is not such an exaggeration at all, because in the peak years more than a million vehicles rolled off the Belgian production lines every year. With the production of roughly a hundred cars per thousand inhabitants, Belgium was the record holder for the number of cars assembled per head of the population. No one at that time gave a thought to the possibility that this situation might ever come to an end.

A portent

There was a rude awakening from that dream on 27 February 1997. News editors received an invitation to attend a press conference that was to be held in a Brussels hotel on that same day by the management of Renault. Everyone present was taken completely by surprise by the announcement that the Renault plant in Vilvoorde, which at that time built the Mégane, was to close. Employees, employers' organisations, politicians – everyone, in fact – reacted with incredulity to this bombshell, even though it had been known for some time that there was overcapacity in the car market. But the announcement that the Renault factory had to close still came like a bolt out of the blue. We have to go back to 1981 to find anything to compare with this event, when British Leyland, which at the time was struggling to survive, decided to close its factory in Seneffe, making 2,200 workers jobless overnight.

The closure of the Renault Vilvoorde plant cost 3,100 jobs. The factory was occupied, lawsuits were instigated against Renault for failure to comply with the rules on mass redundancy and the Belgian sculptor Rik Poot created 'De Vuist' ('The Fist'), which was erected on a roundabout in Vilvoorde, where it stood as a

sign of protest. People declared that they would never buy another Renault. But despite all this, the assembly plant shut down for good. This brought to an end the building of Renault cars in Belgium which had begun seventy years earlier. It was just the start of a series of factory closures in the car industry.

But why did Renault end its assembly activities in Belgium? The basic explanation is simple: Renault was not selling enough cars. That had been the case for years; the figures were deeply in the red and the losses were piling up. Renault had therefore been cutting costs in all its operations for some time. In practical terms, this meant that it was winding down factories and making workers redundant. In his memoirs, the then head of Renault, Louis Schweitzer, pointed to another factor which convinced him that there was no alternative but to close the Renault plant in Vilvoorde. According to him, a major advantage of having a factory in Belgium had disappeared: in the past, Belgian import duties had to be paid on fully assembled vehicles, but this requirement disappeared with the formation of the common European market. It is a stark example of how, as well as being good for the economy, European unification also led to mass redundancies.

One further point: the day after the announcement of the closure of Renault's Vilvoorde plant, the Renault share price rose by 15 percent. Consumers did not stop buying Renault cars – in fact quite the opposite, because Renault achieved a record market share in Belgium in subsequent years. A social plan was drawn up which was intended to help the more than 3,000 redundant workers at the Vilvoorde factory to find new jobs, and ultimately only around a hundred ended up in the unemployment figures. What still survives today is the 'Renault Act' which was introduced in 1998. The Act states that advance notice must be given of mass redundancies and that negotiations must take place first. The government can also demand repayment of any state aid granted. Reference is still regularly made to the Renault Act today whenever there are factory closures. And Rik Poot's 'De Vuist' still stands on the same roundabout in Vilvoorde.

De Vuist (The Fist). Vilvoorde. Artist Rik Poot protesting against the closure of the Renault Vilvoorde Plant

The closure of the Renault factory in Vilvoorde could have served as a wake-up call suggesting that the future of the car industry in Belgium was not assured forever, but the warning was not heeded. Politicians and trade unions continued to believe that car assembly in Belgium had a rosy future. And if car sales should slow down and fewer cars needed to be produced, for many the solution was very simple: redistribute the work among all European factories. It was also consistently asserted that Belgium, in addition to its central location in Europe, had another enormous trump card: its car factories were among the best-performing and most productive in Europe.

A story of decline

Economists were less optimistic about the future of the Belgian car industry. Professor Paul De Grauwe, for example – at that time attached to KU Leuven and today to be found at the London School of Economics – had the courage to say that the future of the car industry in Belgium lay behind us. He described a further decline in employment in the industry as 'inevitable'. According to De Grauwe, there were three reasons for this: globalisation (cars destined for the Belgian market no longer needed to be built in Belgium); delocalisation (companies were moving their factories to countries where it was cheaper to manufacture); and technological progress (new production machinery meant carmakers could produce more with fewer workers).

Captains of industry also took a sombre view of the future. Top industrialist Karel Vinck, for example, did not mince his words when he declared a few years ago that 'Car assembly will eventually disappear from Belgium. The scope for technological breakthroughs has been exhausted and we are saddled with high wage and energy costs. In such a situation, the only conclusion a government can reach is that it needs to run down car assembly in a controlled way while it looks for alternatives. That's something that you have to start doing a few years in advance.' That did not really happen, however.

A fundamental element running through the story of the decline of the car industry in Belgium is that the car industry in the whole of Western Europe has been in deep crisis since the middle of the 1990s (and in fact not just in Europe: the car industry in the US is also fighting for survival). The European automotive market had shown healthy growth of several hundred thousand vehicles every year since the Second World War, reaching a peak of 13.5 million vehicles in 1990. The first major downturn came in 1993, when the market slumped to 11.5 million units. Many believed this was just a blip, which they were convinced would be rectified when annual growth of around 3 percent resumed.

This proved not to be the case, however: the car market stagnated. The number of new people wishing to buy a car failed to grow, and many existing owners put off replacing their current vehicle for as long as possible. On top of that, more and more Japanese and Korean cars came onto the European market: in 1993 there were 1.3 million Asian cars in Europe, with a market share of 12 percent; by 2007 that number had increased to 2.6 million and the market share was more than 18 percent. Automotive analyst Vic Heylen said it five years ago: 'The European car industry will have to produce between four and five million fewer vehicles annually than planned. That means there are almost fifteen car plants too many in Europe. It's as simple as that.'

The consequences were inevitable. First came the restructuring operations, with many redundancies: 117,000 jobs were lost in the European car industry in the period 2000-2006, roughly 70,000 of them from 2004 onwards. Jobs were also lost in Belgium, at Ford in Genk, at Opel in Antwerp and at VW in Vorst. As an example, around 3,000 of the total of 5,000 jobs at VW were scrapped in 2006, when VW Vorst was relaunched as Audi Brussels. The new operation retained 2,200 workers, though they had to take a 20 percent pay cut. This development was hailed by politicians as a great victory. The then Prime Minister, Guy Verhofstadt, declared triumphantly: 'The 2,200 jobs and the new models are proof that the car industry still has a future in Belgium.' Barely 24 hours later it was announced that the Opel factory in Antwerp was to scrap 900 jobs, on top of the 1,400 redundancies that had already been announced. Like VW Vorst, Opel Antwerp had halved in size within the space of just a few years.

During this period there was some hopeful news to be gleaned from the Ford factory in Genk: the plant had succeeded in winning the contract to build the Mondeo, but at the price of pay cuts. The deal would mean work for the next ten years, according to those involved. Even then, however, the first gloomy reports were already appearing in the American business newspaper *The Wall Street* Journal. Ford was putting together a plan to scrap surplus production capacity in its European factories, according to the report, and the plant in Genk might be in the firing line. Following these reports, uncertainty about the future of Ford Genk grew.

In order to shore up employment in the car industry, employees made sacrifices and governments made efforts to provide clarity. Government leaders travelled to the headquarters of the car manufacturers to listen to their concerns and to point out the advantages that Belgium had to offer. All kinds of incentive measures were rolled out to entice carmakers, and governments also came up with cash – lots of cash. Precisely how much money was involved is something that no one has ever been able to discover, because as well as the federal government, the regions, provinces and cities kept dipping into their purses too.

None of these efforts helped. In early 2010 it was announced that the Opel plant in Antwerp was to close for good, and on 15 December of that year the last car rolled off the production line. The remaining 2,600 workers found themselves without a job. Many of them looked for work in similar companies such as Volvo Cars in Ghent, Audi Brussels or the bus assembler Van Hool. Some of them looked for work in a completely different sector such as the construction industry, the hospitality industry or even in the funeral services sector. After two years, 25 percent of the victims were still without work.

The end of the story?

At the end of 2012, it was finally announced that the Ford plant in Genk would close at the end of 2014. The plant had lost out in the competitive battle with other Ford factories. Because while car showrooms compete against other makes, factories belonging to the same manufacturer compete with each other. Production of the Galaxy, Mondeo and S-Max will move from Genk to Valencia in Spain, where wage costs are apparently 42 percent lower. The Ford plant in Genk currently employs around 4,000 people and is therefore still one of the biggest employers in the province of Limburg, and in Flanders. But it is worth remembering that twenty years ago, in 1993, more than 13,000 people – more than three times the present number – earned their living at the Ford Genk factory.

That leaves just one car assembly plant in Belgium: Volvo in Ghent, which employs more than 4,800 people and produces the successful V40, S60 and XC60 models. Doubts are now growing about the future of this plant, too, however. During a visit by the Flemish Prime Minister, Kris Peeters, earlier this year, the head of Volvo made it clear that 'urgent structural reforms are needed in order to improve the competitiveness of Belgian industry.' Wage costs need to be reduced, in other words. Whether that actually happens, and if it does whether it will be enough to allow Volvo to survive in Ghent in a shrinking car market, remains to be seen.

It is therefore increasingly looking as if car production in Belgium is coming to an end. True, the Japanese carmaker Toyota still coordinates its European marketing and sales activities from Brussels, has enlarged its European research and development centre in Zaventem and employs a total of around 4,500 people in Belgium. But there is no industrial activity at these locations. Despite everything, though, Flemish Prime Minister Kris Peeters tries to remain upbeat and even sees new opportunities for the future: 'I believe that Flanders can produce the car of the future: first a hybrid, then an electric car and later perhaps a hydrogen car.' Perhaps. Bonnet closed. ■

Translated by Julian Ross

Ford

VOLVO

d = f (a-s)

Wim Crouwel, a timeless 20th Century Designer

Design is the product of function and aesthetics-minus-subjectivity. This formula could be used to represent Crouwelian design, the visual manifestation of a lifelong pursuit of objective, functional communication, with inadvertent but pleasing interference from subjective aesthetics. A retrospective exhibition, *Wim Crouwel, a Graphic Odyssey*, presented Crouwel's work and viewpoint in 2011, first at the London Design Museum and then at the Stedelijk Museum in Amsterdam.

Crouwel was born in Groningen in 1928, an extraordinary year for architecture and design. It was a year of eager innovation, in which hope and ideology seemed to rise from one and the same source. In 1928, Milanese architect Gio Ponti founded the design and architecture magazine *Domus*, which is still considered to be an authority even today. Later editors include Alessandro Mendini, the chief architect of the Groningen Museum. In La Sarraz, Switzerland, Le Corbusier founded and directed the first International Congress for Modern Architecture. At the Bauhaus, Hannes Meyer took over from Walter Gropius, changing course towards urbanism with a more socialist slant. The German type designer Jan Tschichold, who called himself Iwan for a time as a mark of his admiration for Russian constructivism, published his essay *Die neue Typographie*, in which he distanced himself from classical humanist book design. Later, however, he came to reject this view and instead promoted neoclassical design. Geometrically designed typefaces were enjoying a boom. Paul Renner, an advocate of the German Bauhaus, designed Futura, his bestselling constructivist typeface. The London sculptor and designer Eric Gill created the equally well-known humanist sans-serif typeface Gill Sans, which owes much to Johnston, the London Underground typeface designed by Edward Johnston.

And in that same year of 1928, Wim Crouwel was born. *Datum est omen?* One thing is certain: Crouwel imbibed this largely modernist idiom from an early age.

To the letter

The artist Job Hansen lived next door to Crouwel's grandparents, in Grachtstraat in Groningen. Hansen helped the young Crouwel to develop an artistic eye, and he started to create his own paintings. "The man was a great influence on me,"

Crouwel later said. As a boy, Crouwel was also very interested in architecture and fashion, and designed clothes for his mother. From the age of nineteen to twenty-one, he studied art at the Minerva Academy in Groningen. This course, however, was firmly lodged in the Arts and Crafts tradition and Crouwel soon moved on to study typography in Amsterdam, at the college that would later become the Rietveld Academie.

Crouwel had found a sample of Cassandre Bifur at the library, a typeface designed by the famous French poster designer A.M. Cassandre which, he says, "made a great impression on me". The geometric, almost architectural construction of the letters was a revelation for him. Architecture would continue to inspire Crouwel for the rest of his life, including and especially in his two-dimensional work. In Amsterdam he became an assistant to the renowned poster designer Dick Elffers and in 1953–54 he worked at the Enderberg exhibition company, where he learned to design exhibitions and became acquainted with two Swiss designers, Karl Gerstner and Gerard Ifert.

"I think 3D is wonderful," said Crouwel, as is amply demonstrated by his career, with examples such as his contribution to the Dutch pavilion at the 1970 World Fair in Osaka and his many museum exhibitions.

However, it was typefaces that captured Crouwel's attention and would not let him go, serving as a constant source of inspiration and playing a dominant role in his work. Crouwel researched the use of fonts, finding beauty in their functionality. He may not yet have come across the phrase "Form follows function," coined by American architect Louis Sullivan, the mentor of Frank Lloyd Wright, but it soon became clear that functionality would be Crouwel's rational, investigative and systematic standpoint.

In the 1950s, Crouwel became familiar with the work of the Bauhaus and the Swiss Style. Back in the 1930s, Bauhaus designer Max Bill had introduced an asymmetric layout, for which he designed a grid based on geometric proportions and the use of his favourite sans-serif typeface, Akzidenz Grotesk. Although, at that time, there was generally a formal distinction between art and applied arts, the work of artists such as Hans Albers, Paul Klee and Wassily Kandinsky was already characterized by an aesthetic style that had an almost utilitarian structure.

The Swiss Style – young, new, fresh – was a graphic design methodology that had been able to take root in Switzerland before WWII, sheltered as it was by its political neutrality. Expanding on the work of the Bauhaus, a relaxed and sober kind of graphic design developed in Zurich and Basel. Typical characteristics of the layout were the use of sans-serifs, asymmetric typography, a grid system, real-time photography and photomontage. Armin Hoffmann and Joseph Müller-Brockmann were the teachers who, both as designers and theorists, underpinned this concept and gave the Swiss Style a name that would resound all over the world: the International Typographic Style.

In 1957, Wim Crouwel met Joseph Müller-Brockmann. In that pre-computer era, lead typefaces were a serious and costly investment. As a result, most printers were able to offer only a limited selection, usually consisting of classic typefaces such as Garamond and Bodoni. The purchase of an early sans-serif typeface was a matter for lengthy consideration. The features of new, sans-serif typefaces were very critically scrutinized by designers and praised or reviled. In principle, Müller-Brockmann would employ only one typeface: Akzidenz

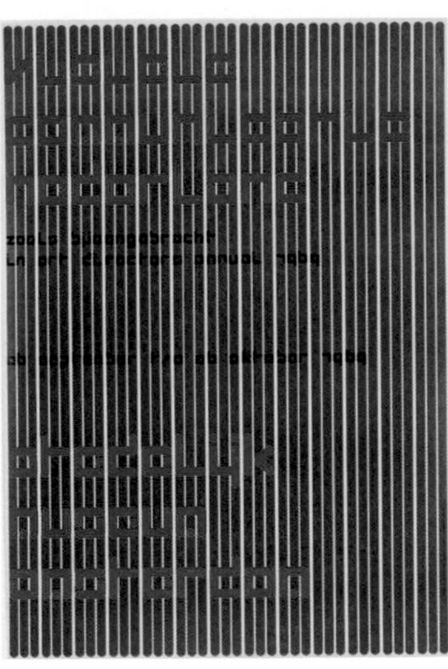

Grotesk, released in 1896. Wim Crouwel, however, has always been less rigid. Like many of his contemporaries, he also appreciates other typefaces, such as Futura, Gill Sans, Univers, and the more machine-like Helvetica, internationally regarded as an icon of the Swiss School. Wim Crouwel, seen by many as the ultimate modernist in Dutch graphic design, has gone so far as to express his aversion to what he calls the "petty individualism" of the early-twentieth-century modernists. Wim Crouwel likes Akzidenz Grotesk primarily because of the hand-designed typeface's touching imperfections. Is this an inconsistency in his functionalist approach? No. His fellow type designer Chris Brand once neatly explained such a paradox with reference to his own practice: "The deficiency of the hand is the charm of the drawn letter." Wim Crouwel has expressed his own view as follows: "We need the machine since we have no time," but "the machine cannot replace the precision of the human eye and human feeling."

Crouwel's work was strongly influenced by the International Style, but what he introduced to the Netherlands was still a very distinctive, structural graphic design based on typographical and spatial invention: rational, systematic, minimalist at times, and yet, perhaps inevitably, poetic.

"I am a functionalist troubled by aesthetics," Wim Crouwel said in an interview with design critic Max Bruinsma. At the same time, he spoke out against "individual subjectivity" in the design process.

Letters on posters

In 1955, when he started out as an independent designer, Wim Crouwel met Edy de Wilde, the director of the Van Abbe Museum in Eindhoven. De Wilde became his first major client and the one he would work for longest. The flood of posters and catalogue covers designed by Crouwel focused primarily on the museum rather than the work of the artists. The museum was viewed as the "creator" of the artist. This was a new and sensational concept. At first, Crouwel employed occasional images of the artists' work, but before long his posters consisted simply of an atmospheric area of colour with a specially constructed typeface as its central element, which sometimes functioned as a logo. These methods were purely typographical, but with a personal, minimal hint about the nature of the art on display. Disengaged? Certainly. Poetic? Subtly so.

In 1963, Edy de Wilde became the director of the Stedelijk Museum Amsterdam and Wim Crouwel went with him as designer. Willem Sandberg was their famous predecessor; both as director and designer, Sandberg had put the Stedelijk on the world map. He was a kind-hearted, enthusiastic generalist who had provided a platform both for the poetry of the Vijftigers (the Dutch angry young poets of the 1950s) and for European modern art in the Netherlands.

The freshly appointed duo gave the Stedelijk Museum a new focus and a new image. Amsterdam's intellectuals and designers watched with great interest and – it may be safely said – some prejudice. Crouwel's designs became even more streamlined: no images of artists or works of art, just typography, typeface and colour. The museum as a provider of information. Full stop. This approach also needed some defending within the museum. Curators can be rather conservative at times.

During this period, Wim Crouwel set out his principles as a designer clearly. In an interview to mark his London exhibition, he expressed his vision as eloquently as ever: "I have always tried to be a no-nonsense designer. Straightforward, no baroque, no fantasies; just readable, well-structured typography." Aiming for standardization, he based all of his designs on an underlying grid. In a quote that has become classic, Crouwel once compared the grid to the lines of a football field: "You can play a great game inside the lines or a lousy one outside them." Crouwel still believes that De Wilde was the ideal client: "He gave me criticism only after the work was finished."

But there was muttering – and some sneering, too. That was all part and parcel of Amsterdam and the Dutch cultural scene in the 1960s and '70s. When the Stedelijk Museum's new graphic identity was introduced, a new logo dominated the posters and other printed material. It consisted of two capital letters: SM. The cries of "How dare you?" were deafening. Making art, in its own temple, subordinate to typography?! How could anyone even think of attempting to unite the sacrosanct diversity of artists under one single banner? SM – Stedelijk Museum or sadomasochism?

At a later stage, Crouwel began to use images on his posters after all, but in a rather disengaged way. This approach caught on and is still typical of the work of many Dutch designers even today: the functional separation of image and typography. The image – whether a photograph or some other element – forms a foundation, with a top layer of typography. This makes it seem as though two designers have been involved in every design: one for the typography and the other for the pictorial component, with the typographical concept as the starting point. This practice differs fundamentally from graphic design in other European countries, such as France, England or Poland, where designers are more likely to start out from a "general idea" or, in other words, a form of "thinking in words and images", where the design begins with an integrated form and the result is an amalgam of image, text and meaning.

Inventive type designs

A characteristic feature of Crouwel's graphic design is his fondness for constructing new characters, which are created initially as functional lettering, constructed within the grid of a poster design, and consisting of the required letters for the title, and then often subsequently developed into a complete alphabet as a result of the designer's pure and logical fascination with the form. His inventive fonts combine to form a marvellous and diverse mini-oeuvre within his body of work, made up of alphabets such as Fodor, for the museum of the same name, and Gridnik for the Olivetti electronic typewriter. Wim Crouwel's liking for grids led fans and friends to give him the affectionate nickname "Mister Gridnik".

However, Crouwel's interest in inventive lettering is not confined to pragmatic on-the-spot solutions or mere creative doodling. Wim Crouwel looks to the future - he has always looked to the future. When new printing technology was introduced in the 1960s, Crouwel was horrified to see the clumsy coarseness and illogicality of the first attempts to design digital typefaces. Forward-thinking, he started work, back in those early days of computerization, on a character that was made up entirely of horizontal and vertical lines. He presented the results in an exhibition: New Alphabet, a typeface that was visionary, logical and elegant, but not easily legible. This naturally prompted many reactions, both positive and negative. His fellow designer Piet Schreuders scornfully referred to it as "the only font that requires subtitles". Wim Crouwel admitted that, for its time, New Alphabet was indeed "over the top" and that it was more of an experiment and never really intended to be used for reading. Even so, the New Alphabet became one of the most widely discussed creations of Crouwel's career. It appeared in British music magazines, usually in some distorted form or as an adapted version that was easier to read, as in the 1988 album cover for post-punk band Joy Division's *Substance*. The alphabet ultimately underwent further development and came to be used as a proper typeface.

In 1963, the Total Design studio was founded by Wim Crouwel, industrial designer Friso Kramer, graphic designer and architect Benno Wissing, and the brothers Paul and Dick Schwartz, who were responsible for the organization and financing. This was the first large design studio in the Netherlands to develop a multidisciplinary, full-service practice, based on the model of British studios such as the Design Research Unit (DRU), F.H.K. Henrion and Fletcher/Forbes/Gill (later Pentagram). The motivation behind the company's creation was that prestigious Dutch design commissions were all too often being awarded to foreign studios. The direct trigger was when F.H.K. Henrion swiped the contract to create branding for KLM. Henrion explained this success by saying that "Institutions like to talk to institutions", which served as an eye-opener for Total Design.

Total Design grew into a company that worked for industry, the government, the cultural sector, trade and commerce. It meant a completely new approach to design in the Netherlands. The notion of corporate identity emerged, followed by a plethora of logos – a marketing concept. This was not, however, the full-service practice of what at the time was perceived as the typical American advertising agency, answering the client's question of "What time is it?" with "What time do you want it to be?"

Total Design was multidisciplinary, shaping visual information and rigorously checking quality at all the required stages and across a range of media: documentation, concept, design, photography, production. It was Wim Crouwel who established and maintained the aesthetic standard, and who was behind many of Total Design's numerous successes. He was omnipresent. Strict. Principled. But still he encouraged his colleagues' own ideas and respected other opinions. Clarity was always of prime importance, both visually and socially, according to the Dutch tradition of consensus. Crouwel has always been a critical observer, but also a diplomat. As the British newspaper *The Guardian* said, "His revered body of work, which spans 60 years, has a deep humanity and an artistic quirkiness that combines precision with emotion."

Headed by Wim Crouwel for over twenty years, Total Design had a great deal of highly unpleasant criticism heaped upon it in the late 1960s and '70s. Those were the years of the Vietnam War and anti-Americanism, of the generation of '68, in short, of social activism. The idiom of Wim Crouwel, based on modernism, was dismissed as the work of "crouwel and his cronies". That's right, "crouwel": the fashion at the time was for small or lowercase letters. Even worse, Crouwel was labelled a "grid freak" by his more progressive colleagues and a "pattern freak" by students. His work was denounced as "colouring inside the lines". Conservative elements among the cultural classes described his work as exhibiting "perpetual baldness", and his 1977 number stamps as "hazy". Author Renate Rubinstein called the telephone directory that Crouwel designed with Jolijn van de Wouw, which featured no uppercase letters, the ultimate example of "the New Ugliness". Crouwel and co were accused of taking a one-size-fits-all approach to Dutch design and making the entire country "total designed".

In 1987, *Vrij Nederland* journalist Rudie Kagie reassessed the development of Total Design: "When it was founded in 1963, Total Design was innovative. It soon became 'timeless' and in 1986, following the departure of Wim Crouwel, the last of the founding members, it became dated."

Designer Karel Martens says that, "It was actually quite difficult to avoid Wim Crouwel's work. In the 1960s the Netherlands was inundated with posters, catalogues and stamps designed by him, even the telephone book."

Be that as it may, Crouwel, as a designer, thinker, and finally as a director of Total Design, has had a huge, structural influence on the way visual information is presented in printed matter in the Netherlands. Crouwel's younger colleague, type designer Anthon Beeke, who at first, when observing from a distance, had called the "dictatorship" of Total Design "criminal" and was subsequently invited by Crouwel to come and tackle it from the inside, later said, "When I was working there, I suddenly saw what a blessing that studio was for Dutch industry and business, as Total Design threw a marvellous blanket over the communication process in the Netherlands, where very many things were indeed going wrong. And I have to say, because of the way TD dealt with companies that had a lot of printing work, it always turned out well."

The value(s) of design

"Ethics is the aesthetics of the future." This was wishful thinking on the part of Vladimir Ilyich Ulyanov, alias Lenin, the son of a Russian aristocrat. In the Dutch design scene in the 1970s, there was growing discussion about the socio-cultural implications of the profession. Famous graphic designers such as Jan van Toorn, Gert Dumbar and Anthon Beeke turned against Wim Crouwel's uncompromising standpoint that it was possible to practice the profession of designer objectively and without reference to personal values.

The dispute culminated in 1972 in a public debate between Crouwel and Van Toorn at Museum Fodor in Amsterdam, about the (im)possibility of objective design. As a socially oriented thinker who employed design to communicate a vision, to comment on society, to stir political awareness, Jan van Toorn perceived design as visual journalism that both liberates and enriches the recipient, with strong images that can be "read" and which are an indicator of the age. Aesthetics are an incidental extra. Jan van Toorn declared, "Forms that are based solely on aesthetics are forgotten in fifteen seconds, as the next pretty picture comes by." There was no winner in this fierce but friendly discussion. Both men were gentlemen. Wim Crouwel expressed his amusement in a later interview: "There were heated debates at the time, but I knew how to handle criticism and I was sure of myself."

This battle of opinions helped to plough and reseed the Dutch design landscape, partly because the new generation of art and design students, in the slipstream of democratization, made their voices heard. In the majority of art academies, programmes were subject to vigorous discussion, which in some cases resulted in coups, with changes of management and teaching staff. The word "beautiful" was declared taboo within the institutions and replaced by "good" and "conceptually sound".

As lecturers too, both Jan van Toorn and Wim Crouwel also contributed to the endless debate about the profession, at home and abroad. Crouwel started teaching in the 1950s, at the Royal Academy of Art and Design in Den Bosch and at the Institute of Applied Art in Amsterdam. From 1965 to 1985, he was attached to the Industrial Design department at Delft University of Technology, first as a member of staff, later as a lecturer, professor and dean. From 1987 to 1993, he was the chair of Art and Cultural Sciences at the Erasmus University in Rotterdam.

As well as the argument about ethics and aesthetics, another debate – about the equalization of "high" and "low" art – was expanded to take in autonomous art and design. Crouwel's position was clear. He did not accept the merging of art and design. In his own words: "I myself cannot stop believing that graphic design is first and foremost a means to inform. That, for me, is the basic rule. Creating complexity and curiosity and raising questions belong to a different domain. In my opinion, the most important issue is always the question of why it is that we do what we do. Is it always about our responsibility towards society?" And: "This very socially aware attitude among designers is most probably a question of time and circumstances. Let the Dutch hammer away all they like, but it's essentially part of a trend."

Hope – and modernism after all

Following all that criticism, it seemed for a while that the "Crouwel era" was drawing to an end. Modernism gave way to postmodernism and its cheerfully referential approach. The image copulated enthusiastically with the letter, and the imagination reigned supreme. The "complexity" referred to by Crouwel is now abundantly evident in the visual culture of the internet.

In 1985, Wim Crouwel became the director of the Boijmans Van Beuningen Museum in Rotterdam and remained in that position until 1993. He did not wish to combine his role as director with the role of designer, but instead brought in the young British studio 8vo (Octavo) for the graphic design, whose studio members Hamish Muir and Simon Johnston were trained by the Swiss typographer Wolfgang Weingart. The studio developed its own visual language based on the Swiss Style. It became a very special collaboration and the museum created exhibitions featuring harmonious displays and graphic design.

The British design scene rediscovered Wim Crouwel's modernism via an unexpected route. I have already mentioned the band Joy Division, and designers Peter Saville and Brett Wickens's use of Crouwel's New Alphabet for their album cover, and the hip music magazines that subsequently embraced this functional style. These hand-drawn, imaginative, constructed typefaces intrigued young designers in particular. This revival – coming after postmodernism – in the form of a futurist-inspired modernism was undoubtedly connected to a need for order and structure in the midst of overwhelming and inescapable visual overload.

This new way of looking at Crouwel's work shows just how remarkable his influence has been on the Dutch design scene, and how much he has since influenced a younger generation worldwide. That said, Crouwel himself wonders if this interest involves nothing more than citing a particular style.

The past hundred years of Dutch Design, one of the country's most important export products, is made up of contributions from a very large number of individual designers and studios and has also paid the bills for many critics. For six decades of that century Crouwel has been an important and influential designer. It was not for nothing that his work achieved cult status, and he is often referred to as one of the founders of Dutch Design. His own reaction is brief and Crouwelian: "The label of Dutch Design is a slogan that is a product of our modern-day one-liner culture. It has become a concept in the trade and represents a fruitless attempt to extend the brief upsurge of design in the Netherlands."

Wim Crouwel has always aimed to be "timeless". Has he succeeded? In an interview he says, "I no longer believe in timelessness. My work from the 1950s is different from what I did in the '60s, '70s, '80s and '90s. But at the same time I hope that it is still recognizable." ■

Translated by Laura Watkinson

FURTHER READING

KEES BROOS, *Alphabets*, 2003, 144 pp., Bis Publishers

MAX BRUINSMA, *Wim Crouwel*, Oeuvre prize for design, 2004, Foundation for Visual Arts, Design and Architecture, Amsterdam, www.maxbruinsma.nl

PATRICK BURGOYNE, *An Interview with Wim Crouwel*, 2007, www.creativereview.co.uk

ESTHER CLEVEN, *Irrationeel, Grafische vormgeving en de context van de beeldcultuur*, Faculty of Humanities, University of Amsterdam, 2007

ESMEE ERDTSIECK, *Idealisme in de context van het modernisme/postmodernisme*, Artez Academie Arnhem, 2009

FREDERIQUE HUYGEN EN DINGENUS VAN DE VRIE, *Het Debat, Wim Crouwel & Jan van Toorn*, [Z]OO producties, www.zooproducties,nl

FREDERIQUE HUYGEN AND HUGHUES BOEKRAAD, *Wim Crouwel*. Zwolle: Waanders, 1995.

HERMAN LAMPAERT, *Chronique de la Forme*, Atelier Perrousseaux, 1997–2002

PAUL MERTZ, *Wim Crouwel*, [Z]OO producties, www.zooproducties,nl

NAGO (Nederlands Archief Grafisch Ontwerpers/Dutch Archive of Graphic Designers), www.nago.nl

IDEA magazine #323, www.iconofgraphics.com

Wim Crouwel: a graphic odyssey, ed. Tony Brook & Adrian Shaughnessy, Unit Editions, London, 2011.

Wim Crouwel: een grafische ontdekkingsreis, www.stedelijk.nl, 2011

Wim Crouwel "in his own words", een selectie van lezingen tussen 1973 en 2006, Lauwen Books, 2011

Flemish Film Beyond the Borders of Flanders?

[ERIK MARTENS]

Back in the 1970s, thousands of young children in Flanders and the Netherlands used to watch the Japanese-Italian children's cartoon *Calimero*. The main character was a small black chicken with half an eggshell on his head that went on all the time in a fretful voice that everything was unfair, 'because she's big and I's small'.

Calimero's experiences were tailor-made for children, and even for the parents the frustration of the powerless in the face of the large-scale was absolutely recognisable. Later, the 'Calimero complex' became a concept in psychology in Belgium and the Netherlands. That concept can also be applied to countries and their populations, especially communities of limited size which, for whatever reason, feel they have had a bad deal.

In the geography of film-producing countries, that sensitivity is also acutely present. The European film industry has always felt weak compared to its powerful big brother from the United States. It is well known that the European market was flooded by American films after the Second World War. Local film production hardly played a significant role of any kind, for all Europeans were mad about American films.

The somewhat larger European film countries, headed by France, still had a handful of big names with an artistic reputation that could counter the lack of popularity. But small film countries, which did not boast any famous filmmakers or have a home audience to fall back on, inevitably had to struggle with a hefty Calimero complex.

Among the small film countries that found the going tough, Belgium was well to the fore. With its central position in Europe and its openness to both the Romance and the Germanic culture, Belgium had a very vibrant, varied film culture. All kinds of films could be seen in Flanders, except Flemish films, since they practically didn't exist. In addition, the market for national production was divided again between a French-speaking and a Dutch-speaking one. For an expensive technological medium that can only recover its costs when a large number of cinema-goers buy tickets, this was – and is – an unfavourable point of departure.

From the sixties onwards, the country was gradually divided up into a Dutch-speaking and a French-speaking community (and a small German-speaking one) each of which developed its own film policy. Both struggle with the lim-

Bullhead
A story of crime and punishment, friendship and lost innocence in the environment of the Flemish hormone mafia

ited nature of their market, for although French-speaking Belgium has naturally linked up with France, and Dutch-speaking Belgium with the Netherlands, in practice their films scarcely cross the border, with the exception of the Dardenne brothers. The cultural border seems to be even tougher than the linguistic border.

One of the problems with which small film-producing entities such as Flanders struggle is that within a context of limited means it is difficult to produce a sufficient critical mass. After all, certain quantity is necessary to keep one's own production apparatus alive, and without a professional production apparatus there can be no qualitative production. Professional expertise and experience cannot develop in a vacuum.

Flemish film has had a number of moments when it seemed that it was approaching a growth phase. Time and again, the film titles concerned appeared from nowhere and gained a surprisingly large local audience. Not all of these films were good quality, but often in their wake they created increased interest in domestic film production for a time.

Loft

Five married men share a loft for their adulterous escapades. When a female body is discovered in the loft, the story changes from misspent decadence to a classical whodunit

A first significant occurrence of this kind was the popular filming of *De Witte* [Whitey] by Ernest Claes in 1934. The film-makers involved were Edith Kiel and Jan Vanderheyden, who were also able to maintain a modest level of film production in subsequent years. In the early 1970s, Fons Rademakers, Hugo Claus and Jan van Raemdonck dug up the Flemish author Stijn Streuvels (1871-1969) to produce a headstrong mix of naturalism and hippie-romanticism with Mira, their film version of his book *De Teleurgang van de Waterhoek*. Here, too, attendance figures were high, and in the years immediately afterwards a number of titles, making use of the same ingredients, attracted a curious Flemish audience.

Until recently the most successful films in Flanders were comedies featuring such popular comedians as Urbanus in the 1990s. Urbanus has the second and third position in the all-time box-office top ten of Flemish films: *Hector* (1987) and *Koko Flanel* (1990), with 933,000 and 1,082,000 viewers respectively.

The films were successful, not exactly because they were exceptional films, but because the comedian in question was successful. There are also a handful of other titles with a comparable effect, such as the historical film *Daens* by Stijn Coninx about the life of the famous socially engaged priest from Aalst (1992). Stijn Coninx, by the way, is the most successful film-maker in the history of Flemish film. He put his name not only to the prestigious *Daens* (848,000 viewers) but also the two Urbanus films, which led to him being able to claim for a long time (until *Loft* in 2008) to have produced all top three of the most successful Flemish films. Flemish film-makers often have a hybrid filmography.

The arrival of commercial television

Apart from these isolated successes, their native language and culture seldom seemed to be a decisive argument for the Flemish viewer to choose local products.

With the arrival of commercial television in the 1980s, this axiom was turned upside-down. In the Flemish TV-viewer there arose an appetite for Flemish fiction that had not existed previously. Since then, Flemish television fiction has experienced a steady advance, initially in the form of long-lasting soaps, in recent years more frequently in the form of clear-cut TV series with a fixed number of instalments. They have repeatedly commanded high viewing figures, and today there also seems to be international interest in Flemish television fiction.

The growth of the television sector over the past 25 years has had a considerable impact on the film sector. The local AV industry increased in size, became more effective and introduced a generation of experienced actors and technicians onto fiction sets.

At a modest Flemish level, local stars emerged: popular television actors who subsequently took their audience with them to the silver screen and who, in the production of television programmes and films, became an element to be taken into account.

Local commercial successes

The first signals of an approaching boom in Flemish film date from 2003. That year Flemish film, with the noir-thriller *De zaak Alzheimer* [The Memory of a Killer], scored its greatest success since the early 1990s: 750,000 people saw the film. Five years later, film director Eric Van Looy confirmed his talent for qualitative entertainment with the film *Loft* [The Loft]. The film was so popular in Belgian cinemas that it broke all previous records. With 1.2 million viewers it became the most popular Flemish film ever.

Since then the indicators have been trending upwards in every respect. In 2003, seven Flemish films were shot; in 2012, there were 30. In 2004, some 566,000 Flemish people went to watch Flemish films in the cinema; in 2012, this figure more than doubled, with 1,462,158. And the market share of Flemish film also doubled to 9.35% of all cinema tickets sold in 2012 – a percentage that has been stable for about the last five years. This trend break did not materialise out of thin air. There are a number of structural factors that have helped shape the new situation.

To begin with, money. Thanks to the federal tax break that celebrates its tenth anniversary in 2013, there are suddenly considerably more means available for the local film industry. The Flemish Audiovisual Fund (VAF), which has been the official public financier of Flemish film production since 2002, adroitly anticipated the dynamic and on several occasions managed to mobilise additional means for film production. Along with the film fund there also came a media fund for the support of TV fiction series, and most recently *Screen Flanders*, an economic fund that invests in productions that are active on Flemish soil.

A second factor that helps to explain the increasing commercial success of new Flemish film is that the new Flemish film-maker also thinks more *commercially* than previously. While the film-maker used to be central to the film concept, audience considerations now tip the scales more than before. Producers and film-makers are no longer averse to commercial concepts. A film-maker such as Jan Verheyen shows in all his films (*Het vonnis*, 2013 *Zot van A*, 2010; *Dossier K*, 2009, *Team Spirit 1 & 2*, 2000 & 2003 etc.) an unerring instinct for the taste of the average Flemish viewer.

It is also revealing that an ever-increasing number of films are being made without financial support from the state. A film business such as Studio 100 has been making profitable commercial productions for children without subsidies for years. The full-length films *Code 37* (Jakob Verbruggen, 2011, based on the TV series of the same name) and *Bingo* (Rudi Van den Bossche, 2013) were shot without support from the film fund. *Frits & Freddy* by Guy Goossens and Marc Punt (2010) got so many people to go the cinema (about 440,000) that it promptly gained a sequel (*Frits en Franky*, Marc Punt, 2013). Both were shot without state support.

Quite a large number of films, however, that have been made *with* support from the film fund are based on equally commercial concepts. Film-makers opt for the well-tried, well-known and easily recognisable and are less interested in the original. Concepts that have already proved successful are taken out and re-used again subsequently.

Recognisability is a two-edged sword. While it may produce a greater number of viewers within the local context, it has a tendency to make a film unrecognisable at an international level.

For the non-Fleming, the apparently accessible house, garden and kitchen nonsense of a comedy such as *Frits en Freddy* is, paradoxically enough, pretty... hermetic. Flemish films that are successful in Flanders are not automatically successful elsewhere in the world. They are tailor-made for Flanders and then only fit a Flemish head.

It is obvious that this prototype of new Flemish film occupies an important place in the statistics of the success of Flemish film. It partakes to a much lesser extent in the debate about the artistic quality of the new generation of Flemish film-makers.

International successes

It would be unjust to assume that Flemish films only enjoy success on the home front. According to the statistics, Flemish films in recent years have more frequently made their mark internationally: in 2012, Flemish films were selected for international festivals on 1,220 occasions. There they won 226 international prizes or nominations.

The export value of the popular film that primarily aimed at the well-known local biotope is usually limited. For films with a broader, or an artistic relevance there is today a well-developed international festival network that is more alive than ever, and within which a great variety of films circulate from all corners of the world.

That festival circuit is not a new phenomenon. Most major festivals emerged in the period after the Second World War and fitted into the context of a reaction against the dominant power position of the American film industry.

Flemish films have been travelling to festivals for some time now. The classic *Meeuwen sterven in de Haven* [Seagulls Die in the Harbour] by Rik Kuypers, Roland Verhavert and the recently deceased Ivo Michiels was shown in the official selection of the 1956 Cannes Festival. In 1960, it was the turn of Emile Degelin with *Si le vent te fait peur* [If the Wind Frightens You], in 1971 Harry Kümel with his *Malpertuis* [The Legend of Doom House]. The international list of awards of the animation-filmmaker Raoul Servais is, quite simply, impressive.

Hasta la vista
Three handicapped youths escape from their over-protective environment and set off on holiday together to Spain, in search of sexual diversion

The Broken Circle Breakdown
Melodrama crammed with Country & Western music about the passionate love of Didier and Elise and their love-child Maybelle, who is going to die of cancer

Have things changed all that much? Well, yes, the scale of things has increased exponentially. On the one hand, the Flemish AV industry has become more highly competitive; on the other hand, the international network has increased enormously. *Flanders Image*, which is the international instrument for promoting Flemish film, has its hands full for, according to official statistics, the world today boasts over four thousand (!) film festivals.

The gigantic international film circuit generates a constantly greater demand for films, to the extent that it has grown into a genuine alternative screening circuit. With the difficult economic situation in which the classic art house circuit finds itself, the festival circuit has taken over part of the screening function.

For the Flemish art house film, which can only fall back on the cinema-loving public, the results at Flemish cinema box-office are, by definition, modest. A respectable number of them pass through smoothly to the international festival circuit with, in the best case, selections at prestigious fora – and, even better, prestigious prizes at these venues. The full-length films made by the duo Jessica Woodworth and Peter Brosens since 2006 (*Khadak*, 2006; *Altiplano*, 2009; and recently *The Fifth Season*, 2012) are the prototype of these. They only registered a few thousand (*Khadak*) to ten thousand cinema-goers (*Altiplano*) in their own region, but the festival trajectory of these films, on the other hand, is remarkable. Similar success was enjoyed by *The Invader* (2011), the first long-length film by the AV artist Nicolas Provost as well as the films by the newcomer Gust Van Den Berghe, whose first film *Little Baby Jesus of Flanders* (2010) and second film *Blue Bird* (2011) were selected for the *Quinzaine des Réalisateurs* in Cannes. The stylised *Noordzee Texas* (2011) by Bavo Defurne had hardly any viewers in Flanders, but in the specialized festivals abroad it was positively received. *Kid* (2013) by Fien Troch was praised in the press, but in the Belgian box-office it attracted only a few thousand film-goers.

Other more or less recent films did manage to combine a respectable local success with a prestigious festival career: *Aanrijding in Moscou* [Moscow, Belgium] by Christophe Van Rompaey was selected in 2008 in Cannes (*Semaine de la Critique*) where it won best screenplay award. It was the same story for *De helaasheid der dingen* [The Misfortunates] by Felix Van Groeningen (2009): 454,336 viewers in Flanders and subsequently a prize in Cannes. His latest film, *The Broken Circle Breakdown* (2012), got 393,000 viewers and a number of international film festival awards, including an Oscar nomination in 2014. And both Hans Van Nuffel (*Adem* [Oxygen], 2010) and Nic Balthazar (*Ben X*) have won the Grand Prix des Amériques at the Montreal Festival (in 2010 and 2007, respectively).

It is not always equally easy to predict success. Take the film *Rundskop* (Bullhead, 2011), the debut film of Michael R. Roskam, which scored a surprising success in the Flemish cinemas (469,576 tickets sold). Surprising, because *Rundskop* is an atypical popular film. It is pretty gloomy, the rhythm is sluggish, the stylisation emphatic and the message sombre.

Rundskop met with broad international recognition in the festival circuit: it was shown at the Berlin festival and carried off an Oscar nomination. The festival effect promoted the actor Mathias Schoenaerts into an 'actor to be kept an eye on internationally', and Roskam was contacted for American projects. *Rundskop* led to Schoenaerts being offered a main role in the French film *De rouille et d'os* [Rust and Bone] by the top film director Jacques Audiard, and made his career accelerate at a speed seldom seen before among Flemish actors.

Careers abroad and commercial prospects

Artistic recognition abroad is fine, but does it also have a financial impact on the career of a film? Does it generate means that enable the film-maker to start new projects?

Just as with the statistics regarding festival selections, the figures for sales abroad follow an upward curve. Rather than provide a general overview of present-day trends, I wish to illustrate the present evolution by means of the career abroad of the film *Hasta la vista* by Geoffrey Enthoven, which, within this field, has followed a remarkable path.

In Flanders, *Hasta la vista* attracted about 250,000 viewers. It was selected for more than 30 international festivals, gained about twenty awards and was sold to about 20 European countries and a further handful outside Europe, including – somewhat surprisingly – Hong Kong and Iran. Often, such sales are mainly symbolical. As in the case of Lithuania, where so far the film has enticed only 196 viewers to the cinema. In other countries, the figures were considerably higher: in the Czech Republic, the film mustered 1,500 viewers, in Russia 2,300, in Poland 6,000, in Hungary 6,000, but in Germany 70,000 and in France

140,000. Including a number of smaller countries, the film quickly amassed more viewers abroad than in Flanders. In this instance, foreign exposure acquires a significance that is more than symbolical.

Art and commerce?

If we are to believe the available figures, Flemish Film is becoming more and more successful; previously, mainly inside its own region, but today increasingly in other countries. Recognition abroad does not, however, immediately lead to great riches for Flemish film producers – but it does create openings for new projects.

Does this success also mean that ever more *quality* and *artistically relevant* films are being made and that the region is slowly but surely acquiring its own place in the annals of film history?

If we consider the issue with the necessary pragmatism, I am inclined to answer moderately positively. The quality and the professionalism of the production apparatus in general has increased. More films are being made, so most probably also more films with artistic virtues. The increasing recognition from abroad points that way in all respects, although that foreign assessment sometimes takes a different direction than our own evaluation. Apart from that, we arrive at a number of hardly shocking conclusions: that Flemish film-makers are increasingly focussed on the commercial success of their work, and that only a limited number of them apply themselves to an artistic path. Flanders has some film-makers that do explore that path uncompromisingly and have produced interesting work, or at least interesting initiatives: I am thinking here of such film-makers as Roskam, Troch, Bal, Van Rompaey, Monsaert, Provost, Grimonprez, Woodworth & Brosens, and a few others. Objectively speaking, there is little that connects them: not even the language or the arena in which their films take place. Or must we see precisely that self-willedness, that urge to follow one's own path as being a connecting element?

There is also a whole group of film-makers who have a striking and obstinate affinity for grotesque distortion. Their films, often black comedies, display expressionistic characteristics, but this Flemish expressionism is only one particular variant.

What applies to all of them is that their trajectories are as yet too short for it to be possible to speak of genuine oeuvres. So for the time being it is a question of waiting for film-makers who make not just one or two interesting films but build up a consistent oeuvre, with a distinctive voice, a personal thematic focus and an international relevance - film-makers whose new films are eagerly awaited internationally, as at present is the case for new films by the Dardenne brothers.

At that level, the Flemish Calimero feeling is still appropriate: we admittedly have the local audience that the French-speaking cinema in Belgium does not have, but so far we do not have any convincing reply to the Dardenne brothers. ■

Translated by John Irons

The Invader
The African refugee Amadoe is washed up on a European shore.
He tries to survive in the urban jungle of Brussels

Futile Scribbles in the Margins of History

The Literary Work of F. Springer

F. Springer, the writer alter ego of the Dutch diplomat Carel Jan Schneider (1932-2011) and the author of eleven novels and novellas and three collections of stories, has been considered a born story-teller since his debut. That debut, a collection of short stories, *Bericht uit Hollandia* (1962), was extremely topical when it was published, in that all three of the stories take place in Netherlands New Guinea, the last remaining part of the Dutch colonial empire in East Asia, which was handed over to Indonesia the same year, under great international pressure. Hollandia was the administrative centre of a colony where, especially in the Baliem Valley, some of the inhabitants still lived in the Stone Age.

Although he regularly refers to work by other writers, the choice between producing literature and telling stories was never difficult for Springer:

> 'I come from a milieu where people have always told each other tall stories. Besides that, in a period like the one in New Guinea I was on tour sometimes for months, with a few Indonesian, Ambonese and Papuan administrative assistants. After sunset, of course, there was nothing to do in the jungle. We used to sit round the campfire near our bivouac then and just tell stories. To be honest there are a couple of stories in *Bericht uit Hollandia* that I wrote up straight from the mouths of a couple of old friends like that from those days.'

In addition, he borrowed lavishly from such trivial sources as stories from school and ships' libraries: tales of Flash Gordon and Winnetou, of Captain Nemo and Robin Hood, and Edgar Wallace's stories about Sanders of the River. There is therefore an element in Springer's work that can best be described as 'boys' books romanticism'. But if he names admired authors with whom he feels he has most affinity, they are F. Scott Fitzgerald, W. Somerset Maugham, Guy de Maupassant or Heinrich von Kleist, for example, not trivial storytellers, nor essayists nor writers with philosophical leanings, but writers of well-paced stories, with a sharp eye for human weakness and incapacity.

The boys' book romanticism is often reinforced by the exotic setting of Springer's work. Apart from Netherlands New Guinea, his stories are set, amongst other places, in Java, the Angolan national park Kissama, Bangladesh, Teheran during the fall of the Shah, and in Kandy in Ceylon. Even when

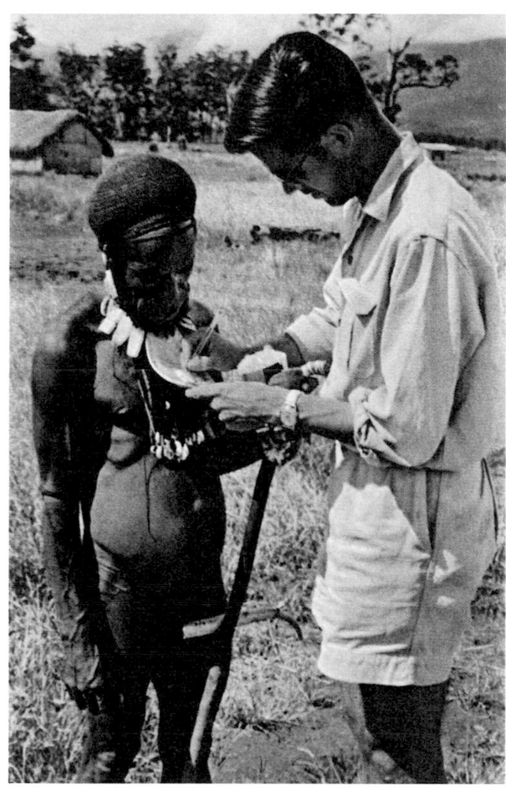

Chief Opinay and Chief Administrator C.J. Schneider, Baliem Valley, Dutch New-Guinea. National Geographic Magazine, May, 1962. Photo by John Scofield

the decor is Berlin, New York or the Dutch village Lutten (in the novel *Quadriga,* 2010; the novella *Tabee, New York*, 1974; and the short story 'De verovering van Bandung' in the collection *Zaken overzee*, 1977, respectively) he succeeds in adding an exotic tone. The author lived in most of these places for a long time, either in his youth or, later, as a diplomat.

The Baliem Valley had only been under Dutch authority for a short while when Springer became the chief administrator (which he was from 1960 to 1962). The clash between the Stone Age and the twentieth century that he experienced at first hand there is the theme of some of his work: the novella *Schimmen rond de Parula* (1966), for example, in which the converts made by an American missionary take his message so literally that they crucify him; and his posthumously published novel *Met stille trom* (2012) – which he actually wrote in 1962 – in which an American anthropologist who wants to allow the original inhabitants to keep their own rituals, including regular tribal wars, clashes with the Dutch authorities. The confrontation between such radically different times and cultures forms a core motif in Springer's work: mutatis mutandis everyone lives in different worlds simultaneously; the tragedy of life is that one seldom or never succeeds in reconciling these worlds with each other.

Two types of characters stand out in his work as far as that is concerned: the escapist and the braggart. Various characters escape from the inclemencies of life in illusions. Sometimes they literally step out of life or disappear without a trace; often they sacrifice hard reality to their imagination. The businessman Charles Enders in *Quissama* (1985) is an example of the latter. He neglects his exploration of the Angolan market because he is completely absorbed by the stories of an impossible love told to him by a fellow countryman who has, in the meantime, tragically died. This is a character who can count one hundred percent on Springer's sympathy. Those who sell their dreams as their successes, on the other hand, do not come off well in Springer's work. In almost every novel there are braggarts like this, braggarts who end up hitting rock-bottom.

Springer is not the type of writer that expressly engages with social or political standpoints; his engagement is in the first instance with the individual that stands his ground in the world by following his dreams. At the same time the realisation that many people cannot hang on to those dreams permeates his work; it is teeming with missed opportunities. Nonetheless, in *Met stille trom*, for example, he makes it clear between the lines that he does believe that the Western ideal of civilisation is right for those still living in the Stone Age. From the fact that his administrators and diplomats generally go about their work without complaining, we can infer that he also believes that they make a useful contribution to the relations between different peoples. But Springer would never use that type of language ('make a useful contribution'). He prefers 'playing embassy' and 'futile scribbles in the margins of history'

In addition to being civil servants, diplomats or businessmen, many of Springer's main characters are, or are forced to become, writers. While writing seems to come easily to them in everyday life (they 'bang out' their reports because they know pretty much what their superiors want to read), it is quite the opposite with their personal writing. It might look as if it has been put together casually, but in fact it is all about sharp phrasing and vivid characterisation, as is the case with his much admired examples. A familiar technique in Springer's work is the comparison of events with scenes from films and characters with film stars; or one hears a song in a scene that adds to the atmosphere - casual manipulations whereby the imagination strengthens the illusion of reality.

A good example of how Springer reflects on his writing can be seen in *Bougainville, Een gedenkschrift* (1981), considered by many to be his most successful novel. In it, the main character Bo, the Dutch Chargé d'affaires in Dhaka (then Dacca), Bangladesh, gets hold of the story of his recently drowned boyhood friend Tommie Vaulant's adulterous love affair with a former school friend. From his own comments on the opening sentence of his story – 'She was so extremely blonde it left me speechless' – it is clear that Tommie realises he is definitely not a writer:

> 'Ah no, that's not how Kleist opened, *Gatsby* didn't start like that. Everything I'd like to say is blocked by her. My friend Bo, who writes (slick) stories and loves pertinent opening sentences, would laugh himself silly if he read "she was so exceptionally blonde". (And anyway, she wasn't blonde). Get some

distance, some perspective, take yourself pretty much out of the equation - that is the only way to make something of it, on paper and elsewhere too. That's what Bo would say. We only spent an hour together this time. He came from the ministry and we had coffee on the Square, in The Hague. They had his collection of short stories in the window of the bookshop there. He bought one for me and, despite the chitchat, the slap on the shoulder, I knew it was important to him to give me that book. I could see him thinking: whatever you do, don't be too serious, don't get theatrical or dramatic.'

The Shah as braggart

Apart from being a literary commentary (in which Springer indirectly trivializes his own writing – 'writes (slick) stories') this is also a life commentary: there is no place for theatricality in stories any more than there is amongst friends. What is really important becomes clear from a person's actions, not from what he says about them. The need to put things into perspective applies not only 'on paper' but 'elsewhere too', in everyday life.

That becomes all the clearer from the passage in this novel describing the talk Bo attended in Dhaka given by the then deathly tired French writer André Malraux. Bo, who has great admiration for Malraux, realises that he is standing 'eye to eye with Grandeur', with an adversary of fascism, the confidant of various great people in the world, but also with the friend of the writer E. du Perron, to whom Malraux had dedicated the novel *La Condition Humaine* and in whose novel *Het land van herkomst* he himself figured as Heverlé. As preparation Bo had read some of *Het land van herkomst*. When he is finally able to shake Malraux's hand, Bo calls himself not an admirer but a compatriot of his friend:

> '"Je suis..." I said, "je suis compatriote d'Eddy du Perron". He took my hand and said something, so softly that I didn't understand, and he had no chance to repeat it as two women suddenly embraced him enthusiastically and shouted loudly that they had admired his work so very much for years.'

Not all of Springer's writers are as conscientious as this Bo. One of them is actually a pure imposter as a writer, in the tradition of Willem Elsschot's characters. This applies to Toby Harrison in *Teheran, een zwanezang* (1991), who gets a commission, just before the fall of the Shah, to write a biography of the Pahlevis in the tradition of James Morier's famous picaresque novel *The Adventures of Hajji Baba of Ispahan,* which was regarded by many in the nineteenth century as giving a true picture of Persia. Harrison knows very well what sort of writer he himself is: 'I sprinkle well-known historical facts with a sauce of highly imaginative noises. [My] books are not meant for clever Swiss clockmakers. I write for nitwits.' In the character of this nonentity, for whom the Shah seems to have more time than for Western diplomats who could help him save his skin, Springer gives a wonderful and often hilarious picture of the unworldliness of a man who fails to see how thin his power and status have worn: the Shah as braggart.

F. Springer (1932 - 2011)

Indonesian background

One element present in all of Springer's novels and stories is the Indonesian background of one or more of its characters, often the main character. Much of this is directly linked to the writer's first thirteen years of life, in Java, and his childhood friendships and loves, and certainly the three years in Japanese camps. Later meetings with former friends play a major role in several of the novels. The sadness at no longer being able to relive the past as it really was and the impossibility of undoing mistakes from the past colours some of these stories. What he reveals of the camps is partly hidden behind a shield of relativity ('some hunger, some homesickness'), but the most harrowing events, such as being separated from his mother at ten years of age, seeing and experiencing misery and death, are clearly mentioned.

In two novels that he wrote after he retired from diplomacy, this period is central. *Bandoeng Bandung* (1993) is the story of an older Dutch politician who goes along on a commercial mission to Java, the land of his birth, as an expert in the field. There he comes into contact with a former classmate of Indonesian origin, to whom he had promised at the end of the war to do what he could to get him out of Indonesia too. But he never fulfilled his promise and feels like a fraud now. The meeting affects him so much that he decides to give up his political and administrative ambitions. He does not want his career in society to hinder his ability to fulfil his real obligations any more.

The other novel is *Kandy, Een terugtocht* (1998), the story of the laborious repatriation of incomplete families after the war. After mothers and children had first been reunited with each other following their years in Japanese camps, it took months, due to chaotic bureaucracy, before they could be reunited with the fathers, who had ended up in Bangkok after their forced labour on the Burma railway. Meanwhile, the mothers and children were stranded in Kandy, in Ceylon (now Sri Lanka), Mountbatten's former headquarters. The subtitle, 'a journey back', applies not only to the events described, it also refers to the way in which the story is told. One of the children of the time recounts his memories, looking back at the secret club in which he and other children had created their own world, remembering the love he never expressed for the girl who was the natural leader of the club and the fact that he might, accidentally, have wounded or even killed their favourite camp waiter with a bow and arrow. Both the question of whether he really was so in love as he remembers now and his doubts about the consequences of his shot take such a hold on him that he goes in search of his companions from back then. Although the meeting results in a brief moment of acknowledgement of what had previously had to remain unsaid, this acknowledgement comes too late. Meanwhile he comments on his nostalgic questions as 'an old fool's sentimental nonsense'. He is a typical Springer character: someone whose nostalgia and disillusionment get in his way. That is also the case, for example, in *Tabee, New York* (1974), the first novel for which Springer delved into his Indonesian youth. In it, a young Dutch diplomat rediscovers his childhood love from Indonesia in the United States. In the meantime she is unhappily married with his erstwhile rival. But when he finally gets his chance with her, he feels it is too late and deliberately lets it go.

It is true that most of Springer's characters, like Bo in *Bougainville*, give themselves up at some point to 'all sorts of sentimental thoughts, distant loves, missed opportunities, deeply buried but never forgotten blunders and a bit of self-pity too.' But then they usually straighten up and tell themselves and the readers: 'What do you bring home from your travels? A handful of wild stories that are embellished with more and more invented true-to-life details at every family get-together – that's all there is to it.' A cast-iron lie that his readers believe again and again with each story and each novel. Thanks to his style, thanks to his humour, thanks to the mixture of perspective and sentiment, and thanks to his refreshing insight into character.

When, in late 1985 – he had just become Dutch Ambassador in East Berlin – he was asked what the most important event of the year had been for him, Springer did not mention his posting to the strange parallel world behind the Iron Curtain, nor the umpteenth summit in Geneva, but a couple of literary facts: the commemoration of the fiftieth anniversary of the death of Kurt Tucholsky and the discovery of a lost poem by Shakespeare. Tucholsky because he had known exactly how to ridicule pomposity; Shakespeare because he had already put down on paper what makes us tick three centuries earlier: power, love, jealousy and desire. In that kind of literature, which is focused on the fortunes and motivations of the individual, history is merely a footnote. ■

Translated by Lindsey Edwards

An Extract from *Bougainville, A Memoir*

By F. Springer

No one will remember, but in 1973, just two years after the state of Bangladesh was born, amid much bloodshed, the Secretary-General of the United Nations made a short visit to the capital, Dacca. And absolutely no one will remember the few short reports announcing that one of the officials that had come from New York with the Secretary-General had had an accident and died during an inspection of the UN food transports in the port of Chittagong. A tragic but unimportant footnote to the visit by the UN top man, who had come, on behalf of all of us members of his organisation, to accept thanks from Sheik Mujibur Rahman for the aid we had provided - and would hopefully continue to provide - him and the millions of his countrymen who had been teetering on the brink of starvation since the state of Bangladesh was founded. Besides, that footnote did not say what exactly had happened to Tommie Vaulant. Obviously he had had a look at those ships full of rice and milk powder in the chaotic port complex in Chittagong, but halfway through the morning he had had enough of it and had driven his UN jeep to Cox's Bazaar, the longest, emptiest, most untouched beach in the world. It's now or never, he must have thought. I knew that, because the night before his death I myself had heard him name a few places in the world that he absolutely wanted to visit if he ever had the chance, because of their exotic names. As a travelling official of the UN he had got through a lot of them already, but there were still some excellent ones on his list.

'When I want to escape from the trials and tribulations of everyday life,' said Tommie, 'I say those names quietly to myself. I'm a first-class, experienced escapist. Cape Farewell in New Zealand, Alice Springs in Australia, Mandalay in Burma, Bougainville in the Pacific Ocean, ah, Bougainville,Cox's Bazaar on the Bay of Bengal. And if ever I have the chance to choose another life in another time, as in the well-known game, I would become a working member of the Royal Geographical Society round 1860 or so. Burton, Speke and all the rest of them.'

I laughed.

'Will you come too?' he asked earnestly.

'Can't get away,' I said. It sounded a bit too self-important.

Swimming in the sea, Tommie was swept away by a sudden undercurrent not far from the neglected Government Rest House in Cox's Bazaar. He was gone, washed up only in the afternoon,

close to the Rest House again, which made the search easier, of course. Well, search is a big word. There was only one witness. She had run backwards and forwards in the hot sand helplessly, wringing her hands. When Tommie ceased to surface she had run to the Rest House, but the telephone there did not work and there were no caretakers (because there were never any guests now). She had run back onto the beach again but there was no Tommie waving in the surf. At breakneck speed she took the jeep to the village further up and finally phoned Chittagong from a police post, but it was already two hours since she had last seen him. In the afternoon, at almost the same time as Tommie, a Red Cross helicopter landed on the beach, and even before the always breathtaking sunset in the Bay of Bengal he had been readied for transport to Dacca.

Obviously I still did not know exactly what had happened when we all – Bangladeshi government dignitaries, diplomats, UN officials – saw the Secretary-General and his entourage off at Dacca airport the following day. I had missed Tommie when we said our goodbyes, but someone said that he was still in Chittagong and would follow later, and I had no idea I was seeing him off too, my old friend, in his coffin in the belly of the UN plane.

Later I saw Bettina sitting in the lobby of the Intercontinental Hotel, in her neat Swiss Red Cross uniform, smoking nervously, looking anxiously at me with her red-rimmed eyes, not answering my greeting. Silently she went with me to my room, I poured her a drink, but she put the glass down on the table, clasped her head in her hands and sobbed and sobbed. 'Gott, Gott!' I heard now and then, and 'warum hab' ich... warum bin ich...'

There had been the official dinner at the Intercontinental two evenings before. On the podium the Secretary-General and his wife sat in a long, formal line with Sheik Mujib and his ministers. The other Bengali dignitaries, important-looking UN people and we local diplomats sat at round tables at their feet. We had started with a glass of pineapple juice, because nothing stronger was served at official functions, but it did not matter, because most of us had, as usual, surreptitiously fortified ourselves with a strong whisky before the start of the party. Beside me was Bettina, the Swiss doctor: good-looking but always stern and professional in public, she had experience in Biafra and other disaster-struck places.Like me, she had been staying at the Intercontinental for months and sometimes, after a long day, she thoroughly enjoyed bending the old elbow with me or others to forget for a while the hopelessness of her work in the Bihari camps. From our seats we could see that the wife of the Secretary-General had long since run out of things to say to Sheik Mujib. We could not help laughing at the determined faces with which the guests of honour on the podium tried to make conversation. It reminded Bettina of the awkward sketches they had had to perform in the hall at her school on the last day before the summer holidays.

Tommie Vaulant slipped into a seat on the other side of me. I had been looking out for him. 'I've written to Sonnie that I've met you,' he said. I introduced him to Bettina: 'An old friend, very important in the SG's cabinet these days.' They shook hands. 'He looks exactly like Montgomery Clift,' said Bettina.

'Well, well, that's a nice compliment,' I said, although I couldn't immediately call to mind what Montgomery Clift looked like. Oh yes, that nervous trumpet player in *From Here to Eternity* - she was right, damn it, Tommie was the image of Montgomery Clift.

Didn't he die young?' he asked.

'Yes,' said Bettina, 'tragic. I was a big fan of his. It's those eyebrows in particular that...'

I did not want to be left behind and said roguishly: 'I've been compared to a film star too, do you know who...?' But the sheik rose to make a speech.

He knew that I was in Bangladesh as Chargé d'affaires; I knew that I could expect him, the UN man, in Dacca. Since '55 we had written each other perhaps ten letters and had exchanged Christmas cards and announcements of our children's births. I had met him once in '65 in New York and we had last seen each other just before I left for Bangladesh, when he phoned me at the ministry. Both pressed for time, we had a coffee somewhere. A lot was left unsaid, which is not unusual between old friends.

Soon after his arrival he knocked on the door of the hotel room where I lived and played embassy, as I had not yet found an office in the chaotic city that Dacca was so soon after independence. On the dressing table stood a typewriter on which I banged out my brilliant reports for the Ministry of Foreign Affairs with two fingers. I used to put them in a postbag with an impressive red seal on the label. I often burned my thumb and index finger sealing the bag. It was and continued to be a dangerous task. Then,

on a three-wheeled bicycle taxi, I brought the bag to the airport, where a young Bengali with the insignia of Thai International Airline on his shirt took the weighty dispatch from me, always with the same words: 'Your Excellency, thank you for entrusting your state secrets to Thai International.'

So there stood Tommie, in my room, and we spent the whole evening talking – well no, that is an exaggeration: actually it was him who talked, non-stop, till about eleven o'clock. About Great Things, such as a Better World, which we would never see; about the poet Robert Lowell, whom he had known personally; about Power and Powerlessness. It was a disappointing meeting, in my opinion. No confidential, intimate conversation between old friends. He seemed to want to avoid any subject of a personal nature.

'I'm tired, Bo, dead tired,' he said suddenly and disappeared, yawning, to his room on the same floor, three doors down from Bettina's – but, of course, he did not know her at that point. ■

Translated by Lindsay Edwards

From *Bougainville. Een gedenkschrift*, Querido, Amsterdam, 1981

The Sculpture of Oscar Jespers in an International Context

From Wieske Baseleer to Little Leda

[JOSÉ BOYENS]

I want to translate the human form into the immobility of stone.
Oscar Jespers

The oeuvre of the Flemish sculptor Oscar Jespers (1887-1970) can easily be divided into a number of periods. These periods coincide with the major developments in European sculpture until about 1935, after which they begin to follow a course of their own. When Jespers prematurely terminated his academic studies in Antwerp in 1911, the dominant movement in the art world was Impressionism. The most brilliant exponent of Impressionism was Auguste Rodin (1840-1917), whose atmospheric figures were often imbued with symbolic significance. Just look at Oscar Jespers's head of *Wieske Baseleer* from 1913, formed in plaster and later cast in bronze (cat. 5), and you immediately notice the refined atmospheric mood of Impressionism that is so closely aligned with Rodin. [1]

According to art critic G.D. Gratama, the influence of Impressionism can also be seen in 'a very Impressionistic portrait of Mia Carpentier',[2] which was shown at the Second Belgian Salon at the Pulchri Studio in The Hague in March 1914. But this was already a transitional work. The hair could, with a bit of good will, be called Impressionistic, but that can hardly be said of the strong facets of the nose. These are closer to Parisian Cubism, as are other works from these early years.[3] This shows that Jespers's interest in Parisian Cubism had already been aroused before he became acquainted, in July 1914, with the fervent anti-Impressionist poet Paul van Ostaijen (1896-1928), with whom he formed a very close friendship. - Mia Carpentier, the subject of this work, became his wife on 1 April 1916; she would support and encourage him for the rest of her life.

Jespers had already become known as an artist in search of his own path when he broke with his art school instructor Thomas Vinçotte in 1911. Vin-

Engel, grafmonument voor de dichter Paul van Ostaijen (Angel, Memorial Stone for the Poet Paul van Ostaijen), 1932, bluestone, 63 x 165 x 60 cm. City Cemetery Schoonselhof, Antwerpen

Left
Wieske Baseleer, 1913, plaster, 25 x 17 x 22 cm. Various collections

çotte had taught him to treat all materials in exactly the same way, be it white marble, clay or plaster. The young Jespers became more and more convinced, however, that each kind of material had its own unique character which had to be taken as the point of departure for the work itself, and that consequently each material deserved its own handling. This respect for the unique character of the material – stone, wood or clay – would lead to the emergence of a highly personal oeuvre that would be recognised both nationally and internationally (though international recognition was for a long time rather scarce).

Cubism

In 1918, '19 and '20, Oscar Jespers replaced the cautious inch-by-inch Cubism of *Mia Carpentier* with a much more daring form that followed the synthetic Cubism of the paintings by Braque and Picasso and the sculptures of Henri Laurens and Jacques Lipchitz from the years 1916 to 1918. A powerful sculpture from that period is *De dode* (The Deceased) from 1918, which was inspired by the death of Jespers's father.[4] Although Paul van Ostaijen thought a great deal of this Cubist work, the sculptor himself eventually became dissatisfied with it and destroyed it. He was unable to do the same with *Frieda* [5] because he had given this Cubist figure away as a gift to his friends René and Frieda Victor-De Meulemeester. Later on, Jespers called these three years his 'laboratory period' [6], a time in which he said he had strayed too far from his own core.

In late October 1918 Paul van Ostaijen fled to Berlin, because he feared that as a Flemish activist he was in danger of being arrested: he and a few others had publicly hissed at the Francophile Cardinal Mercier for his offensive opinion about the use of the Flemish language in Belgium. Van Ostaijen had become a staunch defender of Cubism, and while in Berlin he maintained contact with his Flemish friends, especially with Oscar Jespers. [7] An intensive collaborative relationship developed between them as they worked together on the experimental typography of Van Ostaijen's *Bezette stad* (Occupied City); this would be the first book of Dadaist poetry in the Dutch language. Oscar Jespers provided the experimental typography, as outlined by Van Ostaijen. Working with unusual dedication, he himself published the book at his own firm *Het Sienjaal* in Antwerp in 1921. A second important subject in their correspondence is the publication of the magazine *Sienjaal*, which was announced by Paul van Ostaijen as the organ of emancipated Cubism, but in the end it was never realised. [8]

De pottendraaier (The Potter) is a distinctly Cubist sculpture executed in Euville stone in 1921, 41 cm. high. It shows a certain affinity with André Derain's pre-Cubist *Gehurkte figuur* (Crouching Figure) from 1907, but it is not certain whether Jespers ever saw this work. The stone sculpture by the Parisian painter is disarming in its clumsiness, while *De pottendraaier* is clearly the work of a magister artium by comparison. Jespers contrasted the many rectangles and cubes with five arched forms. As Paul van Ostaijen wrote, here the cube has become the measure of all things. [9] In later exhibitions both at home and abroad (after 1921), *De pottendraaier* often served as the triumphant starting point. The unique thing about Jespers's Cubism, compared with that of the Paris sculptors, was that after making *Frieda* in 1919 he no longer fragmented the human figure. Above all else, Jespers's more synthetic and less dogmatic view of the human figure makes a more vital impression.

This sculpture was followed in the 1920s by a series of animals, a few dozen character heads and some female nudes, all witnessing to a similarly powerful and personal Cubism. The figures were constrained within the rectangular shape of the stone or the cylinder of the tree trunk, and they form a sculptural oeuvre in and of themselves by virtue of their authenticity. In recent years, es-

De pottendraaier (The Potter), 1921,
Euville stone, 41 x 33 x 25 cm.
Bonnefantenmuseum, Maastricht

pecially since 2000, the sculptures from 1921 to 1930 have been classified more and more frequently as works of international modernism due to their severe architecture and rigid forms.

One quite unusual character head is *Perle fine*, which was carved in white marble and shows a secret affinity with Cubism: its height, 22.5 cm., is exactly the same as its depth. [10] Yet this sculpture, in which Jespers made such successful use of asymmetry (in the chin and mouth, for example), is formed for the most part by the expressive intuition that can be seen in the works of Constantin Brancusi (1876-1957), whom he greatly admired. This Romanian sculptor would become a new reference point for many artists after Rodin. He exhibited in 1926 in Antwerp, and Jespers would later visit him in his studio in Paris.

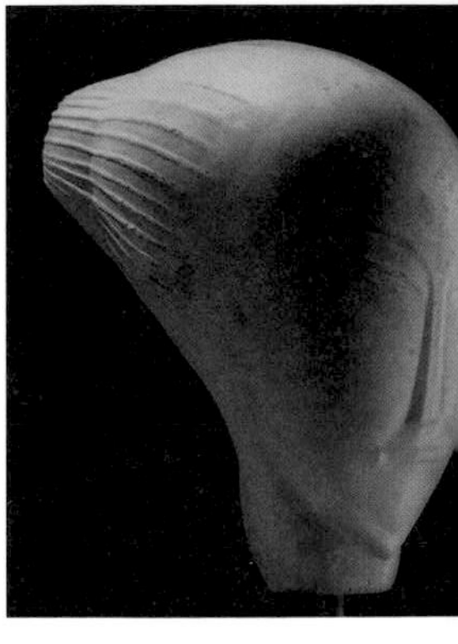

Perle fine, 1925,
plaster, 22.5 x 11 x 22.5 cm.
Musée de Grenoble

In the twenties Oscar Jespers designed a number of reliefs. Reliefs by their very nature are closer to decorative art. The composition of Jespers's reliefs was so complicated that he preferred to start by making a drawing and three-dimensional sketches. That was true with *Kleine ruiter* (Small Horseman), for which he made two sketches in 1924, both 37.5 cm high. In 1924-25, he chiselled the figures of the mother with her child on the hobby horse in white marble, 94 x 72 cm. [11] A detail like the mother's unrealistically high instep links this unusual work with international Art Deco, which had just experienced its apex in the heart of Paris with the famous International Exposition of Modern Industrial and Decorative Arts, from April to October 1925. Other references to Art Deco are the filling of the entire sculpted surface, the stylisation of the forms and the hair style of the mother, modelled after the wig of an Egyptian courtier from the Age of the Dynasties. The frontal presentation of the eyes of the mother and child, even though both are seen from the side, also shows the influence of Egyptian hieroglyphs. Art Deco took such an extraordinary interest in Egyptian art because the discovery of the tomb of King Tutankhamen in 1922 and the decorative riches found there were being followed with great excitement all over the world.

Expressionism

As the thirties approached, Cubist figures began to acquire an inner power: Expressionism was breaking through. Expressionism concentrated on the representation of the essential moments of human existence as they present themselves in lived experiences. Love, birth and ecstasy were therefore permanent themes, along with their opposites: despair, fear and feelings of abandonment. Such essential aspects of life should be expressed as directly as possible without the deliberation of the artisan. Jespers looked to the person of Vincent van Gogh as an important example, which is evident in his early drawings. But he also knew and admired the Expressionist artists of Der Blaue Reiter. Kandinsky once visited his studio. In his own country, Belgium, he had exhibited along with the painters Gustave De Smet (1877-1943), Frits van den Berghe (1883-1939) and Constant Permeke (1886-1952), all of them his friends. There were no sculptors, however, who could inspire him with the Expressionist spirit. So he was forced to find his own way as an Expressionist, and right from the start he displayed a mastery that would remain unequalled in the world of European sculpture.

Even the titles of Jespers's Expressionist works indicate his desire to represent the vitality of life: *Geboorte* (Birth), 1932; *Moederschap* (Motherhood), 1930;

Wiegenkind (Nursling), 1930; *Worstelaar* (Wrestler), 1933. Flemish Expressionism, including that of the painters, was marked by his positive attitude to life.

Broer en zus (Brother and Sister), 1934, bluestone, 56 x 30 x 25 cm. Koninklijk Museum voor Schone Kunsten, Antwerp

In all his Expressionist sculptures, including the monumental *Engel, grafmonument voor de dichter Paul van Ostaijen* (Angel, Memorial Stone for the Poet Paul van Ostaijen), 1931-32, the swelling of the stone, no matter how expansively suggested, is strongly restrained by the basic Cubist form. Like most of the sculptures from Jespers's Expressionist period, this memorial stone is cut from Belgian bluestone, a type of limestone, which filled his studio with a long-lasting and penetrating stench whenever he worked with it. The angel mourns the untimely death of a very gifted poet and keeps watch over his grave.

Broer en zus (Brother and Sister) shows the two of them in their own closed world; it is a sculpture of 56 cm. high, also rendered in bluestone [12] from 1934. The sculpture was first exhibited in 1934 and purchased that same year by the Royal Museum of Fine Arts in Antwerp. All the contours are closed. Nowhere in the volume of the stone is there evidence of an opening. The limbs of the brother and sister are at rest, either vertically or horizontally. The older girl holds her arm around her little brother in a protective gesture; what makes this sculpture Expressionist is the affection and solidarity between the two. It is Expressionism in retreat, however. When the sculptor conceived this work he can only have had one thing in mind: his little daughter, born in 1922, who died unexpectedly in 1927 – the great sorrow of his life – and his son born in 1929. Seen frontally, *Brother and Sister* makes a strong appeal to the viewer. It is a sculpture that radiates a monumental power. In its closed and static character it demonstrates a fundamental kinship with the art of ancient Egypt.

Purity

In 1935 Oscar Jespers began receiving commissions from the Belgian government for monumental decorative works that were mostly destined for world exhibitions. In 1927 he had been appointed professor of monumental and decorative arts at the Institut Supérieur des Arts Décoratifs in Brussels, where architect and designer Henry van de Velde (1863-1957) was the director. None of the designs that Jespers made at this time surpasses *België aan het werk* (Belgium at Work) from 1936-37, executed in embossed yellow copper and measuring 6 x 6 metres. [13] It was intended for the World's Fair of 1937 in Paris, where it dominated the hall of honour of the Belgian Pavillon. The figures in this work who are practising their profession to such a lively rhythm resonate with the Expressionist figures painted by Jespers's friends Gustave De Smet, Constant Permeke and Frits van den Berghe. They also approximate the human forms in the paintings of Dutch magical realism. Compared with the autonomous figures carved by Jespers in Belgian bluestone during his Expressionist period, which ended in 1934, those in *Belgium at Work* are less extreme. This need for a more comprehensible art could also be felt internationally in both the visual arts and literature in the decade before the outbreak of the Second World War.

Oscar Jespers was rather late in discovering the authenticity of the classical sculpture of Aristide Maillol (1861-1944). This French artist, who went to Athens to admire the caryatids of the Erechtheion with his own eyes, helped Jespers realise that his view of the human figure represented something of lasting

België aan de arbeid (Belgium at Work), 1936-1937, embossed yellow copper, 600 x 600 cm. Stadsschouwburg, Antwerpen (Maria Pijpelincxstraat). Commission for the World Exhibition, Paris, 1937

value. This led to the creation of female figures such as *Opschik* (Figure) in 1939 and 1942,[14] and to the highly unusual *Pureté* in 1945, which Jespers first moulded in clay, which he fired, and later had cast in bronze.[15] These sculptures, and *Pureté* in particular, epitomise what the art historian Emile Langui wrote in 1961 about the work of Oscar Jespers: that 'the purity of the plastic Idea was not contaminated by pictorial or literary tendencies'.[16] Because the head and arms are missing in *Pureté*, as with so many figures from Greek and Roman antiquity that were found during excavations, the image retains a higher degree of abstraction than either of the other sculptures. The extremely slender *Pureté* is full of inner life.

Having first been moulded in clay and later cast in bronze, *Pureté* constitutes the transition to the next phase in Jespers's development: that of the bronze female figures from the period 1946 to 1953. Maillol provided inspiration for these works, as did the Italian sculptor Marino Marini (1901-1980) with his heavy, fertile Pomonas. The three female figures that Oscar Jespers called *In de zon* (In the sun) in 1946 and 1947 are all aiming for the spherical, writes art critic Lambert Tegenbosch. 'It is striking how noiseless Jespers is: so silent that even an ecstasy like *In de zon* seems to have become internalised'.[17] The same counts for *Leunende vrouw* (Leaning Woman) of 1950 . Indeed, these figures demonstrate delight in a deeply silent way; what they represent is not reality but a myth, a myth of completeness and fecundity.

A sculptor's sculptor

In the last working period of his life, from 1953 to 1968, Oscar Jespers returned to stone, his material of preference. In *Kleine Leda met de zwaan* (Little Leda and the Swan) from 1965, which is only 34 cm. high, as well as in other sculptures from this period, Maillol's statement is most apt: 'je tache de faire blond'. Jespers explained this statement in 1949: 'that is to say without depths, by which the blondness of the whole could easily violate the unity of the play of light.'[18] The seated Leda clasps the body of the swan, her lover according to Ovid's *Metamorphosis*, with her arms and legs. The sculpture combines not only 'sensitiveness and grandeur' but also two characteristics that rarely go together: strength and sweetness. What *Kleine Leda* has in common with the Expressionist sculptures are the block shape, the static quality and the massive, earth-grounded weight, as well as the representation of a purely vital, non-reflective existence. It does not fit in with the contemporary artistic character of the age, however, so it could be regarded as Post-Expressionist. In *Kleine Leda met de zwaan* Oscar Jespers translated, as in almost all his work, the human form into the immobility of stone.[19]

It was during the years before 1935 that Oscar Jespers participated so intensively in the developments taking place in international sculpture. But this happened at a distance and with little direct international contact. In Paris he was relatively unknown. However, sculptors who themselves were masters in their art regarded him as superior. In this sense he was also 'a sculptor's sculptor'. ■

Translated by Nancy Forest-Flier

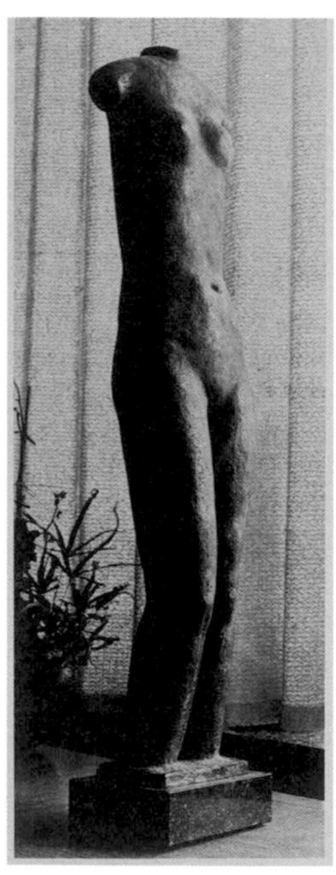

Pureté, 1945, terracotta/bronze, 78 x 18 x 13 cm
Various collections

Leunende vrouw (Leaning Woman), 1950, bronze, 104 x 45 x 58 cm. Koninklijke Musea voor Schone Kunsten van België, Brussel

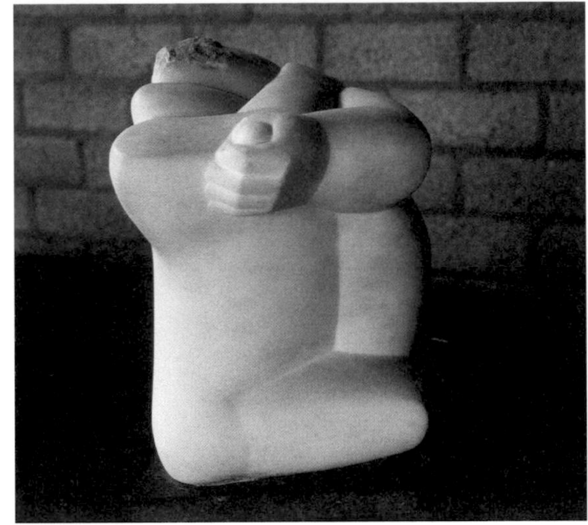

Kleine Leda met de zwaan
(Little Leda with the Swan), 1965,
white marble, 30.5 x 23.5 x 21.5 cm.
Private collection, The Netherlands

NOTES

1. Cat. 5 refers to the number of the sculpture in the catalogue raisonné containing all the sculpted works of Oscar Jespers in *Oscar Jespers, beeldhouwer en tekenaar, 1887-1970* by José Boyens, 2013, pp. 30, 33 and 322.
2. *Onze Kunst*, 1914, XXVI, vol. 13, p. 186. Cat. 4.
3. *Walter Stevens*, kop from 1916, plaster, cat. 21, and *Wim*, 1919, plaster, cat. 37.
4. The sculptor Emile Jespers, 1862-1918. The relief *De dode* was built up in plaster, 350 cm. high, cat. 29.
5. Black painted plaster / bronze (posthumous), 79 cm., cat. 35.
6. Oscar Jespers used this term to refer to his experimental sculptures from the years 1918 through 1920 in a letter of 30 June 1944 to the writer and poet Gaston Burssens.
7. The nineteen letters from Oscar to Paul van Ostaijen were published in 1995 by Pandora in Antwerp in *De genesis van Bezette stad: Ik spreek met de mannen en regel alles wel,* edited by José Boyens. All Paul van Ostaijen's return letters have been lost.
8. See Boyens, note 1, p. 54. The basic text of the announcement folder was printed on grass green paper, as Oscar wrote.
9. Paul van Ostaijen, *Oskar Jespers* in Vlaamsche Arbeid 1924, vol. 24, no. 12, p. 168.
10. See Boyens, note 1, pp.140-145 and 354-355.
11. Ibid., pp. 132-134 and 355.
12. Ibid., pp. 216-218 and 389.
13. Now in Antwerp, placed along the side wall of the city theatre on Maria Pijpelincxstraat. See Boyens, note 1, pp. 235-238 and 395-396.
14. The *Opschik* from 1939, 81 cm. high, as well as that from 1943, were executed in terracotta and in bronze. The version from 1943 is 53 cm. high. During the Second World War it was difficult for sculptors to get hold of good quality stone. Clay was more easily available.
15. All three sculptures are now parts of different collections.
16. Introduction to the catalogue for the exhibition *Oscar Jespers* at the Albert Landry Gallery, New York 1961.
17. 'Beelden zijn blokken bij Oscar Jespers', in *de Volkskrant* of 4 January 1964.
18. O. Jespers in *Het vormprobleem van het beeld*, Brussels 1949 (Mededelingen Koninklijke Vlaamse Academie; afdeling Schone Kunsten, vol. 11, no. 1), p. 13.
19. Oscar Jespers in an interview with José Boyens in 1963, in *Raam*.

Nijmegen Revived

From Roman Settlement to Havana on the Waal

[DAAN CARTENS]

An early Saturday morning in April 2013. The city of Nijmegen is busy. Perhaps less so than in the week of the Vierdaagse, the four day marches, when the population of the city quadruples, but the quayside is full of people and on the other side of the Waal stand row on row of spectators armed with enormous telephoto lenses or film cameras. That morning an arch bridge spanning 285 metres was being placed between the two banks with unprecedented precision. A semicircle, fine and delicate as a Japanese wood carving, particularly in the morning light, it has been lying in wait for this moment for months, like a futuristic trophy. The busy shipping traffic is still, the tide is right, the weather conditions ideal. Just a few hours later this huge operation is complete: in addition to the railway bridge (dating back to 1879) and the 'old' Waalbrug (1936), Nijmegen now has a third connection with the northern part of the city, which is growing explosively. 'Nijmegen embraces the Waal' is also the slogan of the various building activities and the future construction of an island in the Waal.

Within a few decades Arnhem and Nijmegen will draw even closer together, at least in terms of physical expansion. The two cities differ enormously in character, Arnhem being a fashionable administrative city with an art academy, whereas for a long time Nijmegen was a poor labourers' city. The arrival of the Catholic University in Nijmegen in 1923 gave it a new lease of life, and since the eighties the Catholic governors have made way for a leftwing activist movement and a city administration which since 2002 has been composed completely of progressive parties. Since then Nijmegen has earned its reputation as 'Havana on the Waal'. So much for the present, but the history of the city goes back to the decades before our era, when 'De Oversteek' (The Crossing), as the new bridge is known, was still accomplished with boats and rafts.

Roman roots

Another morning, this time a sultry summer dawn on the Kops Plateau, or the Kopse Hof, a high plateau of wooded groves, thickets, paths and moorland, criss-crossed day in day out by dog owners walking their four-footed friends and health freaks jogging off their excess kilos. The atmosphere here is different,

Bombardment of Nijmegen 22/2/1944.

thinner than that of the city; not infrequently the air shimmers and weather changes are clearly discernible. Looking between the bushes, which grow to head height, you can see the Ooijpolder, the unique nature reserve near Nijmegen, popular among walkers and birdwatchers. Further on and deeper down winds the Waal. No coincidence, then, that the Romans saw this as an ideal place for a settlement from which to conquer Germania. They built an enormous 42-hectare encampment on the Hunnerberg, another area of high ground, now a built-up part of modern-day Nijmegen. The camp, surrounded by an earth wall, was also an administrative centre, because the Romans had struck a bargain with the Batavi who inhabited those areas. Nijmegen therefore first appears in history as *Oppidum Batavorum*, more than a century before Emperor Trajan named it *Ulpia Noviomagus Batavorum* in 98 AD.

At around 15 hectares, the settlement on the Kopse Hof was smaller than that on the Hunnerberg, but it was more sophisticated and luxurious. The first stone buildings in Dutch history were built here, and archaeological findings show that this camp also provided quarters for military officers. Trade flourished; the Batavi in particular were sharp businessmen, plying their trade in Lent and Oosterhout, where the 'Waalsprong' area, Nijmegen's extension to the north, is now under development. In 69 AD the Batavi rebelled, tired of the Roman yoke and heavy demands for soldiers for the Roman expansion, which had in any case reached deadlock in Germania. The Kopse Hof was destroyed and the triumphant Romans built a new settlement, elevated to city status by Trajan, on the site of the current Waterkwartier, a famous underprivileged district of Nijmegen. In the second century the city of *Noviomagus* and its surroundings flourished. Around 6000 people lived there, which made it unique at the time. It was a thousand years before another city, Utrecht, achieved so many inhabitants. In the first centuries AD the city centre moved to the Valkhof, which was situated on high ground. The remains of that magnificent site will form the everyday backdrop of many wedding photos from 2014.

As I walk those fields with my dog, not just on summer mornings, but all year round, where the Romans lived and history played out, I realise that Nijmegen has not been particularly creative in its approach to that history. Anyone wishing to imagine those early settlements must visit the Archeon in Alphen aan de Rijn,

Het Arsenaal, former City Archive, now Flemish Cultural Centre. Photo by Hester Quist

where many buildings have been painstakingly modelled. Still, there are enthusiastic researchers and amateurs who often come across surprising discoveries. In 1999, for instance, Professor B. Brus published an interesting article showing that it was the Romans who had laid down seven kilometres of water pipes, remains of which are increasingly found in the ground in the elevated region of Berg en Dal. It was known that the Romans regularly organised 'water games' in their settlements, using more water than was otherwise needed for daily requirements. The system of clay pipes was an ideal method of water transport, proving the technical expertise of the residents. Brus's article has received little attention in Nijmegen, wrongly in my opinion, and there are many other examples.

Anyone wishing to quench a thirst for archaeological findings would do well to visit the Museum Het Valkhof (designed by Ben van Berkel and opened in 1999 by Queen Beatrix), known to Nijmegen residents as 'the swimming pool'. There you will find beautiful displays of jewellery, coins and utensils, the highlight being the Gods Pillar, dating back to 17 AD. There is also a cycle route and road from Nijmegen to Xanten, which really only becomes interesting on the German side of the border, as the requisite Roman past is on show in picturesque Xanten itself. The recently designed walking route through the city is informative but not spectacular. The real question is which city is the oldest in the Netherlands, Nijmegen or Maastricht, and it is this which has long kept bureaucratic minds occupied. Residents of each place insist on their own home territory; historians have found in favour of the Waal city.

Medieval city

In the early medieval period Nijmegen grew up around the Valkhofburcht. In 1230 Hendrik VII gave the city the designation Rijksstad (imperial city). It might be a cliché, but trade grew and flourished due, of course, to the city's unique location on the Waal. In 1273 the church, Stevenskerk, was consecrated by Bishop Albertus Magnus, and it remains the most important city landmark today, viewed from the surrounding area. By around 1560 Stevenskerk had reached its current proportions. The church is now mainly used for (university) meetings, exhibitions and organ concerts. It is a beautiful place, with lighting reminiscent of Saenredam's paintings, the walls in white and terracotta plaster. After the Iconoclasm all the statues of Mary and the saints were removed. The silence and spaciousness are almost dignified. It is a unique place to set the imagination free and be inspired by the essential figures of Nijmegen's history, the Limburg brothers and Mariken van Nieumeghen.

In 2005, some 91,000 visitors to Het Valkhof Museum saw the unique exhibition dedicated to the Limburg brothers' world famous books of hours, Les Très Riches Heures and Les Belles Heures. Since that enormous success, a city charitable foundation, which wants to bring medieval life closer to the people of Nijmegen and its tourists, has organised the annual Limburg Brothers Festival in the last week of August. Who were these famous brothers? Many of Nijmegen's artists worked at the court of the Dukes of Guelders, among them Herman and Willem Maelwael, well-known painters and gilders. The house where their studio was located still stands on Burchtstraat, where you can also see the facade of the medieval town hall. Willem Maelwael's son Jan exchanged the court of Guelders for that of Philip of Burgundy. His sister Metta married the Nijmegen sculptor Arnold van Limburg and their three sons, Paul, Herman and Johan, obtained easy access to the court of Burgundy due to the family connection. There the brothers produced biblical illustrations, which brought them to the attention of art collector the Duke of Berry. It was for him that they made the books of hours, which drew so much attention at the ingenious exhibition of 2005. The brothers visited their birthplace several more times during their lives, but died, probably from the plague, in France. Nevertheless they hold an important place in the Canon of Nijmegen, which was established in 2009 following the form of the Canon of Dutch History.

Of course Mariken is the figure most naturally associated with Nijmegen. *The True and Very Strange History of Mariken van Nieumeghen Who Lived more than Seven Years with the Devil and Kept Company with Him* first came out in print in 1518, published by Willem Vorsterman in Antwerp. The author is unknown, but was clearly familiar with Nijmegen and used many facts from the history of Guelders in the miracle play. Generations of school children have been required to read

Moenestraat. Photo by Hester Quist

Marikenstraat. Photo by Hester Quist

the text and there have been countless famous performances as well as films (by Jos Stelling in 1976 and André van Duren in 2000). The story still appeals to audiences today, perhaps due to its clear moral, very much of its time: even if man sins, he can receive forgiveness through confession and the intercession of Mary. Mariken is a commercial and cult figure in Nijmegen, with generations of girls named after her. The annual women's running event is called the Marikenloop, and the traditional culinary delicacy of Nijmegen is called Marikenbrood. Since 1957 a statue of Mariken by Vera van Hasselt has stood in the Grote Markt square. She must have been immortalised thousands of times by residents and especially tourists, in one of the prettiest locations in the city, between the Waag (weighing house) and the gatehouse leading to Stevenskerk. The statue of Moenen by Piet Killaers stands in the church's shadow. In the nineties the rather sleepy, impoverished shopping scene was refreshed with the construction of Marikenstraat and Moenenstraat, attractive shopping streets with modern apartments above the shops, connecting Burchtstraat with Molenstraat, which flourished in the 19th century, and passing straight through the old city archives, Het Arsenaal, on the way. These are good examples of appealing urban architecture that have clearly brought in more shoppers from outside Nijmegen (especially Germans from the border region).

Fortified city

For centuries Nijmegen was clearly intended as a medieval fortified city, surrounded and delimited by earth walls. The population, housed in small, closely packed cottages, was decimated during epidemics and grew in better times. House building around the fortress was forbidden. In 1875 there were 23,000 people living in Nijmegen in 2,400 houses. Only after the destruction of the ramparts in 1876 could the city expand, and the nineteenth century brought rapid growth. Architects such as Brouwer, Semmelink, Maurits and Buskens built town houses on the main roads, Groesbeekseweg, Annastraat and Graafseweg, which are still lived in or used as offices. From 1591 the Catholic population had no church of their own. That was strange, as they were clearly in the majority, but after the Iconoclasm and intervention of William of Orange, the Remonstrant upper class held sway. Only in 1808 under Louis Bonaparte were two Catholic churches erected. From that moment things moved quickly and the Waal city developed a clear Catholic character, which did not crumble until the years of social resistance at the end of the twentieth century. A Catholic newspaper was published, *De Gelderlander*, a Catholic infirmary, the Canisiusziekenhuis, was founded, and the rapidly growing city was divided into four parishes, served by the Dominicans, Franciscans, Jesuits and secular priests. Catholic entrepreneurs such as Dobbelmann and Terwindt joined the urban elite and in 1898, for the first time in centuries, the city gained a Catholic mayor, Van Schaeck Mathon, who now has a completely reconstructed avenue named after him.

Certainly the most important in this series of Catholic 'conquests', entirely suited to the time of so-called Triumphalism (*Christus regnat, imperat, vincit*) was the foundation of the Catholic University of Nijmegen on 17th October 1923. There was certainly resistance – the city council decided in favour with a majority of only one. Obviously the Catholics were for it, but an unholy alliance

The schommel (The Swing) by Henk Visch. © Stadsarchief Nijmegen

Mariken van Nieumeghen by Vera van Hasselt. Passage to the Stevenskerk. Photo by Hester Quist

of Protestants, liberals and social democrats voted against. Today's Radboud University Nijmegen, which was extended to include an academic hospital in 1956, is now an 'open' community in its thinking, offering a full range of degree courses. In the sixties the towering Talengebouw, or language building, became visible from all directions, underlining the importance of the university, and over the last two decades the sciences have been housed in ultra-modern complexes. Many politicians and administrators were educated in Nijmegen, both at the university and at Canisius College, alma mater of former Prime Minister Lubbers and former Minister of Defence, Minister of Foreign Affairs, and founder of D66, Hans van Mierlo.

If you take a walk from the station through the city, you will certainly recognise much of the medieval street pattern in the completely renovated city centre on the Waal. Nijmegen's allure is further determined by the concert hall *De Vereeniging* (built in 1882) and the nineteenth century streets and avenues, such as Berg en Dalseweg, which is described in detail by A.F.Th. van der Heijden in his cycle of novels *De tandeloze tijd* ('The Toothless Time'). The continuation of the late nineteenth century and early twentieth century city expansion lies on the other side of the Maas-Waal Canal. Since the seventies, districts such as Dukenburg and Lindenholt have been the ideal residential areas for the children of the baby boom generation. Now further expansion in a southerly direction is no longer possible, developers have created the Waalsprong, which offers many opportunities.

But describing it as a continuous line of growth and prosperity does not do justice to history. On 22nd February 1944 the view of the city received a wound which has only recently healed, more than half a century later.

The bombing

A sunny winter's afternoon, a busy station; children were back in class after lunch at home, mothers washing up or shopping, fathers at the office or one of the many factories. Suddenly the sky to the east turned black, aeroplanes dropped their load over the city. Houses and streets went up in flames, vision was obscured by the enormous plumes of smoke. There was great consternation, crying and screaming audible all around. Hours later, as the centre smouldered, the trail of the bombing emerged: from the Valkhof to the east of the centre to the station to the west, the heart of the city was one long scar. In subsequent days, it emerged that the bombardment, carried out in error, had claimed 800 victims and left the centre of the Waal city in ruins. After an interrupted campaign over German territory, Canadian and American bombers had decided to drop their load above the German border city of Kleve, unaware of the terrible fact that they were long past Kleve and were dropping their devastating load over Nijmegen.

In the autumn of the same year, 1944, Nijmegen, along with Arnhem, remained on the frontline and emerged from the war heavily battered, both physically and psychologically. Plans for rebuilding the city were proposed in 1947. The town hall and Stevenskerk were restored, but beyond that people found it difficult to choose between a historicising approach (a nostalgic, traditional view of the city) and a modernising operation (an open, modern city). The choice was never really made. Where whole streets were wiped out, modern nineteen fifties blocks of flats appeared. I myself live in a nineteenth century town house, but neighbours' houses have been rebuilt in a more or less modern style. The centre remained open and empty for a long time, sometimes by choice (Plein 44 became a symbol for the bombing), but generally due to differences in opinion, or lack of financial resources. Only when the money was available, in the prosperous nineties, did the real modernisation take place. The centre is now an amalgam of pre-war properties and streets, utilitarian nineteen fifties buildings (such as the V&D and HEMA department stores) and contemporary streets and houses, such as Marikenstraat and Moenenstraat and the Lux complex, comprising a cinema and conference rooms, largely underground. Not a particularly beautiful centre, perhaps, but cleverly revived and lively, and the leafy lanes, suburbs and surrounding area make up for a good deal.

De Oversteek (The Crossing), new bridge over the Waal (2013). © Stadsarchief Nijmegen

Among the victims of the bombing were many schoolchildren, including those of the Saint Louis Montessori kindergarten, near the town hall, where eight nuns and 24 children died. The newspapers of those days show photos of long rows of grieving family members and relatives on their way to the city's various cemeteries. The nuns and children of Saint Louis were buried in the Catholic cemetery *In Paradisum* on the Daalseweg. A little house, still filled with candles and children's drawings, forms the memorial for a class of innocent young victims, their names written on the walls. In 2000 a monument designed by sculptor Henk Visch, *De Schommel* ('The Swing'), was unveiled where their class once stood. Between the undamaged chestnut trees, it is a beautiful symbol of childlike playfulness and human futility. Since 2000 Nijmegen's mayors have commemorated that February afternoon of 1944 in this quiet place in the midst of the city bustle. They then move to the cemetery with family of the victims and a large group of interested members of the public, to the eternal resting place of the children and their teachers.

Nijmegen has many burial places. The Jewish cemetery is closed to the public. The Holy Land Foundation cemetery borders on the former Biblical Open-Air Museum (now called Orientalis) and has a similar atmosphere. There are also various small parish cemeteries. The victims of the bombing are spread over many of these resting places. The Catholic cemetery *In Paradisum* was consecrated in 1885. Many southern style tombs belonging to rich families exhibit the Catholic grandeur of those years.

A majestic avenue of beeches is preserved as a historic monument. A statue of Christ is clearly visible from all directions, and many priests and missionaries were interred in the priests' crypt nearby. A little further on lies the long forgotten poet Gerard Brüning, who died in 1926, at the age of 28. In his essays and poems he dreamt of a New Time, which he saw represented in fascist Italy. A beautiful statue of Christ by Eduard Overbeeke decorates his neglected grave.

A few steps from this forgotten man of letters, in late June 2012, I buried my beloved spouse Pieter Smals. I would not mention him here, were it not for the fact that he was a member of Nijmegen's city council for years. A representative of a post-war generation, with a strong sense of history, he worked passionately for a modern urban community, a city for *now*, a Nijmegen for 'the crossing'. 'Oh my love / who now lies on peacock cushions / soft, your empire was here, / of this earth, earthly soft, / where I lay you to rest (...),' (From *Op pauwenkussens zacht. Een klaaglied,* 'On peacock cushions soft: A lamentation' 2012).

Against a backdrop of lorries loading and unloading outside the Albert Heijn supermarket, standing among the gravestones I am struck by the juxtaposition of big city and local neighbourhood that characterises Nijmegen, a combination which defines the charm of the old Waal city. ■

Translated by Anna Asbury

All Said Before

Menno Wigman's Ennui

Innovation is impossible. The Earth revolves around the sun, summer gives way to winter, people are born and try to leave a few copies of their DNA behind before they die, and every generation does its best to put the essence of existence into words as if it hasn't all been said before a thousand times. Instead of falling silent or searching for a totally new means of self-expression, we cultivate repetition, which reveals itself in the works of poets, dancers, musicians and visual artists as rhythm. For millennia, the world's poetry has been characterised by periodic repetition, whether we're talking about metrical or musical patterns, graphic regularity on the page or cyclical structures on the semantic level. What's more, poetry owes its indestructibility partly to its being part of a tradition. We are moved or comforted by a sense of being linked to the hundreds of generations that have gone before. For this reason alone, a version of poetry that strives to cut all ties to the past is doomed to fail.

Still, over the last two hundred years in particular, poets and other artists have often tried to radically rejuvenate the tradition, producing free verse, prose poems, cut-up techniques, radical dissociation and furious experimentation in layout and lettering. Baudelaire and Mallarmé, Pound and Eliot, Trakl and Celan have shaken literature and turned it inside out to such a degree that much of what is published today seems, at first glance, to bear little resemblance to the work of Horace, Petrarch, Li Shangyin or Shakespeare. Nonetheless this innovation is relative. Ultimately, even the most revolutionary poets are still concerned with the fundamental rhythms of existence, which remain visible and audible in the most fragmented chaos. This might explain why there have always been poets who deliberately resign themselves to the existence of tradition and renounce all claims to originality.

If there's one Dutch-language poet who is aware of this issue, it's Menno Wigman (b. 1966). His first collection *'s Zomers stinken alle steden* ('Cities Always Stink in Summer'. 1997) includes a poem entitled 'Jeunesse dorée':

Menno Wigman (1966)

I saw the best minds of my generation
bleeding for revolts that didn't come.
I saw them dreaming between the covers of books
and waking in a twenty-two-town hell,
ill-omened as the excised heart of Rotterdam.

I saw them swearing by a newfound drunkenness
and dancing on the sea-bed of the night.
I saw them weeping for the cattle in the trams
and praying under bright and glaring lights.

I saw them suffering from unrequited talent
and speaking in agitated voices –
if it had all been said before, not by them.

They came too late. Their promise unredeemed.
The cities gleamed as black as caviar.

You don't need to study this poem long to see how much it owes its impact to repetition. First, there is a visual pattern in which each new strophe is one line shorter than the previous one, giving a double suggestion of withering and disappearing on the one hand and condensation and reduction on the other. The poem has the fourteen lines of a classic sonnet, but lacks the usual volta. Wigman will use this form, which I like to call the Wigman sonnet, many times in later collections. Second, there's the anaphoric repetition of 'I' – although the speaker defies expectation by presenting himself as a detached observer rather than a participant in what he describes. Of course, this detachment is merely assumed, as the slightly bitter tone betrays an involvement the poet would rather not admit. Third, we have the strong iambic rhythm and the assonance that gives the poem its gloomy resonance.

It's clear that this form is the perfect vehicle for the atmosphere of failure the poem expresses. The *'jeunesse dorée'* dream of revolution and throw themselves into the heady rush of urban night life, but in the end talent and energy peter out into disappointment and boredom. There is no hope. The poem illustrates the fact that everything has been said before, not just by referring to the nonconformist urges we know so well from the poetry of Baudelaire and Rimbaud, but also by citing the first half of a famous quote from Allen Ginsberg's 'Howl': 'I saw the best minds of my generation destroyed by madness, starving hysterical naked'. Even the repugnance for the fact that nothing ever really changes must be expressed in other people's words.

The poem typifies Wigman's work over the last fifteen years. In carefully composed iambic verse, he explores the *ennui* of a man who experiences life as an inane blind alley, giving voice to an attitude towards life that will be familiar to many. As this poetry is also extremely accessible, he has enjoyed great popularity from the outset. His second collection, *Zwart als kaviaar* ('Black as Caviar', 2001) won an important literary prize, and in January 2012 he was appointed Poet Laureate of Amsterdam for a term of two years. At poetry festivals his compelling performances win him a lot of applause. Wigman is an established poet, a fact that he must inevitably see as a source of new discomfort. He is not highly productive. He has published six collections, but one of these (*De droefenis van copyrettes,* 'The Melancholy of Copy Centres', 2009) is a selection of his own work, while *De wereld bij avond* ('The World by Night', 2006) was included in its entirety in *Mijn naam is Legioen* ('My Name Is Legion', 2012).

For all of his oeuvre's thematic and formal consistency, Wigman is not a monotonous poet. Sad childhood memories, a difficult love life, the meagre consolation of alcohol and cigarettes, lonely nights in rainy streets and impersonal hotel rooms – it would all be the elements of a tawdry depression if it wasn't so beautifully written. On top of this, Wigman is also a keen observer of modern urban life. He writes about the ugliness of supermarkets and internet porn, about resentful Islamists and the mentally disturbed homeless, about his demented mother and about the menace of the demise of the book as a cultural phenomenon. For quite some time he has been part of a collective of poets who take turns to write poems for so-called 'lonely funerals', ceremonies for those who have died without friends or family. This too leads to poems that help him to keep a finger on the pulse of contemporary society.

In his first two books, Wigman seems to have deliberately adopted the pose of a nineteenth-century *poète maudit*, flaunting his spleen, his thirst for alcohol and his seedy sex life. He bent, according to a poem in the second collection 'deeper over that past of his/ with all those famous parties, foreign beds/ and infatuated telephone conversations', after which the dejection kicks in with 'years gone up in careless smoke/ and powdered excess'. The reflection doesn't get him very far:

But he saw nothing. Only the thin light
of a back room with nothing to celebrate
beyond two bodies passing on a name,
only a bored and sturdy pair of hands
scraping his last few fibres out of a furnace.

The disgust is superbly worded, but not entirely convincing. The poet revels in his exaggeration of his own revulsion. One drawback is that he leaves little or nothing to the imagination. Wigman's poetry is so explicit that a single reading is usually enough to plumb the depths of each poem, even if the formal refinement is a lasting pleasure. Sometimes his products are no more than a skilful incarnation of Paul Verlaine.

Wigman achieves his greatest perfection in *Dit is mijn dag* ('This Is My Day', 2004). A simply brilliant poem is 'In Conclusion', which starts like this:

I know the melancholy of copy centres,
  of hollow men with yellowed papers,
bespectacled mothers with new addresses,

the smell of letters, of old bank statements,
  of income tax returns and tenancy agreements,
demeaning ink that says that we exist.

And I have seen new suburbs, fresh and dead,
  where people do their best to seem like people,
the street a fair impression of a street.

The thoroughly dispiriting tedium is situated in 'copy centres' and 'new suburbs', both conceived as modern innovations but in reality grim and dingy shops people are forced to frequent and soulless housing developments on the outskirts of large cities respectively. In this context the repetition of the words 'people' and 'street' is exceptionally functional.

The disconsolateness continues in the second half of the poem, again with a lot of repetition:

Who are they copying? Who am I?
  A father, mother, world, some DNA,
you stand there with that shining name of yours,

your head crammed full of cribbed and clever hopes
  of peace, promotion, kids and piles of cash.

And I'm a dog that's kennelled in its cantos

and howls for something new, something to say.
Light. Heaven. Love and death. Decay.
I know the melancholy of copy centres.

Life is one big copy centre, that much is obvious, and in it even the most existential questions have been reduced to clichés. A nice touch is Wigman's choosing Dante's terza rima. The world is an *Inferno*. Whoever enters here must abandon all hope.

With a project like Wigman's, there's a constant danger of the poet getting bogged down in his own material. One must pay a price for cultivating unfathomable dejection. January 2006 saw the release of an uneven volume of ten poems, published and distributed in a print run of many thousands on the occasion of Dutch 'Poetry Day', but after that a six-year silence set in, interrupted only by an anthology. I suspect that Wigman had come up against the walls of his self-made prison, with a formidable writer's block as a result.

The 2012 volume *Mijn naam is Legioen* seems to take a new direction. The poetry is harder and more uncompromising than the work in previous collections. The sorrow and irritation no longer seem to be part of a literary game; the presentation is harsher, the emotions placed in the context of an equally sordid world. The title derives from the Gospel according to Mark, in which a man who has been possessed by evil spirits undergoes an exorcism. Western Europe is a madhouse, but writing may enable the poet to free himself from his demons.

In the first poem, which has the familiar form of the Wigman sonnet, he addresses his penis:

It's getting cold. The days are made of glass,
of armoured glass and Seroxat. If I sought words
for everything that doesn't have a word,
not anymore. I'm an arse, an arse is what
I am for writing poems now. And you,

my dick, what have we achieved today?
Spare me your cut-rate melancholy, come on,
you've slept for days now in my shorts, so tired
of the seething tyrant who rids you of your seed.

Although the poem was already published in 2009, it is a worthy introduction to the disillusionment that follows. The poet is not so much bored and sombre, as angry. That turns out to be a fruitful emotion.

The poem 'Old West' –a title that refers to a scruffy, working-class neighbourhood in Amsterdam that is home to many non-Western immigrants – bears a motto from Rimbaud: 'Merde à Dieu'. It starts like this:

We're living here with Turks, Moroccans, Sikhs,
Afghanis, Kurds and Pakistanis and we
are scared. And I, a stubborn white man,

ni Dieu, ni maître, without the slightest hope
of pleasure gardens when I'm dead, assess
the street from three floors up and see the heated

prayer around the clock, how people lie
on dingy floors and hurry off to places
of worship and constant collection.

If he is here cursing the perverse devotion of uneducated immigrants, we see several pages later that the death of the Christian God has not brought the salvation he covets. This poem is based on a news item about a man who lay dead in his apartment for months. When he was finally discovered, the corpse of his cat was lying on his chest. After the first strophe has sketched this lugubrious situation, the poem continues:

There, in that street, there is a church –
got fitted out with cameras recently.
Is God asleep? No, but thieves abound

and they defy the Allseeing Eye to search
for silver, pulpit bibles and candlesticks,
beheading Mary's statue in its niche.

God has disappeared and surveillance cameras have taken over His job. Or does He manifest Himself in some other way? That's what the last lines of the poem might suggest. Yes, mankind is lonely and abandoned, but there is still some possibility of solace:

remind me of the guy who lay there dead
while his companion paced, miaowed and pined

then nestled finally down upon his chest.

The collection also includes a number of poems in which the speaker clearly differs from the poet's persona. In 'Egmond aan Zee' we hear the voice of a violent youth from a Dutch seaside town: 'Come Friday night, come beer, come coke / and the sea breeze stokes the fire in your head. // Knuckles, blood, a star, a knife and screams. / Our sky above is hard and criminal.' Elsewhere Wigman reproduces a schizophrenic's ranting, complete with spelling mistakes and jangling italics. Apparently it's the psychiatrist who's being addressed:

Blind and deaf, hardjacker & killer
of all I own, I'm warning you.
Sicksofreen & manic, the way you claim.

Well prove that manic and Sicksofreen
for once and all; and write those symtones
down on paper, misery guts & Liar.

That's not very subtle. His account of a prison riot is much more convincing:

A cauldron full of cats and the heat ticking.
All summer long we were steaming in our cells,

the sun a tongue of flame and our heads a hell
*where brutal guards reduced you to a name.**

Remarkably enough, the collection ends with a couple of love poems, which – for the first time in this oeuvre – are not cynical but seem to have arisen from a genuine, heartfelt passion. Although the poems are not especially good and clash with the rest, they do suggest that the poet, even if fictionalising here, has sunk a new well:

The moon has left the sky and I, I think my way to you,
it's three days now that I've been thinking in your scents,
you'd hoped that I might lose my head and how –

the moon has left the sky, what a strange line, that can only be
from Sappho – yes, and now I'm on a roll: she drank,
my god, even more than me, she wrapped me round

with hips and stories, lips and looks, mascara.

Like the decadent ennui and the 'melancholy of copy centres', this love is a thoroughly literary emotion, but it won't do Wigman any harm to read Sappho, Occitan troubadours and Petrarch for a while instead of Baudelaire and Gottfried Benn. I am very curious about the second half of this poetic career. ■

Translated by David Colmer

* This excerpt only translated by Judith Wilkinson

's Zomers stinken alle steden, Bert Bakker, Amsterdam 1997
Zwart als kaviaar, Bert Bakker, Amsterdam 2001
Dit is mijn dag, Prometheus, Amsterdam 2004
De wereld bij avond, Poetry International & Prometheus, Rotterdam/Amsterdam 2006
De droefenis van copyrettes, Prometheus, Amsterdam 2009
Mijn naam is Legioen, Prometheus, Amsterdam 2012

Five Poems

By Menno Wigman

Semper eadem

There are whores in your head
when you turn thirty.

An hour of keen delight
outweighs each word you say.

But sinking ever deeper
into your unwashed grave

you think of who she was
and who has slept here since.

What happened to the wide-eyed awe
of mornings after new delight?

There are whores in your head
when you turn thirty.

From: *Cities Always Stink in Summer*

Semper eadem

Er wonen hoeren in je hoofd
wanneer je dertig wordt.

Een uur van scherp genot
weegt zwaarder dan een woord.

En toch, je ligt steeds dieper
in je ongewassen graf

te denken wie zij was
en wie hier na haar sliepen.

Waar blijft het staren en verbazen
na een nacht van nieuw genot?

Er wonen hoeren in je hoofd
wanneer je dertig wordt.

Uit: *'s Zomers stinken alle steden*

Big-city

What she did *pre*-me? With Hugo she ate lobster,
with Thomas she drove through LA, she slept
with Sander in Berlin, with Rick, with Jim... And I,

so green about the cryptic equations
of our pleasure, whose hair, whose lips,
whose eyes do I recall when I see hers?

She doesn't know her smile's just like Lisa's.
And I don't see how I resemble Hugo.
But now that six or seven weeks have passed,

the ghosts all gather round our bed at night
to watch the slow and tender, dogged way
we strive to exorcise their deepest names.

From: *Black as Caviar*

Grootsteeds

Wat ze vóór mij deed? Met Hugo at ze kreeft,
met Thomas reed ze door LA, met Sander sliep
ze in Berlijn, met Jan, met Stein... En ik,

zo groen in de geheime algebra
van ons geluk: wier haar, wier lippen en
wier oogopslag zie ik bij haar terug?

Ze weet niet dat ze net als Lisa lacht.
En ik zie niet wat ik van Hugo heb.
Maar na een week of zeven staat er 's nachts

een kring van schimmen rond ons bed te kijken
hoe traag, hoe teder en verbeten wij
hun diepste namen uit ons hoofd verdrijven.

Uit: *Zwart als kaviaar*

Hotel night

The libraries have been shut for hours.
The city centre celebrates a street.
Insomnia. Pick up a book and put it down again.
TV it is. To watch the way it creeps.

The city centre celebrates a street
and sniffling taxis stand out in the rain.
TV it is. To watch the way it creeps.
For hours now the weather's been repeats.

The empty taxis drifting through the rain.
At worst you'll have four decades more of days.
For weeks the weather's only been repeats.
You read your palm and hope that you exist.

At worst you'll have four decades more of days.
God knows the kinds of secrets that you keep.
You read your palm and hope that you exist.
Your orphaned spirit gives and starts to slip.

From: *This Is My Day*

Hotelnacht

De bibliotheken zijn al uren dicht.
Diep in het centrum triomfeert een straat.
Insomnia. Drie boeken ingekeken.
Tv dus maar. Toekijken hoe het jaagt.

Diep in het centrum triomfeert een straat
en staan verkouden taxi's in de regen.
Tv dus maar. Toekijken hoe het jaagt.
Al uren wordt het weerbericht herhaald.

Er drijven lege taxi's door de regen.
Je hebt desnoods nog veertig jaar te leven.
Al dagen wordt het weerbericht herhaald.
Je leest je hand en hoopt dat je bestaat.

Je hebt desnoods nog veertig jaar te leven.
God weet wat voor geheim je verzwijgt.
Je leest je hand en hoopt dat je bestaat
nu je verweesd en wel je hoofd uit glijdt.

Uit: *Dit is mijn dag*

Rubbish dump

A knoll of dead things taunts the air.
Nothing is itself. A mass of addled chattels.
Liquid, black liquid leaking from a fridge.
Forever broken, squandered, sick of human hands,
a city of refuse rises up before me.

And I look and I look. And as I walk
I lose my hair, I feel a beard, my coat
grows threadbare on my back and all the clouds
go racing off to Dortmund.

That's just the start: a village church floats through
the water, fish make their homes in city squares,
a wet grey sea from Utrecht to The Hague.

Knowing what I know of time and dykes,
I write this for the future drowned to read.

From: *The World by Night*

Vuilstort

Een terp van dode dingen tergt de lucht.
Niets is zichzelf. Veel jichtig huisraad. Vocht,
zwart vocht dat uit een koelkast welt. Voorgoed
kapot, versjacherd, mensenhanden moe
tijgt me een stad van afval tegemoet.

En ik kijk en ik kijk. En als ik loop
verlies ik haar, ik voel een baard, mijn jas
verrafelt waar ik sta en alle wolken
jagen Dortmund achterna.

Dan gaat het snel: er drijft een dorpskerk door
het water, wier en vis bevolkt de Dam,
nat, grijs, week, dacht je randstad, zag je zee.

Om wat ik van de tijd, van Holland weet
schrijf ik voor wie dit onder water leest.

Uit: *De wereld bij avond*

Sick of Hitler

Berlin. I'd had a fuck but in the shower
the Holocaust was back there in my skull.
I saw my dick and counted tiles, white,
the tiles were white, I counted and a cloud
of breathlessness hid them from sight.

I read I don't know how many books,
kept digging round in Adolf's life,
the seven spoons of sugar in his tea,
Geli, Eva, forelock, whip and testicle –
what good were they to me? Here in this shower,

here in a warm and workaday Berlin,
my shame ran off and gurgled down the drain
and I could never be too lax, too late or all to blame.
And light and fresh and sick to death of Hitler
I made a beeline back towards her bed.

From: *My Name Is Legion*

Hitlermüde

Berlijn. Ik had geneukt en nam een douche.
Toen sloop de Holocaust weer in mijn hoofd.
Ik zag mijn pik en telde tegels, wit,
ze waren wit, ik telde en een mist
van ademnood vertroebelde mijn zicht.

Ik las ik weet niet hoeveel boeken, bleef
maar in het leven van Adolfus wroeten,
de zeven scheppen suiker in zijn thee,
Geli, Eva, teelbal, spuuglok, zweep – wat
moest ik ermee? Hier onder deze douche,

hier in een warm en doordeweeks Berlijn,
hier gleed mijn schaamte in een doucheput weg,
kon ik nooit laks, te laat of schuldig zijn.
En licht en fris en hevig Hitlermoe
stapte ik weer op haar kamer toe.

Uit: *Mijn naam is Legioen*

All poems translated by David Colmer

Over Exposure

The Art of Erik van Lieshout

[FRANK VAN DER PLOEG]

What is going on in today's visual arts? Refinement, precision and finish are often nowhere to be seen. Installations are erected here and there, as raw as life itself. One of the most inventive representatives of what can almost be seen as a genre is the Dutch artist Erik van Lieshout (Deurne, 1968). He draws, paints, builds and makes films. And all with the energy and expressionism of someone with ADHD. Or is this just the way it seems?

'I want too much. I want too much in one image. I want too many topics. I want to belong too much. I want to be accepted far too much. I want to say far too much in a single image. I want to be political *and* abstract *and* do paintings. *And* show people's lives. And I want to make regressive work. I want psychological depth. And abstract beauty. And to achieve great profundity and weight. I want to achieve all this in one artwork.' Halfway through *Sex is Sentimental* (2009), in which the above words are coupled with shots of dung beetles copulating, changing graffiti and Rorschach ink blots, Erik van Lieshout explains these objectives and then tells us that he has lost his way. The reason? His assistant, Suzanne Weenink, has also become his girlfriend. And he is struggling with this. But while struggling he satisfies all the ideals he has sketched out. With as a bonus an ode to art and, why not, to the love of a person. A successful, many-layered artwork.

Memory

Erik van Lieshout is everywhere. It seems that no self-respecting art event is complete without him. In 2012, for example, in Belgium alone his work could be seen in two places at the same time. His film installation *keine Kohle kein Holz* (2009) was given a reprise in a completely new setting at 'Manifesta9' in Genk and as a participant in 'Track' in Ghent he fitted out a former video rental shop with a 'Dutch exhibition'. His film *Janus* (2012) was projected amidst a tangle of carpentry filled with artists' household goods.[1]

Van Lieshout always adopts a position. In this case against the cutbacks in the arts in the Netherlands. As a Dutch artist he sought refuge in Belgium, which in his view has a friendlier cultural climate. To represent/symbolise the

Commission, 2011, still, HD, colour, sound, 49 min. Made for Sculpture International Rotterdam and Hart van Zuid. Courtesy Annet Gelink Gallery, Amsterdam

Netherlands in this installation, he used the colours of De Stijl, a movement he admires. Its original members, including Rietveld (1888-1964), Piet Mondrian (1872-1944), Van der Leck (1876-1958) and the architect J.J.P. Oud (1890-1963), would turn cringingly in their graves at the sight of the rough construction in which Van Lieshout, with good intentions, squanders their rectilinearity in his pursuit of the 'Hollandisation' of the space. He completely subordinated the formality of De Stijl to his inner need to dress up his installation.

Van Lieshout refers to and shows his penchant for De Stijl in other work too. The film at the heart of *keine Kohle kein Holz* features models of furniture by Rietveld, including the 'Zigzag Chair'. This is not so surprising, as the film is a cobbled-together animated tribute to *Misère au Borinage*, the renowned 1933 film by another great Dutchman, Joris Ivens (1898-1981), about miners in a time of crisis. The concept for Rietveld's chair dates from 1932, the same year that Ivens was shooting his documentary. It is an atypical van Lieshout film, because he himself does not appear in it. The installations around it (those of both 2009 and 2012) do comply entirely with the image he is keen to create. Using very few resources (wooden slats and angle plates symbolise the miners and BBQ briquettes represent the black gold) he keeps to the principle of the original film; projected text – in *keine Kohle kein Holz* it is slogans on poster-sized paper – provides the accompanying commentary: *Jetzt ist es genug / Weltkrise / Widerstand von der Bergleute!* The installations surrounding the film bring the crisis atmosphere into the present, in both the personal and political spheres. (The Dutch populist Geert Wilders is a prominent presence, not for the first time and definitely not for the last.)

(Neighbourhood) director/recorder

Erik van Lieshout's usual mental and working processes can be distilled from the film Janus. He combines filmed images of street life – Van Lieshout likes to be among people – with such studio creations as painted works, drawings and collages. This is because Van Lieshout also likes to spend several days alone in the complete isolation of his studio. To keep track of all his visual material

Holland House, 2012, detail, various materials. As exhibited in *Track*, Ghent. Photo by Jhoeko. Courtesy Annet Gelink Gallery, Amsterdam

– the studio works can be used as props for the film, but also become part of later installations – he works with an editor, Core van der Hoeven. This solid figure remains out of shot, though in every interview, which Van Lieshout sees as part of his role as an artist in the world, he gives him the credit he is due. Watching material shot previously and giving an accompanying commentary regularly forms part of the end product. (The finest example is a scene from *Up* (2005), in which Van Lieshout, while looking into the lens, fulminates to Core against his mother's egocentric tone in an excerpt they are watching together at that very moment).

Janus is the result of a project by the Museum Rotterdam, which wanted to make portraits of 'ordinary' people. Van Lieshout ended up in the house of a man who had died four weeks previously, made the acquaintance of his relatives and made arrangements to use some of the household objects for his art project at the museum. The essential ingredient of the film is the run-up to this experience, which was quite extraordinary for the family ('this way we can go and look at his things for a while rather than everything going straight into a skip'). Museum staff appear in shot during and after the viewing of the household objects and the image of the deceased is built up in commentary spoken by the relatives concerned, the compassionate museum people and the neighbours (who are negative). Van Lieshout interlaced these images with more or less philosophical reflections on art, subsidies and so on, which he shares with the theatre-maker Marien Jongewaard. He also reacts – though less than usual – with shots of his own drawings and writings, and local residents turn up here and there too. In an interview on the occasion of 'Track', Van Lieshout himself said: 'Obviously in *Janus* you don't have to expect a film with a beginning, a middle and an end, in that order or otherwise, but neither is it a load of arty-farty inaccessibility.'[2]

But for all that it is still desirable to watch the full 50 minutes to experience any coherence. Little by little the stories emerge about Janus Noltee, the 73-year-old victim of a hospital infection, his relatives and people from the surroundings in the small neighbourhood of Rotterdam South, where the museum was so keen to install an artist. In this instance, Van Lieshout's presence is by his standards relatively modest. He occasionally throws a statement at the camera, such as 'subsidies make for mediocre art... I am a Dutch state artist, I hate the ordinary people', and he has Jongewaard recite theatrical lines while playing the part of 'Erik van Lieshout, the artist'. But he would not be Van Lieshout if he did not take on an extra part for himself too. Under the motto 'an artist is actually a bacteria, a virus' – an idea prompted by the multi-resistant hospital bacteria that spares no one – he dresses up as a bacteria and goes out into the street. By the end of the film he is visiting two of Janus' relatives to tell them that the project has been cancelled due to the cutbacks.[3] *Janus* is no more... There is no mention of the fact that Janus will rise again like a phoenix, this time in a comparable neighbourhood in Ghent, though this was certainly already known at the editing stage.

Erik makes us happy

A year earlier, Van Lieshout moved into empty shop premises in the indoor 'Zuidplein' shopping centre in Rotterdam. It was a commission for Sculpture International Rotterdam and Hart van Zuid. The title of the film was *Commission*. In this typical shopping mall he fitted the shop space out with what he himself called 'a bit of junk', which was intended to be given away. The accompanying film shows the way there, the onsite investigation – the police considered Van Lieshout an alien element and repeatedly questioned him and sent him away – the building of the interior and especially the conversation with the building workers (perhaps stand-builders is a better term) and future fellow shopkeepers. The result is of course a typical Erik van Lieshout installation. And when he reads this in the newspaper it actually disappoints him! But what would

Home Stretch, 2011, collage, 33.5 x 42 cm. Collection Stedelijk Museum, Amsterdam. Photo by Jhoeko. Courtesy Annet Gelink Gallery, Amsterdam

one expect with such slogans as ERIK MAKES YOU HAPPY and REAL LUXURY IS BUYING NOTHING in capitals on the shop windows. So he doesn't sell anything either; though people can just take his things with them. Van Lieshout is disappointed. It has turned into art again. He wonders what added value he has given, and asks others too. Fortunately he is able to end the film with the encouraging words of one of the proprietors at the Zuidplein. This man, who had previously spoken to the camera about sales strategies, observes that Van Lieshout has indeed been seen by his fellow shopkeepers. His hard work and above all his enthusiasm gave them the impression he was a passionate entrepreneur. This is the enthusiasm that the Zuidplein actually really needs. Ergo: added value! And Erik? He's happy again.

Left: Janus, 2012, still, HD, colour, sound, 51 min. Courtesy Annet Gelink Gallery, Amsterdam

Right: Das Museum, 2009, colour, sound, 21 min. Wood. As exhibited in *Im Netz*, Museum Ludwig, Cologne. Photo by: Rheinisches Bildarchiv, Cologne. With the financial support of Rheingold Sammlung. Courtesy Annet Gelink Gallery, Amsterdam

Commitment

Erik van Lieshout comes from a family brought up on left-wing political commitment. While others went on nice picnics, the inhabitants of the Van Lieshout house were dedicated to demonstrations. Taking action is so much in his blood that he became an active member of the 'Youth Against Nuclear Arms' movement. When no cruise missiles were stationed in the Netherlands, he started embroidering large wall-hangings – couldn't help himself? Having made three or four of them, and doing his first drawing, he discovered his inner artist. This is the image of himself that he broadcasts to the world.

Those aspects of his work that are political can be traced back to his early years. He attacks Geert Wilders' populism. The murdered Rotterdam politician Pim Fortuyn crops up regularly too. Having now finally reopened, the Stedelijk Museum in Amsterdam has set up a room containing Van Lieshout's drawings and collages of Fortuyn. Intense and raw, sexually charged, banal. These are the manifestations of Van Lieshout's ideas that show up more in his 'flat' work than his films. As a bonus, he donated a collage to the Stedelijk Museum in which Geert Wilders is sitting on Van Lieshout's back and is reining him in by his bra straps – both men have women's bodies: *Home Stretch* (2011).

As far as art is concerned, he is exceptionally aware of what is in store for him. For an exhibition at the Museum Ludwig in Cologne (*Das Museum*, 2009) he spent the night in the museum. At a certain moment he sighed out the names of such illustrious predecessors as Vermeer, Mondrian and Van Gogh and blissfully added his own name to the list.

What is more interesting, as far as content is concerned, is his awareness of links with people like the Dutch conceptual artist Bas Jan Ader (1942-1975), who is a benchmark. When Van Lieshout himself cried in a therapy session during the shooting of *Up*, he knew at the same time that the camera was there, was able to forget the camera, and was also able to start up the crying for a second time. And he knows his classics. In this case Ader's *I'm too sad to tell you*

(1971). Van Lieshout shares more than just tears with Ader. In his view artists have to be able to bare themselves completely. There is also a practical reason why he so often appears in the films himself. Van Lieshout: 'The films are always about other people. But the problem often lies with me and so I want to solve it myself first. They say it has a liberating effect if you try it out on yourself. When I am at the start of a project, I often try everything out on myself, asking questions. They call that consensus. The result is that you know what you are up to. Other people often have the same problems.' It has to be noted here that those others may not want to spend the time to think so deeply about things, especially when it becomes more intellectual.

Spiderman

At the start of the film *Das Museum*, Van Lieshout transforms himself into Spiderman. The aim is to expose networks. He takes this literally by making a web with lots of lengths of black tape. When he has put on a reasonably successful Spiderman head (red plastic and black tape) he gazes into the camera (with his characteristic black glasses on, of course) and says: 'so now I actually have to do something I suppose?' Nothing ever happens, however, at least not as a superhero. In a metaphorical sense he really is the spider in the web. Not only in the direct sense, with his work, but also regarding its presentation. He is for example a welcome guest on discussion panels and YouTube is full of short films of him at work.

So the invitation to appear on *Zomergasten* (Summer Guests) in 2011 was a gift from heaven.[4] This is a television programme in which a guest is asked to compile his own evening of television using excerpts from programmes and then comments on them with a presenter. Van Lieshout was able to zap through his sources of inspiration and muses in precisely the way he puts his films together: not in a straight line, but with his own logic. Those who can tolerate lots of changes of images and ideas – the children of today – could really enjoy themselves. Van Lieshout knows that – above all as an artist – he exists by the grace of the footlights. At a certain point in the middle of the broadcast he looked around him, sought out the camera and said: 'If you turn off the camera, we can go away, we don't exist anymore.' ■

Translated by Gregory Ball

http://erikvanlieshout.com

Erik van Lieshout lives and works in Rotterdam. He is represented by the Annet Gelink Gallery in Amsterdam (www.annetgelink.com), Galerie Guido W. Baudach in Berlin (www.guidowbaudach.com), Maureen Paley in London (www.maureen-paley.com) and Galerie Krinzinger in Vienna (www.galerie-krinzinger.at).

Up!, 2005, still, DV, colour, sound, 18 min. With the financial support of Beyond, Leidsche Rijn. Courtesy Annet Gelink Gallery, Amsterdam

NOTES

1. Films like Janus and Commission tour various institutions, where the setting (the form of the installation) is often adapted to the location. In 2013 Janus was shown at the International Film Festival of Rotterdam (IFFR) (www.filmfestivalrotterdam.com/films/janus/) and others.
2. Geert Simonis' blog: Gent als oefenterrein (French translation); interview with Erik van Lieshout at http://trackundercover.wordpress.com/category/geert-simonis/.
3. That the cutbacks are not a fantasy is apparent from the fact that since the end of 2012, Museum Rotterdam has disposed of its two fixed locations, the Dubbele Palmboom and the Schielandhuis. For the time being it will be wandering the city streets.
4. Broadcast on 21 August 2011. Can be viewed (without the excerpts) at http://programma.vpro.nl/zomergasten/vorige-seizoenen/zomergasten-2011/erik-van-lieshout.html

Population Shrinkage in the Netherlands

From a Cold to a Warm Approach

Since 2008, the towns of Sluis, Hulst, and Terneuzen have set up shop each year at the annual Emigration Fair under the motto that you really don't have to go abroad to find peace, quiet and elbow room – the Dutch can simply emigrate within their own country. It's one of the measures being taken in Zeelandic Flanders to counter population shrinkage. And it's not only in Zeeland that shrinkage is a top agenda item. Regions such as South Limburg and North Groningen have been losing inhabitants for several years now and have come to be known as 'shrinkage areas'. Other regions such as the Achterhoek, Drenthe, and the Hoekse Waard are regarded by the government as 'anticipation areas': they aren't shrinking yet, but they will in the near future. Ultimately it is expected that half the towns and cities in the Netherlands are going to undergo shrinkage.

This population shrinkage is not difficult to explain. It's all a question of demographics: more and more young people – women in particular – are taking up higher studies and moving from the countryside to the cities. University cities such as Utrecht and Nijmegen have actually become 'women's cities' – they have a surplus of women. Not only is the countryside losing its young people, but it's also losing the children they will eventually bear. This baby drain is going to have a serious impact on education and social activities, inevitably forcing hundreds of village schools in the Netherlands to close their doors in the coming years. In addition, the population of the shrinkage areas is also ageing. On the one hand this is the result of the baby drain (when young people leave the average age goes up), and on the other hand it has to do with increased life expectancy (all of us are living longer).

Shrinkage is posing new problems for regional and municipal governments in the Netherlands. Can shrinkage be stopped, and if so, how? What sort of impact is shrinkage having on local communities? Do we have the means to deal with the growing number of elderly people? New spatial problems are also arising as a result. Sooner or later, the baby drain and ageing are going to lead to fewer inhabitants, causing a surplus of space. A drop in the population is saddling shrinkage areas with unoccupied buildings, not only private homes but also shops, schools, and other facilities. If governing officials fail to act, they must face the threat of a self-sustaining process also known as the Matthew Effect: 'For to him who has will more be given, and he will have

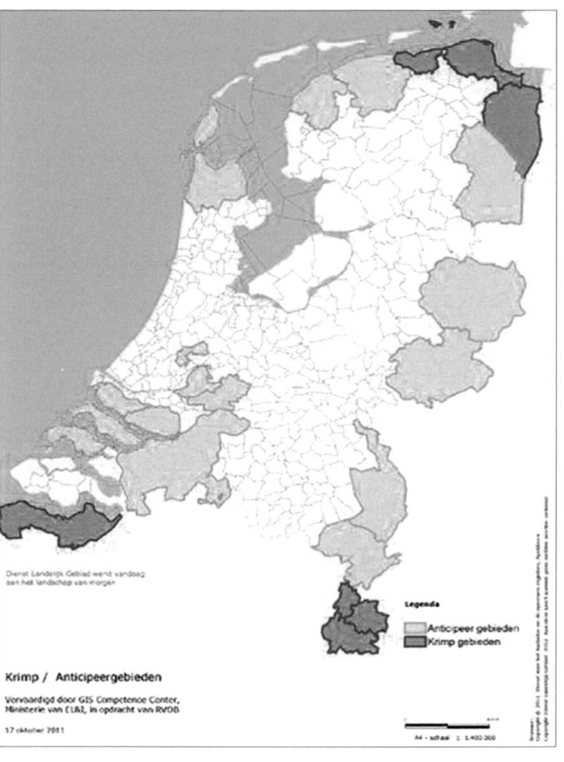

Shrinkage areas *(krimpgebieden)* and Anticipation areas *(anticipeergebieden)*

abundance; but from him who has not, even what he has will be taken away' (Matthew 13:12). In other words: things will go from bad to worse. What can officials do? What works and what doesn't?

Making the mental switch

For the record: shrinkage is not the next big hype, it's a structural development. According to the Netherlands Environmental Assessment Agency, this is only the beginning. Until 2025, new shrinkage areas throughout the Netherlands will be taking their place alongside Zeeland, South Limburg, and North Groningen. It is expected that the population of Parkstad Limburg (Heerlen, Kerkrade and surroundings) and Northeast Groningen will dwindle by 15% between now and 2040. Zeelandic Flanders and the Achterhoek will probably shrink by 10% and 5% respectively during that period. At the same time, the Randstad (the western conurbation that includes Amsterdam, Rotterdam, The Hague and Utrecht) will keep on growing. Demographers predict that traditional growth cities such as Spijkenisse, Vlaardingen, Almere, and Ede will lose inhabitants, however. According to the prognosis, half the municipalities in the country will ultimately be faced with shrinkage, although in the Netherlands this will mainly consist of 'rural shrinkage': 80% of the present and future shrinkage communities are in the countryside.

Naturally these prognoses are also being discussed by local officials. Their reactions are predictable: they either deny shrinkage or they are determined to take action. They are assisted by firms of consultants who apparently see

Strong increase of the ageing population

the shrinkage theme as an interesting growth market. With headlines such as 'Regional exodus is a grieving process' and 'Shrinkage cannot be averted', journalists stoke the flames even higher. Some mayors and city councillors avoid the word 'shrinkage' and prefer to speak of 'zero growth', 'slimming down', or 'transition'. Others are a bit more advanced in their thinking and talk about 'shrinkage with quality' and 'shrinkage as opportunity'. Local officials continue to regard shrinkage as a sensitive subject, however, because they have so little control over it. Growth gives the government influence and the chance to divide up limited space. In addition, the Dutch national government is known to reward growth. Traditionally, laws and regulations have been tailored to growth, while the salaries of city councillors increase with the size of the municipality. By contrast, shrinkage suggests loss, decline and administrative failure. In such a context, it isn't easy to let go of growth-based thinking. Shrinkage, however, demands a shift in mind-set from regional and local officials. And that doesn't only go for governments. Developers, corporations, organizations, schools, and institutions – not to mention the inhabitants themselves – have to learn how to live with shrinkage.

The cold approach to shrinkage

Many officials think that population shrinkage in their area won't be all that bad. They regularly bring the shrinkage figures up for discussion. It is indeed difficult to predict whether a municipality is going to lose 900 inhabitants over the next fifteen years or only 700, so the cliché 'demography is destiny' only partially applies. Yet demographic prognoses are a bit more reliable than economic projections. That's because there are only three variables involved in shrinkage: birth, death, and moving patterns. And even if the population figures at the local level are not indisputable, at least they serve as a guide for the way ahead.

Areas that are already undergoing shrinkage are more willing to look to the figures as a starting point for policy. One popular anti-shrinkage strategy is city and regional marketing. Many a campaign has been launched in the hope of attracting new residents and promoting growth, varying from 'Your new future' (Zeelandic Flanders) and 'South Limburg: the bright side of life' to 'Dronten: discover the wide open spaces' and 'Ranch Fryslan' (Kollumerland). Running parallel with these campaigns are the inevitable building projects. Modern housing concepts are especially popular, such as houseboats, fixer-uppers, farm-type houses and houses for horse lovers. The brochure texts are usually the same: here you can realise your dreams at an affordable price, and in a magnificent environment. The Blauwestad – a large home-on-the-water project in East Groningen – is a classic example of this 'cold' approach to shrinkage. The province of Groningen started the project in 2004 to attract highly-educated, wealthy people from the Randstad who were looking for peace and quiet. Other regions also extol the virtues of their housing climate. Marketing Drenthe, for example, organises trial weekends for the whole family, while other regions offer custom-made get-acquainted programmes.

These cold approaches to shrinkage, which are aimed at outsiders, raise certain questions. Ultimately, regions and municipalities are competing for the same group. A successful recruitment campaign in one place draws residents away from another. In addition, the Dutch have a tendency to stick close to home. Two-thirds of the people who move house in the Netherlands do so within their municipality, while only 7% move from one region to another. We see this in the example of the Blauwestad: of the 1,500 parcels available only 190 have been sold, half of them to people from the neighbourhood. When people who want to move start looking beyond their own region, they decide for themselves where they want to go. Marketing can only work as a trigger. If you still want to attract newcomers, focus your attention on local residents, former tourists, and others who have a feel for the area. A relatively large number of 25 to 35-year-olds from South Limburg move back to their native region. If an area is set on attracting such return migrants, then work availability is a crucial factor. In Twente, a 'Career Centre' has been set up to help find suitable jobs for interested 'hunkertukkers' (former inhabitants of Twente who are itching to come home) and their partners.

Warm approach to shrinkage

Fighting shrinkage by attracting newcomers is almost futile. The relevant question for shrinkage regions is not 'how do we attract new inhabitants?' but 'how do we guarantee the quality of life in the region for the people who never left?' That requires 'warm' policy measures that bind the population to the area and involve them in solving the shrinkage problem. In more and more municipalities, local starters in the housing market are being offered starters loans so they can purchase the house of their dreams. The town of Sluis gives free housing advice to its residents and issues loans so they can renovate part of their house or finance a first mortgage. In many shrinkage regions initiatives are also being taken to maintain the level of amenities within small centres or districts. Here housing corporations tend to take the lead. They might purchase the neighbourhood shop or contribute to a multifunctional facility to accommodate a range of services for the elderly (such as a café or home care).

More and more regions and municipalities are reducing their construction plans for new housing. In 2011, the province of Gelderland cut back the number of planned dwellings in the Achterhoek from 14,000 to 6,000. And more and more local officials are restructuring the existing housing supply. Two examples of warm measures aimed at people who already live in the area are removing the top floor from existing flats and converting row houses to semi-detached homes. In Heerlen, small miners' houses are being combined to form one-family dwellings, while corporations in the Frisian 'Rotten Tooth' project are doing their best to make the 'rotten teeth' (dilapidated buildings that spoil the look of a village) a bit more presentable.

Not all shrinkage communities are interested in searching for new uses for their surplus housing, however. Some deal with the problem of unoccupied buildings by calling in the demolition firm. In the Netherlands, East Groningen and Parkstad Limburg are demolishing buildings on a grand scale. Delfzijl has ordered the demolition of almost 1,600 dwellings and is going to pull down even more in the coming years. Heerlen prefers a different strategy: allowing new construction only if two empty rentals are torn down for every new one that goes up (known as 'un-renting'). Yet it remains to be seen whether the creation of scarcity by demolition is always a good idea. Demolition also costs money (about 45,000 euros per dwelling), and when a building is gone, it's gone. In addition, demolition often meets with resistance among residents, certainly if the municipality doesn't bother to discuss alternatives with them.

In any case, it's always a good idea to involve the local population in problems of shrinkage. Doing so not only creates support for any measures that might be taken, but it also provides surprising insights. For example, researchers recently asked 1,600 residents of the North Groningen countryside how they liked living in a shrinkage area. The result? The villages of North Groningen appear to be alive and kicking despite the shrinkage. Ninety-three percent of the inhabitants even said they were very satisfied living in North Groningen. What makes the region so pleasant to live in is mainly the social cohesion: neighbourhood contacts, a closely-knit community and participation in local activities. It seems that amenities such as shops, schools and sports facilities are not a pre-condition for liveability. Respondents did rank accessibility by car as important. When it comes to amenities and public services, regional accessibility trumps local availability.

Good living without amenities

The Groningen survey is not an isolated case. Research carried out in Overijssel, Zeeland, and Drenthe also indicates that liveability in shrinkage regions does not necessarily depend on services and amenities such as shops, schools, and sports accommodation. Liveability has more to do with the quality of the housing environment and with social factors. Many residents of shrinkage areas do insist that everyday services in the surrounding region be good and safe. All the households in the Groningen hamlet of Niehove have one or more cars. Commuting is a necessity they've learned to live with. When asked about liveability in Niehove, residents said that safety on the country roads left much to be desired. Their priority lists include investment in traffic safety and maintenance of the roadsides and berms – yet this is not something that immediately comes to mind when you think of population shrinkage. So local government

Unoccupied houses as a consequence of shrinkage

officials might ask themselves how residents get around. What groups in the community are less mobile? Can they get a lift with someone else?

Physical accessibility isn't the only important consideration in shrinkage regions. Optimal digital accessibility is also crucial, especially in rural areas. In many remote villages in the Netherlands the internet is still very slow. This is a matter of concern for small creative companies that require a great deal of internet capacity, such as architects, designers, and consultancies. High-speed connections are also needed for new technologies that are responding to the ageing population, such as the 'digital neighbourliness' project in the Achterhoek, which uses a webcam to combat isolation among the elderly in rural areas. 'For most of the outlying area the only internet connection still depends on copper wire,' says the Groningen geographer Strijker. He's calling for the construction of a glass fibre network throughout the Dutch countryside, and for good reason. Fast internet service is the only way to prepare the country's shrinkage regions for home-based work, home automation, and everything that technology still has in store for us.

So the relationship between liveability and the level of amenities and services is more nuanced than many people think. In addition: if there is a particular service that residents think is important, they can contribute themselves to its realisation or maintenance. In more and more shrinkage areas we are seeing examples of 'active citizenship', or to put it another way, the population rolling up their shirtsleeves and pitching in. In Drenthe, for instance, there's a community bus that runs between Beilen and Smilde that is driven by a team of about fifty local volunteers. Go-getters in the town of Warder in Noord-Holland collected 700,000 euros from the local community to save the community centre. And in Elsendorp, Noord-Brabant, residents singlehandedly developed an

Shrinkage areas should be easily accessible

Marketing The Blauwestad (home-on-the-water project)

alternative system of home care under the motto 'care for and by the people of Elsendorp'. Citizens' initiatives are not the solution for all types of services, of course. The skills required for organising home care are completely different from those needed to fix up a community centre. Shrinkage forces government officials to come up with a clear answer as to what is the responsibility of the government and what can be left to the residents themselves.

Flemings in Zeelandic Flanders?

A growing number of regions and municipalities in the Netherlands are struggling with population shrinkage. Many local government officials are trying to combat shrinkage with new building construction and marketing. But this kind of cold approach makes little sense. People don't move house at the drop of a hat and they decide for themselves where they're going to live. It's more realistic to accept shrinkage and learn to live with it. This calls for a warm approach whose aim is to bind present residents to the region by developing more moderate construction plans, renovating existing houses, and making it more attractive for young locals to purchase a home. Further advice: be cautious when it comes to demolition and involve residents in making the area and its facilities future-proof. If government officials wish to respond to shrinkage, their best bet is to begin with the existing residents. If this approach meets with the approval of outsiders, all well and good – but don't let that be the deciding factor. Whoever would have thought, for example, that more and more Flemings would be moving to Zeelandic Flanders? With house prices in the shrinkage area declining in recent years, it has become attractive for Flemings from the border region to pick up and move to the other side. This trend is now proving far more lucrative for Zeelandic Flanders than all the visits to the Emigration Fair put together. The lesson: when it comes to a long-term process like population shrinkage, patience is a virtue. For government officials, that's a message that can't be repeated too often. ■

Translated by Nancy Forest-Flier

Hand Ballet and Reflection

On the Work of Karel Dierickx

[STEFAN HERTMANS]

It is often said of the work of the Flemish artist Karel Dierickx that it has something to do with time. At first glance this type of statement may seem both meaningless and profound. Any artist's oeuvre moves and evolves over time – that is just called evolution, work in progress, or whatever. One might just as well say that every work moves in a double space: real and imaginary, and there's no arguing with that either.

Yet a close critical examination of these two statements might explain something very specific about the work of this withdrawn, virtuoso painter. With a tenacity and consistency reminiscent of Morandi, Karel Dierickx has spent over four decades developing an artistic oeuvre that excels in its circumspection and sensitivity. These qualities are not exactly obvious in the art world at the moment, where effect, brilliant ideas, marketing and sloganizing have become a matter of course.

These days, however, Dierickx's work has acquired an aura and a power of persuasion that would have been unthinkable in the years of cultural snobbery when, as Catherine David once put it bluntly, painting had become an outmoded two-dimensional bourgeois illusion. It turns out that nothing could be further from the truth. The so-called out-dated language of painting is once again more contemporary than ever. Besides painters like Gerard Richter, Luc Tuymans or Michaël Borremans, who have been inspired by the media that developed after painting (photography and film) there are the odd few here and there who have continued to search for the essence of gesture, of subject matter, the appearance of the picture from the movement of the hand. I once characterised the art of Karel Dierickx as that of a 'thinking hand'. By that I meant something very specific: Dierickx's painting originates in the physical impulse of the body, the sensuality, the movement, the presence of the artist in the intimate space where he stands in front of the canvas and is confronted by it. The body seems to know more than any theory, and the reflection of this is the complex, sensitive brushstrokes of the painting hand, formed by its daily ascesis. Thinking and painting occur in and through each other. One might argue that this is true for many painters, and that the lyrical abstract style is to some extent reminiscent of the Cobra credo and action painting. There are indeed some references to this tradition in Dierickx's work, but remarkably his development as a painter has led

The Artist with Jan Hoet (right) in his studio, Ghent, 2011

him away from any sort of fashionable influence, and has obviously been fed by a much more timeless tradition, namely that of the art of drawing as it has existed since the Renaissance. Consequently his work has acquired a surprisingly existential overtone. Dierickx's oeuvre is like one enormous sketchbook - this is how a man who has spent decades expressing himself in quiet concentration, with the cautious movements of his deliberate hand, thinks, breathes and moves. Brush technique, colour, perspective, line, composition: the keywords of the time-honoured tradition in a contemporary, compact form - a form that can at the same time fan out within its given limits into an unlimited variety of possibilities. But there is also - not least - the almost philosophical effort of the draftsmanship.

Ascesis and lyric

The cultural tradition of draftsmanship is indeed more fundamental, older and more timeless than that of painting; it has always been less tied to evolution and fashion. Some of Dierickx's drawings betray an exceptionally sensitive, in-depth knowledge of the draftsmanship of the Renaissance and Mannerism periods, but equally of the draftsmanly qualities in the work of painters such as Degas, Monet and Bonnard.

Tobias, 1997, oil on canvas, 50 x 40 cm.
Private collection

The affinity of the movements that drawing requires with the gestures of painting has some striking consequences. In particular, it means different treatment of the surface, the perception of space, and not hesitating to leave portions of the canvas unpainted. The evocation of transparency and 'thin' application of the paint can easily be combined with matter painting, impasto and dynamic paint application.

This all means that Dierickx's work can move freely within what is nonetheless a personal, recognizable grammar. The ability to combine freedom with recognisability – which is perhaps a good definition of character, of a strong artistic personality. It determines the sovereignty of this oeuvre too. Over the past decades, Dierickx has continued to concentrate in a systematic but intuitive way on a dialectical movement in painting that can only be characterised as the one between appearing and disappearing. As he conjures up old motifs – the landscape, a portrait, a still life – he constantly explores the possibilities of both contemporary and ancient art over and over again in a way that remains surprisingly fresh. Motifs crop up, but in the complexity of the colouring, painterly dynamic and composition, the theme, the subject, the motif or the figure seem at the same time to be absorbed and merge with them. On the verge of recognisability, the forms seem to the viewer to quiver, vibrate and tremble. There is often something touching about this, the drama of becoming visible occurs before our eyes, and sometimes it is as if the picture materialises, opens up, as we watch. This is one of the palpable ways in which time is present in Dierickx's work, as something that comes at us like a moving image in the minutes we spend looking at it, but that also, at a very different level, shows how much this dynamic has developed over the decades of researching how something can be made to appear, something that seems to acquire the ability to withdraw again discreetly into the suggestiveness of the forms. The mental space in which Dierickx explores this process and experiments with it, the way in which the hand moves, brushes, draws, scores and scratches, also conjures up a wide range of reminiscences, while the works themselves continue to have something economical about them, something discreet that begs to be seen as well. A strange, touching dialectic between appearing and disappearing. This combination of ascesis and lyrical animation is the inspirational motor of his work; it is also its great integrity. You need patience to see it. The work requires more than recognisability – it requires the capacity to miss something in what we see and to integrate what we have missed into what we see.

Tranquil radicalism

It is as if Dierickx wants to capture this possibility of missing something, which is intrinsic to every act of looking, on canvas, on the surface of the philosophical frustration that is typical of looking: what we see, always partly eludes us too. Dierickx paints this human limitation with an unbelievable wealth of forms and techniques. Hence this type of painting, once declared to be old hat, triumphs over earlier conceptual trends. It absorbs all the thinking about concept, visibility and philosophical issues and presents it in a form language that becomes increasingly fascinating the more it remains steadfast in its obsessions, repetitions, resumptions, variations, modulations and techniques – in the tenacity

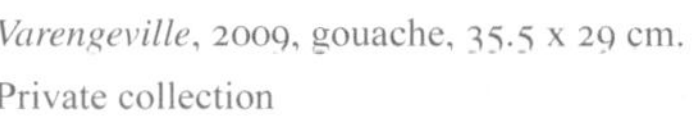

Varengeville, 2009, gouache, 35.5 x 29 cm. Private collection

Portrait of the poet Leonard Nolens, 2010, oil on canvas, 50 x 50 cm. Private collection with which the most fleeting impression can have a great impact on us if it is captured in just the right way, with an autonomy that has something innocent about it. In that sense Dierickx can, without reserve, be called a radical painter – on the understanding that this radicalism, this combination of ascesis and lyricism, is an intense exercise in pictorial reflection, a reflection in which sensitivity, sensuality, impasto light effects and line flow easily one into the other. The painting is not so much a fixed object as the result of a process that is completed in and by looking at it. That is why the observer paints, as it were, with the painter, by learning to understand what was at stake when the painting was still open to change. Potential and completion are therefore extensions of each other, they keep the work open for the next picture, yet within the picture itself there is still the possibility of a certain completion, because at a certain moment it is 'left in peace'. An extremely delicate, carefully balanced and always difficult process.

Bonnard's Studio, 2012, drawing (mixed technique), 60 x 47 cm. Artist's own collection

After all, nothing can have a more dramatic and more suggestive effect than the moment when the painter decides, in the middle of a compelling movement, to lift his hand and decline to complete the line or the composition, or to partly remove it from sight with a well-aimed erasure or smudge. It is the moment at which thought about what can be seen is given the chance to be left in peace again. For this reason there are moments in Dierickx's work that evoke intensity precisely because their possibilities are left open: they show how thought tapers off when painting has become everything or nothing. This is the point at which painting comes close to the stylised radicalism of Morandi, as well as to the gossamer-thin suggestiveness of some Japanese masters. So, Karel Dierickx walks a fine line then, as did the classic modernists: his work is at its strongest where it balances between figuration and abstraction, between tradition and contemporaneity, between what is revealed and what is left to the imagination. In that sense his work is extremely vulnerable, and that is a deliberate choice, a matter of artistic conviction.

A melancholy soldier

It is perhaps not exaggerated to say that the key to this oeuvre is integrity – a difficult category, suggesting an insistence on being morally right, what Nietzsche once called the arrogance of the modest. But this ambivalence in the very concept of integrity may also be understood as striving for integrity: on the one hand being torn between the overconfidence of wanting to paint everything (i.e. uniting the processes of watching and becoming visible), and on the other hand constantly withdrawing to the narrow basis of the self-determined terms of what actually constitutes art.

This means his oeuvre also contains an intrinsic ethic, an unending quest for an ever elusive integrity. The struggle is never easy. Dierickx is a fighter, too, a melancholy soldier, a man who strives for the one unsurpassable, right brushstroke. Aesthetics are accomplished with a sort of moral understanding of rightness and accuracy.

This is noticeable in his sculptures too. His figures are unmistakably the work of a virtuoso draftsman, who rubs, scratches and drafts with paint, a man who waits for the right stroke, as it must manifest itself from the right frame of mind.

Stil Life, 2013, oil on canvas, 31 x 27 cm.
Artist's own collection

His sculptures show this same carefully balanced hand ballet, the restrained touch that leaves an impression, a trace like a paintbrush or charcoal leave, the gesture of the hand that must create the form, knowing that it is exposing itself if it decides after all to add that brushstroke. This is an exhausting demarche, whereby he must constantly put his own existence - the vulnerability and power of it - on the line. Returning to where we started, it is clear that the effects of time and space manifest themselves here in a very specific, urgent way, namely as the categories that make the existence of the painter as an existential movement visible. This is why many of his works initially seem introvert in nature, but appear daring, extrovert and dynamic on closer examination. However melancholy his way of looking and capturing may seem – the half perceptible landscapes, in particular, often excel in their absolutely correct 'deploration' of the imperfections of the human eye – the sensitivity always looks intensely vital, it manifests its poetic sigh as a no-nonsense, tenaciously maintained discipline, as a primary survival instinct in and through observation, mistakes, new starts, struggles with the artist's own consciousness which is itself harassed by looking – and transforms this looking into a reflection on thinking and looking. The circle is at once both particular and universal.

The intimate and radical studio

The extent to which existentialism and integrity are a part of Dierickx's personality is clear from the way in which he speaks of his studio and tries to define this room very personally. Over and over again, in every interview or conversation the overriding importance of the studio as a mental space comes up. Those who visit the studio get the surprise of their lives. This is not the usual industrial-looking open workshop, but a small - you might even call it intimate - back room in a pleasant old villa, overlooking a stylised urban garden, full of light and quiet. The place speaks for itself in its intimacy and radicalism; over the many objects in the room, spotted with endless different shades of colour, the world of the canvas on the easel emanates into space. The stained sink, the dirty cloths, the paint-stained shoes kicked off in a corner, the spots on the walls, on the reproductions pinned to the wall, yes even the vague smudges on a window – they turn reality into canvas, and the canvas on the easel into an integral part of life. The thickly caked palette, the messy open paints stuck together in prehistoric-looking lumps, shining in the daylight, extend the painting into the tiniest corners of the room in which the painter has sat working, all alone, for decades. The power with which this osmosis between painting and living is revealed makes Dierickx's studio a rare sphere of experience in which restraint and freedom, quiet and powerful dynamism, attention and lyricism blend effortlessly. Indeed, one might say, in the well-known words from Wagner's *Parsifal*: space becomes time here. Less mystical perhaps than Wagner intended, but nonetheless at least as charged, at least as complex and fundamental.

'Auf der Suche nach dem eigenen Ich' ran the headline of *Die Welt* back in 1990 with reference to this work. But the search for the self is the same as that for the very essence of painting, and from there to the essence of existence as a looking, thinking being who lifts his hand to reflect something of what is seen and realised. Everything Dierickx makes is created as if from nothing, like work started

Twilight, 2013, oil on canvas, 100 x 80 cm.
Artist's own collection

from zero each time, and ends up being a radical aspiration to say almost everything about looking and realising. Renewal and endless variation, two concepts that are usually opposites, go paradoxically but easily hand in hand in his work.

The freedom of the older master

Because of his existential radicalism Dierickx will always remain aloof from the current generation of Flemish painters, but that aloofness has only strengthened its aristocratic power of persuasion over the years. It is the aloofness, the integrity of someone who is such an integral part of the great painting tradition that he no longer needs, as it were, an environment, a school or a trend. The working of time and space around him is enough for him. It is the breathing of an oeuvre for which the iconographic space of its own intimacy is enough, which is also recognisable quite simply as human lebensraum. It is the freedom of the old master who has reached that stage about which Paul Klee once said that one had only to take the line out for a walk. It is the freedom of the old Matisse: the hand knows its way through the complex ways which the art of painting has amassed for it throughout all these centuries, settled in its own existence. Freedom and rigour, a room full of light and reflection. A work that spreads out into the view in the window. An artist could not ask for much more. ■

Translated by Lindsay Edwards

Left: *In the mirror*, 2013, oil on canvas, 60 x 50 cm.
Artist's own collection

The Everyday is Good

The Novels of Koen Peeters

Conversaties met K. (Conversations with K., 1988), the first novel of Koen Peeters (1959), sports a stamp from the Belgian Congo on its cover. Almost a quarter of a century later the Leuven author published *Duizend heuvels* (A Thousand Hills, 2012), his great novel about the small neighbouring country of Ruanda. Anyone linking these facts might be tempted to think that Peeters' oeuvre forms a close unity, within which the former Belgian colonies are an inexhaustible source of literary inspiration. But that idea is both true and untrue. For though the writer has enduring fascinations, he has travelled a long way.

In the early days Peeters was seen as one of the leaders of a new generation of Flemish postmodernists. He and his colleagues were like the young men who, in the novel *Het is niet ernstig, mon amour* (Nothing Serious, Mon Amour, 1996), set up the Independent Research Center. They had high-flown ambitions. But their *Sturm und Drang* were stifled from the outset by the sensibility of the 1990s. They shone particularly in irony and deconstruction. Peeters' first novels were suspiciously like the Independent Research Center: a promising enterprise without great results. The writer showed himself a master in idiosyncratic, warped mental acrobatics and incisive formulations. But, for all the dazzle, his work remained rather anaemic. Art seemed to the author, in daily life the head of sponsoring and social affairs at a major bank, no more than ritual behaviour at the end of the working day. In an interview he said: 'for me writing is coming home from work, eating, a little later sitting at the table with a bit of paper, and working for an hour or so. Every day, and after two years I've got a book.' A refreshing form of self-irony. But the reader of the first quartet of novels had an uncontrollable urge to wipe the irony off the face with which the writer looked at him from the back cover and to shout at him: 'This is serious, Koen Peeters!'

Divine photo album

Those hoping Peeters would show a little more courage in not simply feigning seriousness were rewarded in *Acacialaan* (2001). The novel is a labyrinth of stories in which the I-figure, Robert, wanders through the oeuvre of

Koen Peeters (1959)

Maurice Gilliams and Louis Paul Boon, through the streets of Brussels and Aalst and through late-twentieth-century Belgium. Interwoven with the book is a wonderful episodic narrative entitled 'My Father'. In it the I-figure describes Father's admission to hospital and death. Before he is anointed, he wants to get something off his chest. 'He saw things very sharply now,' writes Peeters in a strange combination of irony and compassion. 'Up there we'll all be together, in one great mason's hand, a photo album or call it God's eternity.' For Robert it is incomprehensible that their wartime experiences did not afflict his father's generation with existential angst. But he does not ridicule in his incomprehension, and the irony is not deadly. Fascination and emotion carry the day. And Father puts up a fight. 'Don't you think people are too cynical these days? Aren't you like that yourself?'

Father would definitely have had a problem with *Grote Europese Roman* (Great European Novel, 2007). In the 'Mission Statement' the author explains the aim of his Great Project. 'Sweeping and epic, it should sum up the history of European humanity, but from the narrow perspective of people who live or work in Brussels.' We hear an echo of Louis Paul Boon's curses and prayers of the little man confronted with the Great War. Where the young Boon was serious in his rage and hope, Peeters'sentences in contrast drip with sarcasm and he gives short shrift to all high-flown expectations.

Take the mission for which the I-figure Robin scours the European continent: making recommendations for the trade organisation of manufacturers of promotional gifts. On his journey to European capitals he collects local beauties, tourist tips and words in all languages. These do not afford him any deeper insights into the unity of European identity amid the variety of peoples. The main thing he discovers is the emptiness of universal office life.

Yet it is too easy to dismiss *Grote Europese Roman* as an ironic deconstruction of the European dream that ends in cynicism. At the end of his odyssey Robin encounters a youthful love again. Together they savour a thought that brings them close to Father's divine photo album: 'wouldn't it be better to view happiness as a long-term balance, an eternal sum of presents large and small that we receive and give, conversations and chats, exchanged secrets like electric words, slightly smarting wounds, faces that we never forget, and all that added and added and added, perhaps even different lives added together? Perhaps this kind of happiness is built up piece by piece and passed on from generation to generation, families, and dynasties? Like photos in an album?'

Everyday dust

Peeters draws up the balance of family happiness in the novel *De bloemen* (The Flowers, 2009), which was awarded the F. Bordewijk Prize. The novel is 'very loosely based on family stories', notes the writer in his afterword. But it is clear from every line that the characters are very close to home. In *De bloemen* Peeters is better able than previously to create real characters instead of pawns in a literary game. In wonderful prose he paints intimate portraits of his grandfather Louis and his father René.

Flowers bloom and fade in a trice. But like a twenty-first-century Heraclitus, Peeters sees in what vanishes the germ of the new, and in motion what endures. In the chapter 'Dandelions' the I-figure sweeps the dust out of his house. 'What I see in my hands, I can scarcely give a name. It is the wind of what keeps us going, the movements of intentions, conversations, and thoughts. It is the simple, negligible, everyday things that constantly reappear in the movements in a house, especially through the wind that blows in when the windows are opened in the morning to let in the birdsong.'

De bloemen is an attempt to capture this dust, slow down time, find the eternal in the transient. The way Peeters reaches for eternity by stringing together the stories of the generations is almost mystical: 'If I can now go on writing in the right way, time will no longer exist, and we shall all be the same.'

Endless practice in watching your words

That the right kind of writing can move mountains is also shown by Peeters' latest novel *Duizend heuvels*, which was awarded the E. du Perron Prize. The book is a thousand things at once. A quest for what more there is to Ruanda than a country torn apart by genocide. An ode to the Kinyarwanda language and Ruandan mythology. A portrait both empathetic and harsh of the community of White Fathers, who came full of good intentions, but were silent when their Christian consciences should have spoken out. An intimate biography of the Ruandan scholar Alexis Kagame, who fought against the white accusation that his country had no history and transcribed the ritual texts of the Ruandan dynasty that went back to the twelfth century, but saw his life's work traduced by Belgian researchers. A jolly novel of manners on the academic community of Ruanda experts. And most of all a web of secret literary paths around such themes as colonial guilt and reconciliation.

It is tempting to read the novel as an indictment of the Westerners who have made such a mess in Ruanda. Peeters quotes the White Father Van Overschelde who saw the Tutsis as 'the aristocracy of the black race' and 'whites in disguise'. Following in his intellectual footsteps, the colonial administration made absolute the previously fluid distinction between the population groups. First the Belgians appointed only Tutsis as vassals of the ruling power, but shortly before independence church and state suddenly took the side of the previously oppressed Hutus. In this way they sowed the divisions that later did their devastating work. An old Ruandan sage argues in *Duizend heuvels* that Belgians exported their language struggle to Africa. 'So Flemings, who felt treated like second-class citizens in their native Belgium, sympathised with the Hutus. And so the Belgians mentally organised the Hutu-Tutsi division.' But before the novel opens, the writer has already warned the reader and the reviewer: 'Every quotation taken out of context is untrue.'And opposed to the vision of the old sage, there is that of a younger Ruandan postgraduate, who says of the genocide: 'We did it. Not you. Our complexes from the past that we had kept hidden for years suddenly surfaced.'

Duizend heuvels is not a political pamphlet, but a polyphonic work that undermines facile judgements and unambiguous truths. In contrast, with a kaleidoscope of narratives and perspectives, Peeters shows that there are many truths which, despite the fact they clash, may be equally true. But amid all the ambiguity a core idea does nevertheless seem to take shape. Shortly after the horrors of the genocide have taken place, the Brussels boy Louis, who is visited at night by Ruandan dreams, asks for an explanation of how to weave baskets. 'From now on when everyone sees the big picture, I shall see the little one.' When he is incarnated as the I-figure in the final section of the book and no longer visits Ruanda in his dreams but in reality, he meets the sixty-eight-year-old Abbé Donatien.'Everyone must practice endlessly in watching their words,' says the abbé. In the eyes of the old clergyman, only when people abandon the big words and raging anger and meet in everyday, simple friendliness can Ruanda be saved.

The attention to small things that Louis and Donatien cherish fits in perfectly with the philosophy that emerges from *De bloemen*. Whether it be in the nearby Kempen or distant Ruanda, Peeters' literary universe expresses an unclamorous devotion to the small and the everyday. The postmodern mocker has turned into a serious collector of fragile happiness. ■

Translated by Paul Vincent

Two Extracts from *Great European Novel*

By Koen Peeters

Mission statement

I want to write a book in the style of the Great American Novel, disguised as a Great European Novel. I've googled it and there's no such thing as yet. Sweeping and epic, it should sum up the history of European humanity, but from the narrow perspective of people who live or work in Brussels.

I'd like to write this novel in the form of the periodic table. Like the Italian Primo Levi - each chapter a chemical element. Yes, each chapter of my novel should be about a capital city, as if each city were a chemical element in an ingenious Brussels system. With characters in search of all-consuming love, promising and impatient. Or else driven by a past that has made them wise and sad.

I'd like to describe the beauty of Administration, the eroticism of the Brussels business world. With you, in a European way. In conference centres, airports and hotels we'll examine how we, strangers, are nevertheless able to find one another. How we sometimes delight in misunderstanding one another. How we feel one another out with hands full of language. How there are some secrets we can only entrust to people we've never seen before and will never see again. The Portuguese writer Pessoa talked about ants that 'communicate amongst themselves using tiny antennae which work a thousand times better than our complex language which eludes all comprehension'.

Everyone knows the miracles in the Bible, the beetle story by the German Czech Kafka, and Ovid's Metamorphoses, in which gods and demigods are turned into trees and springs.

Stories like this are about the fluidity of things, the rearrangement of bodily atoms, forever on the move. Or, as in the tradition of the Talmud, we should interpret texts, adapt and comment on them time and again, until we've forgotten how the first text went. Or like that story about the ship...

Consequently, any resemblance to persons or cities is coincidental. Even dates have been moved around effortlessly here and there. Because, even now, someone has to prepare the rooms for the future, fold the sheets tightly on the beds and lay out clean clothes for the travellers. The first arrived last night, and the fastest, the most intelligent are already running through our streets.

Nicosia

Brussels, the 1950s. Theo had recorded the monthly figures and discussed the new targets with his colleagues. Next, he entered the profit in the ledger. Everyone was working away diligently. The stationery sported the company name in a very vigorous red: MARCHAND NV/SA, Avenue Louise/Louizalaan. 'Marchand' was in sturdy, broad capitals. The red of the letters was not the signal red of warning signs or stop signs. Nor was it the colour of fire, of glowing, hot ash just before it turns into dead, white powder. No, it was the warmest, the most commercial red possible.

Marchand then. But didn't this young man used to go by a different name? Marcus or Maerski? Or Marcowicz? Or something to that effect? Perhaps these were silly questions, because the mercantile red was meant to draw attention to the brand name Marchand, if only to command business success, or as publicity, or as a guarantee of profit.

Theo did good business after the war. He chose the publicity industry and specialised in promotional items,which even then people began to call 'gadgets'. He bought and sold. He was the sort of young, dynamic person who has hushed conversations, whispers or shouts, swallows softly and murmurs, or places eye-catching advertisements. Their words slip away skittishly when you grasp them, their thoughts curl. All year round, these men dress in timeless black tailor-made suits, white shirts, and the latest fashion in ties.

Whenever Theo rang a European business contact, he always asked what the weather was like where they were. In Madrid, scorching heat. In London, cloudy. In Paris, rain.

'Then it will soon be drizzling here in Brussels', said Theo, and all these international reports made him feel liberated and rich.

He was i n t e r n a t i o n a l, E u r o p e a n.

To him, these telephones represented freedom, progress, prosperity. He put up a European country map in his office. He had decided that people speak more passionately if there's a map on the wall. It gave more weight to their words. *Navigare necesse est*, he thought, we have to sail, we have to explore the world - travel, trade and talk uninhibitedly. He talked about the helicopter view, big gestures. But not about our deepest desires, because we don't really know what they are.

Although he'd always written with soft blue ink in his youth, now he wrote in a cheerful, post-war turquoise. He remembered how this colour materialised in the words on the page as he wrote. For a moment the colour was greenish, the green of mint and eucalyptus, before turning turquoise. He leaned back with his hands behind his head and studied the ceiling. His ultimate ambition was a public limited company with one hundred employees.

Naamloze vennootschap, nv.

Société Anonyme, SA.

Aktiengesellschaft, AG.

Public Limited Company, PLC.

Because he thought he could have a perfect overview of one hundred employees, like before with his linguistic family tree and his constellations. He could just manage to know them all personally still.

Theo was the inspired, driven type. He could fire off ideas the way you can separate water from mud if you beat it gently. He clapped people on the back in a studied fashion. He did that to get closer to his people, to inspire them. He even remembered the names of most of his employees' children, but perhaps that was just to do with his passion for lists.

In 1958, Brussels hosted the World's Fair. The city was appropriated by cheery foreigners. That's what tourists are like, open, inquisitive, always in high spirits. Theo was amazed at the optimism which the concrete and the metal called out to him.

Everything will be O.K.!

We are human progress!

Alle Menschen werden Brüder!

Brothers! Frères! Fratres!

At the American theatre, beneath flowering Japanese cherry trees, he watched as letters appeared between the branches. He could read them easily: an N, an I, a C, no, an O, and he tried to make out the rest of the letters that spell 'Nicosia', the capital of Cyprus. He knew that from his stamps. But a curly S appeared, the prongs of an E, an X in the intersection of some twigs. And X. And another X. Theo fell in love with a woman, and shortly afterwards he finally had sex for the first time. His thoughts dissolved into something pink, something heavenly white, something with the sensitivity of eyelashes. So this was it, this momentary, inward-focused deafness.

This soft, graceful underside of things.

When he came, words flew at him out of nowhere. He listened to the echo of the ejaculation. What did the words mean? He didn't know. It was something from his innermost depths, from gaps and chinks in his being. Something which managed to rise to the surface before evaporating. Every time they made love, he was beset by messages he was completely unable to identify.

His girlfriend said he was quiet, non-communicative. Sometimes she called him antisocial, self-absorbed, far too sober. Her resentment mounted.

The relationship broke up. Theo's second girlfriend was someone who came up to him one day and told him she was in love with him. It all happened very quickly. She taught him to drink alcohol, but Theo remained on his guard the whole time, afraid as he was of spluttering, staggering people who talk too much. She insisted he spend the night with her.

In the morning, they were awoken by the sound of children playing in a nearby school. They had sex, and when Theo came, all he heard were the little fools shrieking relentlessly in the playground. He looked outside, looked at the commotion of the children. It was as if someone was daubing paint with an invisible hand. Theo wanted to hear messages he couldn't make out. Should he go back to the watermill of his youth sometime?

Nothing came of that relationship either.

When Theo drove to the watermill a month later, a board with a primitive drawing of a watermill was hanging from the gable. The mill had been turned into a restaurant with a small bird park around the back. Theo accompanied the manager as he went from cage to cage dishing out apples and alfalfa. There were partridges and a hoopoe, a magpie without a tail, a reddish bird from America. Under eucalyptus trees, large black grouse were being reared.

'Tetraotetrix', said Theo, and he surprised the manager even more as they stood in front of the cages with a stork, falcons and a sick cuckoo. Theo just came out with it:

Ooievaar, stork, Storch, cigogne, ciconia.

Valk, Falke, falcon, faucon, falco.

Koekoek, cuckoo, coucou, Kuckuck, cuculus.

In the restaurant, Theo saw a photograph of the man and woman who had taken him in during the war years hanging beside the parchment lampshades.

'Is that the miller?' asked Theo.

'Yes, they died one shortly after the other ten years ago. Do you know them?'

'No,' lied Theo, 'but it would make sense for you to have a photo of them here.'

'Will you be eating here tonight?' asked the manager. 'We have wild boar on the game menu, and confit de canard.' Theo assured the man he would, but he drove back to Brussels without stopping. ■

Translated by Rebekah Wilson

From *Great European Novel*

(Grote Europese Roman. Amsterdam-Antwerpen: Meulenhoff/Manteau, 2007)

An Extract from *A Thousand Hills*

By Koen Peeters

Hello young man, come in. How nice of you to come and shave me.

I close my eyes.

Does this interfere with your work?

I can't see you, but I can feel you.

I like the sharpness of your knife, I quite like the way it rasps. The bare sound cleanses me. Mind my throat, I'm not an ox.

All my archives are here in this splendid head you now hold in your hands. *Enchanté*, my name is Alexis Kagame, Abbé du Clergé indigène de Ruanda– Catholic priest, Doctor of Philosophy and lecturer at the University of Ruanda. I am celebrated, renowned; I am the man of Ruanda's history. Don't forget to trim my nostril hair.

Thank you for your attentions, I'm as good as new again. It's going to be an unusual day, I can feel it. I fear it won't be much longer.

In the 1950s, the African world changed radically. From then on, we lived in modern times, and I travelled regularly to Belgium. In Tervuren, in their royal Belgian institutes, they studied us.

Us, *les Africains*.

At the time I was still one of the exceptions. As a Ruandan, I published books about our armed forces, cattle breeding, overviews of dynastic poetry, races, the tribes. They contained photos of bare-chested Twas and Hutus, but the Tutsis were serious, tall and wore white clothes.

In 1952, I was at the carnival in Stavelot with Father Hulstaert. There were men in loose-fitting clothes with long red noses. Confetti, pigs' bladders. I, the African, thought: look at these primitives. In Ruanda we don't have any masks.

We're not Congolese.

Some people say our language is our mask. They say we're proud, complicated, elitist. We don't need any masks.

In Belgium, I learned how I should behave in Belgium. I mean, how they would like me to behave. For example, if you don't know the way, you should act as if you're exceptionally helpless. They like that. Only then will they help you. I liked that play-acting. In Luxembourg, I found I'd run out of money. Apparently in Luxembourgish my name - Kagame - means 'no money left', *keigei meh*.

The Europeans thought that was so funny when I told them. I repeated it as often as they wanted to hear it. In 1953, in the Royal Belgian Colonial Institute, I was the only black member of the assembly. This made me proud and angry at the same time. I, the Ruandan historian, was allowed to address the gentlemen. I wasn't just anybody, I realised. I told them how our cultures were kindling each other. A spark that landed in a pile of dry grass. There were bound to be flames. Yes, these were recent, modern times and I, Rwandese, bore a Belgian stamp. We were Belgian Africa. This history, this now, had to be recorded too. Suddenly I had to live more carefully, I thought, and continue carefully to write our new history. From now on, there were thousands of witnesses, Belgian and Ruandan. There were no omniscient old men any more, I was just one of the spectators of the events.

The events. *Les évènements*.

We Ruandans believe the man who says he's seen it. I've seen a lot. In the 1950s, political parties started to emerge in Ruanda, Hutus against Tutsis. Aprosoma, Parmehutu, Rader, Unar. Our King was not happy about this. Since the Hutus, Gitera in particular, were so angry about the Karinga, the ancient drums were hidden.

By whom? I shan't say.

In July 1959, King Mutara went to see a film in Usumbura, *Les Seigneurs de la Forêt*. Mutara III had been drinking with friends, heavily according to some. Some said he was addicted to alcohol, but I'm not saying that.

Others claim his own mother said he was mad, that he was suffering from tuberculosis of the spine. Or something to do with syphilis. I don't think so.

Did I hear his confession before he departed?

I'm saying nothing. Of course not, I'm a priest.

In Usumbura, our King went to see Doctor Vinck, who gave him an injection of megacillin, after which he collapsed. Brain haemorrhage, dead on the pavement. Some say he poisoned himself to invoke the shadow of revenge. Most said the Belgians had murdered him.

But I'm saying nothing.

Just like our country, I was shocked, saddened. Our earth shook. I mourned. The King had always supported me, we talked to each other like colleagues, and our King had no heir.

We say: 'The days pass, but they don't resemble each other.'

We say: 'No-one knows which way the ram's horns will grow.'

We say: 'The things of tomorrow are told by the people of tomorrow.'

Every country needs a leader, to know where evil lurks, solve problems, protect the weak. I pulled my curtains shut, considered and reflected on everything the King had said to me. I had to retrieve every royal word, and I did so. The King isn't just any dead person. The Hutus were in favour of democracy. That was fine by me, but I wanted a king to realise this democracy. History prescribed it, I was a historian and did what I had to do. I knew the ancient secret texts that dictated how the transfer of power should take place after the king's death. I knew the *Ubwiru* and therefore I felt responsible.

On 27 July 1959, I was in my room working on old war poems. All of a sudden I smelt burning wood, charcoal from the hills. I was informed of the death of the King. Then I heard the sound of bones breaking in the poems on my desk, they were crying out to me. 'Shout away, old poems,' I said, 'set fire to each other', and sure enough the poems, with their embellishments and frills, caught fire, as blue flames shot up and burned my fingers. I doused the flames.

I had to do something. In any case, the King had given me an order before. Perhaps I was also curious about my authority.

I doused the flames of the poems. I made telephone calls, paid visits, I had my contacts. That night, we decided on a successor. The abiru and I. I wrote a confidential letter to Monseigneur Perraudin. I reminded the Bishop that the ceremony of the *Ubwiru*, for which I possessed the secret texts, had to be followed, even though we were burying a Christian king. The childless Mutara had told me personally who was to be his successor. I was the *umwiruw'ljambo*.

It was his young half-brother Jean-Baptiste Ndahindurwa, also a son of Musinga. The young man was only twenty-one years old. I said that the new King should bear the name Kigeli V, as custom - *la coutume* - prescribed, and be designated before the funeral of his predecessor.

Bishop Perraudin did not answer me.

My house was being watched by men working for the Belgian Colonel Logiest. In those days, he had already quite clearly chosen the side of the Hutus. The Belgians: first they used the Tutsis to govern the country, then they used the Hutus to block our independence.

At the funeral on 28 July, on Mwima Hill near Nyanza, many people were gathered with spears. There was shouting. A lot of whites discreetly carried revolvers. Deputy Governor Harroy read out condolences from the Belgian King Baudouin. Around the coffin people began jostling and pushing, clapping wildly, and Francis Rukeba, his inside pocket full of banknotes, stirred the people up.

He shouted out that they must know the name of the new King immediately.

Or was it Kayihura, from the family of the guardians of the Karinga, who shouted that out?

Kayumba was there too, the grandson of Gashamuza, though not a true umwiru himself, because he didn't know the whole code. In the commotion, Kayumba said the name I had told him.

Or was it Kayihura, after all, who said the name of the successor in a doubtful voice, because he was made to by Bideri? In any case, it was in either case the name I had said. The name the King had told me.

Jean-Baptiste Ndahindurwa gave a start. I was standing right beside him, whispered to him that he would do well. The Belgians knew nothing about it. They were stunned. They had no choice but to accept the new King. Harroy nodded uncomfortably, nodded and nodded again. He said he was ready for the official inauguration of the new King.

We say: 'Drink the white man's milk while it's still fresh. If you wait until it curdles, it will be spilled.'

We say: 'A mouth that is not used murders its owner.'

We say: 'I wear my pagne inside out, not my heart.'

Under my breath, I said: 'We must show the successor to the crowd now', and Musinga's son was lifted onto the shoulders of four men. He was carried around in celebration. He was a half-brother of Mutara, Jean-Baptiste Ndahindurwa, and he was given the royal name Kigeli V. Some people called it a coup, but it wasn't. The old, dead King was buried, long live the new King. He would make our country independent. Or not. ■

Translated by Rebekah Wilson

From *A Thousand Hills* (Duizend heuvels. Antwerpen: De Bezige Bij, 2012)

The Difference Between Language and Dialect in the Netherlands and Flanders

[MARC VAN OOSTENDORP]

Perhaps the real puzzle is why there is so much variation. The small geographical area of the Netherlands and Flanders is home to hundreds of dialects according to some counts –some of them mutually unintelligible, all of them divided over two languages: Dutch and Frisian.

In this delta area in the northwest corner of Europe variation has been ingrained from time immemorial. Even in the wildest nationalistic fantasies of the nineteenth century, the inhabitants were descended not from one people, but from at least three Germanic tribes who settled here: the Franks, the Saxons and the Frisians. We also know that when these tribes set foot on it, the area was by no means uninhabited. Even if little is known about the previous inhabitants, there are traces of their language in present day Dutch.

So from the very beginning the linguistic landscape here was also a delta, with influxes from elsewhere mixing with local elements in continually changing combinations, gradually giving rise to all these varieties.

Add to that a variety of political developments. The fact that the Netherlands formed an autonomous nation in the seventeenth century set the linguistic border between Dutch and German. As such, the Dutch dialects do not differ that much more from High German than the original Northern German dialects when it comes to justifying a sharp boundary, but the political reality increasingly became a linguistic reality. The intermittently shifting borders in the south too, between the Northern and Southern Netherlands, and between the Dutch-speaking and French-speaking areas, have left traces in the everyday language.

Only relatively recently has there been any semblance of unity. A written form of the standard language was created in the seventeenth century, a century in which Dutch culture flourished and Protestantism became very powerful. The result was the *Statenvertaling*, the 'States Translation', a translation of the Old and New Testaments put together by a special parliamentary commission (the 'States General', hence the name) to be comprehensible to readers throughout the region. In order to achieve this, choices were made: in Dutch dialects the word *himself* can be rendered as *z'n eigen, zijn or hem*. In the Statenvertaling *zichzelf* was chosen, which then became the standard Dutch form.

However, the mix was far from neutral. In the majority of cases the examples came from the dialects of Holland or those of the regions that are now Antwerp and

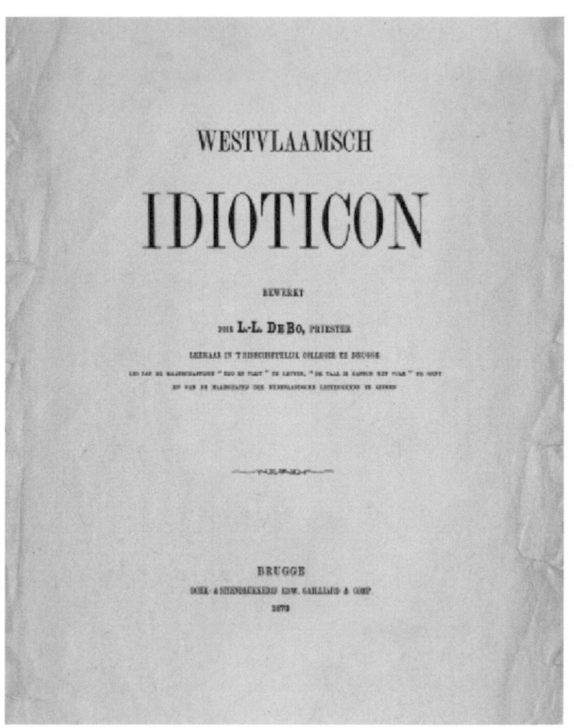

WESTVLAAMSCH

IDIOTICON

BEWERKT

DOOR L.-L. DE BO, PRIESTER

BRUGGE

BOEK- & STEENDRUKKERIJ EDW. GAILLIARD & COMP.

1873

Flemish Brabant, the economic centres of the Southern Netherlands. In the seventeenth century a great many wealthy, industrious people also came to Holland from those areas, mainly to escape religious persecution. This substantially strengthened Holland's position and introduced elements of the Antwerp dialects and others into the dialects of Holland, making them look more like the standard language.

Standardisation of spoken Dutch took longer, and probably came about spontaneously in university cities such as Leiden, where the well-to-do youth from various regions lived together for several years, adhering to a common standard pronunciation, which they then spread when they returned as ministers or notaries to their home villages. Only in the course of the twentieth century, with the introduction of mass media such as radio, films, TV and particularly the telephone, did a standard spoken language become established.

In fact then the standard language has only existed for a short time in the history of the Dutch dialects. According to some (such as Professor Joop van der Horst from Leuven) it has already had its heyday. He believes people throughout Europe will pay less and less attention to the arbitrary state borders that are supposed to determine where one language differs from another.

Logically the internet should reduce the need for a uniform standard language. Traditional media, from print to television, from film to CD, had to achieve wide circulation. Production was expensive and the only way to earn back the costs was to serve as large a group as possible simultaneously, requiring a standard language. The spread of the internet removes that obstacle. A YouTube video or weblog allows people to reach a small, local group without incurring high costs. Somewhat ironically, the effect of the worldwide web in the Low Countries, as elsewhere, has been to breathe new life into the local community.

Language – dialect – accent: the difference is political

How many dialects are there precisely in the Dutch language region? It is impossible to give an exact figure. This is not down to lack of research: in the twentieth century language variation was mapped very precisely in a couple of big language atlases. Even now dozens of detailed studies are published every year; new database techniques are applied to make clearer maps with improved computer graphics.

The problem is also different: it is impossible to establish a scientific definition of dialect, to distinguish it once and for all from the concept of language on the one hand, and accent on the other. Two languages, for example, generally differ more from one another than two dialects of the same language, but exactly where the threshold lies varies from one country to another: the so-called dialects of Chinese differ more than Italian and Spanish, for instance, according to one particular method of analysis.

A similar effect applies to the boundary between dialect and accent. People use the latter when the difference is solely in pronunciation. Two dialects must therefore also differ in vocabulary and grammar, but what if the difference affects only a handful of words and one or two grammatical constructions?

In fact the terms language, dialect and accent are distinguished primarily socio-politically. It is power that determines that the varieties of Chinese are 'insufficiently' different from one another, and the fact that Italy and Spain (or the Netherlands and Germany) are different countries pushes the decision in the other direction.

Since the concept of 'dialect' is socio-political, one might expect different results in the Netherlands and Belgium. To a certain extent that is the case, although I believe this is more down to cultural differences between the two countries than conscious politics. In the Netherlands, particularly in the provinces of North and South Holland, where Amsterdam, Rotterdam and The Hague are located, many people assume that they 'automatically' speak the standard language and 'therefore' automatically speak more or less 'correct'

Dutch, whereas in Flanders there is a greater awareness of distance between the dialects spoken by individuals and the standard language.

That difference is primarily a matter of time. In Flanders, too, the distance between dialect and standard language is shrinking – a variety known as *tussentaal* ('in-between language') or *Verkavelingsvlaams* ('housing estate Flemish') has developed, somewhere between the traditional dialects and the formal standard language. This makes the difference between standard language and dialect, as in the Netherlands, less of a sharp division (you speak one or the other) and more of a continuum, where people shift one way or the other, depending on who they're talking to.

It is even uncertain whether variation is decreasing. We do know that in the last 150 years the standard language has made great strides. Almost everyone in the Low Countries speaks a form of standard language, and everyone certainly understands it, but this knowledge certainly need not come at the expense of dialect - people can easily master a variation.

In some respects the dialects have even gained a new lease of life. They are now used in places one would not have found them fifty years ago, such as pop music and advertising. It is important to see such dialect use in context: it primarily serves to convey a feel, rather than to make the message of the text as clear as possible. All native Dutch and Flemish-speakers who can read and write can read and write standard Dutch. No one turns to dialect to make a message clear; in fact, many people in Limburg probably read Dutch more fluently than Limburgish, simply because they are more used to it. It seems that this dialect use has increased over the last decade or so (although we cannot be certain of this).

The European Charter for Regional or Minority Languages

There has been a long-standing discussion on the question of precisely which varieties should be called language, and which dialect. A good example is the discussion around *The European Charter for Regional or Minority Languages*. About twenty years ago, in 1992, the Netherlands became one of the first countries to sign this document produced by the Council of Europe, which primarily served to protect regional vernaculars. The Charter sets out a wide range of measures governments can take to protect these languages. In signing the Charter, a country commits to applying a proportion of those measures, to be decided by the individual country, for instance in education, broadcasting and the language used in government. (There is a minimum, but each country decides for itself where the measures are desirable and feasible).

When the Netherlands signed the Charter, everyone thought it would only apply to Frisian. Historically the Frisian dialect group is relatively distant from the dialects that form the basis of standard Dutch and since the 17th century there has been a battle in the Frisian region for recognition of that dialect group as a language in itself. This would formalise and reinforce the measures for the protection of Frisian.

Belgium, on the other hand, has never signed the Charter, for a number of reasons relating to its already complicated political linguistic situation, with three standard languages, Dutch, French, and German. There were fears that the French-speaking minority in Flanders would apply for the status of a minority language. (In Switzerland this happened with speakers of Rhaeto-Romance outside the cantons where it is the official language.)

A couple of years after the Netherlands signed, further eventualities emerged. Germany had also signed the Charter and one of the languages to be recognised was Low German, the large northern dialect group stretching from Berlin deep into the west. How deep? There is really no good reason for excluding the north-eastern Dutch dialects: people do not speak any differently on either side of the border. Well, Germany could hardly go granting recognition to languages in another country, but this led local politicians on our side of the border – such as the liberal members of parliament Johan Remkes and Henk Kamp, who both later became ministers and who were already reasonably influential in their party at the time – to hope that the Netherlands might grant recognition.

A power struggle developed based on these scholarly arguments. The State Secretary of the Interior initially did not want to know, arguing that the Charter was only intended for languages, not dialects, and ignoring the fact that there are no watertight criteria for the difference between language and dialect, as mentioned above. In a couple of months it became clear to the State Secretary that he could not prevent recognition of 'Nedersaksisch' (Low Saxon) – the collective name for the dialects of Groningen, Drenthe, Overijssel and parts of Gelderland and Friesland – on scientific grounds. Well-known dialect researchers began to show an interest and added that the eastern dialects had contributed very little to standard Dutch, and consequently really could not be called dialects of Dutch, a dubious argument in itself, as there are no scientific criteria for determining how little is 'too little'. In the end, however, the State Secretary conceded that Nedersaksisch was also a language and required recognition, which was indeed forthcoming, albeit with a peculiar twist. A clever civil servant noted that there were three parts to the Charter: parts 1 and 2 set out general provisions and definitions, whereas the actual measures are described in part 3. Frisian was recognised 'in accordance with part 3', Nedersaksisch 'in accordance with part 2': the Kingdom of the Netherlands recognises it as a language but won't put a single penny towards it.

Small as the significance of such recognition may be, it appears it was desirable enough. Soon the province of Limburg approached the government for recognition of Limburgish – which was also forthcoming, again in accordance with part 2 – but the story took another twist. Limburg is also spoken across the border – this time in Belgium. The Belgian Limburgers wanted their language recognised now too and approached their own government. Unfortunately neither Belgium nor Flanders had signed the Charter. The Flemish government directed the Limburgers to the Nederlandse Taalunie, the Dutch Language Union. Although the Dutch and Flemish governments officially outsource their Dutch language policy to the Taalunie, the union had never been asked for advice on this subject.

One people, one country, one language?

The Nederlandse Taalunie was founded in defence of standard Dutch, so perhaps it was not surprising that it now sided against recognition. Moreover the General Secretary of the Nederlandse Taalunie declared that it would have been better not to have granted Nedersaksisch and Limburgish recognition in the first place. According to the Charter previous decisions could not be revoked: languages once recognised cannot be unrecognised. Johan Remkes, who had meanwhile been appointed minister of Interior Affairs, promised that he would always consult the Taalunie on future applications, thereby blocking for other varieties what he had achieved as a cabinet minister for his own regional language, Nedersaksisch.

This emerged a few years later, in 2002, when the province of Zeeland requested recognition for Zeelandic. The Taalunie said no, so recognition was refused. The province of North Brabant, which was already preparing an application for Brabantian, took it as read that they had no chance and abandoned their application.

Most Dutch provinces have proceeded with their efforts to achieve official recognition despite past refusals, and most now have a regional language official – someone who is paid directly or indirectly by the provincial government to promote the interests of the province's 'own' language. They help local dialect groups draw up dictionaries and grammars, organise concerts for dialect singers, and give lectures here and there in the province.

It would be cynical to suspect an underhand power struggle behind such amiable activities. All the same, those provinces are unlikely to undertake such work without reason, or simply because there is a Member of the Provincial Council who has such warm feelings for the regional mother tongue. The Dutch provinces have long been under pressure at an administrative level; the turnout is never lower than for provincial elections, with the possible exception of the water boards. It is clear enough why you would vote for your local authority or national government, but the province has yet to prove its worth. Having one single language is a sign of unity. Since the nineteenth century, the slogan 'One people, one country, one language' has taken root, inspiring the European states to consider their own languages important, and the idea that a serious administrative unit should have its own language has remained a driving force for many administrators. ■

Translated by Anna Asbury

Otto Dix, *Shock Troops Advance under Gas* (detail) (Der Krieg, 1924)

Chronicle

The Golden Key to Happiness

Alex van Warmerdam's 'Borgman'

"A sly, insidious and intermittently hilarious domestic thriller that is likely to remain one of the most daring selections of this year's Cannes competition", raved the professional journal *Variety* with regard to *Borgman*, Alex van Warmerdam's eighth feature film. It was the first Dutch feature film for thirty-eight years considered to be good enough for the main competition at the most important film festival in the world. A historic moment, although the film failed to win an award.

What is *Borgman* about? Or better put, who is the main character that the film takes its name from? Vampire, vagabond, leader of a satanic sect or devil in disguise? A filthy messiah with unkempt hair, a passive-aggressive robber-chief, a shaman, alien, Rasputin, commander of a sect-like group of evil intruders? One could speculate forever, but there can be no doubt that Borgman is a manifestation of evil. "A sorcerer", says a child in the film. Satyr is maybe the closest: a bearded forest creature that follows its instincts, with a partiality for wine and anarchy; or (according to Borgman himself) the younger, vindictive brother of Jesus, a pain in the neck who's only concerned with himself, who has been sent to earth to instil some order into things.

Van Warmerdam begins his satirical miracle play with a quasi-biblical motto, redolent of the Apocalypse. "And they descended upon earth to strengthen their ranks." After that a priest starts the hunt for Camiel Borgman, aided by armed henchmen and an Alsatian. Like two of his assistants, Borgman hides in an underground hut in the woods. But Borgman – himself more hunter than quarry – escapes and looks for a fresh hiding-place in an affluent suburb. Under a false name he rings at the door of various villas asking if he can take a bath. When the somewhat short-fused, arrogant television producer, Richard, opens the door and beats the uninvited guest up after an exchange of words, his wife, Marina later offers him shelter in their summerhouse, because she feels guilty – without her husband knowing anything about it. This provides Borgman with the opportunity to gradually and stealthily increase his hold on the inhabitants of the concrete grey, cubist villa, exploiting the nagging guilt feeling to the full, and "the [effortless] ability to bring out the malice lying dormant in the good citizens of suburbia", as *Screen Daily* wrote. In the process he turns their garden paradise into a cesspit of vice.

Actually, what's wrong with the paradise-like existence of the happy, well-heeled family? Surely they aren't lacking anything? Aren't they respectable people? Borgman definitely knows better. He tells the family's children a fairytale about a white child from the clouds. It was imprisoned at the bottom of a deep pond by a beast that guarded the golden key to happiness. While Borgman tells of failed attempts to rescue the child, one gets the feeling that it is very possibly the fair-skinned children themselves who are living at the bottom of this proverbial pool. With selfish parents who have handed the care of their children over to an au pair. Three grey cars are parked under the carport: a Jaguar for father, a Mini Cooper for mother, and a family car that is only used by the au pair for the children. Repressed tensions are denied to the outside world, uncontrolled emotions don't fit the picture.

But under the slick surface hides a disturbed emotional existence, which has its roots in guilt feelings about the way in which material prosperity is accumulated. However often people in the film take a bath, their conscience is never any cleaner. Relentlessly Van Warmerdam unmasks the polite, manicured life of the well-heeled family as false and pretentious. In *Borgman* evil is dressed in misleading, pure white. They are all wolves in sheep's clothing. "There's something around us", says Marina to her husband Richard. "Pleasantly warm, but bad. I feel so guilty. We are happy and happy people must be punished." Richard rejects the idea: "Nonsense. We live in the West. The West's affluent. We can't do anything about it."

Still from *Borgman*

In *Borgman* there are more fatal sacrifices than in any of Van Warmerdam's previous work. In an interview, Van Warmerdam himself analysed the film as "darker and tauter" than his earlier work. More abstract but also more explicit.

The sly complications that have mutual knock-on effects follow each other at a swift pace. With black humour and visual jokes, abetted by horror effects and conventions to do with good taste, *Borgman* is constantly balanced on the edge of where the viewer ceases to find it funny. The action is often silent, swift and sickeningly efficient. Dialogues are short and measured, and the clichés of everyday speech are given short shrift. There is nothing more deceptive than the young woman who says: "It'll all turn out alright madam." Surrealistic scenes, fantasies, horror, in *Borgman* anything goes. The tone swings between deadly serious, irony and gallows humour. This irresistible mix makes the film ineluctable in its allegory on the well-to-do middle classes.

The name of the main character Borgman contains a play on words. The Dutch word *borg* means security. Borgman is not a man who provides 'security' in the sense of certainty and protection; he comes to collect caution money, the security demanded by a dissatisfied lender, be that God, the devil or Van Warmerdam himself. Significant in that respect is the scene in which the director, playing one of Borgman's accomplices, with a cool pair of sunglasses perched on his nose, drives an excavator that rips up the family's pond at a rate of knots.

International critics compared the film to the enigmatic unease in the dramas of Michael Hanek, Luis Buñuel's satires on the middle classes, the absurd humour of Roy Andersson, and Jean Renoir's *Boudu Saved from Drowning*, a film made in 1932 in which a well-heeled family also take a tramp into their home. With their miracle-play the brothers Van Warmerdam (Alex the director and Marc the producer) have proved themselves to be the present day successors of the brothers Grimm.

Karin Wolfs
Translated by Sheila M. Dale

Purveyors to the Court of Modern Variety

The Ashton Brothers

Stage performances are by definition fleeting, and to a greater or lesser extent the same thing applies to theatre genres. In the Dutch language area, for example, the farce machinery of yesteryear and the radio play, if not yet dead, have become seriously marginalised. One genre that has suffered the most from the urge to experiment in theatre and the dawn of the new media is the time-honoured revue and the related variety show.

In the Netherlands, the popular comedian André van Duin (° 1947) is one of the last - perhaps the very last - to practise this genre in a professional blend of familiar and more contemporary forms of entertainment. But Van Duin is not the only one at work under the more general label of 'stage entertainment'. Although they probably appeal to a different – mainly younger and more theatre-oriented – audience, the four members of the Ashton Brothers also take inspiration from the elements of old-fashioned variety.

The Ashton Brothers, or simply the Ashtons, as they are often called, are Pepijn Gunneweg, Pim Muda, Joost Spijkers and Friso van Vemde Oudejans. They got to know each other as students at the Amsterdam Academy of Popular Entertainment. Having completed their course, in 2001 they decided to put on a show together. They took the name Ashton Brothers from a group of early 20th-century Australian circus artists.

The Tragedy of the Base, derived partly from study assignments from their time at the academy, was an immediate bull's-eye. The impresario Jacques Senf discovered their talent at the International Theatre School Festival in Amsterdam and scheduled a tour for the following season. The show, expanded and adapted, opened in December 2002. The audience and the press were enthusiastic about it and its sustained success enabled them to schedule a second season, including several performances abroad. *The Tragedy of the Base* thereby set the tone for a long series of successes both in the Netherlands and abroad.

This first show contained all the ingredients that would characterise the later productions. It won the Ashtons the Pall Mall Export Prize, an award for striking young talent in the Dutch culture sector. Here's a quote from the jury report: 'The Ashton Brothers make use of the variety tradition, but in an innovative form, and they overwhelm us with their unbridled youthful energy. The components of their show are acrobatics, slapstick and music, where humour is rapidly alternated with emotion and grand theatrical effects with moments of close intimacy.' This is a description of the content of the Ashton shows that is equally valid today; in each new production the balance may change, but not the ingredients.

The Ashtons made their international breakthrough with their second show, Ballyhoo!, which they also performed at the Fringe in Edinburgh. Partly because there is hardly any spoken text in the performances, and because the foundations are universal theatre arts, the Ashtons' idiom is understood all over the world. There is barely any textual depth to their shows and so their quality can be measured only by their entertainment value. And the strength of this is clearly demonstrated by the fact that *Ballyhoo!* kept going for two years and three hundred performances. On 3 October 2007, the group put on a show in Ljubljana at the invitation of the Dutch embassy in Slovenia, in the presence of the present King and Queen of the Netherlands.

Spring 2008 saw the premiere of their third show, called *Charlatans, a Medicine Show*. This piece remained on the group's repertoire for a very long time, though this was not simply as a result of its resounding success, but mainly because the initial touring schedule could not be completed due to a serious, long-term illness that Friso van Vemde Oudejans had to contend with. It's true that a replacement was sought and found, but even so about seventy performances had to be cancelled. In the end, the original foursome, including Van Vemde

© L. van Velzen

Oudejans, now declared cured, continued performing *Charlatans* until 2012.

In the meantime, other makers of music and theatre have discovered the extra dimensions yielded by collaborating with the Ashton Brothers. After a previous collective performance with the Dutch Wind Ensemble in *A Midsummer Night's Dream* (2009), during the 2011-12 season, the Ashtons appeared as guest performers in *Tales of 1001 Nights* by *Het Zuidelijk Toneel*, a major theatre company from the south of the Netherlands. With their musical talent, their daredevil feats and perfect sense of timing, they gave the performance the dynamism it occasionally lacked at other moments.

Since December 2012 they have been performing their tenth anniversary show, *Treasures*, a treasure trove of previously performed acts, now perfected even more, plus new material, all in a fantastic set with inventive use of perspective tricks. Van Vemde Oudejans says of the older numbers: 'You can perform them twenty times and yet still change them every time, though of course only the details. They can be polished like a diamond. There is always a facet that can be made sharper, flatter or shinier.'

Treasures will be touring at least until the end of April 2014. It once again comprises the typically masculine, morbid and above all magical elements we are used to from this foursome. Unfortunately it is impossible to describe exactly what one experiences and enjoys in just a few sentences. Is it possible for anyone who has never seen the Ashtons to imagine, for example, a goat singing *Ave Maria* and then, after being fatally shot, taking a hilarious minute to die? Or the vain attempts by the actor Pepijn Gunneweg to reanimate a goldfish? Or two half-naked men playing rival penises?

But there are also a great many subtle and delicate moments. Though perhaps slightly too few to help determine the rhythm of the performance. In general the scale is grand, but there are also the minor grievances, and there are brilliant musical episodes when the laughter fades to make way for silent emotion. The actors' teamwork sometimes takes the spectator's breath away and audiences are full of wonder for their physical and mimetic skills.

It is no surprise that the quartet's antics rejoice in constant attention and that others try to take advantage of this too. Not only the Dutch Wind Ensemble and *Het Zuidelijk Toneel*, but for example the organisation that was responsible for the festive opening of the transformed *Rijksmuseum* in Amsterdam on 13 April 2013, too. Once again the Ashtons performed there in the presence of royals. It is an agreeable notion that even the most elevated circles have the opportunity to wonder at these Purveyors to the court of modern variety.

Jos Nijhof
Translated by Gregory Ball

www.ashtonbrothers.nl

Kaiser Turned Woodcutter

Huis Doorn, Home of the Exiled Wilhelm II (1920–1941)

It is a photograph that went all around the world: the German Kaiser Wilhelm II pacing up and down the platform at the Dutch border station at Eijsden in the province of Limburg. The date was 10 November, 1918, and the Kaiser had travelled in a convoy with his retinue from the German headquarters at Spa to Eijsden, where the imperial train was waiting for him. The day before, the Republic had been proclaimed in Berlin. The Kaiser had requested political asylum in the Netherlands. On the platform, local Limburgers and Belgian refugees called him *"Schweinhund"* and *"Mörder"*. *"Vive la France!"*, they shouted, and *"Kaiser, wohin? Nach Paris?"* The go-ahead was given after a number of telephone calls and a telegram from Queen Wilhelmina, and the imperial train steamed off to Maarn near Utrecht, where the Dutch Count Bentinck extended hospitality to Wilhelm at Kasteel Amerongen. Queen Wilhelmina and the Dutch cabinet would tolerate the Kaiser as a private individual, and that was to remain the official line, in order to pacify both disgruntled populace and angry Allies. Much to Wilhelm's frustration, Wilhelmina would never officially receive him and never visit Huis Doorn herself.

On 28 November, 1918, at Amerongen, Wilhelm signed his abdication as German Kaiser and King of Prussia. Heels clicking, a farewell was bid to *Seine Majestät*. The empire was dead, but Prussia still had a little life left in it. His obedient and devoted wife, Augusta Victoria, who had given Wilhelm seven children, came to join him that day. Wilhelm was to remain Bentinck's guest not for days or for weeks, but for almost two years. In May 1920, he finally took up residence nearby at Huis Doorn, which he had discreetly purchased. Fifty-nine train carriages had transported imperial household goods, furnishings, art and kitsch from the Hohenzollern palaces in Berlin to Doorn. The Kaiser was able to maintain a certain level of grandeur. He was wealthy enough to keep a household of German retainers and – to the irritation of the local nobility – generously remunerated Dutch staff. When the Empress died in 1921, she was given a massively attended funeral in Berlin. The Kaiser got married again the following year, to a widowed German princess, Hermine von Reuss. This second marriage, to an overbearing intrigant who was almost thirty years younger than him, was not a popular one. And so the deposed Kaiser settled into his routine as a redundant monarch who hoped against hope that one day he would be called back to Germany. He received monarchist visitors at Doorn, including Queen Mother Emma and later Princess Juliana and her new German husband, the money-grubbing Bernhard. The future Queen Beatrix lay asleep in her pram. However, Göring also came to visit a few times before Hitler seized power in 1933. The Kaiser hoped the Nazis would restore him to the throne; the Nazis wanted to secure the support of the Kaiser, and therefore of the Prussian-minded nobles and officers. Wilhelm did not like the Nazis, though, and soon they no longer had any need of the side-lined Kaiser. In May 1940, when the German soldiers reached Huis Doorn, the Kaiser gave them breakfast and champagne. When they took Paris, he sent a telegram to congratulate Hitler, whose response was respectful, but cool. In reality, the Kaiser was discreetly being held captive at Doorn – by German soldiers. When, after a woodcutting session, Wilhelm talked to one of those German soldiers, and found that he no longer recognized him, he realized that his world was over. The Kaiser died on 4 June, 1941. The day before, he had welcomed the German invasion of Crete with enthusiasm: *"Das ist fabelhaft. Unsere herrlichen Truppen!"* Hitler wanted the Kaiser's body to be taken to Potsdam, as he hoped to pass off as the Kaiser's successor at the funeral, but Wilhelm's will stipulated that his body should only be transferred to Germany if the land was a monarchy. And so he was bur-

Kaiser Wilhelm II's mausoleum at Huis Doorn
© Huis Doorn

ied in the park at Huis Doorn. His two wives were laid to rest in the park at Sanssouci in Potsdam. It was a glorious day at Doorn: *Kaiserwetter*. Those who followed the coffin included Seyss-Inquart, the Reichskommissar of the occupied Netherlands, and Admiral Canaris, the head of the German military intelligence service. Canaris was later executed at Flossenbürg concentration camp after the failed assassination attempt on Hitler, while Seyss-Inquart was executed in Nuremberg after the war. There were swastikas at the funeral, which the Kaiser would not have wanted, and a wreath from Hitler.

The family elected not to open the mausoleum at Huis Doorn to visitors. Peering through the window, I catch a glimpse of the Prussian flag with its black eagle draped over a casket. I walk around the park: the horses, the deer, the graves of the five imperial dogs; the spot where the Kaiser, methodically, obsessively, needlessly, turned thousands of trees into stumps; the majestic trees in the watery autumn sunshine. I wander through the castle, past the dinner services and the silver, the tapestries and the snuffboxes that once belonged to Frederick the Great, a role model for Wilhelm, his epigone. The abundance of knickknacks and bric-à-brac is wearying, but the portrait of the delightful Queen Louise of Prussia, who charmed Napoleon at Tilsit, hits me square in the face: this woman married at seventeen, gave birth to ten children, and died at the age of thirty-four.

I see the dining room with its table laid for eternity, where no one will ever dine again, and the special fork with three tines, one of which also served as a knife for a Kaiser who had a withered left arm. I amble through the bedrooms that once belonged to the Kaiser and his two wives, the smoking room, the study, the library of this amateur archaeologist; the Empress's modern toilet, neatly concealed in an antique closet. This is a place where people lived. Survived. Maintained the appearance of a court in exile. With a Kaiser who read aloud from the Bible every morning to his assembled staff. And who then went out for a walk, to chop wood, eat lunch, have a siesta, answer correspondence from all over the world, dine from plates that were whipped away the moment His Majesty had finished eating. A routine designed to provide meaning in a meaningless life.

Huis Doorn, confiscated after the war, is now the property of the Dutch state. Subsidies have recently been scaled back, but an army of volunteers keeps the place open and running. Whatever happened to the Kaiser's large financial legacy remains a mystery. The House of Orange, the Dutch state, the House of Hohenzollern and the banks provide no clarity. I came to Doorn with the notion that I would find one of the few WWI *lieux de mémoire* on Dutch soil. However, what I encountered was more like a *trou de mémoire* of the Great War, and I walked around, somewhat bewildered, within *a lieu de mémoire* of European absolutist empires and monarchies, perhaps a last echo of the *Ancien Régime*, surviving in a form that is both tragically ironic and slightly grotesque. After all, the grandmother of Wilhelm (who remained "our Willy" to the British branch of the family) was Queen Victoria and the last tsar was his first cousin by marriage. Huis Doorn? It's most definitely worth a visit.

Luc Devoldere
Translated by Laura Watkinson

www.huisdoorn.nl/eng/

The American Dream in Antwerp

The Red Star Line Museum

At the beginning of the twentieth century Arthur Rousseau, a young building-trade worker from Deinze in the East of Belgium, went to seek a better life in America. He was one of my great-grandmother's brothers and ended up eventually in St. Clair Shores, 18 miles or so from Detroit. He set up a building business there. As with so many European migrants the story of his emigration began in Antwerp, from where he left Belgium on one of the ships of the Red Star Line. Between 1873 and 1934 this shipping company carried more than 2 million passengers from Antwerp to New York and a small number to Canada. Less than 10% of them were Belgians. The majority of the Red Star Line passengers came from Eastern Europe and a considerable proportion of them were Jews.

At the end of September 2013 a new museum was opened in the old buildings of the shipping company. It tells the stories of these millions of emigrants. They all had the same aim: they were seeking happiness and a better life. The stories start from the moment the migrants left their original dwelling-place. Poverty, war or racial hatred compelled them to leave. Very few left out of a sense of adventure. Usually one family member went ahead of the rest. That was often the father. This meant that families were often split up for years. Some travelled by train halfway across Europe to reach Antwerp. Most had bought their ticket somewhere near home and it specified their entire journey. The price included their train journey, accommodation in Antwerp, the boat ticket and frequently also the train journey to the final destination in America.

The throngs of emigrants added colour to Antwerp. At the height of the Red Star Line several thousand emigrants were arriving every week. Once they reached the station most of them were accompanied to the shipping company's premises, where they were subjected to rigorous inspection. Their clothing and luggage were disinfected and they themselves had to shower. Then there followed

Postcard issued by the Red Star Line, 1901

a thorough medical examination. Anyone who was not deemed healthy could not go on the voyage. The reasons for this stringent policy were simple. The American authorities were afraid the large numbers of immigrants might bring in all kinds of illnesses, and anyone who entered the country via Ellis Island had to undergo a further thorough check. Anyone who failed to pass the inspection was sent home at the expense of the shipping company, without further ado.

The stringent controls applied particularly to the third class passengers. Most of them only stayed for a short time in the Belgian port, but for those who failed to get through the controls the stay could be longer. They were often taken in by relief organizations or ended up in local hospitals. The Red Star Line Museum tells the tale, among others, of Ita Moel, a Russian girl who emigrated to America in 1921 with her mother and brothers, following their father, but she was turned back with an eye infection. She had to travel back on her own to Antwerp, where she was taken in by Ezra, a Jewish relief organization. It was not until 1927 that she was able to rejoin her family.

The migrants also inspired some artists. They were a source of inspiration for Eugeen van Mieghem (1875-1930) especially. His parents had a café directly opposite the entrance to the Red Star Line sheds. Van Mieghem was continually sketching and painting the emigrants who passed his door. His works have a pessimistic aura. For a few years now Van Mieghem has had his own museum in Antwerp, within walking distance of the Red Star Line Museum. The mass migration was also a theme in the work of Constantin Meunier and Eugène Laermans (1864-1940). The latter's imposing canvas *The Emigrants* also hangs in the museum.

Once all the checks had been gone through, the emigrants could board ship. Over the years the company had 23 ships. The flagship of the company was the *Belgenland II* which, moreover, had been built in the same shipyard as the *Titanic*. *The Belgenland II* could carry 500 passengers in first class, 500 in second and 1500 in third class. For the latter category the voyage was often no joke. They were kept strictly apart from the other passengers, deep in the bowels of the ship. Until late in the 19th century the travellers slept in narrow bunk beds, on straw mattresses. They ate in the same space. If weather permitted they were allowed up on deck. There they could see the promenade decks where the first and second-class passengers enjoyed luxury conditions. After 1889 the conditions for third-class travellers were slightly improved, for commercial reasons.

Sailing past the Statue of Liberty was a very emotional experience for the emigrants. The end of a long and arduous journey was in sight and they were about to be able to begin a new life. But first they had to go through yet another thorough check. In the case of the first and second-class passengers, this was only done if they appeared ill. All the rest were put through a rigorous medical and administrative check-up on Ellis Island. Between 1892 and 1924 around 12 million immigrants passed through it. Of these, 2% were sent back with no right of appeal, others ended up in the Ellis Island sick bay for some considerable time. The museum tells the tale of a Ukrainian girl, Basia Cohen, who had to wait a further 8 months on Ellis Island after her arrival because she had a fungal infection.

After their arrival in New York, the majority of the emigrants travelled on immediately to their final destination in America, where they were for the most part awaited by family members or compatriots who had gone before them. This is how real immigrant communities were formed, of which traces can still be seen to this very day. The Belgians had their own communities too, with their own clubs and periodicals. Whether all those emigrants fulfilled their American Dream remains uncertain. Some of them returned after a few years – from homesickness, to find a partner, or simply because they had not found what they hoped to find on the other side of the ocean.

The decline of the Red Star Line began in the twenties, when the American government tightened the laws around migration. The shipping company tried to turn its fortunes round with tourist travel, cruises and car transport, but in 1934 it went into permanent liquidation. The buildings were assigned another use and the Red Star Line slowly faded from the memories of the people of Antwerp. But not from the memory of dockworker Robert Vervoort who had begun to collect everything to do with the Red Star Line. He managed to acquire over 5000 items, including the original foundation charter. It was his mania for collecting that provided the basis for the new museum that is now housed in the original buildings. The American architectural firm Beyer Blinder Belle Architects and Planners, which also redeveloped Ellis Island, built this new museum. The showpiece of the building is a brand new tower from which visitors have a beautiful view over the Schelde and Antwerp. In the museum itself a circuit has been set out in which visitors follow the route the emigrants had to take, through the control area, the showers, over the pedestrian bridge to the bowels of the ship, until they reach Ellis Island. Everywhere the voices of real migrants are to be heard, because there are stories being told here, it's not just a display of artefacts. You become acquainted with unknown travellers, but also with people who are famous the world over, such as A. Einstein who sailed with the Red Star Line

Ellis Island, 1930 © Library of Congress

on various occasions, and Irving Berlin, the well-known composer of *White Christmas* and *There's no Business Like Show Business*, who emigrated from White Russia as a five-year old and sailed to America on the *SS Rhynland*. His family donated one of his pianos to the museum. He is an example of one of those emigrants who did make their American Dream come true via Antwerp. But the museum also looks at migration in general and shows that this is a story from all times and all places.

Whether Arthur Rousseau made his American Dream come true, I know not. I only have twenty or so of his letters that bear witness to his life in America in increasingly deteriorating Dutch. Maybe I should donate them to the Red Star Line Museum. Then his tale will become part of the extensive collection of stories that the museum staff have been able to assemble in recent years.

Dirk Van Assche
Translated by Sheila M. Dale

www.redstarline.be

Americans in Occupied Belgium 1914-1918

Americans in Belgium witnessed the German invasion, occupation and retreat. They described what they saw in letters, memoirs, newspaper reports and magazine articles. Prior to America's entry into the war, these accounts from Belgium were of wide interest in the United States. However, once America joined the war on April 7, 1917, interest in Belgium waned. Battles fought by the American Army in France became the primary focus, which is understandable. Today, the experiences of Americans in Belgium during the war warrant barely a mention in histories of the First World War. We sought to correct that omission in *Americans in Occupied Belgium 1914-1918*. As the following excerpts illustrate, Americans were in Belgium from the first hours of the invasion until the final liberation.

On August 4, 1914, the Imperial German Army crossed the German border and invaded Belgium, a country about the size of the state of Vermont. The Army's first major objective was the Belgian city of Liège. A major railway hub, Liège was the key to the Belgian rail system. Miss Glenna Lindsley Bigelow from New Haven, Connecticut, was a guest at Château Nagelmackers near Liège, literally in the path of the invading army. Monsieur Nagelmackers was very well connected; his cousin was the wife of a member of the Kaiser's Imperial Court. Consequently, General von Moltke, the Chief of the General Staff, issued written orders protecting the château and its owners during the invasion and occupation. In her memoir, Glenna Bigelow described tending Belgian wounded in a nearby church: 'August 13 . . . charred bodies with no suggestion of faces - just a flat, swollen, black surface, with no eyes, nose nor mouth. Some of the wounded lay on beds, others in the middle of the floor or wherever there was space, and each was holding up hands burned to the bone'[1]. That evening Glenna met the invaders. After nursing the wounded all

Mrs. Winterbottom, née Gladys H. Appleton of Massachusetts, in her Rolls Royce driving to one of the outer Antwerp forts to retrieve wounded. The thirty-three- year-old Boston socialite served with a British hospital group during the Siege of Antwerp (1914), *Le Miroir*, 1914

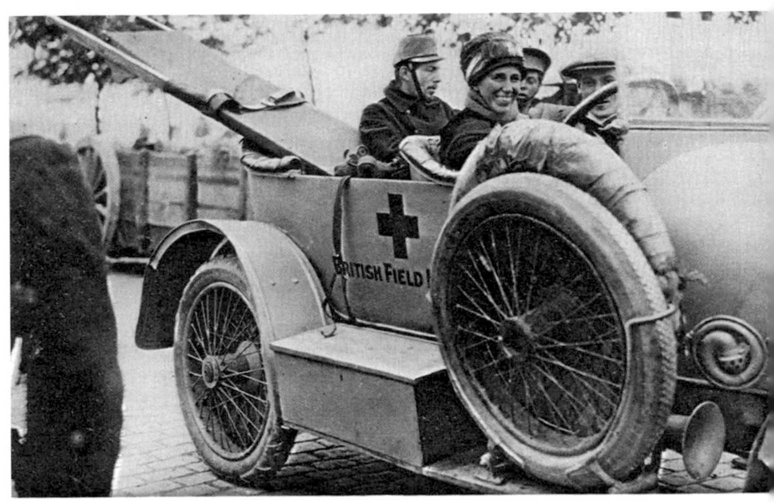

day, she was required to dine and make small talk with the officers responsible for the horrors. Château Nagelmackers, where Voltaire had once stayed, where Liszt had composed, now hosted the masters of the new 'German *Kultur*'.

In Brussels, Brand Whitlock awaited the invaders at his post as head of the American Legation. The forty-five-year-old American Minister and his wife, Nell Brainerd Whitlock, arrived in Brussels in February 1914 and would remain until April 2, 1917. He was a former mayor of Toledo, Ohio where, as a progressive, he fought corruption, big business, political bosses and other special interests. He was against prohibition, advocated decriminalizing prostitution, and was against capital punishment. For these "radical" views, he often incurred attacks from Toledo's pulpits. Mayor Whitlock, defender of the underdog, saw the Brussels appointment as a European sabbatical during which he would have time for his two hobbies: golf and writing fiction. The sabbatical ended when the German Army invaded Belgium. However, before the German Army marched into Brussels, an invasion of American journalists, writers, and war tourists arrived to see the action. After dealing with the Americans and the Germans, there was hardly time for golf.

In 1914, Belgium was home to a large American colony, e.g. people working for U.S. corporations, diplomats with the American Legation and Americans in the arts - Brussels was cheaper than Paris. One of those in the arts was the American novelist Julia Helen Twells. She resided in Brussels throughout the war. Even though in her seventies, Ms. Twells pedaled around the city on her bicycle, sporting a small American flag. She witnessed the entrance of the Imperial German Army into Brussels on August 20, 1914, and she watched its retreat four years later. It was only on November 18, 1918, that the last German troops left the city. On the outskirts of Brussels, the departing soldiers held open-air bazaars to turn loot into cash. Julia Twells described the shopping: 'At Forest and other suburban parts of the city, great car-loads of material, looted from shops and private houses probably months or years ago, - for the dry-goods shops of Brussels had been cleaned out quite two years before, - were offered at absurdly trivial prices. Silk-velvet, which could not be had in Brussels for less than two hundred francs, went at a mark a yard; warm woolen stuffs, which the shivering population, thinly clad in dyed cotton, could not obtain at any price in the shops, were sold - to such as deigned to buy - for an equally small sum. . . . all manner of other things, as if from some pirates' cave, were bartered back to those who had been robbed of them'[2].

Americans were present at all the major battles fought by the Belgian Army. They were present during the siege of Antwerp and at the Yser Front. As the most industrialized country in Europe, Belgium depended upon trade and food imports. The war isolated Belgium and wholesale starvation was imminent in the fall of 1914.

Herbert Hoover and his Commission for Relief in Belgium raised funds to purchase and import foods to sustain Belgium. Idealistic American volunteers (including a number of Rhodes scholars) supervised food distribution in the occupation zone assuring foodstuffs went to Belgians and not to the German Army. At the front in Belgium, hundreds of Americans served (illegally, at peril to their citizenship) in the British and Canadian Armies. Even after America entered the war on April 7, 1917, the German Army permitted some Americans to remain in Belgium. When the United States finally did enter the war, there was considerable concern at home about the country's 'preparedness'. To gain battlefield experience, American medical schools sent teams of physicians and nurses to work with the Royal Army Medical Corps. The R.A.M.C. assigned them to field hospitals and postes de secours during the Third Battle of Ypres. However, not all Americans were with the Allies; some were journalists embedded with the German Army and not a few were soldiers serving the Kaiser. At the time, German-Americans accounted for one of the largest ethnic groups in the United States.

The American experience in Belgium was very multifaceted and complicated. Consequently, the writings of these American men and women are a unique record of Belgium during the seminal event of the twentieth century, the First World War.

ED KLEKOWSKI & LIBBY KLEKOWSKI

ED KLEKOWSKI & LIBBY KLEKOWSKI, *Americans in Occupied Belgium* 1914-1918, Jefferson / McFarland Press, N. C. / London, available spring / summer 2014 (ISBN 978 0 7864 7255-0).

NOTES:

1. GLENNA LINDSLEY BIGELOW, Liège - On the Line of March, John Lane, New York / London, 1918, p. 46.
2. J. H. J.H. TWELLS, In the Prison City, Andrew Melrose, London, 1919, p. 270.

The *Gazette van Detroit* Celebrates its 100th Anniversary

The *Gazette van Detroit* is the only remaining Flemish-American newspaper in the United States. It is an unaffiliated, apolitical, non-profit publication written by and for North Americans of Flemish descent and Dutch-speaking Belgians. Its goal is to serve as a cultural bridge between North America and the Dutch-speaking region of Belgium. It will reach the hundred-year mark on August 13, 2014.

The *Gazette van Detroit* was the brainchild of Camille Cools, a Flemish immigrant from West-Flanders. He moved to Detroit, Michigan, with his family as a fifteen-year old boy in 1889. Camille Cools was very active in many organizations, from the archery club to the theatre. News from Flanders was scarce, and Camille Cools turned to existing Flemish newspapers in America such as *De Gazette van Moline* (Moline, Illinois) and *De Volksstem* (De Pere, Wisconsin). He took his first steps as a publisher in 1913, when he printed his *Vlaamsche Almanak*. Encouraged by other Flemish-Americans who shared his passion and recognized his leadership, Camille Cools published the first edition of the *Gazette van Detroit*. He was its founder, editor, and publisher. The newspaper provided information about the activities of various organizations, about new immigrants, and announced upcoming social and sporting events. Significantly it contained news from Flanders about World War I in Dutch for Flemish immigrants. The articles in the weekly publication were aimed mostly at craftsmen and farmers with no more than an elementary education, hence they were written in simple Dutch. Camille Cools died unexpectedly, age 43, in 1916.

In 1920, Peter Corteville (1881-1966) and his brother-in-law Leo Leplae acquired control of the *Gazette van Detroit*. They changed the company's name to The Belgian Press and later in 1940 to Corteville Printing Co. Ms. Hortense Leplae (1879-1963), Leo Leplae's niece, became

Gazette van Detroit
SINDS 1914

the driving force behind the *Gazette* in the early 1920's and would remain editor for thirty-five years. She expanded the *Gazette* into a full-size eight-page weekly with more than twenty correspondents in the US, Canada and South America. The newspaper stayed true to its origins: the language remained simple and sprinkled with dialect. It was criticized as 'archaic' by some, but despite such criticisms the *Gazette van Detroit* continued to grow. The *Gazette* also grew by absorbing another weekly, *De Detroitenaar*, just after World War I and by taking over *De Gazette van Moline* in 1940.

Richard Corteville's death in 1974 marked the beginning of a difficult period for the *Gazette*. René de Seranno, a native of Moline, Illinois, grew up in Tielt (West Flanders), reorganized the *Gazette* under a new moniker 'Belgian Publishing Company' as a non-profit corporation. This new entity was born in 1974 with the donation of $5,000 from 18 Flemish Americans.

In 1977, the *Gazette* became a biweekly. Articles in English were added to attract younger generations, as many no longer knew their parents' language. Unfortunately with René de Serrano's death in 1983 the *Gazette* went through another difficult period of declining subscribers and increased costs. The *Gazette* navigated through this period with the support of a donation from the *Nederlandse Taalunie* and a dedicated group of volunteers. Father Karel Denys, a Flemish priest ministering in the Detroit area, led the *Gazette* from the 1980s until well into the 2000s. After Denys, the *Gazette* found itself for the first time without a Dutch-speaking, Flemish-born editor. To appeal to a younger audience, the paper moved from a black-and-white Flemish front page to a more English-centric format.

In the mid-2000s the *Gazette van Detroit* received a new lease on life through the efforts of Ms. Leen de Donker, an expat from Antwerp, who brought her energy and bilingual skills to the *Gazette*. She recruited new volunteers, among them Elisabeth Kahn (née van den Hove), and introduced a number of innovations. The paper moved from an 8-page *boterblad* in black and white to a 24-page full color production and introduced the e-Edition. Importantly Elisabeth Kahn secured formal recognition from the IRS of the tax-free status of Belgian Publishing, Inc. These innovations generated new hope and interest in De *Gazette van Detroit* on both sides of the Atlantic.

Boosted by the leadership of David Baeckelandt since 2012, the *Gazette* proactively reached out to many Flemings in the US and Belgium to support the *Gazette* and ensure its future. The *Gazette* is now a monthly twenty-four-page periodical with articles and features in both English and Dutch. Inspired by their Flemish roots, the new wave of volunteers works hard to make the *Gazette* the hub for the Belgian community in the US and Canada. The *Gazette* is not immune to the economic challenges of print media. In 2014 it has started the transition from print to digital, while staying true to the spirit of Camille Cools and the mission of the paper.

JEROEN VAN CAUWELAERT

www.gazettevandetroit.com

Pinkster in New York

The earliest reference to a Dutch Pinkster celebration in America dates back to 1655, when the Court of Fort Orange gave permission to the burgher guard of Beverwijck, the later Albany, to organize *papegaaischieten* (parrot shooting) on the third day after *Pijnghsteren* (Pentecost). Later sources confirm that Pinkster continued to be celebrated until the mid-nineteenth century in areas in New York and New Jersey that once formed New Netherland. American sources on Pinkster all confirm the massive participation of African Americans, to such a degree that in the nineteenth century it was primarily perceived as a celebration of the black community.

The most famous description of an American Pinkster festival was provided by James Fenimore Cooper, author of the historical novel *The Last of the Mohicans* (1826). Since he spent his childhood in Upstate New York, where the Batavian bastion Albany was the nearest city, Cooper was quite familiar with Dutch culture. His wife Susan De Lancey also had close relatives in Fishkill who were of Dutch heritage. In the spring of 1828, Cooper visited the Low Countries for the first time and he later returned there twice, in 1831 and 1832.

In his novel *Satanstoe* (1845), set in the mid-eighteenth century, Cooper describes the Pinkster festival through the eyes of Cornelius —'Corny'— Littlepage, a New Yorker of mixed English-Dutch descent. During his visit to New York City on Pinkster day, Corny is accompanied by two friends, one of whom, Dirck Van Valkenburgh, is of Dutch descent, while the other one, Jason Newcome, is a New Englander from Connecticut. According to Corny, one of the most notorious differences between New Yorkers and New Englanders is the distinctive way in dealing with people of other races, because 'there is something in the character of these Anglo-Saxons that predisposes them to laugh, and turn up their noses, at other races,' whereas '[a]mong the Dutch, in particular, the treatment of the negro was of the kindest character.' The cultural differences between the friends are notable in the description of the festival. While Dirck and Corney are familiar with the African-American Pinkster attractions, Jason was 'confounded with the noises, dances, music, and games that were going on'.

Cooper's interest in Pinkster is connected to the 'Anti-Rent War' that began with the 1839 death of *Patroon* Stephen Van Rensselaer, whose tenants owed him 400,000 dollars. When Van Rensselaer's sons attempted to collect these debts, the tenants bluntly refused to pay. After the Judiciary Committee had sided with the landlords in an 1842 decision, angry tenants formed the 'Anti-Rent Movement' that violently resisted legal action. The movement grew considerably in the next decade and gained political importance when anti-renters decided to back specific candidates, both Whigs and Democrats, who favored their positions. Cooper, who was personally acquainted with some of the land-owning families involved in the dispute, considered anti-rentism 'the great New York question of the day'. He felt that the anti-renters' behavior represented an opportunistic distortion of republican principles that represented a threat to the nation's future.

In *Satanstoe*, Cooper reacted to the anti-rent war by marking the difference between two types of America, one with an exclusively English background as opposed to one with a Dutch-English background, or what he called 'a *melange* of Dutch quietude and English aristocracy.' Irritated by what he considered to be the populist, selfish behavior of the anti-renters, Cooper focused on America's Dutch heritage in order to distinguish between New Englanders, who essentially interpreted the notion of freedom as individual freedom in an Anglo-Saxon tradition, and New Yorkers, whose understanding of freedom had been shaped by the Dutch community-oriented mentality in a bourgeois tradition.

Omitting the fact that, in places such as Suri-

A present day celebration of Pinkster in the United States

name, Dutch slaveholders were considered among the cruelest in the world, Cooper interpreted the treatment of slaves owned by Dutch-American families as a reflection of the tolerant and community-oriented Dutch mentality. The English refusal to consider slaves to be part of their own community, on the other hand, reflected the same problem that was at the heart of the Anti-Rent War: the evolution of the United States into a nation where citizens do not perceive themselves as brothers and sisters of one and the same community but rather act as selfish individuals.

Cooper's *Satanstoe* stands, as such, at the beginning of what would become a tradition in American literature—from Mary Mapes Dodge's *Hans Brinker* (1865) to Russell Shorto's *Amsterdam* (2013)—to idealize the Netherlands as a nation characterized by a strong commitment to tolerance, diversity and solidarity and to use this image as a mirror for readers in the United States. Due to New York's Dutch heritage, this strategy did not simply have a comparative value but rather served as a vision of what America could have been. No other Dutch tradition better represented this utopian vision of a harmonious society than New York's Pinkster festival.

JEROEN DEWULF

Language

A Biography of the Dutch Language

In the introduction to his new history of the Dutch language Roland Willemyns boasts that his is the first such history written in English. A few pages later he corrects himself, however, and acknowledges the publication of Bruce Donaldson's *Dutch. A linguistic history of Holland and Belgium* (1983) exactly thirty years earlier. This contradiction is a rare hiccup in an otherwise excellent book. Actually, Willemyns is full of admiration for Donaldson's work, just as he is for the Frenchman Brachin's *La language néerlandaise* (1977) and its English translation by Paul Vincent (1985). Why have we had to wait thirty years for a new linguistic history of Dutch in English? Lack of expertise amongst Anglo-Saxon *neerlandici* or, more likely, lack of time? Reluctant publishers? A combination of these? Whatever it may be, the need for an updated history of Dutch has been keenly felt in the Anglo-Saxon world of Dutch Studies since Donaldson went out of print. But it is not just for that reason that the appearance of Willemyns' book is a cause for celebration.

A great deal has changed over the last thirty years, not only in the Dutch language itself, but also in our knowledge of its history. Yet Willemyns goes much further than charting that history in all its facets: he also sketches a contemporary portrait of the language and discusses possible scenarios for its future development. In all this, his angle is clear: "The story of Dutch is predominantly a story of language contact and conflict." The Dutch standard language emerged through contact between and with other languages, and contact with other languages has always influenced it. Inherent in that contact is conflict, which remains a characteristic of Dutch today. This thread is the recurring theme of Willemyns' linguistic history of Dutch, and what emerges is a sympathetic portrait, without value judgements, of a language that continues to develop.

Contact and conflict are even reflected in the names for Dutch through the ages and in other languages. The first chapter is about these names, including the interesting English word *Dutch* itself. It is also about the geography of the language and its border with the surrounding languages: German and Frisian, and especially French. This is followed by five historical chapters covering, respectively, the precursors and contemporaries of Old Dutch (or Old Low Franconian, up to 1100), Middle Dutch (1100-1500), Early Modern Dutch (1500-1800), the nineteenth century and the twentieth century. The next two chapters investigate the colonial traces of Dutch and the history of Afrikaans. Willemyns concludes his book with a careful and measured reflection on the future of Dutch in the 21st century in the light of a number of recent developments.

The five historical chapters do not follow a set pattern, but allow their structure and focus to be determined by the matters in hand. Thus, the chapter on Middle Dutch stresses literary production in the context of the first careful steps towards a standard language, whereas the Early Modern Dutch chapter tells us about the first grammars and dictionaries that appeared in the 16th century. Sometimes the focus is on the north, at other times on the south, for example the steps towards further standardisation in the Dutch Republic and the 19th-century emancipation of Flanders. Such a balance between the Netherlands and Flanders is often absent from more superficial descriptions of Dutch. This is very helpful for students of Dutch outside the Low Countries who are often unaware of the wider context of the language, including the fact that it is not just spoken in Holland. And Willemyns clearly has these students in mind, given his criteria for the selection of his material. Not only does he want to give the best possible description of the development of modern Dutch, but he also wants to highlight those aspects of Dutch that are most interesting "for non-native speakers having learned Dutch as a foreign language and for other foreigners taking an interest in Dutch".

In over 40 years of research into the history of Dutch, Willemyns has studied many of its aspects, but perhaps not so much the colonial heritage of the language. Nevertheless he rightly dedicates two chapters to it, but they necessarily depend more than other chapters on the work of other scholars. Sometimes this results in a noticeably different, more noncommittal tone in these chapters, whereas elsewhere he tells a more inspired story and readily sounds a critical note. One example: the comment that "Creoles have generally been regarded as degenerate variants" begs for more discussion of the concept of Creole languages, and this would also have provided an opportunity in the penultimate chapter to investigate the extent to which Afrikaans can be called a Creole. However, Willemyns' inspiration is back in full flight in the final chapter where he discusses the concepts *Poldernederlands* and *Verkavelingsvlaams*. The former refers to changes in the pronunciation of standard Northern Dutch, especially widening of the diphthongs /—i/ (written <ij> or <ei>), /œy/ (written <ui>) and /—u/ (written <ou> or <au>). The latter, which is also known as *Schoon Vlaams* or *Tussentaal*, refers to colloquial speech in Flanders that takes an intermediary position between standard Dutch and dialects (hence the label *tussentaal*, 'in-between language'). It is characterised by a wider range of features than is *Poldernederlands* in the Netherlands, including pronunciation, morphology, lexis and syntax. Willemyns subjects these concepts, which are seen by some people as two completely new, divergent varieties of standard Dutch, to deservedly critical examination.

Oxford University Press, Willemyns' publisher, has recently also published two linguistic histories of German: Ruth Sanders' *German. Biography of a Language* (2010) and Joe Salmons' A *History of German* (2012). This calls for a comparison, not least because of the almost identical titles of Sanders and Willemyns. However, Willemyns' book is much better and much more balanced than Sanders'. On the other side of the comparison, Willemyns' focus is explicitly on external linguistic history, whereas Salmons concentrates on internal linguistic history. The two books do not refer to each other, but they should. After all, Dutch and German have a large part of their history in common and Salmons therefore provides excellent insights into the internal linguistic history of Dutch. Moreover, many Anglo-Saxon students of Dutch tend to learn the language after they have already acquired German. For that reason it is to be hoped that Oxford University Press, unlike Donaldson's publisher in the 1980s, will soon allow a second edition of Willemyns' book to appear which can refer to Salmons. That would also provide an opportunity for a number of editorial improvements, for example in the use of English tenses. A number of maps and illustrations are not clear enough (e.g. on p. 95, where the difference between the Spanish Netherlands and the Dutch Republic has got lost), require an English version (e.g. the legend of the table on p. 136 is in German), and/or need an acknowledgement. An extensive list of recommended websites would be a further improvement.

Despite such imperfections, *Dutch. Biography of a Language* brilliantly closes a 30-year gap. It is required reading for students of Dutch not just in Anglophone countries but all over the world, even in Flanders and the Netherlands.

Roel Vismans

ROLAND WILLEMYNS. *Dutch. Biography of a Language.* Oxford: Oxford University Press, 2013.
ISBN 9780199858712. 289 pp.

LITERATURE

Pierre Brachin. 1977 *La langue néerlandaise.* Paris: Didier Hatier.
Pierre Brachin. 1985. *The Dutch Language: A Survey. Trams.* Paul Vincent. Cheltenham: Stanley Thornes.
Bruce Donaldson. 1983 *Dutch. A linguistic history of Holland and Belgium.* Leiden: Martinus Nijhoff
Joseph Salmons. 2012. *A History of German. What the past reveals about today's language.* Oxford: OUP.
Ruth Sanders. 2010. *German. Biography of a Language.* Oxford: OUP.

Cees Nooteboom as Nomadic Writer

For a British scholar to have produced a major monograph on a prominent, internationally known Dutch writer would be a coup in itself. However, Jane Fenoulhet's ambitions extend much wider than the establishment of Cees Nooteboom's 'national canonical status'. (As is well known, until comparatively recently Nooteboom's critical acceptance in the Low Countries lagged behind international recognition, notably in Germany.)

What this book seeks to do, and does with admirable clarity, is examine the 'transnational nature' of Nooteboom's literary presence. The key concept of 'nomadism' is defined with reference to such literary and sociological theorists as Gilles Deleuze, Rosi Braidotti and Michael Cronin. Focus is on the increasing porousness of national literatures and the role of translation in cross-border transfer.

Part 1 of the text concludes with the key chapter 'Nomadic Subjectivity and Identity, Or Cees Nooteboom and Dutchness'. It includes a wide-ranging contextualisation of the author's position as a national outsider, a condensed biography and a brief discussion of the autodidacticism he shares with his contemporaries Mulisch and Claus. Fenoulhet writes of her own approach to Nooteboom: 'I portray him as fundamentally nomadic with a multiple, shifting identity, emphasising the effect of his extreme mobility on his subjectivity – his sense of himself and his sensibilities.' A little later he is characterised as being 'without a trace of nationalistic pride' and adopting 'a firmly cosmopolitan position'.

In Part 2 the major components of the oeuvre are surveyed. In particular, the somewhat neglected poetry is reinstated at the core of his writing, as representing a 'home base' in language. Nooteboom's consistent production of verse from the 1950s on is given the attention it deserves. Here, though, one is struck by the absence of any mention of Nooteboom's predecessor Jan Jacob Slauerhoff (1898-1936), surely the archetypical nomadic writer ('Only in my poems can I dwell') and an obvious antecedent. A fascinating exercise in close reading is the comparison of three English versions of the 'Basho' sequence.

In the travel writing Fenoulhet draws an illuminating parallel with the Italian writer Claudio Magris, biographer of the River Danube. There is a fuller analysis of the three major collections of travel writing, translated into English as *Roads to Santiago, Nomad's Hotel* and *Roads to Berlin*, quoting among other sources J.M. Coetzee's essay 'Cees Nooteboom, Novelist and Traveller', which identifies the development of a deeper matrix in the later travel writing 'within which to reflect on the deeper currents of life of a foreign culture'. Fenoulhet sees this, in my view rightly, as a fruitful concept. In *Roads to Berlin* there is striking appeal to an endangered sense of European cultural community.

A chapter is devoted to Nooteboom's 'English after-lives' in translation, reviewing his narratives of 'fictions of becoming' and highlighting his post-modernism, intertextuality, 'rhizomic' (i.e. subterranean associative structures), narrative complexity and characteristic 'vitalism in muted form'. The critical reception of the work is touched upon, but not dealt with in any great depth. There is an interesting and puzzling section on the contrasting fortunes of the German and English translations of the early novel *Philip en de anderen* (Philip and the Others): the former became a bestseller (in a second translation) while the latter remained rather marginalised. No explanation is proffered apart from the book's atypical, non-nomadic vision.

The conclusion of this study reiterates its guiding principle: 'I proposed a complex way of approaching a writer and his work which does not see literary texts as intrinsically connected with the country of the writer's birth, while in the second part I put it into practice.' One can say unequivocally that that stated aim is substantially achieved.

This book is an important contribution to literary studies and one that will undoubtedly engender further research and publication: on Nooteboom himself, and (*pace* the premises of this work) Dutch literature, as well as in the general literary and translation field.

PAUL VINCENT

JANE FENOULHET, *Nomadic Literature. Cees Nooteboom and his Writing*. Oxford: Peter Lang, 2013.

Cees Nooteboom © Simone Sassen

A Poet in Love with Words

Lucebert Translated into English

Lucebert © Rob Bogaerts / Nationaal Archief

No other twentieth-century Dutch poet made an entrance quite like Lubertus Swaanswijk, alias Lucebert (1924-1994). He seemed to come out of nowhere. Although the picture turns out in retrospect to be slightly romanticised, Lucebert led a wandering existence in the years after World War II. He began to gain a reputation as an artist and painter among his immediate circle; however his poetic talent remained hidden for a long time, even from his friends. The poets Gerrit Kouwenaar and Jan G. Elburg, who were in close contact with the experimental artists of the CoBrA movement and knew Lucebert as a visual artist, were dumbfounded when he recited some of his poems one evening.

With the 'birth' of Lucebert as a poet, Dutch poetry suddenly gained an incomparable voice. What's more, Lucebert's work had connections to traditions that were unknown or barely known in the Netherlands, such as mysticism, German Romanticism, Dada and other modernist trends. He brought a new élan to the type of experimental poetry that had had scarcely any following in the northern Netherlands since the pioneering work of the Belgian Paul van Ostaijen. With his poetry and performances, in which there was also an element of wanting to shock the middle class, Lucebert showed the way to a group of young poets named after the decade in which they began to make their mark: The Fiftiers (*De Vijftigers*). One happening, which culminated in a riot, saw Lucebert crowned emperor of the group (wearing fancy dress).

It is now twenty years since his death, and for many people in the Netherlands Lucebert still stands on the pedestal on which he, with his sense of irony, put himself. Poet, novelist and critic Ilja Leonard Pfeijffer writes: "Not everyone realises it yet, but in ten years' time there'll be no doubt left in anyone's mind that, Vondel aside, Lucebert is the greatest Dutch poet of all time. I look on him as my teacher." Yet Lucebert often provoked disapproving reactions too. As early as 1953, two years after Lucebert's debut in book form, writer Bertus Aafjes came to the rather hysterical conclusion that Lucebert's work ushered the SS into Dutch poetry. In 2010, the poet Maria Barnas took the measure of the Lucebert anthology selected and introduced by Pfeijffer, and again was ultimately negative in her conclusion.

The key to this disapproval lies in the subtitle that literature professor Thomas Vaessens gave to *De verstoorde Lezer* (The Unsettled Reader), his book about Lucebert, namely *Over de onbegrijpelijke poëzie van Lucebert* (Lucebert's Incomprehensible Poetry). Lucebert's poems are particularly difficult for anyone who approaches them logically and rationally. Sound and rhythm are the basis for a language game that is as virtuosic as it is boundless, and that bursts with associative mental leaps and references to sources often largely hidden from or unknown to the reader. Literature professor Anja de Feijter, for example, has demonstrated the theory that, in his early work in particular, Lucebert was influenced by the Jewish mystical tradition of the Kabbalah, among other things. Lucebert's method of working has also been convincingly compared with the way in which jazz musicians improvise.

The same De Feijter has written the foreword to the first part of *Lucebert: The Collected Poems*, the ambitious undertaking of translator Diane Butterman, who plans to render Lucebert's entire body of work into English. Lucebert's poetry is so complex that Butterman's intention seems arrogant to anyone who has not read her translations. Butterman herself gives a detailed account of her choices, but in order to really assess the quality of her achievement, it is a good idea to consider a few examples of what makes Lucebert's poetry difficult, and translating it even more difficult.

One tricky issue is Lucebert's penchant for ambiguous words. Other languages seldom possess words with exactly the same meanings. The following poem illustrates this point:

haar lichaam heeft haar typograaf
spreek van wat niet spreken doet
van vlees je volmaakt gesloten geest
maar mijn ontwaakte vinger leest
het vers van je tepels venushaar je leest

leven is letterzetter zonder letterkast
zijn cursief is te genieten lust
en schoon is alles schuin
de liefde vernietigt de rechte druk
liefde ontheft van iedere druk

de poëzie die lippen heeft van bloed
van mijn mond jouw mond leeft
zij spreken van wat niet spreken doet

her body has her typographer
speak of what cannot be spoken of
of flesh your perfectly closed spirit
but my awakened finger reads the verse
of your nipples venus' hair your waist

life is typesetter without printer's draw
its italics is lust to be enjoyed
and beautiful is all that is oblique
love destroys the standard print
love frees from every imprint

poetry that has lips of blood
that lives on my mouth your mouth
they speak of what cannot be spoken of

Apart from the sound play of rhyme and alliteration, there is the insurmountable problem of the words "leest" and "druk", the double meanings of which cannot be preserved in English. "Je leest" at the end of the fifth line is particularly problematic. It can be read as both "you read" and "your waist". Butterman chooses the second option; translating is a matter of accepting there will necessarily be some loss. In any case, Butterman's translations succeed in safeguarding the vitality of Lucebert's poems, despite the fact that much is lost (something Butterman readily admits to in her notes), for example that quality of Lucebert's work that "builds poems from the swirling quasars of individual words", as Pfeijffer puts it.

Lucebert is a poet in love with words who, time and again, allows himself to be led by the richness of sounds and the ambiguity of language. He is fond, for example, of using words that can be read as both verbs and nouns, such as "saw" and "neck". Because he uses no punctuation, there is often no single authoritative reading. Both meanings are intended, but the translator is forced to choose. What is commendable is that Butterman does so without reservation. However difficult this must have been, it is important that the reader who cannot speak Dutch is served up a good poem and not an integral rendering of all possible sounds, figures of speech and layers of meaning. And Lucebert's poems are good in English too. The resulting clarity would perhaps be undesirable for the poet, but it is not unpleasant for the reader.

In such a comprehensive and ambitious project, some decisions are always going to be debatable, but Lucebert holds his own surprisingly well in English, and consequently the translator does too.

Mischa Andriessen
Translated by Rebekah Wilson

Lucebert: The Collected Poems volume 1, translated from the Dutch by Diane Butterman, with an Introduction by Anja de Feijter, Green Integer, Los Angeles, 2013, 664 p.

Minimalist Grandeur

The Paradoxical Pop Music of Balthazar

You could certainly call 2013 a great year for Flemish rock group Balthazar. They have played at pretty much every big Belgian summer festival and reviews have been unanimously full of praise. Since the summer they have also been on tour with the British band Editors, opening the way to performances in very large concert halls in certain European countries. 2012 was just as good: the entire Belgian musical press (and some of the Dutch) placed Balthazar's second album *Rats* high on their list of best albums of the year, and in France they were also predicting an international future for the band.

Balthazar is one of a handful of rock groups that have cropped up in recent years in the rich, almost oversaturated musical landscape of Flanders, with their eye on the international scene. Of all bands, how did they succeed in striking a sensitive chord?

Balthazar's story begins in 2004 in a shopping street in Kortrijk, where teenagers Maarten Devoldere and Patricia Vanneste busked together, and their contemporary Jinte Deprez did likewise but on his own. The trio joined forces, and from then on things moved quickly, with prominent participation in music competitions, including weekly magazine *Humo's* Rock Rally in 2006, the most important springboard for young rock musicians in Flanders.

They seemed ready to take the world by storm, but Balthazar deliberately stepped out of the fast lane: their debut album *Applause* only appeared in 2010. The five young people used those four years – an eternity in pop music – to gain stage experience and find their own sound. They have tried everything: folk, dance (such as their first single 'This Is a Flirt'), pop with an artistic twist (their second single 'Bathroom Lovin': Situation') and even hip hop. In the meantime their two front men, Devoldere and Deprez, have been studying music production, allowing them to present their

Balthazar

musical ideas in optimal form. Balthazar's first record *Applause*, produced by Devoldere and Deprez themselves, sounds unusually mature for a debut album. Typically for the idiosyncrasies and evolution of the group, their first two singles, mentioned above, are missing from *Applause* despite the fact that both have been radio hits and live favourites. "These tracks just don't reflect who we are anymore," was their simple explanation.

Applause doesn't contain the profusion of ideas many young bands use to make an impression; instead the songs are reduced to their bare essence. Clear melodies supported by minimalist, danceable rhythms, occasionally pleasantly interrupted by a rasping violin or clashing piano. This restraint of expression intrigues the listener and puts the musical press to the test: where reviews of young groups are generally teeming with references to other bands, they judged this debut album primarily on its own merits. People often talk about Balthazar in terms of oppositions: complicated songs that sound easy; a familiar sound that you cannot quite place; melodies simultaneously echoing euphoria and sadness; cool songs with a warm glow; music as charming as it is sombre. In short, from the outset Balthazar had found their own unique sound, moving to and fro between artistic pop and danceable rock, and well suited to live performance. On stage Balthazar emerges as a band with flare, a solid groove machine combining nonchalance with precision.

The CD entitled *Applause* also wins real applause from all quarters (a Music Industry Award in Belgium for best album and mentions in many end of year lists) and the group is gaining new momentum. Balthazar have signed a European record contract, which brings their debut album to French, German and Scandinavian shops, and more. In 2011 the band also performed in these countries, sometimes on their own, sometimes as a supporting act for Belgian's foremost rock export, dEUS, whose experienced manager also took them under his wing.

Expectations of Balthazar were sky high, but the group fulfilled them completely in 2012 with their second album *Rats*. Their idiosyncrasies showed this time in unusual choices of location: recordings were made in cellars, bedrooms and on the Brussels metro. Anyone listening carefully – headphones bring more of the rich sound to the surface – will even hear birds chirping and a horse neighing.

Notably, where Balthazar's debut largely avoided comparisons, in *Rats* the influences emerge: Bob Dylan, Leonard Cohen and Serge Gainsbourg, surprisingly classic for such a young band, who even claim not to listen to other people's music much, although it explains the timelessness of Balthazar. These three influences culminate in 'Sinking Ship' and 'The Man Who Owns the Place', the crowning glory of *Rats*. Devoldere sings emphatically, almost slurring the notes (Cohen); his texts are fascinating, if sometimes rather cryptic (Dylan); bass and drums provide an apparently rippling but eventually insistent rhythm (Gainsbourg).

In *Rats* Balthazar again excels in restraint: the songs sound even more Spartan than in their debut album, with more space for silence between the notes. Now restraints are even imposed on the rhythm, which went in all directions in *Applause*. They play slowly, sometimes almost coming to a halt, laying extra emphasis on melodies and established grooves. What at first sounds monotonous, turns out to be very subtle. It is precisely because *Rats* is stripped of all ballast that the album stays interesting after multiple listenings. Every touch of the guitar, melodic shift or tempo change takes on a special significance. It is a daring approach, but the good news is, it works. It gives Balthazar's tracks a nonchalant class and creates an effect which can only be described paradoxically as minimalist grandeur.

PIETER COUPÉ
Translated by Anna Asbury

www.balthazarband.be

Caro Emerald at Hampton Court Palace in Richmond upon Thames © A. Mouthaan

Caro Emerald Gladdens Our Hearts

A Diva Without the Whims

Her name is Caroline Esmeralda van der Leeuw, and she was born in Amsterdam in 1981. She started singing at a very early age and has made a career of it. In 2005 she left the Jazz Department at the Amsterdam Conservatoire. Two years later - in the meantime she had been working as a backing singer and a singing teacher - she recorded a demo for some producer friends: *Back It up*. It was put on a shelf somewhere, but people starting asking for it after Caroline sang the song live on Amsterdam's ATV television channel in 2008. The creative team behind the song kept everything under their own management from the beginning. Grandmono is the name of the company, the label and the orchestra for which the singer became responsible in her twin roles as employer and employee. The concept of retro glamour pop with a dance beat, fronted by a voluptuous fifties-look vamp, really took off.

In 2009 *Back It up* became an instant hit. The CD *Deleted Scenes from the Cutting Room Floor* (2010) was a sensation and *A Night Like This* brought the international breakthrough. We had heard things like this before, as a pastiche and with only short-term success, but 'La Emerald' is something quite different. The melodious swing style is in her blood. When she sang *Mad about the Boy* on Jools Holland's New Year show on the BBC in 2010, he told her 'You make me happy'. In her black satin dress she had the look of a Rita Hayworth, an Ava Gardner or a Hedy Lamarr.

It was from a glamour photo of Lamarr that Emerald's stylist took the pose and oversized hat for the cover of *The Shocking Miss Emerald* (2013). The title is taken from the film *The Shocking Miss Pilgrim* (1947) with Betty Grable in an uncharacteristic part as a nineteenth-century advocate of female emancipation. The same idea lies behind Caro Emerald's act, which projects the notion of an intelligent modern woman who acts out the story that she was able to command success on her own terms at some time in the past.

The secret of the success is the music itself, which is at times a brilliant cocktail of happy ingredients from the lucky dip of musical history, an original synthesis of a thousand and one parts of a great puzzle. When you recognise the ingredients, the pleasure is even greater. The Caribbean element of Emerald's background (her mother is Aruban) finds its way into such Latin elements as the sound of the marimba, a mambo rhythm or the bandoneon, the instrument that provides the backdrop to the tango (e.g. *Tangled up* with Carel Kraaijenhof). David Scheurs and Jan van Wieringen cut and pasted and played around brilliantly with loops of Duke Ellington piano, surf sounds, oompah music, Phil Spector's 'Wall of Sound', disco, Prince, ballad clichés and film music effects. Emerald turns it all into a flowing whole with her timbre and timing. The lyrics are not so deep, but sometimes they produce a smile, for example when, in *Liquid Lunch*, she sings about the Martini brand, which used *A Night Like This* in an online advertising campaign, as the cause of her hangover.

In 1955 the American Julie London set the standard for ageless crooning in the rock 'n roll era, in 1982 the British ex-punk Vic Godard and his band Subway Sect, with their *Songs for Sale*, made the perfect retro album in the midst of MTV 'synthpop', and Caro Emerald came along at just the right moment to liven up a fatally fatigued pop world with a well-tried recipe: making a new thing out of something old that has proven its worth, using the most advanced means.

In the Netherlands the Caro Emerald circus is invariably a sell-out. On 5 September 2013 she started on her first major European tour. In autumn 2014 she will do a wide-ranging tour of Great Britain, her second base. She thinks nothing of a cover of Amy Winehouse or Adele, and these remakes show just how subtle her imitations are.

Having been showered with prizes, and performing at venues that others can only dream of, it will be hard for Caro Emerald to continue surpassing herself. Once the first shine has gone off it, what awaits next is usually the circuit of musicals, casinos and dinner shows. Which is why the Emerald firm is making sure it milks the success now, with acoustic versions, remixes, dance versions, merchandise and apps. It may be that the lapse into dull routine is just around the corner, but Caroline van der Leeuw is now already legendary as a diva without the whims. With that mentality you can always start all over again.

Lutgard Mutsaers
Translated by Gregory Ball

www.caroemerald.com

The Power of the 'Intermediate Sphere'

The Passage to Europe

The history of the European Union has been written many times. Books have been published in every language describing how in the years after the Second World War, six European countries signed a treaty to set up institutions which would henceforth manage the coal and steel industries in these six founding member states. More than half a century later, the radius of action of the European Union has expanded spectacularly, and the number of EU citizens has increased almost fivefold. The intervening period has been one of breakthroughs and new treaties, but also of arguments and conflicts.

Rarely has that history been written in such a penetrating, idiosyncratic and compelling way as in Luuk van Middelaar's *The Passage to Europe*, which was first published in Dutch-language edition (*De passage naar Europa*) in 2009. Van Middelaar has not been idle since then: he became a speechwriter for the first President of the European Council, Herman Van Rompuy. Time has not stood still within the European Union either, with the difficulties surrounding the euro plunging Europe into an existential crisis. That crisis forms a good test case for the book: in 2009, Van Middelaar described how the Union succeeds time and again in adapting to unforeseen situations. Every time a crisis arises, there are analysts who predict the break-up of the Union, but every time Europe manages to come out stronger and with a deeper level of unity.

The common theme running through Van Middelaar's book is the observation that the ultimate stimulus in European politics has always come from the collective of member states. It is not so much the institutions of Europe (what he calls the 'inner sphere') that are the driving force, nor is it the case that each individual member state (the 'outer sphere') has control. Rather, it is an 'intermediate sphere', in which member

The Berlaymont Building in Brussels, headquarters of the European Commission © TPCOM

states sit around the table together and are able to learn about coinciding interests, which gives direction to the integration. It is the challenges from outside the Union, such as the economic crisis in the 1970s, the fall of the Berlin Wall or the 9/11 attacks, which prompt member states to decide jointly on whether or not to give a new dimension to European integration.

Van Middelaar's take on history is more original than it first appears. Traditionally, there are two main theories about the history of European integration. One argues that the dynamic emanates mainly from the European institutions themselves: the European Commission or the European Court of Justice set the direction and create an ever more integrated Europe; whether or not the member states want this to happen does not matter very much. The other theory asserts that the individual member states ultimately always have the last word and each looks at whether it is in its own interests to take the next step.

The reality is rather more complex than either theory would suggest. Ultimately, member states decide to take new steps out of a sort of common realisation. This is perfectly illustrated by the euro crisis, which appears to demonstrate the ability of the Union to reinvent itself infinitely. In the response to the crisis, taboos were broken and red lines crossed. Within the space of two years the power of the Union increased spectacularly: henceforth, the economic policy of the member states will be controlled from Europe. These decisions were taken in that 'intermediate sphere', especially during meetings of the leaders of the member states, who came to see that their common interests and the choices made in the past meant they now had no alternative but to work together.

This take on history explains why Van Middelaar is so interested in the intrigues, the discussions, the informal agreements, the details. It is during the debates and the wrangling between member states that this common realisation is born and grows. All this makes the book a very enjoyable read. It is anything but an encyclopaedic overview of dates, names and statistics. Rather, a number of key moments are highlighted and recounted using pleasing anecdotes: lots of 'little history', and largely based on memoirs. In order to place these events in context, it does help if the reader already has some awareness of the broad brush strokes of the history of European integration. When presented in this way, history emerges as a concatenation of intriguing, often tense and sometimes bizarre events.

Luuk van Middelaar also devotes a lot of attention in his book to a theme that has long been forgotten by European policymakers: public opinion. Europe has never been as lively a place as it is today. The same debates are raging everywhere and the same topics dominate the media across the Union. This is in stark contrast to earlier decades, when it was nigh on impossible to engage the interest of the public at large in Europe.

Europe has tried to engage that interest in a variety of ways. There was for example the 'German' strategy of trying to create a European sense of 'togetherness'. That strategy foundered on the distrust of the member states. Or there was the 'Greek' approach, aimed at involving the public in politics. That was also a failure, as demonstrated by the low turnouts at European elections. And there is the 'Roman' strategy: the way to engage the public is to make better provision for 'bread' and 'games'. The 'bread' means the tangible things that improve people's lives: reducing the costs of mobile phone calls in Europe or subsidising farmers in deprived regions. Public enthusiasm remains limited, however. The 'games' are the political knockabout, the conflicts, played out on a knife-edge. The euro crisis produced sharp oppositions in public opinion in the different member states, but at the same time the crisis ensured that, for the first time in history, 'Europe' became deeply embedded in all national debates. In fact, the fiercest debates about Europe rage in a country where the euro has not even been introduced: Great Britain. In the English-language version of his book, Van Middelaar launches into a discussion of the referendum on Europe that has been promised by Prime Minister David Cameron. That creates an imperative to think carefully about the usefulness and added value of European integration, not just in Great Britain, but in all member states.

This book is much more than an academic quest to find the ultimate driver of European integration. It looks at events from sometimes surprising angles; it is an enjoyable read; it is very well documented; and it is written in an extremely witty style – something that is sadly lacking in the traditional literature on European politics. That alone makes *The Passage to Europe* worth reading.

HENDRIK VOS
Translated by Julian Ross

Luuk Van Middelaar, The Passage to Europe,
translated from the Dutch by Liz Waters,
Yale University Press, 2013 (ISBN 978 0 300 18112 8).

From Plato to the European Union
The Road to Democracy

Democracy is probably the most famous 'contested concept'. That means that there is quite some disagreement about what it exactly means. There are thus many good reasons for investing a bit in a good understanding of the concept and of its many components. One possible and always quite fruitful approach is to look back, to see how democracy came about, how it evolved, how aspects of it were criticized, changed and rethought along the way.

In *The Road to Political Democracy* Robert Senelle, Emile Clément and Edgard Van de Velde opt for that approach. They want to trace the history of political democracy from Plato to the fundamental Rights of the European Union. That is a long journey, and the road is winding and complex, with many side roads and dead-ends. One of the reasons for that is of course the multidimensional nature of democracy. For the authors of the book, political democracy means "(...) a formal democratic system wherein political and economic freedom is guaranteed and in which an equilibrium between equality and liberty can be established. The rule of law and the redistributionist principle are inherent features of such a system" (p. 26). That is a lot. Political democracy thus refers among other things to rules about participation and representation, to the right to govern the people, to a political culture of equality, to policy goals like redistribution, to (supreme) courts and their role in safeguarding the rules, and to human rights.

The book has an interesting and original format. Between the foreword of Stephen Breyer, Justice of the US Supreme Court and the postscript by Herman Van Rompuy, President of the European Council, there are two parts. The first one is written by the authors and describes the 'red wire' in the history of democracy from Antiquity till today. It does so by looking at four major issues. The first is the question whether there is indeed a need for societies of men to be ruled, i.e. whether a society can function properly without politics. The second is an endeavour to classify political systems and in particular to search for a distinction between democratic and other systems. The third is the question of the grounds on which a ruler has the right to govern. Rule by turn, the importance of a middle class, the rule of law and the need for education are then – based on Aristotle – the topics that the authors explore. They do so by pointing at the contributions of major political thinkers. The usual suspects of political theory and philosophy are presented in sequence and confronted with each other in their search for the best way to govern society.

The second part – which is actually the bulk of the book – presents the road workers and a few of the important building blocks assembled by them. The road workers include authors like Plato, John Locke, Montesquieu, Rousseau, Benjamin Constant, Tocqueville, John Stuart Mill, Friedrich Hayek, Hannah Arendt, Robert Nozick, John Rawls and Francis Fukuyama. The building blocks include the Magna Carta, the Habeas Corpus Act, the French Declaration of Human and Civil Rights (1789) and the Charter of Fundamental Rights of the European Union. For each of these the authors of *The Road to Political Democracy* have selected excerpts of the writings or of the document, and each of them is situated in its historical perspective. This works quite well. One can travel leisurely along the road towards political democracy, and appreciate the importance of many problems that have been discussed and discussed again in the course of the last 25 centuries.

'The road to political democracy' is not a book that one can read from cover to cover. The road to democracy is too long for that, and requires that one takes a rest once in a while. It is a book that should be savoured in little pieces, allowing each of them to sink in and allowing oneself to travel back and forth, which is actually what democracy has also done. In the end, the reader will know

a lot about the difficult quest for that intriguing thing called democracy. However, this reader was still a bit disappointed. I found very little on the current debates about democracy. There is very little on decision-making procedures, on elections and electoral rules, on varying notions of representation, on the evolution of the nation states in which a formal political democracy has developed and on the transfer of decision-making powers from the nation state to other actors. If one listens to the current debates, it is difficult to say that the quest has been completed with the European Charter and that democracy has been fully developed and consolidated.

Even without all the things that I missed, this fascinating and nicely presented book has over 1000 pages. That probably tells us something about democracy as a contested and multi-dimensional concept.

Kris Deschouwer

Robert Senelle, Emile Clément & Edgard Van de Velde, *The road to political democracy from Plato to the Charter of Fundamental Rights of the European Union*, Academic and Scientific Publications, 2012, 1071 p.

More Radical than Spinoza

Adriaan Koerbagh (1633-1669)

The seventeenth-century Dutch Republic was an oasis of tolerance in the Europe of the day, but that did not mean its inhabitants could say or write just anything with impunity. So much is evident from the fate of the doctor and lawyer Adriaan Koerbagh (1633-1669), a passionate Enlightenment thinker who was in many respects more radical than Spinoza himself. Not for nothing was Spinoza's motto "caute" (with caution); and the fact that he wrote in Latin, only published one book under his own name, and kept his major work, *Ethics*, in a drawer (the book was not published until after his death) sheltered him from the storm that Koerbagh chose to brave.

The English translation of Koerbagh's work *Een Ligt Schijnende in Duystere Plaatsen, om te verligten de voornaamste saaken der Godsgeleerdtheyd en Godsdienst* (A Light Shining in Dark Places, to Illuminate the Main Questions of Theology and Religion, edited and translated by Michiel Wielema, Brill, Leiden) makes this major early, radical Enlightenment source available to a wide public once again, and provides me with the opportunity to shed light on the dramatic final months of this so-called heretic.

On Friday 27 July 1668, at 10 o'clock in the morning, a prisoner is brought into the torture room in the Town Hall of the City of Amsterdam, the present-day Royal Palace of Amsterdam. It is the 35-year-old doctor and lawyer Adriaan Koerbagh. He listens to demands for his right thumb to be severed, his tongue to be bored through with an awl, his possessions to be seized, his books to be burned, that he should pay all legal costs, and be sentenced to thirty years' imprisonment in the Rasphuis jail in Amsterdam.

Why? Koerbagh was brought to trial because he had written two blasphemous books: *Bloemhof (Flower Garden)*, a dictionary of loanwords, and *Een Ligt Schijnende in Duystere Plaatsen*, a polemical tract. Armed with a razor-sharp pen, he had openly ridiculed the dogmas of the public Reformed Church. He used *Bloemhof* as a vehicle to cheerfully poke fun at the Bible, the doctrine of the Holy Trinity, original sin and predestination. The way in which Koerbagh desecrated the Bible in *Bloemhof* caused huge public outrage. He defined the word 'Bible' as a term derived from the Greek that simply meant 'book', and that could just as well be used for a collection of folk tales about Reynard the Fox or Eulenspiegel. When the controversial loanword dictionary was published in February 1668, the sheriff of Amsterdam moved immediately to seize as many copies as possible. The author was summoned to report for questioning to the Town Hall in Amsterdam. However, rather than appearing in court, Koerbagh sought refuge in 'Cuylenburg' (Culemborg), which in the seventeenth century was a free town with its own legislation and jurisdiction.

Temporarily safe from prosecution by the sheriff of Amsterdam, he began working feverishly and in secret on his second book, *Een Ligt Schijnende in Duystere Plaatsen*. Koerbagh wrote Ligt as a philosophical justification of the radical views he had expressed in *Bloemhof*. The light in the title is a symbol of truth, of science, and the 'dark places' are a metaphor for lies, religious belief. Koerbagh argues that the story of creation out of nothing is a fiction that originated at some time or other from a mistaken translation of the original Hebrew text of the book of Genesis. He also refutes the doctrine of the Holy Trinity as a fabrication made up by confused theologians. There is no reference to it in the Bible, he asserts; moreover, as a logical contradiction, it is an absurd concoction. How could a God consist of one and three beings? By denying the existence of the Holy Trinity, Koerbagh also denies the divinity of Jesus. In retrospect, *Ligt* is without a doubt the most radical and merciless written criticism of the public Reformed Church produced during the seventeenth century.

Koerbagh's brother Johannes, who was two years his junior, managed to persuade an Utre-

The Rasphuis jail in Amsterdam, where Adriaan Koerbagh died

cht printer, Johannes van Eede, to print the book. However, shocked by the radical content of *Ligt*, Van Eede stopped the presses as he read and printed the eleventh sheet of paper, and reported both brothers to the sheriff of Utrecht. The matter was betrayed. In a bid to escape arrest, Koerbagh fled from Culemborg to Leiden, but the authorities were hot on his heels and on 18 July 1868, at 6 o'clock in the morning, he was taken from his bed and arrested, before being transported from Leiden to Amsterdam in a cart *pede ligato* (with the feet bound).

During the legal cross-examination, Koerbagh confessed that he was the author of both *Bloemhof* and *Ligt*. The sheriff and magistrates were chiefly concerned with discovering whether anyone else had helped Koerbagh write the two works, something he firmly denied. Reports of the trial give the impression Koerbagh had decided to take all the blame himself, despite the fact that it is very likely he was helped by his brother and a number of friends. For example, it sounds implausible that his brother Johannes should not have read *Bloemhof* until the proofs were completely ready. Equally suspicious is his flat denial of having discussed his work with Spinoza (himself suspected of atheism), despite admitting to having been in contact with the Jewish philosopher.

Although the final sentence was more lenient than the original harsh demands, it was still a heavy punishment for the time. His thumb was not severed, nor his tongue pierced, but he was sentenced to ten years in the Rasphuis jail. Just one year later, on approximately 12 October 1669, Koerbagh died in the Rasphuis. On 15 October, he was carried out to burial from his Amsterdam home, Oude Nieuwstraat 6, before a large crowd of onlookers. When a black hen alighted on his coffin as he was being borne away, the rumour quickly went round that the devil in person had come and taken away his soul.

Bart Leeuwenburgh
Translated by Rebekah Wilson

FURTHER READING

Adriaan Koerbagh, *A Light Shining in Dark Places, to Illuminate the Main Questions of Theology and Religion*, edited and translated by Michiel Wielema, Brill, Leiden.

Bart Leeuwenburgh, *Het noodlot van een ketter: Adriaan Koerbagh* (1633-1669), Vantilt, Nijmegen, 2013.

Marc Van Montagu, Winner of the World Food Prize

In autumn 2013 Marc Van Montagu, emeritus professor of molecular biology at Ghent University, won the World Food Prize 2013. He shared the honour with two American colleagues: Mary-Dell Chilton and Robert T. Fraley. The trio were awarded the prize for their individual breakthroughs as pioneers of modern green biotechnology, further development of this field, and the creation of applications. Van Montagu is the first Belgian to share in the Nobel Prize for Food and Agriculture.

Marc Van Montagu (° 1933) is a pioneer of genetically modified crops. For donkeys' years this subject, so central to the food we eat, has met with serious resistance in certain circles (environmental organisations such as Greenpeace). Opponents speak of genetic *manipulation*, and land with genetically modified experimental crops, once tracked down, often becomes a target for activists, to Van Montagu's horror. He accuses his opponents of using emotional arguments and claims they do not shrink from systematically spreading misinformation.

It all started at the end of the 1970s in the molecular biology laboratory at Ghent University. Van Montagu, born in a working class district in Ghent, the only child of a "militant socialist family" with his nose constantly in a book, was keen to continue with his studies - anything to avoid the dusty world of the textile worker. At seventeen he went on to study chemistry. In the fifties, when James Watson and Francis Crick unravelled the double helix structure of DNA, Van Montagu fell under the spell of molecular biology. After receiving his doctorate in 1965, he was made professor of molecular genetics at Ghent and founded the VIB (*Vlaams Instituut voor Biotechnologie*), which he directed until his retirement in 1999.

In that modest laboratory, "kept open by hook or by crook", lies the origin of gene technology that dominates large scale agriculture today. It was groundbreaking work. Van Montagu and his colleagues had to achieve what results they could with limited means and a good deal of hard work. At the end of the seventies that led to the development of what is called the Ti plasmid: DNA transferred to a plant's genes by the soil-dwelling bacterium *Agrobacterium tumefaciens*. The genetic transfer became all the more interesting when it was discovered that the bacterial DNA could be replaced by other DNA, from external hereditary material.

Marc Van Montagu

In 1982 Van Montagu and his colleague Jozef Schell (1935 - 2003) started the company Plant Genetic Systems, a spin-off from his laboratory at Ghent University. A year later they presented their first genetically modified plant in the prestigious scientific journal Nature: a tobacco plant made antibiotic-resistant by a "new" gene. This genetic defence mechanism in plants offered new perspectives on alternatives to chemical weed killers. For that reason the discovery attracted a great deal of attention, including that of the University of Washington and the multinational agricultural giant Monsanto, home to both other winners of the World Food Prize 2013.

The development of genetically modified crops with the associated higher yields and health benefits (a famous example being Golden Rice with vitamin A) is of great significance to agriculture and world food production. In 1998 Van Montagu was closely involved in the founding of CropDesign, another spin-off from Ghent University, involved in biotechnology and genetic modification of crops. Van Montagu hopes his innovations will provide "food security" for the entire world population and enable us to farm less intensively, with less pollution. In 2000 Van Montagu set up the Institute of Plant Biotechnology Outreach, an institution at Ghent University which aims to meet the needs of less-developed countries with training, technology transfer and scientific research into plant technology.

Genetically modified maize and soy are used "invisibly" in many products in the United States, but in Europe, even thirty years after their introduction, genetically modified organisms (GMOs) still meet with substantial resistance in some quarters. Van Montagu can become very worked up about this: an interview in the Flemish newspaper *De Standaard* on 29th June 2013 carried the headline "Opposition to GM is a crime". Looking back on the past thirty years Van Montagu believes he was too slow to stand up to what he considers a misleading and false impression of the issues as presented by his opponents. For example, he mentions the myth of suicides by small farmers in India, who were reportedly forced by Monsanto to work with their genetically modified seeds. "Completely false," according to Van Montagu.

Van Montagu claims that GMOs enable farmers to achieve bigger harvests sustainably and at lower costs. Seeds in the lab developed and tested on experimental plots have higher nutritional value thanks to their genetic modification, or are more resilient when faced with drought, poor soil, disease, or pesticides. "We're just getting started," says Van Montagu. "Genetically modified crops are an effective weapon against hunger and good for the environment. Genetic change in crops is as old as the world. Since the invention of agriculture humans have been making genetic changes by crossbreeding plants. Current techniques for modifying plants are very precise methods for something that has been in vogue for thousands of years."

DIRK VAN DELFT
Translated by Anna Asbury

A Cassandra in the City

Joris Luyendijk

The Dutch journalist Joris Luyendijk (° 1971) embodies the future of his profession in more ways than one. The fact that his name has become almost a brand in its own right illustrates the still embryonic but unmistakable emancipation of journalists with respect to their media. Through his work as a financial blogger for *The Guardian* in London, Luyendijk demonstrates that impersonal, engaged reporting need not stand in the way of objective quality.

Admittedly, not all his colleagues like Joris Luyendijk. And some of them have good reason. The US-dwelling Dutch columnist Charles Groenhuijsen, for example, was recently described by Luyendijk as "an idiot. And I don't mean that tongue in cheek; he really is a criminally naive idiot." The reason for this is that Groenhuijsen believes that NSA whistleblower Edward Snowden is a traitor, while Luyendijk considers him a hero.

Subjecting members of his own profession to (highly) critical scrutiny is something of a trademark of Joris Luyendijk. While many accuse him of soiling his own nest, his robust but always carefully argued media criticism always provokes thought and reflection. He is a qualified anthropologist, and that is evident in the way he looks at news and reporting. For example, he finds it difficult to reconcile himself with the notion that a correspondent – be it abroad, in a war zone, in the political or financial/economic sector - should actually become part of the exclusive biosphere about which he or she reports.

It was on precisely this topic that he wrote the booklet *People like us*[1], a critical review of his earlier spell as a Middle East correspondent for various Dutch media between 1998 and 2003. In the book he shatters the illusion that foreign correspondents are able to make sense of the world from their location. While they can occasionally put their own slant on a report, generally they simply carry out instructions given to them by the editorial teams at home base. That explains why when browsing through newspapers and zapping between news programmes you will often keep on seeing the same images and the same stories. The way it works is this: the men and women in the editorial teams are of course smart, but they don't have an overview of the world; rather, they have an overview of the news agencies, from which the boss, or "chief" in the jargon, makes a selection.

The essay caused something of a furore. *People like* us became the subject of heated debate, was reprinted more than 20 times, and even drew a response in book form from other reporters seeking to restore their professional honour. It gave Luyendijk himself fame in his native Netherlands: in 2006 and 2007 he was invited to host the popular Dutch chat show programme *Zomergasten* (Summer Guests), and in 2008 hosted the winter version of the same programme, *Wintergasten* (Winter Guests).

In *Je hebt het niet van mij, maar...* (You didn't hear it from me, but..., 2010) he refined his media criticism. He spent a month as an undercover reporter in the Dutch Parliamentary world in the seat of the Dutch government in The Hague. His report provided a penetrating insight into the "media-political complex". It demonstrated with painful accuracy that the political world is not only a rarefied environment that is far removed from the normal world, but also that, apart from politicians, journalists and lobbyists also play an active and interconnected role within that network.

One result of this is that reporters take a rather short-sighted view of the tactical and personal aspects of politics, and invest less in independent research. To illustrate the point, Luyendijk wonders rhetorically what difference it would have made if the Dutch public had simply stopped following the political news completely since the last elections. "What would you really have missed?" he asks. "Lots of opinion polls, lots of debates in which the puppets attempted to outdo each other; analyses of those attempts; efforts to form a government; reports of what all those puppets thought about it all?" It is an analysis that does not just apply to Dutch political reporting.

In 2012 he moved from the Dutch daily newspaper *NRC Handelsblad* to *The Guardian* in London to report from the financial centre that is the City. The appointment gave Luyendijk an opportunity to pursue his anthropological/journalistic approach in a logical, consistent manner. Press conferences, stock market prices and sales figures do not interest him. As a scientist, he interviews financial workers high and low about how the financial world is functioning after the crisis. The succession of interviews posted on his *Banking blog* present a picture of the sector that is both human and frightening. Human because many interviewees are very aware of the risks that are still being taken in the banking world; frightening because no one appears to have the power to stop the machine. Luyendijk has now finished his blog - a book is on the way - but the final picture that emerges is decidedly dark. It carries a great, Cassandra-like predictive power about the inevitability of a new systemic crisis in the near future.

Original, empathic, (self-)critical, and always with an open mind: Joris Luyendijk is the modern-day embodiment of engaged journalism. The fact that he has acquired some fame along the way merely confirms his status as the standard-bearer of New Journalism. As his own quality mark, the new journalist is less and less dependent on a medium in order to communicate with the public.

Bart Eeckhout
Translated by Julian Ross

This English translation by Michele Hutchison was published in 2009 by Soft Skull Press in New York. The original Dutch version (*Het zijn net mensen*) was published in 2006.

The 'Commedia dell'Arte' of Peter Vos

Dutch artist Peter Vos (1935-2010) was 'one of the best draughtsmen the Netherlands ever knew', as the obituaries unanimously proclaimed a few years ago. He was, as he stated most resolutely, an illustrator. He produced thousands of drawings, tens of books, as well as work for magazines (he worked for student newspaper *Propria Cures*, and weekly magazine *Vrij Nederland*). Vos's passion was drawing, but it also became his way of evading life, combating his shyness and healing his wounds - the deaths of his father and brother. Although he was exuberant in life, a heavy drinker even, it was only in drawing that he found a way of "disguising" himself. He would have liked to dress up as a bird and like other great artists such as Grandville, Doré or Le Brun, he adorned the people in his drawings with feathers and beaks.

Peter Vos was the son of Cornelis Vos, an alcoholic journalist, well known at the time, who had been paralysed by meningitis. A bohemian, he liked to sit in the cafés of Utrecht, but passed his final years 'lonely at home, one leg amputated, cared for by his sons'.

One of the two sons, Peter Vos, emerged as a bird-loving illustrator, gifted at depicting sparrows, in the words of one of his fans, head cocked to one side, picking at an invisible crumb, or dejected, head hunched between shoulders. That was what he loved doing, illustrating 'animal books', fairy tales and stories which express human nature through animal characters. He drew not only sparrows, but also owls, frogs and herons, even shrews, grasshoppers and horned frogs. Vos had natural talent, designing covers and beautifully illustrating many stories by Jules Renard, fairytales by Perrault and fables by La Fontaine. He went drawing in *Artis* zoo in Amsterdam, where he reproduced what he saw in

Peter Vos, *The Metamorphosis of Pierus's Daugthers into Magpies*, 2003

the animal kingdom as faithfully as possible. His many animal character studies really portrayed humans: the animal fable as mirror image. Vos was a sharp observer, always carrying a sketch-book. "We're here to watch," was his artistic creed, "not to be watched."

Vos learnt Italian at the academy and was introduced by his teacher to the drama of Carlo Goldoni, master of masquerade and *commedia dell'arte*, where characters creep into all sorts of skins, sometimes even becoming animals. Vos did the same in his drawings. Critic Carel Peeters described him as 'the Dutch version of commedia dell'arte', a melancholy clown.

Vos dressed humans as animals, as so often happens in theatre. People could be characterised by wings and feathers. Personally he was very shy, withdrawing into his alcoholism. He did not enjoy attention, avoiding holding exhibitions of his own work and preferring to exhibit with others, particularly writers, such as Renate Rubinstein (with whom he lived for a while), Rudy Kousbroek (1929-2010) and of course Anton Koolhaas (1912-1992), who often wrote about animals with human characteristics.

Since his youth Vos had been intrigued by Ovid's *Metamorphoses*, especially the stories in which people changed into birds. That was his last big project: with Ovid in mind he set out to explore how people could change and transform. Effectively this was the way he had sought to protect himself from the beginning, as a timid boy, against the world he found so difficult. He drew his figures in graphite and pen, rarely in colour, because he wanted camouflage. Vos's *Metamorphoses* were exhibited in the Rembrandt House in Amsterdam until the beginning of October 2013 and previously in the *Institut Néerlandais* in Paris, which has since closed.

According to Giorgio Vasari's famous biographies of the greatest painters, sculptors and architects, the 10-year-old Giotto was quick on the uptake for his age. As he tended the flocks and wandered his father's estate with the animals, his natural aptitude drove him towards drawing. Wherever he went, on stones, soil or sand, he drew what he saw in nature or whatever popped into his head. That must have been Peter Vos's experience. His art has led many people to greater enjoyment of the animal kingdom.

Paul Depondt

Translated by Anna Asbury

Contributors

Maarten Asscher
Writer and Bookseller
m.asscher@wxs.nl

Mischa Andriessen
Writer and Critic
misschaandriessen@gmail.com

Dirk Van Assche
Deputy Editor Ons Erfdeel vzw
dirkvanassche@onserfdeel.be

Annelies Beck
Journalist
annelies.beck@vrt.be

Derek Blyth
Journalist
derekblyth@lycos.com

José Boyens
Art Historian
jose.boyens@hotmail.com

Georgina Boyes
Music Critic
georgina@nomasters.co.uk

M.C. Brands
Em. Professor of History
brawier3@hotmail.com

Daan Cartens
Literary Critic
daurge@hotmail.com

Jeroen Van Cauwelaert
Legal Counsel
jommevc@gmail.com

Piet Chielens
Director of the In Flanders Fields Museum Ieper
piet.chielens@ieper.be

Pieter Coupé
Secretary *Ons Erfdeel. Vlaams-Nederlands cultureel tijdschrift*
onserfdeel@onserfdeel.be

Christophe Declercq
Lecturer Translation Studies University College London
c.declercq@ucl.ac.uk

Dirk van Delft
Science Journalist
dirkvandelft@museumboerhaave.nl

Dominiek Dendooven
Scientific Researcher at the In Flanders Fields Museum Ieper
dominiek.dendooven@ieper.be

Paul Depondt
Journalist and Art Critic
paul.depondt@skynet.be

Kris Deschouwer
Professor of Political Science
kris.Deschouwer@vub.ac.be

Luc Devoldere
Chief Editor Ons Erfdeel vzw
luc.devoldere@onserfdeel.be

Jeroen Dewulf
Professor in Dutch Studies at the University of California
dewulf@berkeley.edu

Bart Eeckhout
Journalist
bart.eeckhout@demorgen.be

Piet Gerbrandy
Poet and Critic
psgerb@xs4all.nl

Theo Hermans
Professor of Dutch and Comparative Literature at University College London
t.hermans@ucl.ac.uk

Stefan Hertmans
Writer
stefan.hertmans@telenet.be

Arnold Heumakers
Critic and Writer
heumakers@hotmail.com

Gert-Jan Hospers
Professor of Economic Geography
g.j.hospers@utwente.nl

Ed Klekowski
Em. Professor of Biology
edk@bio.umass.edu

Bart Leeuwenburgh
Historian
bart@lee.tte.nl

Erik Martens
Film Critic
eiae@telenet.be

Lutgard Mutsaers
Music Critic
lut@ision.nl

Jos Nijhof
Theatre Critic
nijhof@xs4all.nl

Marc van Oostendorp
Senior Researcher at the Meertensinstituut Amsterdam
marc@vanOostendorp.nl

Ewald Pironet
Journalist
ewald.pironet@gmail.com

Frank van der Ploeg
Art Critic
info@artaz.nl

Nicholas J. Saunders
Lecturer in the Department of Archaeology and Anthropology at the University of Bristol
briquet55@yahoo.co.uk

Sophie De Schaepdrijver
Professor of Modern European History at Pennsylvania State University.
scd10@psu.edu

Geert Setola
Graphic Designer
geert@setola.com

Dirk Steenhaut
Journalist
dirk_steenhaut@hotmail.com

David Stroband
Art Critic
davidstroband@zonnet.nl

Dirk Vandenberghe
Journalist
dirkvdb71@gmail.com

Luc Vandeweyer
Historian
luc.vandeweyer@arch.be

Tomas Vanheste
Journalist
t.vanheste@kpnmail.nl

Alex Vanneste
Em. Professor of French
ppa.vanneste@skynet.be

Ilja Veldman
Art Historian
ilja.veldman@tiscali.nl

Paul Vincent
Translator and Critic
p-vincent@btconnect.com

Roel Vismans
Reader in Dutch
r.vismans@sheffield.ac.uk

Hendrik Vos
Professor of European Studies
hendrik.vos@ugent.be

Jeroen Vullings
Critic
jeroen.vullings@me.com

Karin Wolfs
Film Critic
mail@karinwolfs.nl

Ad Zuiderent
Poet and Critic
ad.zuiderent@xs4all.nl

Translators

Anna Asbury
Gregory Ball
Pleuke Boyce
David Colmer
Sheila M. Dale
Lindsay Edwards
Chris Emery
Nancy Forest-Flier
Sam Garrett
John Irons
Yvette Mead
Julian Ross
Paul Vincent
Laura Watkinson
Judith Wilkinson
Rebekah Wilson

Advisor on English usage
Lindsay Edwards

Colophon

Institution

This twenty-second yearbook is published by the Flemish-Netherlands Institution 'Ons Erfdeel vzw', with the support of the Dutch Ministry of Education, Culture and Science (The Hague), the Flemish Authorities (Brussels) and the Provinces of West and East Flanders.

The Institution 'Ons Erfdeel vzw' also publishes the Dutch-language periodical *Ons Erfdeel* and the French-language periodical *Septentrion. Arts, lettres et culture de Flandre et des Pays-Bas,* the bilingual yearbook *De Franse Nederlanden – Les Pays-Bas Français* and a series of books in several languages covering various aspects of the culture of the Low Countries.

Address of the Editorial Board and the Administration

'Ons Erfdeel vzw', Murissonstraat 260,
8930 Rekkem, Flanders, Belgium
T +32 56 41 12 01, F +32 56 41 47 07
www.onserfdeel.be, www.onserfdeel.nl
thelowcountriesblog.onserfdeel.be
VAT BE 0410.723.635

Philip Vanwalleghem *Head of Administration*
Adinda Houttekier *Administrative Secretary*

Aims

With *The Low Countries,* a yearbook founded by Jozef Deleu (Chief Editor from 1993 until 2002), the editors and publisher aim to present to the world the culture and society of the Dutch-speaking area which embraces both the Netherlands and Flanders, the northern part of Belgium.

The articles in this yearbook survey the living, contemporary culture of the Low Countries as well as their cultural heritage. In its words and pictures *The Low Countries* provides information about literature and the arts, but also about broad social and historical developments in Flanders and the Netherlands.

The culture of Flanders and the Netherlands is not an isolated phenomenon; its development over the centuries has been one of continuous interaction with the outside world. In consequence the yearbook also pays due attention to the centuries-old continuing cultural interplay between the Low Countries and the world beyond their borders.

By drawing attention to the diversity, vitality and international dimension of the culture of Flanders and the Netherlands, *The Low Countries* hopes to contribute to a lively dialogue between different cultures.

ISSN 0779-5815
ISBN 978-90-79705-177
Statutory deposit no. D/2014/3006/1
NUR 612

Printed by Die Keure, Bruges, Flanders, Belgium
Design by Henk Linskens (Die Keure)

Prices for the yearbook 2014, no. 22
Belgium € 37, The Netherlands € 39, Europe € 39

Other Countries: € 45
All prices inclusive of shipping costs

You can order this book from our webshop at www.onserfdeel.be and pay by credit card

As well as the yearbook The Low Countries, the Flemish Netherlands Institution 'Ons Erfdeel vzw' publishes a number of books covering various aspects of the culture of Flanders and the Netherlands.

Wim Daniëls
Talking Dutch.
Illustrated; 80 pp.

J.A. Kossmann-Putto &
E.H. Kossmann
The Low Countries.
History of the Northern and Southern Netherlands.
Illustrated; 64 pp.

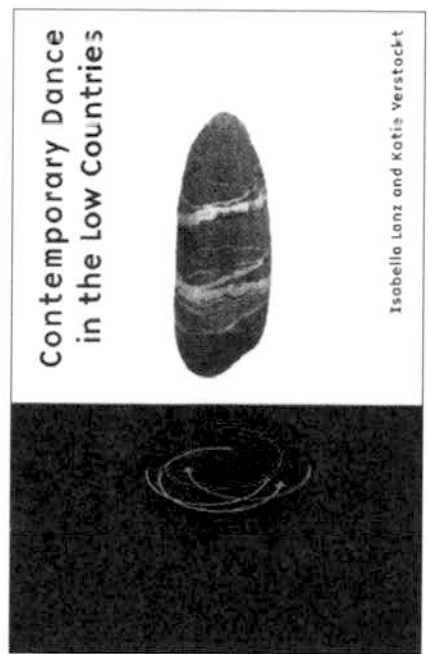

Isabella Lanz &
Katie Verstockt,
Contemporary Dance in the Low Countries.
Illustrated; 128 pp.

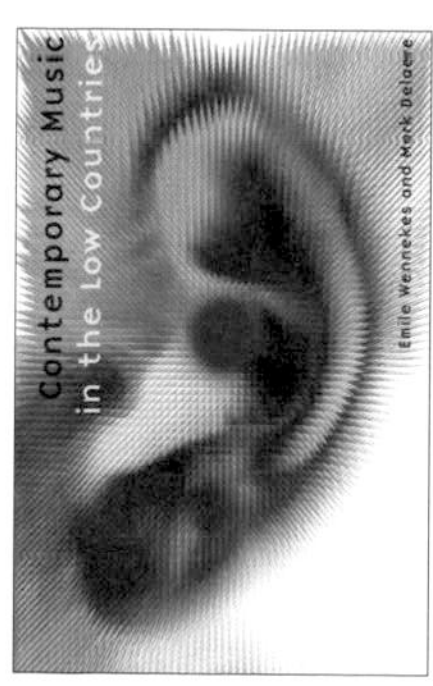

Mark Delaere &
Emile Wennekes,
Contemporary Music in the Low Countries.
Illustrated; 128 pp.

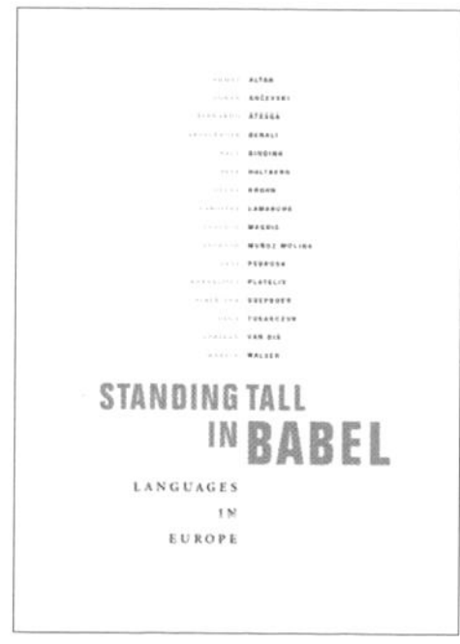

Standing Tall in Babel.
Languages in Europe.
Sixteen European writers about their mother tongues.
Hardcover; 144 pp.

Between 1993 and 2013 the first twenty one issues of the yearbook *The Low Countries* were published.

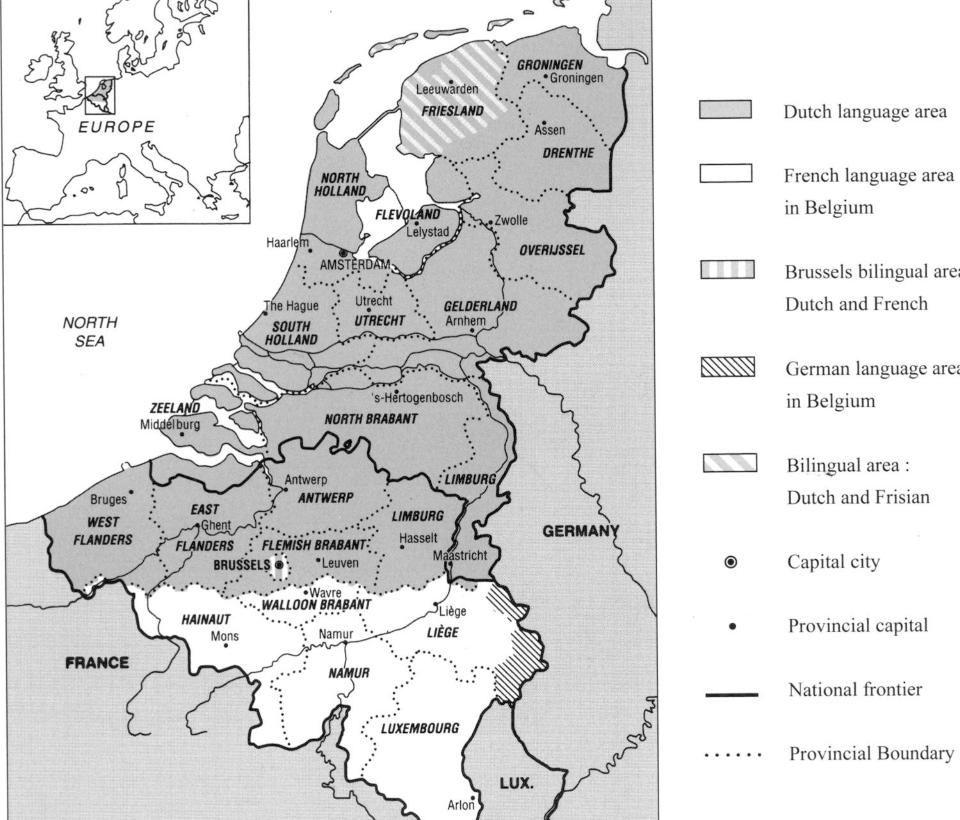
EUROPE
NORTH SEA
GRONINGEN
Groningen
Leeuwarden
FRIESLAND
Assen
DRENTHE
NORTH HOLLAND
FLEVOLAND
Lelystad
Zwolle
OVERIJSSEL
Haarlem
AMSTERDAM
The Hague
Utrecht
UTRECHT
GELDERLAND
Arnhem
SOUTH HOLLAND
ZEELAND
Middelburg
's-Hertogenbosch
NORTH BRABANT
LIMBURG
Antwerp
ANTWERP
Bruges
WEST FLANDERS
EAST FLANDERS
Ghent
LIMBURG
FLEMISH BRABANT
Hasselt
BRUSSELS
Leuven
Maastricht
GERMANY
Wavre
WALLOON BRABANT
Liège
HAINAUT
Mons
Namur
LIÈGE
FRANCE
NAMUR
LUXEMBOURG
LUX.
Arlon
0 km 50
© Carto
Dutch language area
French language area in Belgium
Brussels bilingual area : Dutch and French
German language area : in Belgium
Bilingual area : Dutch and Frisian
Capital city
Provincial capital
National frontier
Provincial Boundary